T0366222

Knowledge Management Strategies:
A Handbook of
Applied Technologies

Miltiadis D. Lytras
University of Patras, Greece

Meir Russ
University of Wisconsin-Green Bay, USA

Ronald Maier
Leopold-Franzens-University of Innsbruck, Austria

Ambjörn Naeve
Royal Institute of Technology, Sweden

IGI PUBLISHING

Hershey • New York

Acquisition Editor:	Kristin Klinger
Development Editor:	Kristin Roth
Senior Managing Editor:	Jennifer Neidig
Managing Editor:	Jamie Snavely
Assistant Managing Editor:	Carole Coulson
Copy Editor:	Ashlee Kunkel
Typesetter:	Amanda Appicello
Cover Design:	Lisa Tosheff
Printed at:	Yurchak Printing Inc.

Published in the United States of America by
    IGI Publishing (an imprint of IGI Global)
    701 E. Chocolate Avenue
    Hershey PA 17033
    Tel: 717-533-8845
    Fax: 717-533-8661
    E-mail: cust@igi-global.com
    Web site: http://www.igi-global.com

and in the United Kingdom by
    IGI Publishing (an imprint of IGI Global)
    3 Henrietta Street
    Covent Garden
    London WC2E 8LU
    Tel: 44 20 7240 0856
    Fax: 44 20 7379 0609
    Web site: http:/www.eurospanbookstore.com

Library of Congress Cataloging-in-Publication Data

Knowledge management strategies : a handbook of applied technologies / Miltiadis Lytras ... [et al.], editors.
-- Regular ed.
    p. cm. -- (Knowledge and learning society book series ; 5)
  Summary: "This book provides practical guidelines for the implementation of knowledge management strategies through the discussion of specific technologies and taxonomies of knowledge management applications. A critical mass of some of the most sough-after research of our information technology and business world, this book proves an essential addition to every reference library collection"--Provided by publisher.
  Includes bibliographical references and index.
  ISBN-13: 978-1-59904-603-7 (hardcover)
  ISBN-13: 978-1-59904-605-1 (e-book)
  1. Knowledge management. 2. Organizational learning--Management. I. Lytras, Miltiadis D., 1973-
  HD30.2.K637697 2008
  658.4'038--dc22
                2007037719

British Cataloguing in Publication Data
A Cataloguing in Publication record for this book is available from the British Library.

All work contributed to this book is original material. The views expressed in this book are those of the authors, but not necessarily of the publisher.

"Knowledge management-still going strong"

To all the people who are enthusiastic about improving the way individuals, teams, organizations, and the society handle knowledge

Knowledge Management Strategies:
A Handbook of
Applied Technologies

Table of Contents

Preface

The *Knowledge Management Strategies: A Handbook of Applied Technologies* is the fifth book in the *Knowledge and Learning Society Book Series*. Three titles are already available in the bookstores:

- *Intelligent Learning Infrastructure for Knowledge Intensive Organizations: A Semantic Web Perspective*
- *Open Source for Knowledge and Learning Management: Strategies Beyond Tools*
- *Ubiquitous and Pervasive Knowledge and Learning Management: Semantics, Social Networking and New Media to their Full Potential*

This book is complementary and is published together with the 5th book of the series entitled:

- *Technology Enhanced Learning: Best Practices* (Editors: Miltiadis D. Lytras, Dragan Gasevic, Patricia Ordonez De Pablos, and Wayne Huang)

For mid 2008, two more edited volumes which contribute further to our vision for the knowledge society are also planned:

- *Knowledge and Networks: A social Networks Perspective* (Editors:Miltiadis D. Lytras, Robert Tennyson, Patricia Ordonez De Pablos,)
- *Semantic Web Engineering for the Knowledge Society* (Editors: Jorge Cardoso, Miltiadis D. Lytras)

Introduction

Knowledge management (KM) is a buzz word of late 1990s. In an era of business transition, the effective management of knowledge is proposed as a strategy that exploits the organizational intangible assets. This fact has intrinsic market attractiveness and a great interest for practical guidelines for the implementation of knowledge management strategies. However, the term of knowledge management has been used to describe many different applications. In some cases the tag "knowledge management product" is attached to several software programs purely for marketing reasons.

The motivation for this book was based on the fact that literature on knowledge management rarely concentrates on the practical aspect of KM. Moreover, in the situations where a book discusses KM technologies, this is based on a taxonomy which is difficult to align with real world situations. This book recognizes knowledge management as a complex sociotechnical phenomenon where the basic social constructs such as person, team, and organization require support from information and communications technology (ICT) applications. This is not only due to the complexity of the phenomenon but also due to the contextual nature of knowledge.

The inevitable relation of knowledge and strategy formation seems to be taken for granted in most approaches. From this perspective knowledge management is a contextual phenomenon and its performance has to be secured through enormous effort of codifying strategies that deploy specific technologies.

Figure 1 provides an initial stage for analysis: knowledge management infrastructure within business organizations facilitates project teams that work towards the achievement of deliverable *n* given deadlines. Of course teams are not the only level of analysis. KM is recognized as a critical enabler of qualitative achievements in the organizational and interorganizational level as well.

The book intends to give answers to problems that business organizations face when they try to implement knowledge management. Mainly two critical issues are addressed:

Figure 1. The basic scenario in a knowledge-intensive organization

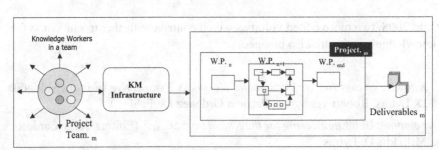

- Which technologies to use for specific KM problems?
- Which strategy can guide the implementation of KM that corresponds to the answer of the above problem?

The ultimate objective of the book is to provide practical guidelines for applied knowledge management through the discussion of specific technologies. Or, in another words, which components provide the basic KM infrastructure and how the selection of several technologies can be justified through specific knowledge management strategies.

The whole book is organized around the following pillars of the knowledge management research agenda:

ARTIFACT LEVEL

- Managing Documents
- Managing Metadata and Semantics
- Managing Taxonomies

INDIVIDUAL LEVEL

- Constructing Yellow Pages of Experts
- Managing Individual Profiles
- Managing Tacit Knowledge

TEAM LEVEL

- Managing Workflows
- Managing Discussion Forums
- Exploiting Collaborative Work Systems
- Managing Team Dynamics

ORGANIZATIONAL LEVEL

- Building Best Practices
- Developing Knowledge Maps/Ontologies
- Managing Competencies
- Managing Organizational Memory

INTERORGANIZATIONAL LEVEL
- Managing Interorganizational Network
- Managing Projects
- Future Technologies

Our wonderful journey in the research and vision for the Knowledge Society has one more stop. In September 2008 [and in each forthcoming September], we organize the 1st World Summit on the Knowledge Society, http://www.open-knowledge-society.org.summit.htm].

The World Summit on the Knowledge Society aims at becoming the leading forum for the dissemination of latest research on the intersection of Information and Communications technology (ICT) and any area of human activity including production, economy, interaction and culture, and will be organized annualy in Greece.

Athens World Summit on the Knowledge Society brings together:
- Academics
- Business People, and Industry
- Politicians and Policy Makers
- Think Tanks
- Government Officials

The underlying idea is to define, discuss and contribute to the overall agenda on how emerging technologies reshape the basic pillars of our societies towards a better world for all.

This is why these five general pillars provide the constitutional elements of the Summit:

- Government in the Knowledge Society
- Research and Sustainable Development in the Knowledge Society
- Social and Humanistic Computing for the Knowledge Society
- Information Technologies for the Knowledge Society
- Education, Culture, Business, Tourism, and Entertainment in the Knowledge Society.

Last but not least we invite you to read the just published special issue on Semantic based Knowledge Management special issue we developed for the IEEE Internet Computing Magazine Issue: Sept/Oct 2007, Guest Editors: John Davies, Miltiadis Lytras and Amit Sheth.

We do believe that this edition contributes to the literature. We invite you to be part of the exciting knowledge management research community and we are really looking forward for your comments, ideas, and suggestions for next editions.

Structure/Editing Strategy/Synopsis of the Book

When dealing with **knowledge management** it is really of no sense in trying to be exhaustive. Not only because of the fast pace in technologies that support KM strategies but mostly due to the many different aspects of the domains. Moreover, when you are trying to investigate the new insights of KM, like social networks and the Semantic Web, then the mission becomes even more complex.

This is why from the beginning we knew that our book should be selective and focused. In simple words we decided to develop a book with characteristics that would help readers to follow several different journeys through the contents. We also decided to open the book to big audiences. While we could pursue through our excellent contacts and great network of collaborators a publication aiming to promote the discipline, we decided that it would be most significant (from a value adding perspective) to develop a reference book. And this is what we made with the support of great contributors: a reference book for KM strategies providing an excellent overview of the emerging research agenda and the state of the art. Having already the experience of the edition of four edited books and getting feedback from 100s of researchers from all over the world, we decided to keep the same presentation strategy. We tried and we think that we really have managed to develop a book that has the following three characteristics:

- It discusses the key issues of the relevant research agenda,
- It provides practical guidelines and presents several technologies, and
- It has a teaching orientation.

The last characteristic is a novelty of our book. Several times editions seem like a compilation of chapters but without an orientation to the reader. This is why every edited chapter is accompanied by a number of additional resources that increase the impact for the reader.

In each chapter we follow a common didactic-learning approach:

- At the beginning of each chapter authors provide a section entitled **Inside Chapter,** which is an abstract-like short synopsis of their chapter.

- At the end of each chapter there are some very interesting sections, where readers can spend many creative hours. More specifically the relevant sections are entitled:

  ○ **Internet session:** In this section authors present one or more Web sites relevant to the discussed theme in each chapter. The short presentation of each Internet session is followed by the description of an **Interaction** where the reader (student) is motivated to have a guided tour of the Web site and to complete an assignment.

  ○ **Case study:** For each chapter, contributors provide "realistic" descriptions for one case study that readers must consider in order to provide strategic advice.

  ○ **Useful links**: They refer to Web sites with content capable of exploiting the knowledge communicated in each chapter. We decided to provide these links in every chapter, even though we know that several of them will be broken in the future, since their synergy with the contents of the chapter can support the final learning outcome.

  ○ **Further readings:** These refer to high quality articles available both in Web and electronic libraries. We have evaluated these resources as of significant value and readers can definitely find them significant.

  ○ **Essays:** Under this section a number of titles for assignments are given. In the best case essays could be working research papers. The general rule is that we provide three to six titles for essays and in the abstract titles readers can find an excellent context of questioning.

Next, we will elaborate on the theoretical framework for this book.

Knowledge Management Strategies Underpinnings: Dynamic Flows in Business Organizations

In Figure 2, we depict two entities that are the main actors in projects within knowledge-intensive organizations: the person who carries experiences, skills, knowledge, cognition, and a learning capacity, which are realized in behavior and attitudes; and the project team, which utilizes the team synergy in order to achieve the desired objectives, and is a qualitative whole in a knowledge-intensive organization. The concept of culture is also important here, since the concept of team is not a solid whole with distinct borders, but rather a dynamic formation. Shared meaning emerges through any action that is undertaken while working in a project.

The simple interaction presented in Figure 2 is not representative of practice. In knowledge-intensive organizations, several individuals and a number of project teams interact, forming a spaghetti-like group of relationships (Lytras & Naeve (eds.) 2005). A kind of network is realized with the various nodes playing an important role that merits research investigation.

The dynamic flows between these two entities are rarely explicit in nature. The dynamics of individual and team working together on a project formulate a contextual environment where information technology is used to facilitate the value exchanges. Four kinds of dynamic flows are depicted: team formation, knowledge flow, behavioral change, and learning. These "flows" are knowledge transformation mechanisms. The knowledge capacity of each person is in a continuing exchange with the environment of the individual, which can be the team or the organization (Naeve et al. 2007).

The knowledge flow relates to the characteristic of humans to constitute teams that share a common objective and thus facilitate the exchange of knowledge. In this context the critical question is the nature of knowledge. To this end, a number of knowledge category models (McAdam & McCreedy, 1999) have been proposed.

Figure 2. Dynamic flows in knowledge intensive organizations

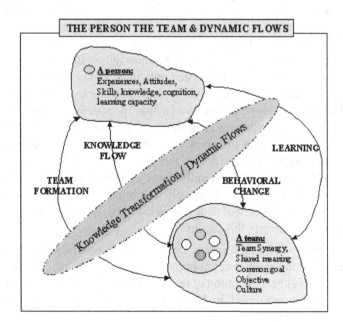

A number of characteristics of knowledge have been distinguished providing the dimensions for categorization. The traditional approach seems to be the selection of two characteristics and the justification of a two-dimensional matrix where the specified kinds of knowledge are presented. Such abstraction is easily understandable but perhaps too simplistic. In the literature a number of knowledge categories models can be identified. The model by Boisot (1987) recognizes two critical characteristics of knowledge: diffusion and codification. Proprietary, personal, public knowledge, as well as common sense are the four suggested types of knowledge. A criticism of this model is that a distinction of personal knowledge according to whether it is uncodified or undiffused does not assume that this knowledge is not exploited. The person in daily practice refers to this knowledge and acts according to specific context. Hahn and Subramani (2000) provide a very interesting approach that investigates a framework of knowledge management systems using two basic dimensions: the locus of knowledge and the level of the a-priori structure. These two dimensions determine the boundaries for four quadrants, where several applications are positioned in order to support knowledge management. In each quadrant, specific knowledge types are determined providing an overview of knowledge types that require specific support through ICTs. Nonaka (1994) and colleagues (i.e., Nonaka & Takeuchi, 1995) promote the well-known distinction of tacit and explicit knowledge which seems to be a manifestation in knowledge management, since in its simplistic categorization describes the admission of hidden and revealed knowledge.

The learning flow corresponds to the archetype of human behavior, that through action and feedback, promotes the understanding and adoption to the environment. The contextual character of learning is of critical importance. Individuals, teams, and organizations have a learning capacity, which is not simply a cumulative result of individual contributions. A number of theories concerning learning have been identified for every context mentioned earlier. In an organizational context, Argyris (Argyris, 1976, 1991, 1993; Argyris & Schön, 1978) proposes a double loop learning theory, which pertains to learning changing underlying values and assumptions. Kim (1996) describes the relations between individual and organizational (single- and double-loop) learning, a theme that is expanded further by Naeve et al. (2007). Double loop theory is based upon a "theory of action" perspective outlined by Argyris and Schon (1974). This perspective examines reality from the point of view of human beings as actors. Changes in values, behavior, leadership, and helping others are all part of, and informed by, the actors' theory of action. An important aspect of the theory is the distinction between individuals' espoused theory (what they say) and their "theory-in-use" (what they actually do); bringing these two theories into congruence is a primary concern of double loop learning. Typically, interaction with others is necessary to identify this conflict.

There are four basic steps in the action theory learning process: (1) discovery of espoused theory and theory-in-use, (2) invention of new meanings, (3) production of new actions, and (4) generalization of results. Double loop learning involves applying each of these steps to itself. In double loop learning, assumptions underlying current views are questioned and hypotheses about behavior are tested publicly. The end result of double loop learning should be increased effectiveness in decision making and better acceptance of failures and mistakes.

At the individual level many learning theories investigate the phenomenon of learning. Two interesting approaches are provided by Bloom and Krathwohl (1984) and Shuell (1992). Bloom's taxonomy of educational goals and the concept of learning function describe the concept of educational objectives while Shuell promotes a value carrier. Lytras, Pouloudi, and Poulymenakou (in press), through an integration of educational goals and learning functions, propose nine learning processes that potentially set the context of learning.

At the team level a number of theories promote the role of a group as a learning facilitator. Action learning (ARL-Inquiry 1996; Watkins & Marsick 1993) can be defined as a process in which a group of people comes together more or less regularly to help each other to learn from their experience. Cooperative learning (Bossert, 1988: Kagan, 1992) is a generic term for various small group interactive instructional procedures. Students work together on academic tasks in small groups to help themselves and their teammates learn together. In general, cooperative learning methods include three-step interview, roundtable, focused listing, structured problem-solving, paired annotations, structured learning team group roles, send-a-problem, value line, uncommon commonalities, team expectations, double entry journal, and guided reciprocal peer questioning.

The team formation is one more dynamic flow, which needs further investigation that goes beyond the scope of this paper. The coherence of the team requires flows that prove to the members the value of the integration. Bird (1989) and Hackman (1990) have identified five parameters that promote the effectiveness of a team. These are vision, values, processes, structure, and perceived business performance.

Finally, behavioral change (Bandura, 1977) enlightens the way in which individuals transform their behavior according to feedback they gain from participation in bigger social constructions. According to the behaviorists, learning can be defined as the relatively permanent change in behavior brought about as a result of experience or practice. In fact, the term "learning theory" is often associated with the behavioral view. The focus of the behavioral approach is on how the environment impacts overt behavior. The psychomotor domain is associated with overt behavior when writing instructional objectives. In the behavioral approach, we assume that the mind is a "black box" that we cannot see into. The only way we know what is going on in the mind, according to most behaviorists, is to look at overt behavior. The feedback loop that connects overt behavior to stimuli that activate the senses has to be studied extensively.

The previous analysis sets a context through the admission that some patterns of relationships contextually describe knowledge transformations without taking into account the sociotechnical nature of the phenomenon. In other words the relevance of KM applications to support these relationships is something that needs justification. If we expand the basic construct by adding the organizational level, then a richer picture of relationships is revealed. In Figure 3, the person, the team, and the organization define dynamic flows that are of critical importance in knowledge-intensive organizations.

The learning and knowledge flow link together person(s) and organization as well as team(s) and organization. Of course team-to-team linkages can be defined as well as person-to-person relationships (these are not depicted in Figure 3 for simplicity). These patterns of relationships imply specific scenarios of knowledge exploitation. The next step in our research approach is focusing on the sociotechnical dimension of the phenomenon of knowledge transformations and dynamic flows.

Knowledge Management Support Frameworks

The justification of an application as a knowledge management one has to be based on a context. In the KM literature several ways for categorizing KM applications can be found (Binney 2001; Lee & Hong, 2002; Nissen, Kamel, & Sengupt, 2000). Lee and Hong (2002) link IT applications to a four stages knowledge life cycle. Binney (2001) recognizes six elements on the KM spectrum (i.e., transactional,

Figure 3. The knowledge management intra-organizational landscape

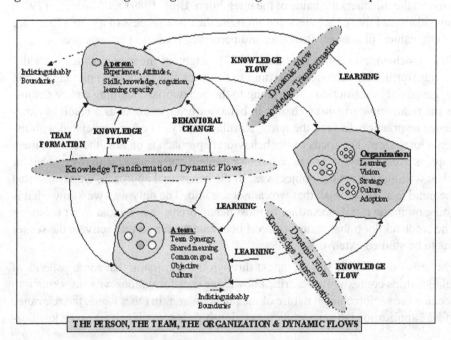

analytical, asset management, process, developmental, innovation, and creation) and links various knowledge management applications and enabling technologies to each element.

A common approach in knowledge management is the analysis of the phenomenon from two perspectives: the process-centered and the product-centered approach (Hansen, Nohria, & Tierney, 1988; Koehn & Abecker, 1997). Woods and Sheina (1998) promote a categorization of applications that support these two aspects of knowledge management using the two basic approaches of knowledge management and mapping several KM applications in a two dimensional structure. Figure 4 provides an overview of the suggested positioning. Applications include file management systems, shared files, full-text retrieval, push technology, real time messaging, e-mail, semantic analysis, Intranet, knowledge maps, structured document repositories, white-boarding, automatic profiling, net conferencing, and discussion groups.

The depicted allocation of applications seems to be very interesting since it gives an overview of technologies and two coordinates can be assigned to each position. A critical question concerning positioning is which is the scale in each dimension? What is the maximum considered abstraction of a knowledge product? Are there any ingredients that incrementally are realized through the employment of specific technological components? And in the knowledge as a process dimension, despite

Figure 4. The process-centered and product-centered approaches in KM software (Apostolou & Mentzas 2001) (Adopted from Woods & Sheina, 1998)

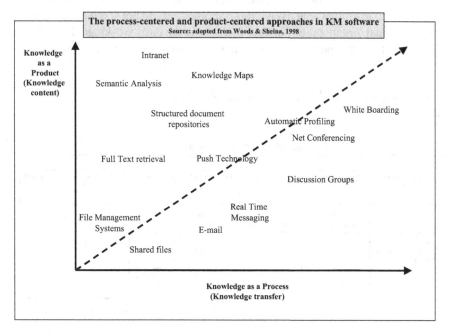

the simplification of emphasis on knowledge transfer, we have to answer the critical question concerning scaling. In this approach several other contributions provide insight. Especially in the case of knowledge as a process, the relation of applications to several knowledge processes is a common approach. Nissen et al. (2000) provide an interesting approach concerning this aspect. They distinguish three levels of knowledge management, namely organizational level KM, group level, and individual level. In Figure 5 we present their classification; the figure pays special attention to the distinction of the three levels. Their presentation is based on an amalgamated KM model which is a result of the integration of four others models (Nissen, Despres & Chaveul, Gartner Group, Davenport & Prusak). This model recognizes six knowledge management processes: create, organize, formalize, distribute, apply, and evolve.

At the organizational level, Nissen et al. provide a number of applications and practices that seem to support each specified KM process. At the stage of knowledge creation, they depict the importance of business intelligence, the R&D practices, the benchmarking approach, and data mining as well as artificial intelligence. In the subsequent phases they emphasize the importance of knowledge maps, semantics networks, data warehouses, and reports. It is obvious that the distribution process, where a number of systems and practices are recognized, has a special role in the whole continuum.

At the group and the individual level the depicted practices and systems present an accumulation in the organize and distribute phase. It seems that the key issue in KM support is the distribution of knowledge. But the critical question is how can the distribution of knowledge be secured if in a previous stage the extensive codification of knowledge is not promoted? Moreover this classification does not pay any attention to learning capacity. All these applications do not stand in any context (team, individual, organization) just for facilitating the daily workload. Knowledge management from this perspective is weak if we do not reveal its capability to sup-

Figure 5. Organizational level systems & practices (Adopted from Nissen et al., 2000)

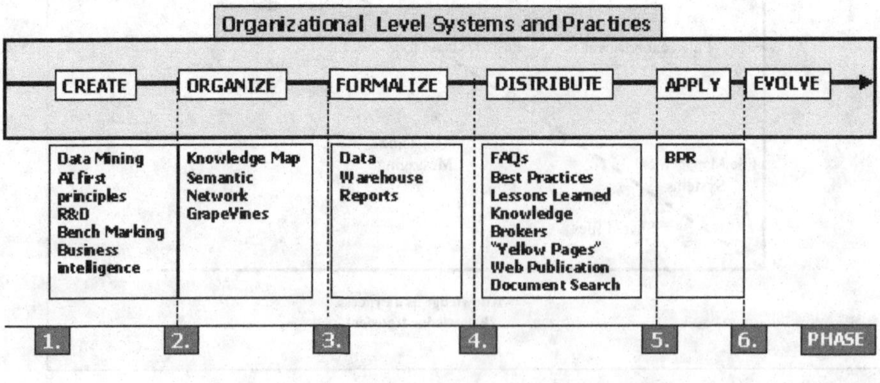

port learning initiatives that increase the capacity for effective action. Moreover the learning dimension is underlying in any system since if their users will not be able to align their behavior and attitudes to the requirements of the systems then their usage would be limited. Unfortunately the intangible nature of knowledge makes the ROI analysis of knowledge management systems a difficult task. This process-oriented approach provides an insight to the phenomenon of knowledge management, and in the environment of knowledge-intensive organization, it can justify implementations.

A similar approach is provided by Lee and Hong (2002), who recognize a four-stage KM life cycle and they associate specific IT applications with each stage. Figure 7 provides the overview of their proposition.

In this approach, the learning dimension of knowledge management is also disregarded. This is really a very weak point in the models if we consider knowledge management as a sequential indication of stages. The knowledge infrastructure in an organization must not be considered using a librarian perspective of knowledge management. In this dimension the empowerment of learning capability in an organization is a continuing process where specific technologies must secure the human resources management. Drucker (1992) states that "it is safe to assume that anyone with any knowledge will have to acquire new knowledge every four or five years or become obsolete."

Figure 6. Group & individual level systems & practices (Adopted from Nissen et al., 2000)

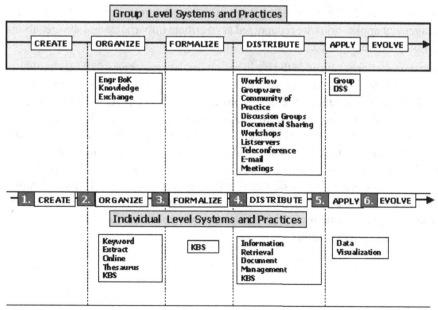

Figure 7. IT applications and KM life cycle (Lee & Hong, 2002)

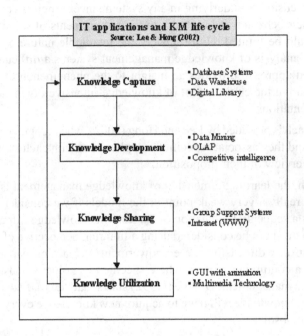

An interesting categorization of KM technologies is provided by Binney (2001). In this mapping in the developmental stage of the spectrum, a number of knowledge management applications are recognized as of critical importance and some enabling technologies are depicted.

In the next section we provide the basic notion for the categories of KM technologies that will be discussed in the relevant chapters of this book. Knowledge exploitation as a dynamic flow requires the development of extensive practical capabilities in the direction of building competences. All the depicted dynamic flows in previous sections do not stand for just descriptive reasons. The revelation of the underlying logic forces the extensive analysis of infrastructures that support the realization of these flows. One of the most important obstacles in knowledge management is the persistence to descriptive models that unfortunately provide only formalization with limited practical implications. In this direction the proposed book expands further the ideas and the research presented in two published papers in the *Journal of Knowledge Management*.

Figure 8. Enabling technologies mapped to the KM spectrum (Binney, 2001)

Enabling Technologies mapped to the KM spectrum, Binney (2001)						
	Transactional	**Analytical**	**Asset Management**	**Process**	**Developmental**	**Innovation Creation**
Knowledge Management Applications	• Case –Based Reasoning (CBR) • Help Desk Applications • Order Entry Applications • Service Agent Support Applications	• Data Warehousing • Data Mining • Business Intelligence • Management Information Systems • Decision Support Systems • Customer Relationship Management (CRM) • Competitive Intelligence	• Intellectual Property • Document Management • Knowledge Valuation • Knowledge Repositories Content Management	• TQM • Benchmarking • Best practices • Quality Management • Business Process (Re) Engineering • Process Improvement • Process Automation • Lessons Learned • Methodology • SEI / CMM ISO 9XXX, Six Sigma	• Skills Development • Staff Competencies • Learning • Teaching • Training	• Communities • Collaboration • Discussion Forums • Networking • Virtual teams • Research and Development • Multi-disciplined Teams
Enabling Technologies	• Expert Systems • Cognitive Technologies • Semantic Networks • Rule-based Expert Systems • Probability Networks • Rule Instruction Decision Trees • Geospatial Information Systems	• Intelligent Agents • Web Crawlers • Relational & Object DBMS • Neural Computing • Push Technologies • Data Analysis & Reporting Tools	• Document Management Tools • Search Engines • Knowledge Maps • Library Systems	• Workflow Management • Process Modeling Tools	• Computer-based training • On-line Training	• GroupWare • Email • Chat Rooms • Video Conferencing • Search Engines • Voice Mail • Bulleting Boards • Push Technologies • Simulation Technologies
	• Portals, Intranets, Extranets					

Knowledge Management Strategy and Technology Convergence

In the quest of a knowledge management strategy and technology convergence we have carried out systematic research in the past 4 years investigating the relationship of these two concepts, mainly capitalizing on knowledge and learning dimension. In a recent publication (i.e., Lytras et al. 2002) we propose the integrated e-learning knowledge management framework, which recognizes two basic transformations. In Figure 9, this model is provided through a general presentation of the idea for dynamic e-learning environments (Lytras et al. 2002). The two circles in the figure represent two basic transformations. One is summarized by a 6-stage KM life cycle model that is responsible for general knowledge management purposes and a learning-oriented KM life cycle, which is responsible for the adoption of general learning object to reusable learning content. The second circle is based on a clear position that learning content is not guaranteed from general information/knowledge resources unless a specific adoption process for learning is undertaken. The second cycle depicts six learning-oriented processes, namely relate, adopt, attract, engage, learn, and use. The underlying concept is that a kind of learning product is the value carrier in a learning context. The ingredients of this product include needs, knowledge, motivation elements, team synergy, problem solving capacity, and packaging, which are realized through the employment of the six learning-oriented processes. In parallel to the two approaches for the analysis of knowledge management, this approach is two-fold, since the learning case investigates learning as a process and learning as a product.

In close relation to the practice by Nissen et al. (2000) the anticipation of learning as a process gives an opportunity to map specific applications to each stage (Lytras & Doukidis, 2001). The depicted applications in Figure 10 give an overview of applications or application modules that empower a learning environment. Tools for needs assessment and online survey tools help the recognition of learning needs and promote the personalization and customization to learning needs. One of the most important problems in e-learning is the static content that limits the performance and the willingness of learners to enroll in e-learning courses (Lytras & Pouloudi, 2001). In the adoption phase the information resources are manipulated in order to match educational objectives and to become meaningful learning units. Special

Figure 9. The integrated e-learning knowledge management framework

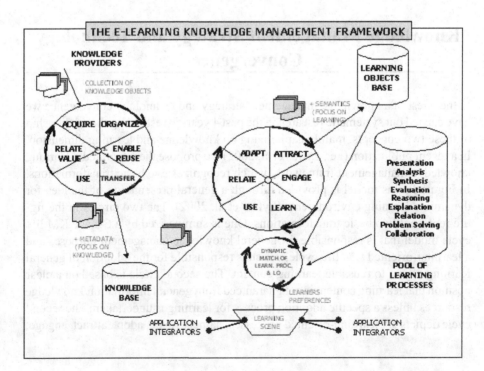

Figure 10. IT applications for learning support (Adopted from Lytras & Doukidis, 2000)

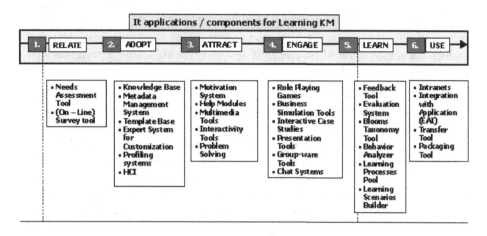

attention is paid to metadata and semantics as well as profiling systems and templates according to HCI theories is paid. In the stage of attract, where the subject of research is the realization of motivational elements, help modules, multimedia and interactivity tools, as well as systems that promote problem solving are very important. The stage of engagement facilitates the active participation of (e-)learners to the learning content, and from this perspective a number of applications are considered to promote the engagement: role-playing games, business simulation tools, interactive case studies, presentation tools, GroupWare, and collaboration tools. In the phase of learn, the learning effort must be evaluated. Given the complexity of the phenomenon of learning, this stage requires sophisticated systems that in general are absent in the majority of learning management systems. Such applications include feedback tools, evaluation systems, Bloom's taxonomy tools, learning processes pool, learning scenarios builder, and behavior analyzers. Finally in the stage of use, transfer tools, packaging tools, Intranets, Extranets, Internet, integration, with critical business applications (EAI) expand the information highways that bring together learners and content.

Lytras, Skagkou, and Doukidis (2001) investigate a number of application modules according to the proposed multidimensional dynamic e-learning model (Lytras & Doukidis 2000; Lytras & Odman, 2001; Lytras & Pouloudi, 2001; Lytras & Pouloudi, 2001; Lytras et al., 2002) which recognizes three critical dimensions for the effectiveness of learning initiatives that utilize information and communication technologies: knowledge management, e-learning pedagogy, and application integration. The justification of dynamic learning environments requires enormous effort in applications that investigate the complex nature of learning.

A first implication of our approach is the capability to propose a two-dimensional map according to the model proposed by Woods (1998), which gives emphasis on the categorization of several applications that support learning. In Figure 11, learning as a process and learning as a product are depicted on the two axes. In each dimension there is a scaling according to the distinctions that where made; learning product is a combination of six elements and there are six learning processes that describe the life cycle of learning.

This two-dimensional abstraction can be used in order to provide an overview of technological components that potentially empower the learning performance within business units or organizations. In most cases, descriptive knowledge management models lack practical implications since they only pay attention to the modeling of knowledge flows without taking into account how descriptive narrations can support instrumental and normative aspects of practice. The proposed categorization of Figure 11 provides insight into how several applications support specific value constellations within a business context from a learning perspective. In this categorization the specified scaling permits the anticipation of the potential capacity of each technological component to realize the several value components of learning product as well as to support specific learning processes. For several applications this could be a multifaceted consideration for their placement in the theoretical abstraction.

Figure 11. The process-centered and product-centered approaches in learning software

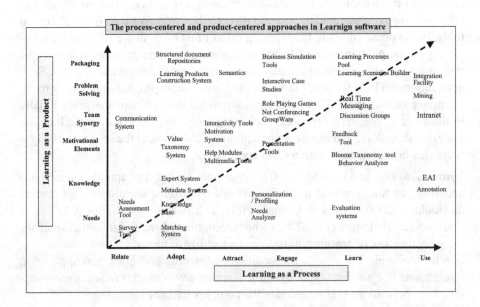

This map requires an extensive explanation. The basic idea is that the two-fold approach to learning can be realized in business units if a number of infrastructures provide knowledge and a learning Web. The word infrastructure refers not only to IT applications but also to "soft" issues that reveal the role of the social parameters that constitute a sociotechnical environment. In this direction the research work of Hahn and Subramani (2000) proposes an interesting approach for categorization. In contrast to traditional matrix models that usually specify types of knowledge according to specific characteristics, Hahn and Subramani map KM infrastructures according to two very interesting characteristics: the locus of knowledge and the level of a priori structure. In Figure 12 their proposed model is depicted. A first comment is the fact that knowledge is considered to be either on artifacts or in individuals. This distinction poses a critical question: Knowledge cannot be found in teams or organizations? Or perhaps this distinction implies that these two locations are the final points of reference, since organization and team are considered to be a social integration of persons. In our opinion this distinction is really useful and quite sophisticated in its simplicity but it could be expanded further. Locus of knowledge could be the team as well as the organization, and in a way, the interorganizational environment as well. Concerning the second dimension of Hahn and Subramani's model, we have to argue that the structured or unstructured knowledge can support many different scenarios of exploitation. In our proposition, knowledge is considered to be the capacity for effective action and from this perspective one

Figure 12. Hahn, J. and M. Subramani, "A framework for lnowledge management support"

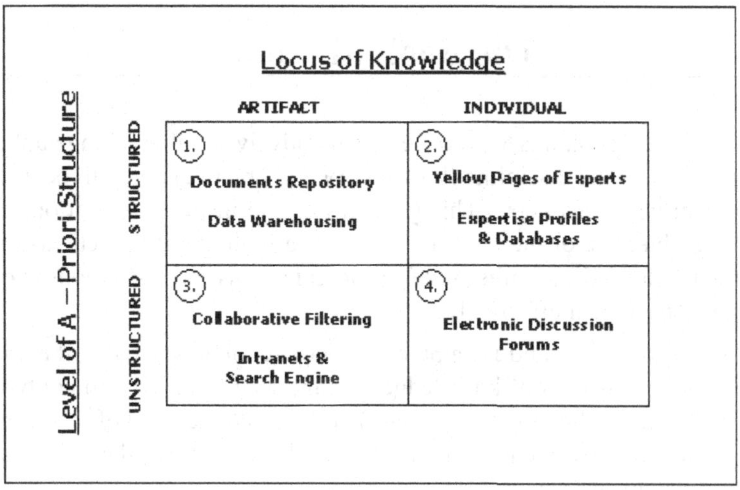

xxvi

critical concern is to reveal the capacity of learning to provide a continuous loop that increases knowledge sharing and knowledge creation towards the quest for organizational performance.

The proposed framework of knowledge management support is based on the work of Hahn and Subramani but incorporates two basic revisions. First of all it recognizes that the locus of knowledge or learning is not only an artifact or a person but also a team and the organization as a whole. Knowledge and learning dynamics are critical characteristic of teams and organizations. From this perspective the level of a priori structure can have two different concentrations: on the one hand, knowledge as a knowledge product, and on the other hand, learning as learning content. This addition to the perspective of Hahn and Subramani (2000) modifies their model, and the four cells that they distinguish become 16.

In Figure 13, the revised model is presented. In each of the 16 cells, specific IT applications are depicted according to their capacity to promote the main scope of knowledge management. The propositions of the model describe in synopsis the underlying logic that is summarized by the knowledge management and learning convergence. This framework guides business managers as well as academics in the way that it correlates IT applications to specific knowledge and learning dynamic flows. The concept of flow is basically justified if we describe a channel that diffuses a kind of an intangible product. In each cell of the proposed model a number of applications are highlighted. Of course in an organization the establishment of dispersed infrastructures according to the propositions of the framework is not the point. The critical question is if we can establish a learning and knowledge management infrastructure that can provide integrative services that match the requirements of the applications in the various cells. It sounds challenging but it is just the only way to establish effective knowledge management infrastructures with embedded learning capacity.

The Book Mission

Our mission for this book was to produce collaboratively "a value adding publication which will promote the discipline (both theory and practice) and will be accepted in the relevant target markets." This general mission inspires several objectives. The ultimate objective of the book is to deliver a high quality practical-oriented book that will help business units as well as organizations and institutions to deploy knowledge management effectively.

We see a tremendous demand for a practical book (cookbook) that will explain in depth the practical aspects of knowledge management (e.g., how to apply a KM strategy and which technologies to deploy). The target audience of this book can be distinguished into two general segments. We decided to call them the learning industry and the business market.

Figure 13. A proposed framework for knowledge management support from a learning perspective

"A Framework for Knowledge Management Support from learning perspective"			
Locus of Knowledge			
ARTIFACT	INDIVIDUAL	TEAM	ORGANIZATION
1. Documents Repository Data Warehousing	2. Yellow Pages of Experts Expertise Profiles & Databases	3. Work Flow Systems Collaborative Work Systems Project Deliverables Repository Team Profiles	4. Enterprise Application Integration Best Practices, FAQS Knowledge Maps Knowledge Brokers OLAP
5. Collaborative Filtering Intranets & Search Engine	6. Electronic Discussion Forums	7. Virtual Teams Group Ware Systems Chat/ Conferencing List Servers E-mail	8. Teleconference Intranets Extranets CRM Search Engines Data Mining Help Desk Applications
9. Learning Objects Base Learning Templates Base Metadata Mgmt system Learning Scenarios Builder	10. Semantics Competences Description Learning Expertise Profiles	11. Expert Systems for Personalization Lessons Learned FAQS	12. Profiling System Lessons Learned Programs FAQS Learning Infrastructure
13. Search Engine Keywords Extract	14. Annotations Needs Assessment Tool Motivation System Evaluation System	15. Role Playing Games Business Simulation Brainstorming	16. Benchmarking Business Intelligence

(Rows: KNOWLEDGE – STRUCTURED/UNSTRUCTURED; LEARNING CONTENT – STRUCTURED/UNSTRUCTURED; Level of A – Priori Structure)

In the learning industry five subsegments are highlighted:

• Students enrolling in KM courses
• Special interest groups on KM; for example, associations, public bodies, and so forth
• Adult trainers
• Educational policy makers (with special interest in KM)

Respectively, in the business market five more subsegments are distinguished:

• Managers (interested in implementing KM)
• KM specialists
• Knowledge officers
• Human resources management officers
• Business consultants
• IT managers

The specific added value we see in this book is by facilitating the creation of the ubiquitous business intelligence space. Knowledge management, learning technologies, and the Semantic Web in the last 5 years have gained a significant interest in the information technology research community. The integration of these fields will create a significant business interest for specific products and services, some of which are discussed in this book.

The contribution of this book to the literature of IT is significant. Information technologies are analyzed as sociotechnical systems. Business intelligence based on advanced knowledge management strategies that guide the deployment of technologies and infrastructures provides the context for the exploitation. Learning and knowledge jointly formulate a challenging landscape for the deployment of information technology since their performance is directly related to behavioral-soft issues.

Miltiadis D. Lytras, Research Academic Computer Technology Institute, Greece

Meir Russ, University of Wisconsin - Green Bay, Wisconsin

Ronald Maier, Martin Luther University Halle-Wittenberg, Germany

Ambjörn Naeve, Royal Institute of Technology, Sweden

August 2007

References

Argyris, C. (1976). *Increasing leadership effectiveness.* New York: Wiley.

Argyris, C. (1991, May/June). Teaching smart people how to learn. *Harvard Business Review.*

Argyris, C. (1993). *On organizational learning.* Cambridge, MA: Blackwell.

Argyris, C., & Schön, D. A. (1978). *Organizational learning: A theory of action perspective.* Reading, MA: Addison-Wesley.

ARL-Inquiry. (1996). Developing an infrastructure for individual and organizational change: Transfer of learning from an action reflection learning program. In E. Holton, III (Ed.), *Academy of Human Resource Development 1996 Conference Proceedings* (pp. 41-48). Austin, TX: Academy of HRD.

Bandura, A. (1977). Self-efficacy: Toward a unifying theory of behavioral change. *Psychological Review, (84),* 191-215.

Binney, D. (2001). The knowledge management spectrum: Understanding the KM landscape. *Journal of Knowledge Management, 5*(1), 33-42.

Bird, B. J. (1989). *Entrepreneurial behaviour.* Glenview, IL: Scott Foresman and Co.

Bloom, & Krathwohl (1984). *Taxonomy of educational objectives, handbook I: Cognitive domain.* New York: Addison-Wesley and Co.

Boisot (1987). *Information and organizations: The manager as anthropologist.* London: Fontana/Collins.

Bossert, S. T. (1988). Cooperative activities in the classroom. *Review of Educational Research, 15,* 225-250.

Drucker, P. (1992, September-October). The new society of organizations. *Harvard Business Review,* 95-104.

Hackman, J. R. (1990). *Groups that work and groups that don't.* (pp. 1-35, 479-504). San Fransico: Jossey-Bass.

Hahn, J., & Subramani, M. (2000, December 10-13). *A framework of knowledge management systems: Issues and challenges for theory and practice.* Paper presented at the 21st Annual International Conference on Information Systems, ICIS 2000, Brisbane, Australia, (pp. 302-312).

Hansen, M. T., Nohria, N., & Tierney, T. (1988, March-April). Whats your strategy for managing knowledge? *Harvard Business Review,* 107-116.

Heldund & Nonaka (1993). *Models of KM in the West and Japan. Implementing strategic processes change, learning and cooperation* (pp. 117-144). London: Mackmillan.

Kagan, S. (1992). *Cooperative learning* (2nd ed.). San Juan Capistrano, CA: Resources for Teachers.

Koehn, O., & Abecker, A. (1997). Corporate memories for knowledge management in industrial practice: Prospects and challenges. *Journal of Universal Computer Science, 3*(8), 929-954.

Lee, S. M., & Hong, S. (2002). An enterprise-wide knowledge management system infrastructure. *Industrial Management & Data Systems, 102*(1), 17-25.

Lytras, M. D., & Doukidis, G. I. (2000, November 20-23). *E-learning evaluation criticism. The multidimensional dynamic e-learning model.* Paper presented at the Fourth IASTED International Conference on Internet and Multimedia Systems and Applications (IMSA 2000) [CD Proceedings], Las Vegas, (pp. 368-373).

Lytras, M. D., & Doukidis, G. I. (2001, March 26-29). *E-learning pedagogy: Define the value.* Paper presented at the Technology in Education International Conference & Exposition (TechEd 2001), Southern California.

Lytras, M. D., & Odman, H. (2001, June 26-27). *Fulfilling organizational learning on concurrent enterprises: The Multidimensional Dynamic Learning model for knowledge management exploitation.* Paper presented at the 7th International Conference on Concurrent Enterprising (ICE 2001), Bremen, Germany.

Lytras, M. D., & Pouloudi, A. (2001). E-learning: Just a waste of time. In D. Strong, D. Straub, & J. I. DeGross (Eds.), *Proceedings of the Seventh Americas Conference on Information Systems (AMCIS)*, Boston, (pp. 216-222).

Lytras, M. D., & Pouloudi, N. (2001, June 25-30). *Expanding e-learning effectiveness. The shift from content orientation to knowledge management utilization.* Paper presented at the Word Conference on Educational Multimedia, Hypermedia and Telecommunications (ED-MEDIA 2001), Tampere, Finland [CD Proceedings].

Lytras, M. D., Pouloudi, N., & Doukidis, G. (2002). A framework for technology convergence in learning and working. *Educational Technology and Society, Journal of International Forum of Educational Technology & Society and IEEE Learning Technology Task Force.*

Lytras, M. D., Pouloudi, N., & Poulymenakou, A. (in press). Dynamic e-learning settings through advanced semantics. The value justification of a knowledge management oriented metadata schema. *International Journal on E-Learning.*

Lytras, M. D., Pouloudi, N., & Poulymenakou, A. (2002). Knowledge management convergence: Expanding learning frontiers. *Journal of Knowledge Management, 6*(1), 40-51.

Lytras, M. D., Skagkou, T. N., & Doukidis, G. I. (2001, April 1-5). *Value dimension of the e-learning concept. components & metrics.* Paper presented at the 20th ICDE World Conference on Open Learning and Distance Education, Dusseldorf, Germany.

McAdam, R., & McCreedy, S. (1999). A critical review of knowledge management models. *The Learning Organization: An International Journal, 6*(3), 91-101.

Nissen, M., Kamel, M., & Sengupta, K. (2000, January-March). Integrated analysis and design of knowledge systems and processes. *Information Resources Management Journal, 13*(1), 24-43.

Nonaka, I. (1994). A dynamic theory of organizational knowledge creation. *Organization Science, 5*(1), 14-37.

Nonaka, I., & Takeuchi, H. (1995). *The knowledge-creating company: How Japanese companies create the dynamics of innovation.* New York: Oxford University Press.

Shuell, T. J. (1992). Designing instructional computing systems for meaningful learning. In M. Jones & P. H. Winne (Eds.), *Adaptive learning environments: Foundations and frontiers* (pp. 19-54). New York: Springer-Verlag.

Watkins, K. E., & Marsick, V. J. (1993). Sculpting the learning organization: Consulting using action technologies. In L. J. Zachary & S. Vernon (Eds.).

Wiig, K. (1998). *The role of knowledge based systems in knowledge management.* Paper presented at the Workshop on Knowledge Management and AI, Washington D.C.

Woods, E., & Sheina, M. (1998). Knowledge management: Applications, markets and technologies. *Ovum Reports.*

Acknowledgment

The time has come for us to express our deepest appreciation and respect to the 30 contributors of this edition. Their knowledge, expertise and experience are evident in every line of this edition. It sounds typical, but it is the ultimate truth. Every edition is just an outlet, where the world of ideas is seeking a fertile ground. And this ground is not self-admiring. It requires the interest and insights of people. Hence our profound thank you goes to our readers in academia, industry, government, and in society in general.

It is also typical to acknowledge the publishers and all the supporting staff in all the stages of the book production. But in IGI Global, we have found more than just publishers and excellent professionals. We have found great supporters of a shared vision to develop books/editions and knowledge for a highly demanding society. So Dear Mehdi, Jan, Kristin, Jessica, Anthony, Meg, please accept our warmest compliments for your encouragement and inspiration. You prove to us every day that IGI Global is not only a high quality publishing organization but also a community that cares for its people.

If you judge the type of our "job" then you have to admit from the beginning that editing books is not an income generating case. We must laugh when we go to DHL with a bulk package of all the required materials for the book and they ask us to pay about 250-300 euros for sending them to the United States. We are joking and saying that with this money one of us could fly in person to the States. But when we have posted the package, the Ithaca is there and we really enjoyed the trip, so our only real anxiety is to open our book to our audiences. So, once again, the journey was full of exciting experiences and we are really grateful to all the people that stand by us.

We are looking forward to the next one.

A personal note from Miltiadis: I want to thank from the bottom of my heart Patricia, for the new journey we started together concerning our magazine about China, ORLY, and D++, a lifetime project, and also my filos Ambjörn and Meir that recently we don't have the time to enjoy our frie3nship, and to Ronald for his good spirit and positive energy.

A personal note from the rest of us (Ronald, Ambjörn and Meir): We would like to thank Miltiadis for inviting us to contribute to the compilation of this book, and for convincing us with his enthusiasm for its potential impact on the KM practitioners of the knowledge society. Miltos, you are a very special person that is able to combine the utopian vision of a better world for all with the energy to actually contribute to this vision with all your different publications and initiatives – while at the same time teaching 30 hours a week!

Chapter I

Knowledge-Based Strategies and Systems:
A Systematic Review*

Meir Russ, University of Wisconsin – Green Bay, USA

J. Greg Jones, Berea, Kentucky, USA

Jeannette K. Jones,
American Intercontinental University – Online Campus, USA

Abstract

Knowledge management strategies and implementation of knowledge-based systems have gained importance over the last decade. However, many organizations are not able to develop "winning" knowledge-based strategies and others waste significant monies when the knowledge-based systems they invest in fail to produce the desired results. To address the challenges faced by these organizations, a recently developed framework for strategic dilemmas was proposed by Russ, Jones, and Fineman (2006) to aid in the development of knowledge-based (KB) strategies. The framework (C^3EEP) identifies six dilemmas that organizations should balance when considering their knowledge management and business strategies. Examples of such dilemmas include the balance between concealment (secrecy) vs. transparency, complementary vs. destroying, and the balance between exploitation and ex-

ploration. The framework compliments the six stages in the life cycle of KB systems (KBS) as identified by the academic literature that discusses the development and implementation of KBS from the information systems (IS) perspective (e.g., Lytras, Pouloudi, & Poulymenakou, 2002; Nissen, Kamel, & Sengupta, 2000). This interaction/linkage between KB strategies and systems is crucial for the success of both. Academic research supports the complex relationship between the two. However, there is no conclusive formula for managing this relationship to achieve success. The purpose of this study will be to identify crossovers between the two streams (strategy and systems) of research by using a systematic literature review. For example, is the academic literature focusing mostly on the learning aspect (late stage in the life cycle) of the exploration strategy while largely ignoring the discussion about attracting the appropriate knowledge (early stage in the life cycle) for this kind of strategy? Or does the academic literature focus on populating a KBS with appropriate complementary knowledge while largely ignoring the dynamics of the transfer of destroying knowledge (learning aspect)? The authors hope to accomplish three goals in this study: (1) to continue the validation of the two (C^3EEP and KBS life cycle) frameworks; (2) to identify new research opportunities; and (3) to focus managerial attention on areas of importance in KB strategies and systems that lack depth of academic discussion.

Introduction

Academic research conducted in the last decade within the economic and accounting disciplines suggests that knowledge and intellectual capital account for a significantly unexplained wealth created within the economy and value created by firms (e.g., Blair & Wallman, 2001; Brooking, 1996; Lev, 2001; Nakamura, 2001). Therefore, to capture knowledge and intellectual capital, companies spend significant amounts of money on systems that are not necessarily effective, efficient, nor do they create value. Even though at the macro and cumulative level of analysis it is clear that such investments have a positive impact on the economy at large, and a specific company's performance (e.g., Brynjolfsson & Hitt, 2000), the ultimate investment results are inconsistent. Based on the inconsistent results of systems investments, a large number of practitioners and academics view knowledge management (KM) as a fad (e.g., Lev, 2000; Ryan & Hurley, 2004). First generation KM (at least in the U.S.) was propagated by information systems (IS) providers that over-promised and under-delivered, by suggesting that knowledge sharing and new knowledge development was as simple as installing appropriate IS (e.g., Groupware or data warehouse) or artificial intelligence (AI) software (e.g., expert systems or case-based reasoning). This failure was followed by the realization that knowledge that creates value to the organization by definition is unique (Barney, 1991), complex, and sticky (Szulanski, 1996). As such, managing existing knowledge is seen as complicated and strenuous at best. And as important and complex as managing existing knowledge is, new knowledge development is where most of the competitive value is created through novel business models and strategies (e.g., Coulson-Thomas, 2004; Malhotra & Majchrzak, 2004). As a result, the second generation KM is moving away from the simplistic notion initiated by the knowledge-based systems (KBS)/IS system "pushers" and the proponents of AI: "we build, and they will come." Still, large numbers of organizations have difficulties with managing their knowledge and even more difficulties developing a "winning" KM strategy that is formal, explicit, and supports or drives their business strategies (Bose, 2004).

To address the challenges faced by these organizations (as described above), companies have to address both KB/KM strategic and systems issues simultaneously. A recently developed framework for strategic dilemmas was proposed by Russ et al. (2006) to aid in development of KB strategies. The framework (i.e., C³EEP) identifies six dilemmas that organizations should balance when considering their KM and business strategies. The framework complements the six stages in the life cycle of KBS as identified by the academic literature that discusses the development and implementation of KBS from the IS perspective (e.g., Lytras, Pouloudi, & Poulymenakou, 2002; Nissen, Kamel, & Sengupta, 2000). This interaction/linkage between KB strategy and systems is crucial for the success of both (Hung, Huang, Lin, & Tsai, 2005). Academic research supports the complex relationship between the two; however, there is no conclusive formula for managing this relationship to achieve success (Paoli & Prencipe, 1999).

The purpose of this study will be the first step in this excursion. Specifically, the goal of this study is to identify crossovers between the two streams (strategy and systems) of research by using a systematic literature review. The authors consider this intersection of the strategy and systems to be of extreme significance because this crossover is where human elements of high level strategic decision making and daily practical aspects of the use of the knowledge embedded in the system meet to form reality. The authors hope to accomplish three goals in this study: (1) to continue the validation of the two (C³EEP and KBS life cycle [KBS LC]) frameworks; (2) to identify new research opportunities; and (3) to focus practical managerial attention on areas of importance in KB strategies and systems that lack depth of academic discussion.

This chapter will report on the attempt of such an effort. This chapter will also discuss the methodology used, the findings of the research, the conclusions and implications, and finally the next steps. Figure 1 depicts the pertinent frameworks discussed in this chapter.

Figure 1. Research methodology and pertinent frameworks

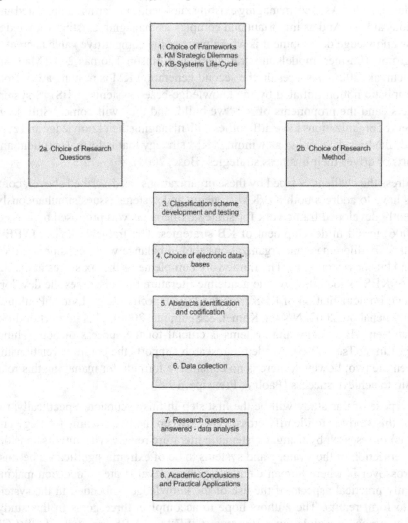

1. Choice of Frameworks
a. KM Strategic Dilemmas
b. KB-Systems Life-Cycle

2a. Choice of Research Questions

2b. Choice of Research Method

3. Classification scheme development and testing

4. Choice of electronic data-bases

5. Abstracts identification and codification

6. Data collection

7. Research questions answered - data analysis

8. Academic Conclusions and Practical Applications

Theoretical Background

To begin, a brief discussion of the major frameworks and concepts used by this research is provided.

C³EEP

The following will briefly describe the dilemmas and provide limited illustrations. More in-depth discussion can be found by Russ et al. (2006).

Codification (Explicit) vs. Tacitness

Should the company concentrate on codifying its knowledge or would it be better off upholding the knowledge as tacit (Conner & Prahalad, 1996; Leonard-Barton, 1995; Schultz & Jobe, 2001)? Tacitness might sustain the company's competitive advantage by making it more problematic for competitors to emulate (Conner & Prahalad, 1996). If, on the other hand, the company decides to codify the knowledge and make it explicit and/or embedded, then the diffusion of the knowledge within the company can be accelerated (Leonard-Barton, 1995). An example of this dilemma would be where the company invests in KBS to corroborate employee's knowledge sharing or where the company supports employee travel for the purpose of personal contact (Persaud, Kumar, & Kumar, 2001). Based on this strategic choice, the company should then decide whether, and how, to reward employees for using KBS (Zack, 1999b).

Complementary vs. Destroying

Should the company focus on developing knowledge that is complementary with its current KB or would it be better off destroying its existing KB by developing new-to-the-company knowledge (Barley, 1986; Bower & Christensen, 1995; Hill & Rothaermel, 2003)? The destroying strategy can be seen as a strategy focused on developing a new KB base while destroying the value of the current KB base in order to develop an exclusive competitive advantage that will allow the company to transform its industry (Hill & Rothaermel, 2003). A rising number of established companies are embarking on incorporating some aspects of the destroying strategy (Casillas, Crocker, Fehrenbach, Haug, & Straley, 2000; DeTienne & Koberg, 2002; Stringer, 2000). Complementary strategy is a strategy based on developing and using only knowledge that is compatible with the currently used KB (Hill & Rothaermel, 2003). Such knowledge can be "new-to-the-world" development, but still be supportive of the existing KB of the company (e.g., Hargadon, 1998).

Concealment (Secrecy) vs. Transparency

Would the company be better off keeping its knowledge concealed or would it be better off if the knowledge is transparent (Gray, 1988; Inkpen, 1998; Lamming, Caldwell, Harrison, & Phillips, 2001; Radebaugh & Gray, 1997; von Furstenberg, 2001)? Secrecy (in international accounting) was identified as a value that indicates inclination toward confidentiality; as an example, limiting disclosure of knowledge within the legal limits to constituencies on a need-to-know basis that would be the most directly impacted, such as finance and management. Transparency was defined as being publicly open and accountable (Radebaugh & Gray, 1997). For example, Inkpen (1998) identifies the subject of how shielding the partners of their KB as a critical aspect of the knowledge acquisition process among partners in strategic alliance. Inkpen (1998) also details the preference that Toyota made about being more transparent then one would anticipate with its partner/competitor (i.e., GM) and the possible rationalization for such a transparency. Along the same line of thinking, Tapscott and Ticoll (2003) suggest that companies should not view transparency as a threat, but as an opportunity to build trusting relationships with both internal and external constituencies (e.g., suppliers).

Exploration vs. Exploitation

Should the company focus on receiving the most from its existing knowledge or would the company be better off exploring new knowledge (Levinthal & March, 1993; March, 1991; Pitt & Clarke, 1999)? An exploitation strategy of the company KB can be described as a strategy based on using and refining its available knowledge. The exploration strategy can be described as a strategy using mostly inventions and innovation in order to create new knowledge (March, 1991; Levinthal & March, 1993). The KBS and IS that will be most effective for each strategy might be different (Pitt & Clarke, 1999). For example, IS are fairly ineffective in supporting creativity and innovation that are seen as crucial for exploration, but can be very efficient for sharing accessible knowledge that is important for exploitation.

External Acquisition vs. Internal Development

Should the company's KB be developed internally or would the company be better off acquiring the knowledge needed from external sources (Appleyard, 1998; Bierly & Chakrabarti, 1996; Jones, 2000; Parikh, 2001; Pitt & Clarke, 1999)? Developing technologies for a new product, acquiring new processes from outside the firm through interorganizational arrangements, or developing new processes internally are examples (Appleyard, 1998; Pitt & Clarke, 1999; Zack, 1999a). There is a vast academic body of research suggesting that large companies are acquiring new knowledge from the outside, mostly from small and entrepreneurial companies (e.g., Jones, 2000). Jones (2000), for example, suggests that since the mid-1990s U.K.-based pharmaceutical companies considered such an R&D option as another "make-or-buy" choice. Additionally, Quinn (1999) postulates that companies are considering strategic outsourcing for value (not cost savings) propositions, suggesting that companies can employ such outsourcing arrangements to enhance their intellectual depth, innovation, and worldwide reach. Alliances and partnerships (as well as outsourcing) are adding to the complexity of the strategic decision of external vs. internal development. Partnerships in this context can be seen as a third option, or as a combination of the two options (Canez & Probert, 1999; Kurokawa, 1997; White, 2000).

Product vs. Process

Should the company concentrate on the KB that is sustaining the process and creating the value or should the company concentrate on the value creation and the KB supporting its product/service (Abernathy, 1978; Jones, 2002; Smith & Reinertsen, 1998)? The early 1990s brought the realization that companies need to manage all of their processes significantly better (Davenport, 1993; Martin, 1995; Teece, Pisano, & Shuen, 1997). The realization was that the "what" they produce might be as important as the "how" they produce. Recently, there have been a number of attempts to integrate process management with KM (Burlton, 1998; Davenport, Jarvenpaa, & Beers, 1996; Sanchez & Mahoney, 1996). For example, Claycomb, Droge, and Germain (2001) found that when the life cycle of the product is short, process knowledge has a positive effect on the company's performance. Another example is described by Jones (2002), who suggests that companies loosing their revolutionary innovative abilities are starting to focus on value creation through process efficiencies.

Finally, companies rarely use the genuine form of an archetype and are usually striking a balance between the two extreme cases (for each one of the six dilemmas described above) which might serve them better (Russ et al., 2006).

Based on the authors earlier research (Russ et al., 2006) the coding scheme for the six strategic dilemmas was developed (see Table 1 in Appendix A).

Knowledge-Based Systems' Life Cycle (KBS LC)

Nissen et al. (2000) proposed a process model for knowledge systems encompassing the following six stages: create, organize, formalize, distribute, apply, and evolve. Consistent with their three-level proposal (i.e., organizational, team, and individual) and with the focus of this chapter, this research focuses only on the organizational level of KBS and adopted their proposal as the basic framework for the life cycle (LC) of a KBS.

Lytras et al. (2002) expanded the above mentioned model into the e-learning KM by incorporating an additional cycle of KM processes that included a similar six-stage process: relate, adapt, attract, engage, learn, and use. This framework was incorporated into the six LC stages described above.

To enrich and to add to the above mentioned models, the authors reviewed the *Handbook for Evaluating KBS* (Adelman & Riedel, 1997). Based on the three identified sources, the coding scheme (see Table 2 in Appendix A) for the six stages of KBS LC was developed.

Bohn's Scale

Bohn (1994) proposed a framework for classification of knowledge growth. The scale in Bohn's (1994) classification extends from an initial point where knowledge is at the very tacit stage through a final stage where knowledge is absolutely codified. Specifically, the low end of the scale is where there is very little known and the knowledge is mostly tacit. In the midrange, there are some aspects that are understood so some of the knowledge is documented. The classification ending stage is where the knowledge is codified in equations and scientific formulas where a complete knowledge subsists. The authors used this classification to code the state of knowledge illustrated within the abstracts. The specifics of the scale used in this study can be seen in Table 3 in Appendix A.

Layers of Organizational Strategy

As mentioned earlier, this research focuses on the organizational strategy level of analysis. But within this level, the literature identifies four layers of strategy (Thompson, Strickland, & Gamble, 2007, p. 39): operational, functional, business unit, and corporate. The focal point in this framework is the business unit strategy. The business unit strategy might be applied to a stand alone company (e.g., a small business or large multinational company) or a business unit of a corporation. In corporate strategy, one focuses on a portfolio of business units which might be in different products/markets or industries. Functional strategies' (e.g., marketing, purchasing) role is to support the business unit or corporate strategy. Operational strategies support functional or business unit strategies; for example, the strategy of the decision-making process for purchasing that supports the decision to make or to buy within the corporation. This four-layer framework of organizational strategies was used in this research.

Research Perspectives and Methodologies

The following two research perspectives were identified: descriptive vs. prescriptive. Descriptive theories can be portrayed as "what is" vs. prescriptive theories that can be portrayed as "what will be" (Dubin, 1978).

The authors also characterized the abstracts of the literature as being conceptual or empirical. Empirical would refer to an application-based study, or a case study, while conceptual would refer to theory building, confirming, and so forth.

The abstracts were also coded based on the use of specific research methodologies (e.g., case study, applications/prototypes, and surveys) identified within the abstract itself.

Methodology

A number of literature review studies were identified in preparation for this study (e.g., Alavi & Leidner, 2001; Chen & Chen, 2006; Martensson, 2000; Petty & Guthrie, 2000; Robey, Boundreau, & Rose, 2000; Thorpe, Holt, Macpherson, & Pittaway, 2005). This indicated to the authors that the topic is mature and vast as a subject matter for a systematic review. No previous review study was identified discussing KM strategies and system at the organizational level. The use of a systematic review as a research method provides a number of advantages: transparency, clarity, focus, broad coverage, synthesis, and allows the authors to minimize any subjective biases researchers might have had when selecting articles for a literature review (Thorpe et al., 2005). Despite that, it is possible that some biases might be incorporated into the study design or into the classifications.

The Study Process

The first step was to specify the specific research questions intended for the study focus. The authors decided against a thematic review and instead decided to focus on mapping the study area. This decision was based on the authors' limited resources and the infancy of research in this area. In fact, it is believed that this effort is the first of its kind.

The following questions were identified as appropriate for this early stage:

A.   *Research content questions:*

1. Are all six KM/KB strategic dilemmas (as identified by the C³EEEP framework) covered by the research?
2. Are all six KBS LC stages covered by the research?
3. Are all 36 cells of the matrix of KM/KB strategy (six) by KBS LC (six) covered by research?
4. Is the coverage equal for Questions 1, 2 and 3, or do some aspects get a higher rate of coverage?
5. Within each strategic dilemma, are the two anchors covered equally and/or simultaneously?
6. When deliberating KB strategy and systems, are specific KM tools discussed?
7. When deliberating KB strategy and systems, are specific industries discussed?
8. When deliberating KB strategy and systems, are specific countries/geographic scope discussed?
9. Are some layers of organizational KM strategy (e.g., functional, corporate) preferred?

B. *Research context questions:*

10. Are some research perspectives (e.g., prescriptive, descriptive) used more frequently?
11. Are some research methodologies (e.g., case study, applications) used more frequently?
12. What is the frequency of publications (increase, steady over the years)?
13. What are the research outlets/journals?
14. Using Bohn's scale, what is the state of knowledge in this area?

The inclusion and exclusion criteria used in this research will now be described.

Inclusion—Round 1

The major acceptance criterion of the literature studied for this research was that the abstract of the chapters would discuss both KM/KB strategies as well as KBS. Since some of the systems used to support KM/KB strategies might not be identified as KBS, the authors also included in the first round those abstracts that identified IS. The following was the key word search string used.

[(Knowledge management or knowledge based) and strategy] and [(knowledge base or information) and systems] and after 1/1/1990; and scholarly journals including peer-reviewed.

The authors decided the screening criteria for the literature would be those abstracts with a publishing starting date of January 1, 1990. KM became popular in the mid 1990s and the assumption was that going back to 1990 was sufficient. This assumption is consistent with other reviews of KM (e.g., Alavi & Leidner, 2001; Chen & Chen, 2006; Martensson, 2000; Petty & Guthrie, 2000; Thorpe et al., 2005). As such, the authors assumed that there were not many articles written on the subject before that timeframe. This assumption was confirmed by the findings (see below).

One key aspect of the research was the focus on KM strategies or KB strategies, and *not* on KM at large. To illustrate this point, Alavi and Leidner's (2001) review covered KM and KM systems and discussed KM at the different levels: individual, organizational, and so forth. This review focuses on strategies related to KM/KB at the organizational level only. A distinction between business (or business unit) level strategies, functional, operational and higher corporate, or portfolio of business strategies, will come later.

Exclusion

The authors looked for abstracts that discussed organizational-based KM/KB strategies only. There were individual, team, regional, and national KM/KB strategies located. However, these will *not* be covered and were excluded from the authors' research.

Inclusion—Round 2

For round two, the authors added individual- and team-based KM strategies if the KM strategies were within the context of an organization (e.g., biases that allow a purchaser to make decisions within the context of their function were included and classified as an operational strategy, *not* a functional strategy).

Abstract Identification

For the first round, the authors used four of the most popular electronic data bases: ABI/INFORM, Ebsco-Business Source Elite, Emerald Full text, and Wilson-Business Full Text. During the first round, which was conducted on December 2, 2006 and January 16, 2007, 122 abstracts in ABI, 24 in Ebsco, 12 in Emerald, and 4 in Wilson were identified. No abstract was eliminated because of the quality of its source, as suggested by Salipante, Notz, and Bigelow (1982). The abstracts were read by the first author twice. First, consistent with the exclusion criteria, abstracts that discussed national and regional KM strategies were excluded. Also, abstracts that discussed IS/KBS in a general approach and were not detailed enough for LC stage identification, were excluded. Also, consistent with exclusion criteria and inclusion Round 2, individual and team KM strategies were excluded where appropriate. When in doubt, the abstract was left for the next reading (Salipante et al., 1982). Duplication between the two electronic data bases was eliminated. After exclusions were determined, 80 abstracts were left.

In the second reading, the specifics of the classifications were coded (see below). If at this point, there was not at least one KM/KB strategic aspect and one KBS LC stage aspect coded, the abstract was excluded. That left 76 abstracts for the analysis.

Since this sample size was seen as too small by the authors, a third round was conducted. This time, the authors used only the ABI database, being the most productive in the first round, and their personal files. To increase the sample size, the authors investigated each of the six specific strategic dilemmas using specific key words used in the coding of the dilemmas (see Appendix A), for example, a search for codification and tacitness was done by:

[(stickiness or embeddedness or situated or tacitness or codification or codifying or tacit or explicit) AND (knowledge and strategy) AND (system?)] and after 1/1/1990 and scholarly journals including peer-reviewed.

For the six dilemmas, a total of 795 abstracts were identified. The same procedure for inclusion and exclusion as described earlier was used. After excluding duplications and abstracts that did not meet the criteria described earlier, a total of 154 abstracts were identified. As such a total of 230 abstracts were identified as appropriate for this study. The abstracts are listed in alphabetic order in Appendix C. The authors realized that despite their best effort, it is possible that a few abstracts were missed, either because of misclassifications (see weaknesses discussion below) or because some of the journals that published abstracts that might be of interest were not listed within the databases used. As such, the authors refer to data collected as a sample, not a comprehensive database.

Classification

The classification scheme used in screening and classifying the abstracts was developed by the first author based on the academic research covered in the background discussion and screened by the other two coauthors. Minimal changes were incorporated. The classification scheme (see Table 4 in Appendix A) and the coding scheme are available in Appendix A. The abstracts were coded by the first author and verified by the second author with minimal changes that were mutually agreed upon.

Findings

The findings below are reported following the order of the research questions identified earlier.

A. Research Content Questions

Questions 1 and 4: Are all six KM/KB strategic dilemmas covered by the research? Is the coverage equal or do some aspects get a higher rate of coverage?

The authors found that all six of the strategic dilemmas proposed by the C³EEP framework are covered by the literature (see Table 1 in Appendix B). The coverage varies, between the lowest coverage by the literature that discusses the complementary-destroying with about 25% of the abstracts, up to about 82% of the abstracts that discuss the product-process dilemma. The other two aspects that are covered below the average are concealment-transparent (about 26%) and the external acquisition-internal development dilemma with about 34% of the abstracts. The other two dilemmas that are covered above the average are the exploration-exploitation (about 62%) and the tacitness-codification (about 63%) dilemmas. That the three aspects of tacitness-codification, exploration-exploitation, and the product-process are covered above the average is not surprising. The three aspects have a solid and long tradition of academic research, as mentioned earlier. It is also not surprising that the complementary-destroying dilemma has low coverage because of its relative novelty in the strategic literature (Bower & Christensen, 1995). What is a little surprising is the low rate of coverage of the concealment-transparent and the external acquisition-internal development dilemmas. One would expect that when sharing the knowledge within or between companies is a major concern to organizations (Bansler & Havn, 2003; Taylor & Wright, 2004), and when outsourcing is a common strategic option considered by many companies (Jiang & Qureshi, 2006; Pati & Desai, 2005), that there would have been more research discussing those strategic aspects.

Questions 2 and 4: Are all six KBS life cycle (LC) stages covered by the research? Is the coverage equal or do some aspects get a higher rate of coverage?

The authors also found that all six stages of KBS LC are covered by the literature (see Table 2 in Appendix B). The coverage varies between the lowest coverage by the literature that discusses the distribute/sharing stage (about 5%), up to about 69% of the abstracts that discuss the apply/implement stage. The other stage that is covered significantly above the average is the stage of create/develop (about 45%). The other three stages are covered a little below the average level: organize (about 27%), formalize (about 25%), and evolve (about 25%). Again, the surprise here is the low coverage of the distribute/sharing stage of the system, which supports the similar finding about sharing knowledge mentioned above.

Questions 3 and 4: Are all 36 cells of the matrix of KM/KB strategy by KBS LC covered by research? Is the coverage equal, or do some aspects get a higher rate of coverage?

Table 3 in Appendix B details the findings relevant to this question. Please note that here every abstract was codified to include all the mentioned KB strategic dilemmas and KBS LC stages. All the 36 cells of the matrix are covered with one abstract being the lowest (complementary-destroying x distribute) and one 133 abstracts being the highest (product-process x apply), with a total of 1,337 items mentioned.

The other highest and lowest frequencies (in Table 3, Appendix B) are consistent with the results mentioned above. A slight surprise is the relatively low coverage of the evolve stage, which covers the improvements of the KBS, specifically, but not surprisingly in the context of complementary-destroying, concealment-transparent, and the external acquisition-internal development dilemmas.

Question 5: Within each strategic dilemma, are the two anchors covered equally and/or simultaneously?

Table 1 (in Appendix B) presents very intriguing findings. For one, it seems that only the dilemma of tacitness-codification resembles some kind of a balanced discussion. Fifty abstracts covered both topics while 94 covered one of the two. Not surprisingly, within the context of KBS, the vast majority of the abstracts (64) discuss codification and only 30 discuss tacitness. In light of the first generation KBS approach, this data reflect "good news." The other five dilemmas are mostly one sided. For example, the exploration-exploitation aspect is significantly tilted toward the exploitation aspect (69 vs. 37) and only 36 abstracts discuss both aspects (vs. 106 focusing on one). An even more extreme case is the product-process aspect where only 37 abstracts cover both aspects (vs. 151 covering one aspect), while 145 of them focus on the process aspect and only 6 on the product aspect. A similar picture can be seen in the other three dilemmas, with maybe the most extreme aspect, the concealment. This is definitely disturbing when sharing knowledge within an organization, between organizations, and between organizations and other constituencies (e.g., boards, investors) is a major issue, and when individual's knowledge is seen as power and an insurance policy against being fired (Riege, 2005), or when "make-or-buy" decisions and which areas to outsource and which to keep as core competency are frequent business decisions (e.g., Henard & McFadyen, 2006). There were only 21 abstracts that discussed both of them in the context of KB strategy and systems. Lastly, more and more companies realize that the dilemma of destroying their own knowledge base is not a luxury or an option because if they do not make this decision, the competition may make the decision for them. However, this research could find only five abstracts discussing this dilemma in the KBS context.

Question 6: Are specific KM tools discussed when deliberating KB strategy and systems?

The abstract search revealed (see Table 4 in Appendix B) that less than half (101 out of 230) of the abstracts discussed specific KM/IS tools in the context of KB strategies. The specifics of the tools are detailed in Table 5 in Appendix B. Over all, 69 specific KM/IS tools were identified in the abstracts. Fifteen of them were mentioned more than once with the top four being enterprise resource planning (ERP) (11), expert systems (ES) (10), decision support systems (DSS) (9), and customer relationship management (CRM) (7). This resulted in a total of 124 mentions of KM/IS tools in the abstracts.

Question 7: Are specific industries discussed when deliberating KB strategy and systems?

The abstract search also revealed (see Table 6 in Appendix B) that less than half (109 out of 230) of the abstracts discussed specific industries in the context of KB strategies and systems. The specifics of the industries are detailed in Table 7 in Appendix B. Overall, 117 specific industries were identified in the abstracts. Fifty of them were in the manufacturing sector and 42 were in the private service sector. The rest of the abstracts were distributed between others sectors of the economy.

Question 8: Are specific countries discussed when deliberating KB strategy and systems? Is the multinational/global/international scope covered as well?

The abstract search also revealed (see Table 8 in Appendix B) that 54 of the abstracts discussed specific countries and that 20 abstract had an international perspective in the context of KB strategies and systems. The countries specifics are detailed in

Table 9 in Appendix B. Twenty countries are mentioned, with the USA being most frequent (23 out of 54).

Question 9: Are some layers of organizational KM strategy (e.g., functional, corporate) preferred?

Four layers of organizational strategy are discussed by the academic literature (see background earlier). Table 10 in Appendix B describes the findings. The business unit strategy and the operational strategy are most frequently discussed while the functional and the corporate strategies are less frequently discussed. Please note that corporate strategies are rarely discussed.

B. Research Context Questions

Question 10: Are some research perspectives (e.g., prescriptive, descriptive) used more frequently?

It seems that the theoretical (conceptual, prescriptive) perspectives (153 and 156, respectably) are used more frequently than the practical, empirical (139, and descriptive (109) perspectives (see Table 11, Appendix B).

Question 11. Are some research methodologies (e.g., case study, applications) used more frequently?

It seems that the research is mostly driven by specific applications/prototypes (48 out of 230) or by qualitative approaches, like literature reviews (65 out of 230) or case studies (80 out of 230) and much less by quantitative methodologies, like quantitative analysis (18 out of 230) or surveys (19 out of 230). See Table 12, Appendix B for results. This is indicative of a young academic area and as such, should not be surprising.

Question 12: What is the frequency of publications (increase, steady over the years)?

The findings are consistent with Chen and Chen (2006, p. 31-32) which identified that 1999 and 2000 were two years that represented transition between two phases. In this case, it seems that 1999 is the transition year (see Table 13, Appendix B). One can also identify, if so inclined, three distinct periods: between 1990 to 1994, between

1995 to 2003, and between 2004 to 2007. In either case (either two or three periods), the majority of the abstracts studied (127 out of 230) had been written after 2001. Lastly, the authors used a regression analysis and found that every year, by average, about 1.5 articles are adding (above the previous year) to the subject (beta=1.536; F Ratio=24. 386; Prob. > F = 0.0002). This evidence supports the findings suggested earlier of the relatively early stage of academic research in this area.

Question 13: What are the research outlets/journals?

The research results suggest that the abstracts were published in more or less balanced approaches: 100 abstracts with a MIS perspective, 100 with a management perspective, and 30 with a mixed, MIS, and management perspective. The journals were balanced, more or less, as well. Forty three journals with MIS perspective, 65 with management perspective, and 15 with a mixed, MIS, and management perspective were identified. Therefore, no one paradigm is driving this area. A total of 123 journals were identified as contributing abstracts to this study with no one journal publishing more than 13 (5.65%) papers. See Table 14, Appendix B for the list of journals. The large number of journals that provided the abstracts, as well as the diversity in research perspectives and tools, increases the validity of this study (Salipante et al., 1982).

Question 14: Using Bohn's scale, what is the state of knowledge in this area?

The majority of the abstracts can be classified as being at the low end of the range (levels 2-3), which account for 166 out of the 230 abstracts in this study. The rest split about evenly with 32 abstracts in the medium (4-5) of the range and 32 abstracts in the high end (6-7) of the range (see Table 15, Appendix B). This seems to be consistent with the findings answering Question 9 about the research methodologies, which again suggests an early stage of academic rigor.

Conclusions and Implications

The positive answers to Questions 1-3 and the answer to Question 4 strongly support the validity of the two frameworks that were considered in this study. The study results confirm the belief that academic researchers are indeed using and reporting on the strategic dilemmas and the KBS LC stages as proposed by this study.

It was also determined, based on the research, that there are numerous areas that are underemphasized by academic researchers which also might indicate that practitioners may want to focus more of their attention on those areas. Based on the findings, the authors would recommend that more research be done regarding the strategic issues revolving around the complementary-destroying dilemma, as well as the concealment-transparent and the external acquisition-internal development dilemmas. Each of the three dilemmas has a solid tradition in the strategic literature (e.g., Amit & Shoemaker, 1993; Kim & Mauborgne, 2005; Tapscott & Ticoll, 2003) and should be seriously considered in the KM/KB strategic literature as well. Similar conclusions are relevant for a number of specific anchors of the strategic dilemmas. For example, the relative scarcity of the coverage of the KB Exploitation strategy may suggest that researchers (and some practitioners) are focusing too extensively on the fashionable and interesting topic of exploration/innovation and might indirectly be contributing to the low success rate of KBS and the low ROI that many systems produce (Bose, 2004). Similar conclusions can be made about the product strategic aspect. The "systems" nature of KBS is focusing the discussion (and research) on processes. However, from the business strategic perspective, this approach should be, at least, balanced with the focus on product (e.g., new product development) and the ways KBS can support these areas (Park & Kim, 2005). The external acquisition strategic aspect definitely requires more focus, especially, since the outsourcing of IS (Pati & Desai, 2005) and R&D (Henard & McFadyen, 2006) plays such an important role in organizational strategies. The next two aspects are the most demanding and the authors strongly recommend intensifying their academic coverage. Only recently, the need to revolutionize the industry and reinvent the business (the destroying anchor) became clear as a strategic option for organizations (Kim & Mauborgne, 2005). Clearly, there is a need to identify the KM/KB strategic relevance to support or to drive this strategic option and to identify KBS that might be instrumental in such endeavors. As Tapscott and Ticoll (2003), among many others, suggest, companies need to become more transparent. But this discussion requires honest deliberation of the concealment aspect of strategy, especially when incorporating and balancing the concerns for security (Belsis, Kokolakis, & Kiountouzis, 2005) and recent regulations (at least in the USA) that impact electronic documents discovery (Cortese, 2006; Shelton, 2006) and is significantly lacking from the academic literature (at least in the context of KBS).

The authors would also recommend a stronger need to emphasize research on the distribution stage of KBS. The assumption that lessons learned and best practices will be copied or diffused automatically by others within the organization and that they are easy to be copied is questionable at best (e.g., Bansler & Havn, 2003).

The authors would suggest a more focused research approach on the crossover areas of study that cover the evolve/learning stage of KBS LC within the context of complementary-destroying, concealment-transparent, and the external acquisition-internal development strategic dilemmas (Amit & Shoemaker, 1993; Kim & Mauborgne, 2005; Tapscott & Ticoll, 2003). A similar recommendation is made about the intersection of distribution of the KBS and all six strategic dilemmas (Chua & Lam, 2005).

It is clear that to make KM/KB strategies happen, many different aspects need to "work right" (Massey, Montoya-Weiss, & O'Driscoll, 2002). One aspect is to have more concrete discussion and research about the KBS needed to support the above mentioned strategies. The authors are recommending (similar to a recommendation made earlier by De Long and Fahey [2000}, in regards to culture) that no study, model, or framework of KM can be complete, unless it has a KBS aspect embedded within it.

One aspect of the context of KB strategies and systems studied was the specific industry discussed within the abstract. It seems that the research at the current stage is focusing heavily on the manufacturing sector of the economy. It is recommended that future studies focus on the service sector of the economy in the context of KB strategies and systems. This is especially important since this sector has a history of high labor and low capital intensity.

The second aspect of the context of KB strategies and systems studied was the specific geographic attribute discussed within the abstract. It seems that the current research is focusing heavily on the USA while lacking country specific context and/or an international perspective. It is recommended that future studies have a more explicit geographic focus and/or international characteristics in the context of KB strategies and systems. This is especially important if tacit knowledge and local culture are of interest.

Also, since large multinational companies are the primary users of KBS, the authors also recommend that more corporate level, multiple, and complex portfolio aspects be studied.

Finally, the authors are calling for more rigorous, exploratory, quantitative studies in this area. Having case studies, anecdotal stories, theoretical models, specific applications, and surveys were sufficient for an early stage of a young academic area. It is time to mature and to be able to convince the business community and the skeptic academic community that KM is not a short-time fad.

Weaknesses

There are two major weaknesses in this chapter. First, the authors did not use thematic review due to lack of resources. This is a major limitation on the scope of the research. One intriguing question relevant to the concealment-transparent strategic dilemma is that the majority of the abstracts identified by this study come from the transparent perspective. It seems that the academic researchers (as well as practitioners) take for granted that when systems are in place, people will post their knowledge. But there is an abundance of evidence to suggest that this is not the case (Bansler & Havn, 2003). Therefore, it would be interesting to see if a thematic survey would illuminate this discrepancy. Second, the authors used the abstracts of the papers for the review. It became obvious to the authors during the research that there is a wide variety of quality of abstracts. Some are very to the point, and short, and as such might cause the authors to misclassify the papers. Again, a thematic survey of the complete papers could have been helpful in overcoming this weakness.

Future Research

There are number of potential directions this research could be extended. For example, the authors identified very limited specific evidence of explicit knowledge management strategies. It would be interesting to see if when such cases are present, is this reflected in a context of business unit or corporate strategy or in a context of operational or functional strategies. A different area of study that this research could be extended is in testing if some research methods, for example case study, when used, result in a richer description (larger number of dimensions) of strategic dilemmas. A third potential extension is into the synergistic aspect of strategic dilemmas and KBS. One illustration of such area is the introduction of business process reengineering and KB/IS systems. Does the timing of the introduction make a difference? In another words, is it better to introduce them both simultaneously into an organization, or is better to introduce one of them (which one?) and then the other?

Acknowledgment

The authors want to thank Clyde E. Hull and Boris Durisin for their comments on an earlier draft of the chapter.

Case Study

Compare and contrast two cases:

1.   Dayan, R., Pasher, E., & Dvir, R. (2006). The knowledge management journey of Israel aircraft industries. Part 2: Competence center. In A.S. Kazi & P Wolf (Eds.), *Real-life knowledge management: Lessons from the field* (pp. 35-44).

Knowledge Board. Retrieved May 9, 2007 from http://www.innovationecology.com/papers/IAI%20case%20knowledgeboard%20ebook.pdf

2.   Chua, A. Y. K. (2007, April 28). The curse of success: Knowledge-management projects often look good in the beginning. But then problems arise. *Wall Street Journal, p. R8. Retrieved May 9, 2007, from* http://sloanreview.mit.edu/wsj/insight/organization/2007/04/27/index.php?p=1

Questions:

1.   For each case, identify the KB strategic dilemmas discussed and the strategic dilemmas missed.

2.   For each case identify the KBS life cycle stages discussed and the stages missed.

3.   Now, compare and contrast the two cases: What did you learn? (What worked? What did not?)

4.   What are the practical implications for your organization? (How can you improve?)

Further Reading

Knowledge Management's Social Dimension: Lessons From Nucor Steel By Anil K. Gupta and Vijay Govindarajan (Fall 2000) http://sloanreview.mit.edu/smr/issue/2000/fall/6/

Managing the Knowledge Life Cycle By Julian Birkinshaw and Tony Sheehan (Fall 2002) http://sloanreview.mit.edu/smr/issue/2002/fall/8/

Rethinking the Knowledge-Based Organization By Michael H. Zack (Summer 2003) *http://sloanreview.mit.edu/smr/issue/2003/summer/10/*

Why Don't We Know More About Knowledge? By Michael Hammer, Dorothy Leonard and Thomas Davenport (Summer 2004) http://sloanreview.mit.edu/smr/issue/2004/summer/02/

Successful Knowledge Management Projects By Thomas H. Davenport, David W. De Long and Michael C. Beers (Winter 1998) http://sloanreview.mit.edu/smr/issue/1998/winter/4/

Harvard Business Review on Knowledge Management (Harvard Business Review Paperback Series) (Paperback) Publisher: Harvard Business School Press; 1st edition (September 1998)

Harvard Business Review on Organizational Learning (Paperback) Publisher: Harvard Business School Press; 1st edition (June 15, 2001)

Knowledge and Strategy (Knowledge Reader) (Paperback) by Michael H. Zack (Editor) Publisher: Butterworth-Heinemann (March 23, 1999)

Managing Intellectual Capital: Organizational, Strategic, and Policy Dimensions (Clarendon Lectures in Management Studies) (Paperback) by David J. Teece Publisher: Oxford University Press, USA; New Ed edition (April 27, 2002)

Managing Knowledge: Perspectives on Cooperation and Competition (Paperback) by Georg von Krogh (Editor), Johan Roos (Editor) Publisher: Sage Publications Ltd (December 4, 1996)

Useful URLs

http://www.kmworld.com/

http://www.fastcompany.com/cgi-bin/finder.cgi?query=knowledge%20managem
ent

http://www.brint.com/km/

http://en.wikipedia.org/wiki/Knowledge_management

References

Abernathy, W. J. (1978). *The productivity dilemma*. Baltimore, MD: John Hopkins University Press.

Adelman, L., & Riedel, S. L. (1997). *Handbook for evaluating knowledge-based systems: Conceptual framework and compendium of methods*. Boston/Dordrecht/London: Kluwer Academic Publishers.

Alavi, M., & Leidner, D. E. (2001). Review: Knowledge management and knowledge management systems: Conceptual foundations and research issues. *MIS Quarterly, 25*(1), 107-136.

Amit, R., & Shoemaker, P. J. H. (1993). Strategic assets and organizational rent. *Strategic Management Journal, 14*(1), 33-46.

Appleyard, M. M. (1998). *Cooperative knowledge creation: The case of buyer-supplier co-development in the semiconductor industry* (Working Paper No. 98-06). Darden Graduate School of Business Administration. Retrieved December 26, 2003, from http://papers.ssrn.com/abstract=287855

Bansler, J. P., & Havn, E. C. (2003). Building community knowledge systems: An empirical study of IT-support for sharing best practices among managers. *Knowledge and Process Management, 10*(3), 156-163.

Barley, S. R. (1986). Technology as an occasion for structuring: Evidence from observations of CT scanners and the social order of radiology departments. *Administrative Science Quarterly, 31*, 708-808.

Barney, J. B. (1991). Firm resources and sustained competitive advantage. *Journal of Management, 17*, 99-120.

Belsis, P., Kokolakis, S., & Kiountouzis, E. (2005). Information systems security from a knowledge management perspective. *Information Management & Computer Security, 13*(2/3), 189-202.

Bierly, P., & Chakrabarti, A. (1996, Winter). Generic knowledge strategies in the U.S. pharmaceutical industry. *Strategic Management Journal, 17*, 123-135.

Blair, M. M., & Wallman, S. M. H. (2001). *Unseen wealth.* Washington, D.C.: Brookings Institution Press.

Bohn, R. E. (1994). Measuring and managing technological knowledge. *Sloan Management Review, 36*(1), 61-73.

Bose, R. (2004). Knowledge management metrics. *Industrial Management + Data Systems, 104*(5/6), 457-468.

Bower, J. L., & Christensen, C. M. (1995). Disruptive technologies: Catching the wave. *Harvard Business Review, 73*(1), 43-53.

Brooking, A. (1996). *Intellectual capital: Core asset for the third millennium.* London: International Thomson Business Press.

Brynjolfsson, E., & Hitt, L. M. (2000). Beyond computation: Information technology, organizational transformation and business performance. *The Journal of Economic Perspectives, 14*(3), 23-48.

Burlton, R. (1998, March). Process and knowledge management: A question of balance. *American Programmer,* 16-25.

Canez, L., & Probert, D. (1999). *Technology sourcing: The link to make-or-buy.* Paper presented at the Portland International Conference on Management of Engineering and Technology, PICMET 1999, Technology and Innovation Management (Vol. 2, pp. 47-52).

Casillas, J., Crocker, P., Jr., Fehrenbach, F., Haug, K., & Straley, B. (2000). Disruptive technologies: Strategic advantage and thriving in uncertainty. *Kellogg TechVenture 2000 anthology* (pp. 203-229).

Chen, M., & Chen, A. (2006). Knowledge management performance evaluation: A decade review from 1995 to 2004. *Journal of Information Science, 32*(1), 17-38.

Chua, A., & Lam, W. (2005). Why KM projects fail: A multi-case analysis. *Journal of Knowledge Management, 9*(3), 6-17.

Claycomb, C., Droge, C., & Germain, R. (2001). Applied process knowledge and market performance: The moderating effect of environmental uncertainty. *Journal of Knowledge Management, 5*(3), 264-277.

Conner, K. R., & Prahalad, C. K. (1996). A resource-based theory of the firm: Knowledge versus opportunism. *Organization Science, 7*, 477-501.

Cortese, A. W., Jr. (2006). Proposed amendments to the federal civil rules strike healthy balance. *Defense Council Journal, 72*(4), 354-361.

Colin, C. (2004). The knowledge entrepreneurship challenge: Moving on from knowledge sharing to knowledge creation and exploitation. *The Learning Organization, 11*(1), 84-93.

Davenport, T. H. (1993). *Process innovation: Reengineering work through information technology.* Boston: Harvard Business School Press.

Davenport, T. H., Jarvenpaa, S. L., & Beers, M. C. (1996). Improving knowledge work processes. *Sloan Management Review, 37*(4), 53-65.

De Long, D. W., & Fahey, L. (2000). Diagnosing cultural barriers to knowledge management. *Academy of Management Executive, 14*(4), 113-127.

DeTienne, D. R., & Koberg, C. S. (2002). The impact of environmental and organizational factors on discontinuous innovation within high-technology industries. *IEEE Transactions on Engineering Management, 49*, 352-364.

Gray, S. J. (1988). Toward a theory of cultural influence on the development of accounting systems internationally. *Abacus, 8*(1), 1-15.

Hargadon, A. B. (1998). Firms as knowledge brokers: Lessons in pursuing continuous innovation. *California Management Review, 40*(3), 209-227.

Henard, D. H., & McFadyen, M. A. (2006). R&D knowledge *is* power. *Research Technology Management, 49*(3), 41-47.

Hill, C. W., & Rothaermel, F. T. (2003). The performance of incumbent firms in the face of radical technological innovation. *Academy of Management Review, 28*, 257-274.

Hung, Y., Huang, S., Lin, Q., & Tsai, M. (2005). Critical factors in adopting a knowledge management system for the pharmaceutical industry. *Industrial Management + Data Systems, 105*(1/2), 164-183.

Inkpen, A. (1998). Learning and knowledge acquisition through international strategic alliances. *Academy of Management Executive, 12*(4), 69-80.

Jiang, B., & Qureshi, A. (2006). Research on outsourcing results: Current literature and future opportunities. *Management Decision, 44*(1), 44-55.

Jones, O. (2000). Innovation management as a post-modern phenomenon: The outsourcing of pharmaceutical R&D. *British Journal of Management, 11,* 341-356.

Jones, P. (2002). When successful product prevent strategic innovation. *Design Management Journal, 13*(2), 30-37.

Kim, W. C., & Mauborgne, R. (2005). *Blue ocean strategy: How to create uncontested market space and make competition irrelevant.* Boston: Harvard Business School Press.

Kurokawa, S. (1997). Make-or-Buy decisions in R&D: Small technology based firms in the United States and Japan. *IEEE Transactions on Engineering Management, 44,* 124-134.

Lamming, R. C., Caldwell, N. G., Harrison, D. A., & Phillips, W. (2001). Transparency in supply relationships: Concepts and practice. *The Journal of Supply Chain Management, 37*(4), 4-10.

Leonard-Barton, D. A. (1995). *Wellsprings of knowledge.* Boston: Harvard Business School Press.

Lev, B. (2000). Knowledge management: Fad or need? *Research Technology Management, 43*(5), 9-10.

Lev, B. (2001). *Intangibles: Management, measurement, and reporting.* Washington, D.C.: Brookings Institution Press.

Levinthal, D. A., & March, J.G. (1993). The myopia of learning. *Strategic Management Journal, 14,* 95-112.

Lytras, M. D., Pouloudi, N., & Poulymenakou, A. (2002). Knowledge management convergence: Expanding learning frontiers. *Journal of Knowledge Management, 6*(1), 40-51.

Malhotra, A., & Majchrzak, A. (2004). Enabling knowledge creation in far-flung teams: Best practices for IT support and knowledge sharing. *Journal of Knowledge Management, 8*(4), 75-88.

March, J. G. (1991). Exploration and exploitation in organizational learning. *Organization Science, 2,* 71-87.

Martensson, M. (2000). A critical review of knowledge management as a management tool. *Journal of Knowledge Management, 4*(3), 204-216.

Martin, J. (1995). *The great transition.* New York: AMACOM.

Massey, A. P., Montoya-Weiss, M. M., & O'Driscoll, T. M. (2002). Knowledge management in pursuit of performance: Insights from Nortel networks. *MIS Quarterly, 26*(3), 269-289.

Nakamura, L. (2001). Investing in intangibles: Is a trillion dollars missing from the gross domestic product? *Federal Reserve Bank of Philadelphia Business Review, 4th Quarter,* 27-37.

Nissén, M., Kamel, M., & Sengupta, K. (2000). Integrated analysis and design of knowledge systems and processes. *Information Resources Management Journal, 13*(1), 24-43.

Paoli, M., & Prencipe, A. (1999). The role of knowledge bases in complex product systems: Some empirical evidence from the aero engine industry. *Journal of Management & Governance, 3*(2), 137-160.

Parikh, M. (2001). Knowledge management framework for high-tech research and development. *Engineering Management Journal, 13*(3), 27-33.

Park, Y., & Kim, S. (2005). Linkage between knowledge management and R&D management. *Journal of Knowledge Management, 9*(4), 34-44.

Pati, N., & Desai, M. S. (2005). Conceptualizing strategic issues in information technology outsourcing. *Information Management & Computer Security, 13*(4), 281-296.

Persaud, A., Kumar, U., & Kumar, V. (2001). Harnessing scientific and technological knowledge for rapid deployment of global innovations. *Engineering Management Journal, 13*(1), 12-18.

Petty, R., & Guthrie, J. (2000). Intellectual capital literature review measurement, reporting and management. *Journal of Intellectual Capital, 1*(2), 155-176.

Pitt, M., & Clarke, K. (1999). Competing on competence: A knowledge perspective on the management of strategic innovation. *Technology Analysis & Strategic Management, 11*, 301-316.

Quinn, J. B. (1999). Strategic outsourcing: Leveraging knowledge capabilities. *Sloan Management Review, 40*(4), 9-21.

Radebaugh, L. H., & Gray, S. J. (1997). *International accounting and multinational enterprises* (4th ed.). New York: John Wiley & Sons, Inc.

Riege, A. (2005). Three-dozen knowledge-sharing barriers managers must consider. *Journal of Knowledge Management, 9*(3), 18-35.

Robey, D., Boundreau, M., & Rose, G. M. (2000). Information technology and organizational learning: A review and assessment of research. *Accounting Management and Information* Technologies, *10*, 125-155.

Russ, M., Jones, J. K., & Fineman, R. (2006). Toward a taxonomy of knowledge-based strategies: Early findings. *International Journal of Knowledge and Learning, 2*(1-2), 1-40.

Ryan, S., & Hurley, J. (2004). Have total quality management, business process re-engineering and the learning organisation been replaced by knowledge management? *Irish Journal of Management, 25*(1), 41-55.

Salipante, P., Notz, W., & Bigelow, J. (1982). A matrix approach to literature review. In B. M. Staw & L. L. Cummings (Eds.), *Research in organizational behavior* (pp. 321-348). Greenwich, CT: JAI Press.

Sanchez, R., & Mahoney, J. T. (1996, Winter). Modularity, flexibility, and knowledge management in product and organization design. *Strategic Management Journal, 17*, 63-76.

Schultz, M., & Jobe, L. A. (2001). Codification and tacitness as knowledge management strategies: An empirical exploration. *The Journal of High Technology Management Research, 12*, 139-165.

Shelton, G. D. (2006). Don't let the terabyte you: New e-discovery amendments to the federal rules of civil procedure. *Defense Council Journal, 73*(4), 324-331.

Smith, P. G., & Reinertsen, D. G. (1998). *Developing products in half the time*. New York: Van Nostrand Reinhold.

Stringer, R. (2000). How to manage radical innovation. *California Management Review, 42*(4), 70-88.

Szulanski, G. (1996). Exploring internal stickiness: Impediments to the transfer of best practice within the firm. *Strategic Management Journal, 17*, 27-44.

Tapscott, D., & Ticoll, D. (2003). *The naked corporation: How the age of transparency will revolutionize business*. New York: Free Press.

Taylor, W. A., & Wright, G. H. (2004). Organizational readiness for successful knowledge sharing: Challenges for public sector managers. *Information Resources Management Journal, 17*(2), 22-37.

Teece, D. J., Pisano, G., & Shuen, A. (1997). Dynamic capabilities and strategic management, *Strategic Management Journal, 18*(7), 509-533.

Thompson, A. A., Strickland, A. J., & Gamble, J. E. (2007). *Crafting & executing strategy: The quest for competitive advantage: Concepts and cases* (15th ed.). Boston: McGraw Hill, Irwin.

Thorpe, R., Holt, R., Macpherson, A., & Pittaway, L. (2005). Using knowledge within small and medium-sized firms: A systematic review of the evidence. *International Journal of Management Reviews, 7*(4), 257-281.

Tiwana, A. (2000). *The knowledge management toolkit*. Upper Saddle River, NJ: Prentice Hall PTR.

von Furstenberg, G. M. (2001). Hopes and delusions of transparency. *The North American Journal of Economics and Finance, 12*, 105-120.

White, S. (2000). Competition, capabilities, and the make, buy, or ally decisions of Chinese state-owned firms. *The Academy of Management Journal, 43*, 324-341.

Zack, M. H. (1999a). Developing a knowledge strategy. *California Management Review, 41*(3), 125-145.

Zack, M. H. (1999b). Managing codified knowledge. *Sloan Management Review, 40*(4), 45-57.

Appendix A

Table 1. C³EEP – coding scheme – March 12, 2007

Codification	Tacitness
explicit knowledge	tacit knowledge
codification	tacitness
codifying the knowledge	knowledge situated
store in organizational memory	stickiness
written plan	embeddedness
Complementary	**Destroying**
routine innovations	disrupting technologies
incremental innovations	radical innovation
linear change	discontinuous change
reactive change	discontinuous innovation
complementary	anticipatory change
knowledge that is compatible to the currently existing knowledge base	destroying
congruent	disruptive technologies
supportive and related to the existing knowledge base	
sustaining technologies	
related and supportive of the existing knowledge base	
recombination of existing knowledge	
knowledge compatibility	
knowledge complementarity.	
Adaptive/evolutionary	
Concealment	**Transparent**
secrecy strategy	transparency strategy
not sharing	sharing
minimize revelation	maximize revelation
controlling exchange	facilitate exchange
concealed knowledge	publicly open and accountable
shielding their knowledge	validating and publicizing information
protecting their knowledge	
confidentiality	
disclosure only within the legal limits	
need-to-know basis	
privatizing information	

continued on following page

Table 1. continued

External Acquisition	Internal Development
external acquisition, acquiring new knowledge	internal development
mergers	R&D
networking	
acquired from outside through inter-organizational arrangements	dependencies on internal development
"make or buy"	"make or buy"
dependencies on external sources with their internal development	
outsourcing/external partnership	internal partnership
external knowledge exchange	
absorptive capacity	absorptive capacity
relationships that the employees have with external constituencies	
external sources of knowledge acquisition	
collaboration/cooperation	collaboration/cooperation
Exploration	**Exploitation**
exploration	exploitation
experimentation	
innovation	managing efficiently existing knowledge
creativity	
proactive	reactive
Product	**Process**
product strategy	process strategy
service strategy	process improvement.
"what" they produce/make	process reengineering
product design	process efficiencies
	administrative
	systems
	continuous quality improvements
	investment in IS technology
	"how" they make/produce
	process innovation
	value stream reinvention
	dynamic capabilities
	six sigma
	business process management (BPM)
product life cycle	product life cycle

Table 2. KBS-Life cycle coding scheme – March 12, 2007

Create-1	Distribute-4
acquire	transfer
attract/adopt	share
develop	distribute
create	access
generate/building	

Organize-2	Apply-5
define/organize/extract	deployment/use/launched
collect/search	utilize/demonstrated
capture/understand	engage
map/systematize	implement
bundle	install/adopt
specify/identification	support/maintain/managed
integrate/looking	

Formalize-3	Evolve-6
enable	relate
reuse/retrieve	learn
store	measure/appraisal
codify/accumulate	meaning creation
formalize	evaluate/analyzed
design/plan	
validate/assessment	
verify	

Table 3. Bohn's stages of knowledge growth; Source: Adopted from Tiwana (2000)

Stage	Name	Comment	Typical form of knowledge
1	Complete ignorance	Nothing known	Does not exist anywhere
2	Awareness	Resembles pure art	Knowledge is primarily tacit
3	Measure	It is pretechnological	Knowledge is primarily written
4	Control of the mean	A scientific method is feasible	Written and embodied in hardware
5	Process capability manuals	A local recipe exist	Hardware and operating
6	Process characterization	Tradeoffs to reduce costs are known	Empirical equations (quantitative)
7	Know why scientific	Takes the form of science	Procedures, methodologies, formulas, and algorithms
8	Complete knowledge always	Nirvana	Never happens; but you can hope for it

Table 4. Classification scheme March 12, 2007

Include? Yes/Exclude:	No KB Strategy — *No KBS LC* – Other:
# of the abstract/Year	Journal name and type
Comments/Miscellaneous.:	
Codification	Tacitness
Complementary	Destroying
Concealment	Transparent
External Acquisition	Internal Development
Exploration	Exploitation
Product	Process
Other KM strategies:	

Specific country identified:	International perspective identified:
Create	Distribute
Organize	Apply
Formalize	Evolve
Specific industry identified:	
Bohn's scale 1-7 (?)	
KB/IS Technologies identified:	
Type of Business strategy:	Operational/Functional/Business Unit/ Corporate
Research Methodology:	
Research Perspective:	Conceptual/Empirical/Prescriptive/Descriptive

Appendix B

Table 1. C³EEP frequencies

	A1-Codification A2-Tacitness A	B1-Complementary B2-Destroying	C1-Concealment C2-Transparent	D1-External Acquisition - D2-Internal Development	E1-Exploration E2-Exploitation	F1-Product F2-Process	Average
neither 1 or 2	86	173	170	151	88	42	118.33
1 only	64	44	2	27	37	6	30.00
2 only	30	5	53	31	69	145	55.5
1 and 2	50	8	5	21	36	37	26.17
Percentage mentioned	62.61%	24.78%	26.09%	34.35%	61.74%	81.74%	48.55%

Table 2. KBS life cycle frequencies

KBS Life Cycle Stage	KBS Life Cycle stage not mentioned=0	KBS Life Cycle stage mentioned=1	Percentage mentioned
Create *1*	126	104	45.22%
Organize *2*	171	59	25.65%
Formalize *3*	173	57	24.78%
Distribute 4	218	12	5.22%
Apply *5*	71	159	69.13%
Evolve *6*	173	57	24.78%
Average	155.33	74.67	32.46%

Table 3. C³EEP and KBS-LC frequencies

	Codification-Tacitness A	Complementary-Destroying B	Concealment-Transparent C	External Acquisition –Internal Development D	Exploration-Exploitation E	Product – Process F	Total KBS-LC
Create 1	64	28	27	32	66	86	303
Organize 2	42	19	23	17	36	45	182
Formalize 3	38	18	21	21	34	48	180
Distribute 4	10	1	6	6	9	7	39
Apply 5	97	42	38	55	105	133	470
Evolve 6	38	7	17	16	34	51	163
Total C³EEP	289	115	132	147	284	370	*1337*

Table 4. Use of specific KBS tools

Specific KBS tools used	
No	129
Yes	101

Table 5. Specific KBS tools used

Number	System	System - A
11	ERP	enterprise resource planning (ERP)
10	ES	expert systems (ES)
9	DSS	decision support systems (DSS)
7	CRM	customer relationship management (CRM)
5	DBMS	databases
4	EMSs	environmental management systems (EMSs)
3	CBR	case-based reasoning (CBR)
4	Internet	Internet
3	Intranet	intranet
3	WfMSs	workflow management systems (WfMSs)
2	data mining	data mining
2	data warehousing	data warehousing
2	EDI	electronic data interchange (EDI)
2	GDSS	group decision support systems (GDSS)
2	GIS	geographic information systems (GIS)
1	an argumentation-enabling mechanism	an argumentation-enabling mechanism
1	an associated structured dialogue scheme	an associated structured dialogue scheme
1	AOKBS	agent-oriented and knowledge-based system (AOKBS) for strategic e-procurement
1	autonomic computing	autonomic computing - e-automation correlation engine
1	community-based information networks	community-based information networks
1	CSMILE	computer-supported intentional learning environments (CSILE).
1	decision simulation	decision simulation
1	deductive databases	deductive databases
1	distributed data bases	distributed databases
1	DSS_BN	DSS using Bayesian network (BN)
1	ECIS	electronic commerce information systems (ECIS)

Table 5. continued

Number	System	System - A
1	ECM	enterprise content management (ECM)
1	EIS	executive information systems (EIS).
1	electronic library	electronic library
1	e-procurement	e-procurement
1	e-sourcing	e-sourcing
1	fuzzy sets	fuzzy sets
1	groupware	groupware
1	HRIS	human resource information system (HRIS)
1	ISCA	information systems for competitive advantage (ISCA)
1	ITSS	information technology support system (ITSS)
1	IMkIS	intelligent marketing information systems (IMkIS)
1	IMS	Internet management system (IMS)
1	induction graphs learning	induction graphs learning
1	intelligent software agent	intelligent software agent
1	Intranet/Extranet	intranet/extranet
1	IPR	intellectual property right (IPR) systems.
1	KBCSCM	knowledge-based collaborative supply chain management (KBCSCM) system
1	KBFDA	knowledge-based functional design automation system (KBFDA)
1	KBSDSS	knowledge-based strategic decision support system
1	KBSim	knowledge-based simulator (KBSim)
1	FARSYS	a knowledge-based system for managing strategic change- FARSYS
1	knowledge repositories	"knowledge repositories"
1	language analysis	language analysis
1	learning-based scheduling KB	learning-based scheduling KB
1	LFS	linguistic fuzzy systems (LFS)
1	LKBS	legal knowledge-based system (LKBS)
1	MKIS	marketing information systems (MKIS)
1	mobile agent for e-commerce	mobile agent for e-commerce
1	multimedia	multimedia
1	neural networks	neural networks
1	next-generation knowledge-based systems	next-generation knowledge-based systems
1	NIS	neighborhood information system (NIS)
1	object-oriented systems	object-oriented representation methods

Table 5. continued

Number	System	System - A
1	OMS	order management system
1	PDCS	Web-enabled product definition and customization system (PDCS)
1	process mapping	process mapping
1	process warehouse	process warehouse
1	RBR	rule-based reasoning (RBR)
1	rule-based KBS	rule-based; knowledge-based functional reasoning strategy
1	service supply relationship management	service supply relationship management
1	SMILE	strategic management interactive learning expert system prototype (SMILE)
1	software objects	software objects
1	structural indexing	structural indexing
1	TNS	transnational systems (TNS)
124	**Total**	

Table 6. Industries identified

Specific industries identified	
No	109
Yes	121

Table 7. Specific industries identified

Industry	Number
Agriculture	2
Construction	2
Education	9
Government	5
Manufacturing	50
Not for profits	3
Services	42
Utilities	4
Total	**117**

Table 8. Countries and international perspective identified

Specific countries identified		International perspective identified	
No	109	No	210
Yes	121	Yes	20

Table 9. Specific countries identified

Country	Number
Australia	3
Canada	1
China	1
Germany	2
Greece	1
Hong Kong	3
Hungary	1
India	1
Japan	1
Kuwait	1
Libya	1
Netherland	3
New Zealand	1
Norway	1
Singapore	1
South Korea	1
Sweden	1
Taiwan	2
UK	5
USA	23
Total	**54**

Table 10. Layers of organizational strategy

Strategy	used=1
Operational	101
Functional	42
Business Unit	82
Corporate	5
Total	230

Table 11. Research frameworks

Research Framework	Method not used=0	Method used=1
Conceptual	77	153
Empirical	91	139
Prescriptive	74	156
Descriptive	121	109
Average	90.75	139.25

Table 12. Research methodologies

Research methodology	method used=1	Research methodology	method used=1
Literature review	65	*Literature review*	65

Case study	59		
Literature review & case study	15		
Field Study	2		
Literature review & focus group	1		
Ethnographic	1		
Case study and Interviews	1		
Interviews	1	*Case study and so forth.*	80

Application and prototype	20		
Application and prototype and case study	16		
Literature review and model	4		
Application model	2		
Application and case study	2		
Model and case study	1		
Literature review and prototype	1		

continued on following page

Table 12. continued

Research methodology	method used=1	Research methodology	method used=1
Literature review, model, and case study	1		
Survey and prototype	1	*Application and so forth.*	48

Survey	15		
Survey and case study	3		
Survey and interviews	1	*Survey, and so forth.*	19

Exploratory and quantitative analysis	17		
Lab experiment and survey	1	*Quantitative Analysis*	18

Total	230	*Total*	230

Table 13. Abstract's publication years

Year	1990	1991	1992	1993	1994	1995	1996	1997	1998
#	6	8	9	8	4	7	10	9	5

Year	1999	2000	2001	2002	2003	2004	2005	2006	2007
#	15	5	17	14	16	31	27	38	1

Table 14. Abstract's publication journals

Journals with mixed MIS and Management Perspective	# of Abstracts
Industrial Management + Data Systems	8
Information & Management	5
Logistics Information Management	4
IBM Systems Journal	2
Global Journal of Flexible Systems Management	1
Information Processing & Management	1
Information Systems and eBusiness Management	1
Information Technology & People	1
Information Technology and Libraries	1
Information Technology and Management	1
International Journal of Information Technology and Management.	1
International Journal of Services Technology and Management	1
Journal of Database Marketing & Customer Strategy Management	1
Journal of Enterprise Information Management	1
Journal of Information Systems Education	1
Total	30

Journals with MIS Perspective	# of Abstracts
Journal of Management Information Systems	13
Information Systems Management	9
European Journal of Information Systems	8
MIS Quarterly	5
Decision Support Systems	4
Information Systems Frontiers	4
Omega	4
Communications of the Association for Computing Machinery	3
Computers in Industry	3
Information Management & Computer Security	3
Information Systems Research	3
International Journal of Information Management	3
Communications of the Association for Information Systems	2
Computers & Industrial Engineering	2
Expert Systems	2
International Journal of Electronic Commerce	2
Journal of Information Science	2
Journal of Intelligent Manufacturing	2

continued on following page

Table 14. continued

Journals with MIS Perspective	# of Abstracts
Journal of Systems Management	2
The Journal of Systems and Software,	2
Campus – Wide Information Systems	1
Computers & Security	1
Information and Software Technology	1
Information Resources Management Journal	1
Information Systems Journal	1
International Journal of Computer Applications in Technology	1
International Journal of Information Resource Management	1
Journal of Cases on Information Technology	1
Journal of Electronic Commerce Research	1
Journal of Information Systems Education	1
Journal of Information Technology	1
Journal of Information Technology Case and Application Research	1
Journal of Information Technology Theory and Application	1
Journal of the American Society for Information Science and Technology	1
Journal of the Association for Information Systems	1
Management Communication Quarterly	1
Online Information Review	1
Records Management Journal	1
Software Quality Journal	1
The Journal of Computer Information Systems	1
The Journal of Information Systems Management	1
VINE	1
Total	100

Journals with Management Perspective	# of Abstracts
Accounting, Organizations and Society	1
Business Process Management Journal	7
International Journal of Production Research	5
International Journal of Technology Management	4
Journal of Knowledge Management	4
Decision Sciences	3
IEEE Transactions on Engineering Management	3
International Journal of Operations & Production Management	3
Strategic Management Journal	3

continued on following page

Table 14. continued

Journals with Management Perspective	# of Abstracts
The Journal of Business Strategy	3
Business Strategy and the Environment	2
California Management Review	2
European Management Journal	2
Harvard Business Review	2
Industrial Marketing Management	2
International Journal of Project Management	2
MIT Sloan Management Review	2
Strategic Direction	2
Technovation	2
The International Journal of Quality & Reliability Management	2
The Journal of the Operational Research Society	2
Association Management	1
Banca Nazionale del Lavoro Quarterly Review	1
Business Strategy Review	1
Construction Management and Economics	1
Disaster Prevention and Management	1
Environmental Science & Technology	1
Human Systems Management	1
Interfaces	1
International Journal of Bank Marketing	1
International Journal of Business Performance Management	1
International Journal of Contemporary Hospitality Management	1
International Journal of Human Resources Development and Management	1
International Journal of Knowledge and Learning	1
International Journal of Knowledge, Culture and Change Management	1
International Journal of Market Research	1
International Journal of Production Economics	1
International Journal of Purchasing and Materials Management	1
International Journal of Retail & Distribution Management	1
Journal of Agricultural and Environmental Ethics	1
Journal of American Academy of Business	1
Journal of European Industrial Training	1
Journal of Management Studies	1
Journal of Small Business Management	1
Leadership & Organization Development Journal	1
Long Range Planning	1
Management Accounting Research	1
Management Decision	1

continued on following page

Table 14. continued

Journals with Management Perspective	# of Abstracts
Marketing Intelligence & Planning	1
Marketing Science	1
Planning Review	1
Production Planning & Control	1
Public Administration and Management	1
Public Administration Review	1
Risk Management	1
Strategy & Leadership	1
Target Management Development Review	1
The Academy of Management Executive	1
The International Journal of Bank Marketing	1
The International Journal of Tourism Research	1
The Journal of Business & Industrial Marketing	1
The Journal of Management Development	1
The Learning Organization	1
Total	100

Table 15. Abstract's state of knowledge

Bohn's scale	1	2	3	4	5	6	7
#	0	125	41	9	23	27	5

median=2   mean=3.13

Appendix C

Abad-Grau, M. M., & Arias-Aranda, D. (2006). Operations strategy and flexibility: Modeling with Bayesian classifiers. *Industrial Management + Data Systems, 106*(4), 460-484.

Alavi, M., & Leidner, D. E. (2001, March). Knowledge management and knowledge management systems: Conceptual foundations and research issues. *MIS Quarterly, 25*(1), 107-136.

Amaravadi, C. S, Samaddar, S., & Dutta, S. (1995). Intelligent marketing information systems: Computerized intelligence for marketing decision making. *Marketing Intelligence & Planning, 13*(2), 4.

Apigian, C. H., Ragu-Nathan, B. S., & Ragu-Nathan, T. S. (2006). Strategic profiles and Internet performance: An empirical investigation into the development of a strategic Internet system. *Information & Management, 43*(4), 455-468.

Askari, H., & Chatterjee, J. (2003). Software exporting: A developing country advantage. *Banca Nazionale del Lavoro Quarterly Review, 56*(224), 57-74.

Atkinson, R. A. (1992). Applying the 80/20 rule: Making it work for IS plans. *Information Systems Management, 9*(3), 57.

Awad, N. F., & Krishnan, M. D. (2006). The personalization privacy paradox: An empirical evaluation of information transparency and the willingness to be profiled online for personalization. *MIS Quarterly, 30*(1), 13-28.

Bakos, J. Y., & Brynjolfsson, E. (1993). Information technology, incentives, and the optimal number of suppliers. *Journal of Management Information Systems, 10*(2), 37.

Banipal, K. (2006). Strategic approach to disaster management: Lessons learned from Hurricane Katrina. *Disaster Prevention and Management, 15*(3), 484-494.

Bardhan, I., Whitaker, J., & Mithas, S. (2006). Information technology, production process outsourcing, and manufacturing plant performance. *Journal of Management Information Systems, 23*(2), 13-40.

Barua, A., Ravindran, S., & Whinston, A. B. (1997). Efficient selection of suppliers over the Internet. *Journal of Management Information Systems, 13*(4), 117-137.

Baskerville, R. L., & Stage, J. (1996). Controlling prototype development through risk analysis. *MIS Quarterly, 20*(4), 481-504.

Beckett, A. J., Wainwright, C. E. R., & Bance, D. (2000). Implementing an industrial continuous improvement system: A knowledge management case study. *Industrial Management & Data Systems, 100*(7), 330-338.

Beckworth, G., & Altmann, G. (1997). Defining strategies - measuring quality. *Software Quality Journal, 6*(2), 171-178.

Behara, R. S., Gundersen, D. E., & Capozzoli, E. A. (1995). Trends in information systems outsourcing. *International Journal of Purchasing and Materials Management, 31*(2), 45.

Bergeron, F., & Raymond, L. (1992). Planning of information systems to gain a competitive edge. *Journal of Small Business Management, 30*(1), 21.

Best, W. (1993). Flexible, integrated operations: The new Japanese challenge. *Planning Review, 21*(5), 49.

Bloodgood, J. M., & Salisbury, W. D. (2001). Understanding the influence of organizational change strategies on information technology and knowledge management strategies. *Decision Support Systems, 31*(1), 55-69.

Bodnar, A. A., & Hawley, R. (2001). The role of engineering in knowledge management: The key to wealth creation. *International Journal of Technology Management, 22*(1-3), 263-277.

Borch, O. J., & Hartvigsen, G. (1991). Knowledge-based systems for strategic market planning in small firms. *Decision Support Systems, 7*(2), 145.

Bose, R. (2004). Knowledge management metrics. *Industrial Management + Data Systems, 104*(5/6), 457-468.

Boulet, M.-M., Jebara, F. B., Bemmira, F., & Boudreault, S. (2002). A comparison of three delivery systems for teaching an information technology course. *Association for Computing Machinery. Communications of the ACM, 45*(4), 129.

Bourgault, M., Gagnon, Y.-C., Posada, E. (2004). Investigating the partnering strategy for information technology acquisition in public organisations. *International Journal of Technology Management, 27*(2, 3), 193-208.

Bozarth, C. (2006). ERP implementation efforts at three firms: Integrating lessons from the SISP and IT-enabled change literature. *International Journal of Operations & Production Management, 26*(11), 1223-1239.

Bracke, M. B. M., Metz, J. H. M., Dijkhuizen, A. A., & Spruijt, B. M.. (2001). Development of a decision support system for assessing farm animal welfare in relation to husbandry systems: Strategy and prototype. *Journal of Agricultural and Environmental Ethics, 14*(3), 321

Bradley, R. V., Pridmore, J. L., & Byrd, A. T. (2006). Information systems success in the context of different corporate cultural types: An empirical investigation. *Journal of Management Information Systems, 23*(2), 267-294.

Brockhoff, K. (1991). Competitor technology intelligence in German companies. *Industrial Marketing Management, 20*(2), 91.

Burke, R. R., Rangaswamy, A., Wind, J., & Eliashberg, J. (1990). A knowledge-based system for advertising design. *Marketing Science, 9*(3), 212.

Cardoso, J., Bostrom, R. P., & Sheth, A. (2004). Workflow management systems and ERP systems: Differences, commonalities, and applications. *Information Technology and Management, 5*(3-4), 319-338.

Case Study: JET Employee Benefits Trust Accounting Application. (1992). *Journal of Systems Management, 43*(5), 26.

Cavazza, M., & Zweigenbaum, P. (1992). Extracting implicit information from free text technical reports. *Information Processing & Management, 28*(5), 609.

Chalmeta, R. (2006). Methodology for customer relationship management. *The Journal of Systems and Software, 79*(7), 1015-1024.

Chan, J. O. (2005). Enterprise information systems strategy and planning. *Journal of American Academy of Business, Cambridge, 6*(2), 148-153.

Chen, J.-H., Chao, K.-M., & Von-Wun Soo, N. G. (2005). Combining cooperative and non-cooperative automated negotiations. *Information Systems Frontiers, 7*(4-5), 391-404.

Chen, C. C., & Yih, Y. (1996, June). Indentifying attributes for knowledge-based development in dynamic scheduling environments. *International Journal of Production Research, 34*(6), 1739.

Chen, C.-C., Yih, Y., & Wu, Y.-C. (1999, June 15). Auto-bias selection for developing learning-based scheduling systems. *International Journal of Production Research, 37*(9), 1987.

Cheung, C. F., Wang, W. M., Lo, V., & Lee, W. B.. (2004). An agent-oriented and knowledge-based system for strategic e-procurement. *Expert Systems, 21*(1), 11-21.

Chin, K. S., Yeung, I-K., & Fai, P. K. (2006). Development of an assessment system for supplier quality management. *The International Journal of Quality & Reliability Management, 23*(7), 743-765.

Chong, P. P., Chen, Y.-S., & Chou-Hong Chen, J. (2001). IT induction in the food service industry. *Industrial Management + Data Systems, 101*(1), 13-20.

Chowdary, B. V., & Kanda, A. (2003). A decision support system for flexibility in manufacturing. *Global Journal of Flexible Systems Management, 4*(3), 1-13.

Chung, W. W. C., & Lee, J. Y. P. (2006). Enterprise information system for customer services excellence. *International Journal of Business Performance Management, 8*(1), 5-23.

Clemons, E. K., Gao, G., & Hitt, L. M. (2006). When online reviews meet hyper-differentiation: A study of the craft beer industry. *Journal of Management Information Systems, 23*(2), 149-171.

Clemons, E. K., Thatcher, M. E., & Row, M. C. (1995). Identifying sources of reengineering failures: A study of the behavioral factors contributing to reengineering risks. *Journal of Management Information Systems, 12*(2), 9.

Cowan, J. E., & Eder, L. B. (2003). The transformation of AT&T's enterprise network systems group to Avaya: Enabling the virtual corporation through reengineering and enterprise resource planning. *Journal of Information Systems Education, 14*(3), 325-331.

Curry, B. (1993). Using computers for management decisions. *Logistics Information Management, 6*(5), 7.

Cyr, D., Gehling, L., & Gibson, M. L. (1997). IT power and the postemptive strike. *Information Systems Management, 14*(3), 7-15.

D Amours, S., Montreuil, B., Lefrancois, P., & Soumis, F.. (1999). Networked manufacturing: The impact of information sharing. *International Journal of Production Economics, 58*(1), 63-79.

Dai, R., Narasimhan, S., & Wu, D. J. (2005). Buyer's efficient e-sourcing structure: Centralize of decentralize? *Journal of Management Information Systems, 22*(2), 141-164.

Davenport, T. H. (1998). Putting the enterprise into the enterprise system. *Harvard Business Review, 76*(4), 121-131.

Davies, F. (1005). Construction and testing of a knowledge-based system in retail bank marketing. *International Journal of Bank Marketing, 13*(2), 4.

Dawood, N. N. (1995). An integrated bidding management expert system for the make-to-order precast industry. *Construction Management and Economics, 13*(2), 115.

Downing, C. E., Field, J. M., & Ritzman, L. P. (2003). The value of outsourcing: A field study. *Information Systems Management, 20*(1), 84-89.

Drury, D. H., & Farhoomand, A. (1999). Information technology push/pull reactions. *The Journal of Systems and Software, 47*(1), 3-10.

Duhan, S., Levy, M., & Powell, P. (2001). Information systems strategies in knowledge-based SMEs: The role of core competencies. *European Journal of Information Systems, 10*(1), 25-40.

Earl, M. J. (1996). Information systems strategy ... Why planning techniques are not the answer. *Business Strategy Review, 7*(1), 54.

Espino-Rodríguez, T. F., & Ma Gil-Padilla, A. (2005). Determinants of information systems outsourcing in hotels from the resource-based view: An empirical study. *The International Journal of Tourism Research, 7*(1), 35-47.

Ettlie, J. E., Perotti, V. J., Joseph, D. A., & Cotteleer, M. J. (2005). Strategic predictors of successful enterprise system deployment. *International Journal of Operations & Production Management, 25*(9/10), 953-972.

Evans, G. N., Naim, M. M., & Towill, D. R. (1993). Dynamic supply chain performance: Assessing the impact of information systems. *Logistics Information Management, 6*(4), 15.

Evgeniou, T. (2002). Information integration and information strategies for adaptive enterprises. *European Management Journal, 20*(5), 486-494.

Fan, M., Stallaert, J., & Whinston, A. B. (2000). The adoption and design methodologies of component-based enterprise systems. *European Journal of Information Systems, 9*(1), 25-35.

Feeny, D. F., & Willcocks, L. P. (1998). Core IS capabilities for exploiting information technology. *Sloan Management Review, 39*(3), 9-21.

Fiala, P. (2005). Information sharing in supply chains. *Omega, 33*(5), 419-423.

Fichman, R. G. (2004). Real options and IT platform adoption: Implications for theory and practice. *Information Systems Research, 15*(2), 132-154.

Finnegan, D., & Willcocks, L. (2006). Knowledge sharing issues in the introduction of a new technology. *Journal of Enterprise Information Management, 19*(6), 568-590.

Fitzsimmons, J. A., Anderson, E., & Morrice, D. (2004). Managing service supply relationships. *International Journal of Services Technology and Management, 5*(3), 221-232.

Florida, R., & Davidson, D. (2001, Spring). Gaining from green management: Environmental management systems inside and outside the factory. *California Management Review, 43*(3), 64-84.

Ford, N. J. (2006). The development and evaluation of an information technology support system to facilitate inter-organisational collaboration in HRD. *Journal of European Industrial Training, 30*(7), 569-588.

Fu, H.-P., Chang, T.-H., & Wu, W.-H. (2004). An implementation model of an e-procurement system for auto parts: A case study. *Production Planning & Control, 15*(7), 662-670.

Gadman, S., & Cooper, C. (2005). Strategies for collaborating in an interdependent interdependent world. *Leadership & Organization Development Journal, 26*(1/2), 23-34.

Galichet, S., & Foulloy, L. (2003). Integrating expert knowledge into industrial control structures. *Computers in Industry, 52*(3), 235-251.

Gammelgaard, J., & Ritter, T. (2005). The knowledge retrieval matrix: Codification and personification as separate strategies. Journal of *Knowledge Management, 9*(4), 133-143.

Gert-Jan De, V. (1997). Collaborative business engineering with animated electronic meetings. *Journal of Management Information Systems, 14*(3), 141-164.

Giacomazzi, F., Panella, C., Pernici, B., & Sansoni, M. (1997). Information systems integration in mergers and acquisitions: A normative model. *Information & Management, 32*(6), 289-302.

Giaglis, G. M., Hlupic, V., de Vreede, G.-J., & Verbraeck, A. (2005). Synchronous design of business processes and information systems using dynamic process modelling. *Business Process Management Journal, 11*(5), 488-500.

Gilmour, J., & Stancliffe, M. (2004). Managing knowledge in an international organisation: The work of Voluntary Services Overseas (VSO). *Records Management Journal, 14*(3), 124-128.

Grimshaw, D. J. (2001). Harnessing the power of geographical knowledge: The potential for data integration in an SME. *International Journal of Information Management, 21*(3), 183-191.

Grover, V., Cheon, M., & Teng, J. T. C. (1994). An evaluation of the impact of corporate strategy and the role of information technology on IS functional outsourcing. *European Journal of Information Systems, 3*(3), 179.

Guan, J., Nunez, W., & Welsh, J. F. (2002). Institutional strategy and information support: The role of data warehousing in higher education. *Campus - Wide Information Systems, 19*(5), 168-174.

Gupta, M., & Kohli, A. (2006). Enterprise resource planning systems and its implications for operations function. *Technovation, 26*(5, 6), 687-696.

Haines, M. N., Goodhue, D. L., & Gattiker, T. F. (2006). Fit between strategy and IS specialization: A framework for effective choice and customization of information system application modules. *Information Resources Management Journal, 19*(3), 34-47.

Hackbarth, G., & Kettinger, W. J. (2004). Strategic aspirations for net-enabled business. *European Journal of Information Systems, 13*(4), 273-285.

Hackney, R., Grant, K., & Birtwistle, G. (2006). The UK grocery business: Towards a sustainable model for virtual markets. *International Journal of Retail & Distribution Management, 34*(4/5), 354-368.

Haeckel, S. H., & Nolan, R. L. (1993). Managing by wire. *Harvard Business Review, 71*(5), 122.

Harris, A., Giunipero, L. C., Hult, G., & Tomas, M. (1998). Impact of organizational and contract flexibility on outsourcing contracts. *Industrial Marketing Management, 27*(5), 373-384.

Hall, H. (2001). Input-friendliness: Motivating knowledge sharing across intranets. *Journal of Information Science, 27*(3), 139-146.

Hertog, F., & Wielinga, C. (1992). Control systems in dissonance: The computer as an ink blot. *Accounting, Organizations and Society, 17*(2), 103.

Higgins, L. F., McIntyre, S. C., & Raine, C. G. (1991). Design of global marketing information systems. *The Journal of Business & Industrial Marketing, 6*(3, 4), 49.

Humphreys, P., McIvor, R., & Huang, G. (2002). An expert system for evaluating the make or buy decision. *Computers & Industrial Engineering, 42*(2-4), 567-585.

Hung, Y.-C., Huang, S.-M., Lin, Q.-P., & Tsai, M.-L. (2005). Critical factors in adopting a knowledge management system for the pharmaceutical industry. *Industrial Management + Data Systems, 105*(1/2), 164-183.

Hustad, E., & Munkvold, B. E. (2005). IT-supported competence management: A case study at Ericsson. *Information Systems Management, 22*(2), 78-88.

Hutchison, C., & Rosenberg, D. (1994, June). The organization of organizations: Issues for next-generation office IT. *Journal of Information Technology (Routledge, Ltd.), 9*(2), 99.

Huyet, A. L., & Paris, J. L. (2004). Synergy between evolutionary optimization and induction graphs learning for simulated manufacturing systems. *International Journal of Production Research, 42*(20), 4295-4313.

Hwang, S. (2006). Role of university in the partnership for IT innovations of community development: Utilizing universities' assets for 'neighborhood information system' development. *Public Administration and Management, 11*(2), 75-84, 86-100.

Ip, W. H., & Chen, B. (2004). An enterprise model and the organisation of ERP. *International Journal of Computer Applications in Technology, 21*(3), 79-86.

Irani, Z., Sharif, A. M., & Love, P. E. D. (2005). Linking knowledge transformation to information systems evaluation. *European Journal of Information Systems, 14*(3), 213-228.

Iverson, J. O., & McPhee, R. D. (2002). Knowledge management in communities of practice. *Management Communication Quarterly, 16*(2), 259-266.

Jang, S., Hong, K., Bock, G. W., & Kim, I. (2002). Knowledge management and process innovation: The knowledge transformation path in Samsung SDI. *Journal of Knowledge Management, 6*(5), 479-485.

Jih, W.-J. (2003). Simulating real world experience using accumulative system development projects. *Journal of Information Systems Education, 14*(2), 181.

Jones, R. (2003). Measuring the benefits of knowledge management at the financial services authority: A case study. *Journal of Information Science, 29*(6), 475-487.

Joshi, K. (2005). Understanding user resistance and acceptance during the implementation of an order management system: A case study using the equity implementation model1. *Journal of Information Technology Case and Application Research, 7*(1), 6-20.

Kalfan, A. M. (2004). Information security considerations in IS/IT outsourcing projects: A descriptive case study of two sectors. *International Journal of Information Management, 24*(1), 29-42.

Kallio, J., Saarinen, T., & Tinnila, M. (2002). Efficient change strategies. *Business Process Management Journal, 8*(1), 80-92.

Kakish, J., Zhang, P.-L., & Zeid, I. (2000). Towards the design and development of a knowledge-based universal modular jigs and fixtures system. *Journal of Intelligent Manufacturing, 11*(4), 381.

Kang, D., & Santhanam, R. (2004). A longitudinal field study of training practices in a collaborative application environment. *Journal of Management Information Systems, 20*(3), 257-281.

Karacapilidis, N., Adamides, E., & Evangelou, C. (2006). A computerized knowledge management system for the manufacturing strategy process. *Computers in Industry, 57*(2), 178-188.

Kathuria, R., Anandarajan, M., & Igbaria, M. (1999). Linking IT applications with manufacturing strategy: An intelligent decision support system approach. *Decision Sciences, 30*(4), 959-991.

Kathuria, R., Anandarajan, M., & Igbaria, M. (1999). Selecting IT applications in manufacturing: A KBS approach. *Omega, 27*(6), 605-616.

Kautto, P. (2006). New instruments - old practices? The implications of environmental management systems and extended producer responsibility for design for the environment. *Business Strategy and the Environment, 15*(6), 377.

Kazlauskas, E. J., Pinder, R., & Richardson, J. H. (1990). A review and exploratory investigation of instructional design strategies relevant to library and information management software. *Information Technology and Libraries, 9*(2), 121.

Kim, R. M., & Kaplan, S. M. (2006). Interpreting socio-technical co-evolution: Applying complex adaptive systems to IS engagement. *Information Technology & People, 19*(1), 35-54.

Kim, B.-O., & Lee, S. M. (1996). Logistics information's role within an IT systems architecture in a world-class organization. *Logistics Information Management, 9*(3), 19.

King, S. F., & Burgess, T. F. (2006). Beyond critical success factors: A dynamic model of enterprise system innovation. *International Journal of Information Management, 26*(1), 59-69.

King, W. R., & Sethi, V. (1993). Developing transnational information systems: A case study. *Omega, 21*(1), 53.

Kivijarvi, H., & Saarinen, T. (1995). Investment in information systems and the financial performance of the firm. *Information & Management, 28*(2), 143.

Kodama, M. (1999). Strategic business applications and new virtual knowledge-based businesses through community-based information networks. *Information Management & Computer Security, 7*(4), 186-199.

Kogan, S. L., & Muller, M. J. (2006). Ethnographic study of collaborative knowledge work. *IBM Systems Journal, 45*(4), 759-771.

Koltys, H. (1992). Corporate counsel cut costs with AI: Legal knowledge-based systems. *Information Systems Management, 9*(1), 82.

Koudal, P., & Coleman, G. C. (2005). Coordinating operations to enhance innovation in the global corporation. *Strategy & Leadership, 33*(4), 20-32.

Krasowski, M. D. (1991). Integrating distributed data bases into the information architecture. *Information Systems Management, 8*(2), 36.

Kridan, A. B., & Goulding, J. S.. (2006). A case study on knowledge management implementation in the banking sector. *VINE, 36*(2), 211-222.

Kwan, M. M., & Balasubramanian, P. (2003). Process-oriented knowledge management: A case study. *The Journal of the Operational Research Society, 54*(2), 204-211.

Lai, V. S., & Mahapatra, R. K. (2004). Correlating business process re-engineering with the information systems department. *International Journal of Production Research, 42*(12), 2357-2382.

Lam, W., & Chua, A. (2005). Knowledge management project abandonment: An exploratory examination of root causes. *Communications of the Association for Information Systems, 16*, 1.

Lanfield-Smith, K., & Smith, D. (2003). Management control systems and trust in outsourcing relationships. *Management Accounting Research, 14*(3), 281-307.

Langdon, C. S., & Sikora, R. T. (2006). Conceptualizing co-ordination and competition in supply chains as complex adaptive system. *Information Systems and eBusiness Management, 4*(1), 71-81.

Law, R., & Jogaratnam, G. (2005). A study of hotel information technology applications. *International Journal of Contemporary Hospitality Management, 17*(2/3), 170-180.

Lee, B. S., & Venkataramanan, S. (1991). Knowledge-based systems approach for offshore safety training. *Computers in Industry, 17*(4), 349.

Lefley, F. (2004). An assessment of various approaches for evaluating project strategic benefits: Recommending the strategic index. *Management Decision, 42*(7/8), 850-862.

Lehmann, H. (2006). European international freight forwarders: Information as a strategic product. *Journal of Cases on Information Technology, 8*(1), 63-78.

Levina, N. (2005). Collaborating on multiparty information systems development projects: A collective reflection-in-action view. *Information Systems Research, 16*(2), 109-130.

Liang, T.-P. (1993). Special section: Research in integrating learning capabilities into information systems. *Journal of Management Information Systems, 9*(4), 5.

Liebowitz, J. (2004). A knowledge management strategy for the Jason organization: A case study. *The Journal of Computer Information Systems, 44*(2), 1-5.

Light, B., Holland, C. P., & Wills, K. (2001). ERP and best of breed: A comparative analysis. *Business Process Management Journal, 7*(3), 216-224.

Lindley, E., & Wheeler, F. P. (2001). Using the learning square. *The Learning Organization, 8*(3/4), 114-125.

Lipusz, C. S., Tróznai, G., Bogdány, J., & Szalai, S.. (2006). The Hungarian space research knowledge management project: A focus on the Rosetta Mission. *Journal of Knowledge Management, 10*(2), 76-89.

Maguire, S. (2004). Reconciling the system requirements process in changing business environments. *Information Management & Computer Security, 12*(4), 362-372.

Mak, K.-T., & Ramaprasad, A. (2003). Knowledge supply network. *The Journal of the Operational Research Society, 54*(2), 175-183.

Makuch, W. M., Dodge, J. L., Ecker, J. G., Granfors, D. C., & Hahn, G. J. (1992). Managing consumer credit delinquency in the US economy: A multi-billion dollar management science application. *Interfaces, 22*(1), 90.

Mamaghani, F. (2002). Information technology knowledge sharing using case-based reasoning. *Information Systems Management, 19*(4), 13-20.

Marjanovic, O. (2005). Towards IS supported coordination in emergent business processes. *Business Process Management Journal, 11*(5), 476-487.

Marren, P. (2003). Where did all the knowledge go? *The Journal of Business Strategy, 24*(3), 5-7.

Massey, A. P., Montoya-Weiss, M. M., & O'Driscoll, T. M. (2002). Knowledge management in pursuit of performance: Insights from Nortel networks. *MIS Quarterly, 26*(3), 269-289.

Matthews, D. H., Christini, G. C., & Hendrickson, C. T. (2004). Five elements for organizational decision-making with an environmental management system. *Environmental Science & Technology, 38*(7), 1927-1932.

McIvor, R., Scullion, G., & McTear, M. (1992). SMILE: Development of a strategic management interactive learning expert system. *International Journal of Information Resource Management, 3*(2), 11.

McKiernan, P., & Merali, Y. (1995). Integrating information systems after a merger. *Long Range Planning, 28*(4), 54.

Menkhoff, T., Loh, B., Chiang, R., & Wah, C. Y. (2005). Knowledge management as an enabler of effective career services in institutions of higher learning: The case of the Singapore Management University. *International Journal of Human Resources Development and Management, 5*(2), 204-217.

Menkus, B. (1991). "Hackers": Know the adversary. *Computers & Security, 10*(5), 405.

Merten, Peter P. (1991, July). Loop-based strategic decision support systems. *Source: Strategic Management Journal, 12(5)*, 371-386.

Miles, I., Andersen, B., Boden, M., & Howells, J. (2000). Service production and intellectual property. *International Journal of Technology Management, 20*(1, 2), 95-115.

Mitsuru, K. (1999). Strategic business applications and new virtual knowledge-based businesses through community-based information networks. *Information Management & Computer Security, 7*(4), 186-199.

Mondragon, C. A. E., Lyons, A. C., & Kehoe, D. F. (2004). Assessing the value of information systems in supporting agility in high-tech manufacturing enterprises. *International Journal of Operations & Production Management, 24*(11/12), 1219-1246.

Muckstadt, J. A., Murray, D. H., Rappold, J. A., & Collins, D. E. (2001). Guidelines for collaborative supply chain system design and operation. *Information Systems Frontiers: Special Issue: Supply Chain Management, 3*(4), 427.

Mullin, R. (1996). Knowledge management: A cultural evolution. *The Journal of Business Strategy, 17*(5), 56.

Nedovic-Budic, Z., & Godschalk, D. R. (1996). Human factors in adoption of geographic information systems: A local government case study. *Public Administration Review, 56*(6), 554-567.

Nerur, S., Mahapatra, R., & Mangalaraj, G.. (2005). Challenges of migrating to agile methodologies. Association for computing machinery. *Communications of the ACM, 48*(5), 72-78.

Next generation product development. (2001). *Strategic Direction, 17*(1), 24-26.

Niwa, K. (1990). Toward successful implementation of knowledge-based systems: Expert systems vs. knowledge sharing systems. *IEEE Transactions on Engineering Management, 37*(4), 277.

Nordheim, S., & Päivärinta, T. (2006). Implementing enterprise content management: From evolution through strategy to contradictions out-of-the-box. *European Journal of Information Systems, 15*(6), 648-663.

Nwankwo, S., Obidigbo, B., & Ekwulugo, F. (2002). Allying for quality excellence: Scope for expert systems in supplier quality management. *The International Journal of Quality & Reliability Management, 19*(2/3), 187-205.

Odem, P., & O'Dell, C. (1998). Invented here: How sequent computer publishes knowledge. *The Journal of Business Strategy, 19*(1), 25-28.

Ohl, R., & Gammack, J. (2004). Integrating an Internet management system into a virtual private network. *Journal of Electronic Commerce Research, 5*(4), 254-269.

Ong, M. H., West, A. A., Lee, S. M., & Harrison, R. (2006). A structured approach to evaluating the impact of implementing a component-based system in the automotive engine manufacturing domain. *International Journal of Production Research, 44*(13), 2645-2670.

Oravec, J. (2004). The transparent knowledge worker: Weblogs and reputation mechanisms in KM systems. *International Journal of Technology Management, 28*(7,8), 767-775.

Osborn, C. S. (1998, July). Systems for sustainable organizations: Emergent strategies, interactive controls and semi-formal information. *Journal of Management Studies (Oxford, England), 35*(4), 481-509.

Ottaway, T. A., & Burns, J. R. (1997). Adaptive, agile approaches to organizational architecture utilizing agent technology. *Decision Sciences, 28*(3), 483-511.

Ozimek, J. (2006). The 2005 information management awards. *Journal of Database Marketing & Customer Strategy Management, 13*(4), 309-318.

Pal, K., & Palmer, O.. (2000). A decision-support system for business acquisitions. *Decision Support Systems, 27*(4), 411-429.

Pan, S., Pan, G., & Hsieh, M. H. (2006). A dual-level analysis of the capability development process: A case study of TT&T. *Journal of the American Society for Information Science and Technology, 57*(13), 1814.

Park, K. H., & Favrel, J. (1999). Virtual enterprise - information system and networking solution. *Computers & Industrial Engineering, 37*(1, 2), 441-444.

Participation in Development and Implementation - Updating An Old, Tired Concept for Today's IS Contexts. (2004). *Journal of the Association for Information Systems, 5*(11, 12), 1.

Pflughoeft, K. A., Hutchinson, G. K., & Nazareth, D. L. (1996). Intelligent decision support for flexible manufacturing: Design and implementation of a knowledge-based simulator. *Omega, 24*(3), 347.

Prahalad, C. K., & Krishnan, M. S. (2002). The dynamic synchronization of strategy and information technology. *MIT Sloan Management Review, 43*(4), 24-33.

Prybutok, V. R., & Spink, A. (1999). Transformation of a health care information system: A self-assessment survey. *IEEE Transactions on Engineering Management, 46*(3), 299-310.

Raghunathan, M., & Madey, G. R. (1999, Fall). A firm-level framework for planning electronic commerce information systems infrastructure. *International Journal of Electronic Commerce, 4*(1), 121-45

Ravichandran, T (1999). Software reusability as synchronous innovation: A test of four theoretical models. *European Journal of Information Systems, 8*(3), 183-199.

Ravichandran, T., & Rai, A. (2003).Structural analysis of the impact of knowledge creation and knowledge embedding on software process capability. *IEEE Transactions on Engineering Management, 50*(3), 270-284,

Ribeiro, F. L. (2001). Project delivery system selection: A case-based reasoning framework. *Logistics Information Management, 14*(5/6), 367-375.

Riggins, F. J., & Mukhopadhyay, T. (1999, Summer). Overcoming EDI adoption and implementation risks. *International Journal of Electronic Commerce, 3*(4), 103-23.

Russ, M., & Jones, J. K. (2006). Knowledge-based strategies and information system technologies: Preliminary findings. *International Journal of Knowledge and Learning, 2*(1-2), 154-179.

Russ, M., Jones, J. K., & Fineman, R. (2005). Knowledge-based strategies: A foundation of a typology. *International Journal of Information Technology and Management, 4*(2), 138-165.

Russ, M., Jones, J. K., & Jones, J.G. (2004). Knowledge-based strategies, culture, and information systems. *International Journal of Knowledge, Culture and Change Management, 4*, 427-452.

Saelens, D., & Nelson, S. (1994). Using client/server to enable change. *Information Systems Management, 11*(3), 28.

Salomann, H., Dous, M., Kolbe, L., & Brenner, W. (2005). Rejuvenating customer management: How to make knowledge for, from and about customers work. *European Management Journal, 23*(4), 392-403.

Sanchez, R., & Mahoney, J. T. (1996, Winter). Modularity, flexibility, and knowledge management in production and organization design. *Strategic Management Journal, 17*, 63-76.

Scardamalia, M., & Bereiter, C. (1993). Technologies for knowledge-building discourse. Association for computing machinery. *Communications of the ACM, 36*(5), 37.

Seidmann, A., & Sundararajan, A. (1997). Competing in information-intensive services: Analyzing the impact of task consolidation and employee empowerment. *Journal of Management Information Systems, 14*(2), 33-56.

Serva, M. A., Sherer, S. A., & Sipior, J. C. (2003). "When do you ASP?" The software life cycle control model. Information systems frontiers: Special issue. *Advances in Software Engineering: Theory and, 5*(2), 219-232.

Shah, S. K. (1990). Implementing a manufacturing information system. *The Journal of Information Systems Management, 7*(1), 8.

Sherer, S. A., Kohli, R., & Baron, A. (2003). Complementary investment in change management and IT investment payoff. *Information Systems Frontiers: Special Issue: IT Investment Payoff in E-Business, 5*(3), 321.

Sherif, K. (2006). An adaptive strategy for managing knowledge in organizations. *Journal of Knowledge Management, 10*(4), 72-80.

Sherif, K., Hoffman, J., & Thomas, B. (2006). Can technology build organizational social capital? The case of a global IT consulting firm. *Information & Management, 43*(7), 795.

Sherman, D. G., Cole, A. J., & Boardman, J T. (1996). Assisting cultural reform in a projects-based company using systemigrams. *International Journal of Project Management, 14*(1), 23

Shih, T. K., Chiu, C.-F., Hsu, H.-H., & Lin, F. (2002). An integrated framework for recommendation systems in e-commerce. *Industrial Management + Data Systems, 102*(8/9), 417-431.

Simon, C. (2006). Corporate information transparency: The synthesis of internal and external information streams. *The Journal of Management Development, 25*(10), 1029-1031.

Slaughter, S. A., Levine, L., Ramesh, B., Pries-Heje, J., & Baskerville, R. (2006). Aligning software processes with strategy. *MIS Quarterly, 30*(4), 891-918.

Smith, D., & Dexter, A. Whenever I hear the word 'paradigm' I reach for my gun: How to stop talking and start walking. *International Journal of Market Research, 43*(3),321-340.

Smith, H. A., & McKeen, J. D. (2004). Developments in practice XIV: Marketing KM to the organization. *Communications of the Association for Information Systems, 14*, 1.

Stefanou, C. J., Sarmaniotis, C., & Stafyla, A. (2003). CRM and customer-centric knowledge management: An empirical research. *Business Process Management Journal, 9*(5), 617-634.

Stoddart, L. (2001). Managing intranets to encourage knowledge sharing: Opportunities and constraints. *Online Information Review, 25*(1), 19-28.

Stojanovic, L., Schneider, J., Maedche, A., Libischer, S., et al. (2004). The role of ontologies in autonomic computing systems. *IBM Systems Journal, 43*(3), 598-616.

Tang, Q., & Cheng, H. (2007). Optimal strategies for a monopoly intermediary in the supply chain of complementary Web services. *Journal of Management Information Systems, 23*(3), 275-307.

Tang, N. K. H., Yasa, P. R., & Forrester, P. L. (2004). An application of the delta model and BPR in transforming electronic business: The case of a food ingredients company in UK. *Information Systems Journal, 14*(2), 111-130.

Tannenbaum, S. I. (1990). Human resource information systems: User group implications. *Journal of Systems Management, 41*(1), 27.

Tate, G., & Verner, J. (1990). Case study of risk management, incremental development, and evolutionary prototyping. *Information and Software Technology, 32*(3), 207.

Taylor, W. A. (2004). Computer-mediated knowledge sharing and individual user differences: An exploratory study. *European Journal of Information Systems, 13*(1), 52-64.

Taylor, J., & Oake, J. (1991). Maximising financial services: Sophisticated database marketing. *The International Journal of Bank Marketing, 9*(2), 17.

Tebboune, S. D. E. (2003). Application service provision: Origins and development. *Business Process Management Journal, 9*(6), 722-734.

Tecker, G., Eide, K., & Frankel, J. (1997, August). In pursuit of a knowledge-based association. *Association Management, 49*, 122-30

Teo, T. S. H., & King, W. R. (1997). Integration between business planning and information systems planning: An evolutionary-contingency perspective. *Journal of Management Information Systems, 14*(1), 185-214.

Toomey, S. (1992). Case study: Flying high with IT. *Target Management Development Review, 5*(3), 17.

Trimi, S., Lee, S. M., Olson, D. L., & Erickson, J. (2005). Alternative means to implement ERP: Internal and ASP. *Industrial Management + Data Systems, 105*(1/2), 184-192.

Tuggle, F. D., & Goldfinger, W. E. (2004). A methodology for mining embedded knowledge from process maps. *Human Systems Management, 23*(1), 1-13.

Tuunanen, T., & Vainio, M.. (2005). Communication flows in software product development: A case study of two mobile software firms. *JITTA: Journal of Information Technology Theory and Application, 7*(3), 27-36, 38-45, 48.

Udin, Z. M., Khan, M. K., & Zairi, M. (2006). A collaborative supply chain management: Part 2 - the hybrid KB/gap analysis system for planning stage. *Business Process Management Journal, 12*(5), 671-687.

Vaughn, R. (2006). Come on in. The water's fine. *Risk Management, 53*(10), 10-12, 14, 16-17.

Voelpel, S. C., Dous, M., & Davenport, T. H. (2005). Five steps to creating a global knowledge-sharing system: Siemens' ShareNet. *The Academy of Management Executive, 19*(2), 9-23.

Volberda, H. W., & Rutges, A. (1999). FARSYS: A knowledge-based system for managing strategic change. *Decision Support Systems, 26*(2), 99-123.

Wakefield, R. L. (2005). Identifying knowledge agents in a KM strategy: The use of the structural influence index. *Information & Management, 42*(7), 935-945.

Wang, W., Hawwash, K. I. M., & Perry, J. G. (1996). Contract type selector (CTS): A KBS for training young engineers. *International Journal of Project Management, 14*(2), 95.

Why do we need knowledge management? (1999). *Strategic Direction: Special Issue: Knowledge Management Strategies*, (154), 4-6.

Wilmshurst, T. D., & Frost, G. R. (2001). The role of accounting and the accountant in the environmental management system. *Business Strategy and the Environment, 10*(3), 135.

Winder, M. (1994). Transitional outsourcing. *Information Systems Management, 11*(4), 65.

Yan, W., Chen, C.-H., & Khoo, L. P. (2005). A Web-enabled product definition and customization system for product conceptualization. *Expert Systems, 22*(5), 241.

Yeh, Y.-J., Lai, S.-Q., & Ho, C.-T. (2006). Knowledge management enablers: A case study. *Industrial Management + Data Systems, 106*(6), 793-810.

Zack, M. H. (1999). Developing a knowledge strategy. *California Management Review, 41*(3), 125-145.

Zahay, D., & Griffin, A. (2004). Customer learning processes, strategy selection, and performance in business-to-business service firms. *Decision Sciences, 35*(2), 169-203.

Zahra, S. A., & George, G.. (2002). The Net-enabled business innovation cycle and the evolution of dynamic capabilities. *Information Systems Research, 13*(2), 147-150.

Zhang, W. Y., Tor, S. B., & Britton, G. A. (2002). Automated functional design of engineering systems. *Journal of Intelligent Manufacturing, 13*(2), 119-133.

Zollo, M., & Singh, H. (2004). Deliberate learning in corporate acquisitions: Post-acquisition strategies and integration capability in U.S. bank mergers. *Strategic Management Journal, 25*(13), 1233-1257.

Zutshi, A., & Sohal, A. (2004). Environmental management system adoption by Australasian organisations: Part 1 - Reasons, benefits and impediments. *Technovation, 24*(4), 335-357.

Chapter II

The Intellectual Capital Statements:
Evolution and How to Get Started

Miltiadis D. Lytras, University of Patras, Greece

Leif Edvinsson, Lund University, Sweden, &
The Hong Kong Polytechnic University, Hong Kong

Patricia Ordóñez de Pablos, Universidad de Oviedo, Spain

Abstract

In light of the latest developments in the field of intellectual capital (IC) measuring and reporting (Asia, Europe, and USA), this chapter aims to help managers measure and report the intellectual capital of their companies. Having first-hand experiences in collaborating with firms in the building of the "intellectual capital report" (ICR)—and therefore knowing weaknesses and major mistakes—the authors of the chapter propose how firms should build the ICR, an innovative corporate report with strategic implications for the achievement and maintenance of a long-term competitive advantage. The first section of the chapter presents a historical review of the development of the intellectual capital report since 1992. The second section analyzes intellectual capital reports, discussing firms' definition and goals for these reports; the analysis is based on intellectual capital reports published by 38 firms from Europe (Austria, Germany, Iceland, Italy, Spain, Sweden, and UK) and Asia (India and Japan) during the period 1992-2006. From here, we address how firms can get started building the intellectual capital report, especially regarding the structure of the report as well as the specific indicators.

Introduction

For more than a decade some pioneering firms from Europe and Asia have built an innovative corporate report called the *intellectual capital statement (ICS)*. Based on these intellectual capital reports (ICR) published by these firms and their learning, this chapter presents the evolution up to now on how managers *could now systematize* measuring and reporting intellectual capital (IC), rather than simply describing it.

The chapter is structured in four sections. The first section presents a historical review of the development of the intellectual capital report since the prototype of the first internal intellectual capital report in 1992 to the last advances in the development of intellectual capital guidelines. The second section analyzes intellectual capital reports, discussing firms' definition and goals for these reports. Based on the analysis of intellectual capital reports published by 38 firms from Europe and Asia during the period 1992-2006, we discuss the most frequent weaknesses and errors observed when preparing this innovative report. From here, we address how firms *could build* the intellectual capital report, especially regarding the structure of the report as well as the specific indicators for measuring each intellectual capital construct. The third section covers recommendations for the presentation the intellectual capital report. The last section encourages managers to systematize measuring and reporting knowledge-based resources, showing the tangible benefits derived from these activities. Finally we suggest new avenues for the future of the intellectual capital report.

Historical Review of the Development Intellectual Capital Reports

The very first internal intellectual capital report was prototyped in 1992 and externally published for the first time in 1994. The Swedish stock and Fortune 500 listed the financial and insurance service company, Skandia. This company drew up the first intellectual capital report or statement to be published anywhere in the world. It was based on the Skandia development of the intellectual capital navigator and the newly launched taxonomy of IC, under the leadership of Leif Edvinsson, to visualize the hidden value for a more systematized cultivation.

This publication represented an important milestone in the field of intellectual capital. At that time the attention of the academic and corporate world centered on this pioneering company and the intellectual capital statement that it produced. The great expectation generated by this innovative report resulted in a small group of European companies beginning to prepare and publish this type of statement in 1998. These included the Danish companies Carl Bro, Coloplast, Cowi, and Systematic, Spanish companies BBVA, Bankinter, and Unión Fenosa,and the Swedish company Celemi.

In 2000, the Danish Agency for Trade and Industry (DATI) published, based on work of, among others, professor Jan Mouritsen (Copenhagen Business School), the document entitled *Intellectual Capital Statement-Towards a Guideline*, which represented an initial effort with respect to developing directives for quantifying intellectual capital and the preparation of intellectual capital statements using the results of these quantifications. Later, in 2001 and 2003, the DATI published a series of new directives and also the first law in the world for the preparation of intellectual capital statements.

In 2002, under the support from The Nordic Investment Bank, NORDIKA— term that stands for "Nordic Project for the Measurement of Intellectual Capital"—published the *Intellectual Capital: Managing and Statement*. The report aims to give companies an overview of the vast number of possibilities open to them for using intellectual capital reports to manage and report intellectual capital. It gives priority to practical knowledge to be used for application. The report is targeted at staff that will be in charge of initiating the intellectual capital process.

That same year, MERITUM (2002) also published its own overview, namely *Guidelines for Managing and Statementing on Intangibles*. It was then followed by another important EU project on IC called PRISM (2003), which stands for policy-making, reporting and measurement, intangibles, skills development and management. It is a multidisciplinary European Commission initiative aimed at gaining a deeper understanding of the issues surrounding the management and measurement of intangibles in today's competitive environment.

Since 2003, the BundesMinisterium fur Wirtschaft unt Arbeit in Germany has been prototyping with excellent success a project called Wissensbilanz (www.akwissens-bilanz.org) for a systematized process for generating IC. This is already approaching 100 applications in Germany and there is also a free download of software from its Web site. On the other hand, The Ministry of Economics, Trade and Industry (METI) in Japan is also involved in prototyping IA reporting since some years ago. They introduced a guideline in 2005. Now five of the largest Japanese companies are publishing intellectual assets-based management report. This guideline, compiled by METI, aims to "help corporations (managers) that prepare intellectual assets based management report and those who assess it. Based on the examination of Subcommittee on Management and Intellectual Assets, New Growth Policy Committee, Industrial Structure Council, it provides a guide for information disclosure concerning intellectual assets based management" (2005, p. 3). METI is now, in December 2006, arranging its second annual IC and IA Week to address a number of different perspectives on the subject. Together Germany and Japan seem to be the leading countries on the ICS subject.

As the new economic value is in the longitude—that is, lateral dimensions instead of vertical dimensions—as described in the PRISM Web site (see www.euintangibles. eu), we have to develop more lateral, benchmarking accounting of value creation potential of intangibles (Edvinsson, 2002). We have to acknowledge such new intangible indicators and get the accountants to audit those, as well as annual reports to present transparency of such intellectual capital, to be able to navigate these new organizational value creations.

The *Intellectual Capital Statement made in Germany Project* -where Leif Edvinsson together with Mart Kivikas and his colleagues Manfred Bornemann and Kay Alwert initiated this method for a process report on a method for Intellectual Capital Statements for Germany based on international experiences. It includes 14 prototypical intellectual capital statements as best practice examples in representative German small and medium-sized enterprises (SMEs) from different regions and sectors implemented. The German approach to prepare the intellectual capital report ("the Wissenbilanz") includes four milestones:

- Milestone I: Why? Initial situation; What? Intellectual Capital; How good? Evaluation
- Milestone II: How much? Indicators
- Milestone III: Who? Communication
- Milestone IV: How? Management

This statement proposes an interdependency process flow chart among the major IC components of intellectual capital. All factors of the human capital, relational capital, and structural capital, respectively, are systematized and ranked into a transparent decision oriented map for better knowledge navigation, knowledge investment, and generation of IC.

One of the most refined recent experiences from prototyping intellectual capital reporting at Skandia emerged, during the first years of 2000, at Seibersdorf Research Center, Austria by then Professor Guenter Koch (with his team of Karl Heinz Leitner, Manfred Bornemann, and Alexander Welzl as pioneering IC colleagues such as professor Ursula Schneider, Graz University). In 2002, the Austrian Ministry for Education, Science and Culture issued the new university law (UG 2002): All Austrian universities will have to publish IC reports from 2006 on. According to the UG (2002),

Each university shall submit an intellectual capital report for the past calendar year to the Minister, by way of the university council, by 30 April of each year. This shall, as a minimum, present in itemized form: 1. the university's activities, social goals and self-imposed objectives and strategies; 2. its intellectual capital, broken down into human, structural and relationship capital; 3. the processes set out in the performance agreement, including their outputs and impacts.

During 2003 in Austria a law was implemented requiring all universities and colleges to publish a knowledge capital report annually, showing knowledge goals, knowledge processes, as well as knowledge indicators. The very first prototype was done by University of Kremz (Austria). In Sweden the very first similar prototype has now been launched by CMM-Center for Molecular Medicin at Karolinska Institute (see www.cmm.ki.se) with a special prototyping focus for the science sector.

Since 2006, intellectual capital reporting has become mandatory for all Austrian universities. Back in 2002 the Austrian Ministry for Education, Science and Culture released a new university law for the reorganization of all public Austrian universities. The Ministry's goals were to enhance transparency, foster the management of intangible resources, and set initiatives for performance orientation. As the European Commission states, "The IC statement should serve as a management instrument for the university as well as a communication instrument between universities and the Ministry" (2006, p. 35).

In Spain, professor Eduardo Bueno Campos and his research group at the Intellectus Forum (www.iade.org) developed the Intellectus Model in 2003. The model consists of five fundamental elements: its structures, principles, internal logic, development of the model (definitions), and table of indicators (Bueno, 2003). The structure of the intellectus model is described through the components, elements (E_i), variables (V_i), and indicators (I_j). According to this model, intellectual capital is divided into human capital, capital structural, and capital relational. In turn, structural capital is subdivided into organizational capital and technological capital, while the relational is disaggregated into business capital and social capital

In 2004, one year later, the *3R Model for Intellectual Capital Statements* was developed (Ordóñez de Pablos, 2004). This model proposes three reports for building the intellectual capital statement: (1) the *Intellectual Capital Report*, which shows the situation of the intellectual capital of the firm, and includes information of each of its components (intellectual capital components will be quantified based on indicators that measure diverse categories of each component); (2) the *Intellectual Capital Flow Report* addresses the increases and decreases of intellectual capital during the year as well as the intellectual capital variation or net flow; and finally (3) the Intellectual Capital Memo Report complements and further explain the information included in the two previous reports.

In December 2004 the Directorate General for Research and Technological Development (DGRTD) of the European Commission set up a high-level expert group to propose a series of measures to stimulate the reporting of intellectual capital in research-intensive SMEs. The report by this expert group with Professor Daan Andriesen as Secretary, presents six recommendations to stimulate the reporting of intellectual capital SMEs by raising awareness, improving reporting competencies, promoting the use of intellectual capital reporting, and facilitating standardization (RICARDIS, 2006, p. 7). The acronym RICARDIS reflects the objective of the high-level expert group to stimulate reporting of intellectual capital to augment research, development, and innovation in SMEs (see http://europa.eu.in/comm./research/rtdinfo/index_en.html).

Based on these recommendations another EU sponsored project is now starting to distribute the learning from mainly Germany to cover 5 major European countries, called intellectual capital (InCas) statements. The countries to prototype this are Germany, UK, France, Poland, and Slovenia.

Furthermore Taiwan initiated a Research Center on Intellectual Capital (TICRC) in 2003. Its most important task is promoting industrial intellectual capital research and development, and assisting to progress intellectual capital in this country. The main mission of TICRC is to implement the projects to enhance industrial intellectual capital and accelerate the upgrading of industry. The concrete tasks of TICRC are: strengthening national or industrial intellectual capital policy plans; integrating aggregation of various fields related to intellectual capital; developing intellectual capital key technologies for industries; promoting practical experience of intellectual capital transfers to Taiwan; establishing an environment conductive to intellectual capital development; intensifying the publicizing of intellectual capital management and other achievements; and promoting international research exchange and cooperation. Several countries are now also establishing such IC research centers.

As the IC statements initially were focused on enterprises, starting in 1996 in Sweden, there was another prototyping work by professor Edvinsson to start to report on IC of Sweden as a nation. This was then followed by Israel, Denmark, Holland, France, Finland, and lately Austria. This pioneering work is also looking into IC of regions and cities (Bounfour & Edvinsson, 2005; Viedma, 2004).

It is important to mention the special case of USA, which could be considered as a "special space" in the development of ICRs. It very much started in the early 1990s with the initial work by Professors Thomas Johnson and Robert Kaplan with the book on *Relevance Lost-The Rise and Fall of Management Accounting* (1987), and in the early 1990s with Professor Baruch Lev, then at University California, Berkeley as well as activities by the Conference Board, New York. In 1996, the ICM gathering by Patrick Sullivan, Gordon Petrash and Leif Edvinsson was also formed at Berkley, which focused on the aspects of intellectual capital assets and intellectual property issues.

Professor Baruch Lev together with the Brookings Institute Task Force, Washington published the first white book on intangible assets, in collaboration with Securities and Exchange Commission (SEC). It resulted in Lev's 2001 *Intangibles - Management, Measurement, and Reporting* as well as in Blair and Wallman's 2001 *The Unseen Wealth.* More recently, the U.S. Federal Reserve and the University of Maryland have renewed their research in the field of intellectual capital with "Unmasking the Economy," which appeared in *Business Week* in February of 2006.

The following figure summarizes major milestones in the history of the field of intellectual capital measuring and reporting.

Figure 1. Some milestones in the field of intellectual capital measuring and reporting

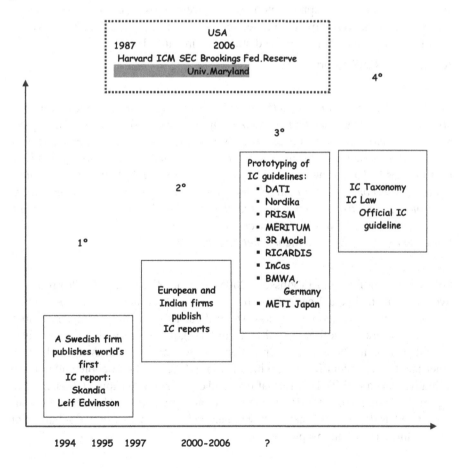

Now there are more and more emerging and generally accepted official directives to guide companies in the preparation and presentation of an intellectual capital statement. In light of the experience of 38 companies from 9 different countries, and the analysis of the intellectual capital statements that have been published during the period of 1992-2006, the proposal put forward by this work is offering and providing managers with recommendations on how to prepare an intellectual capital statement and avoid the weaknesses observed in the statements analyzed and the mistakes made by the companies during their preparation.

The Intellectual Capital Statement

Distinctions and Objectives

What is an intellectual capital statement? Before proposing our own definition, it is advisable to analyze how the pioneer companies in the field define this type of report. You will find some of these distinctions in Table 1.

As the RICARDIS report states

Intellectual Capital Reporting is the process of creating a narrative that shows how an enterprise creates value for its customers by using its IC. This involves identifying, measuring, and reporting its IC, as well as constructing a coherent presentation of how the enterprise uses its knowledge resources [...] it is complementary to a business plan as it shows how value will be created through R&D and what the role is of the various components of intellectual capital. Therefore it can provide – unlike a business plan – transparency into the hidden value drivers of R&D investments and pinpoint the availability (or absence) of key complementary assets crucial to bring the results of R&D to the market. (2006, p. 9)

Following Bounfour and Edvinsson (2005)'s work, RICARDIS (2006) proposes two types of intellectual capital: on the one hand, "autonomous IC" (A), which is less dependent on people and consists of those assets with a secondary market like patents, brands, software, and so forth (A-1), and those without a secondary market such as methodologies, reputation, image, and so forth (A-2); and on the other hand, "dependent IC" (B), which is more dependent on people and consists of innovation capital (B-1), informational and organizational capital (B-2), marketing and distribution capital (B-3), and relational capital (B-4). These resources are considered as dependent because they are embedded in the corporate organization and are therefore of an inseparable nature.

Table 1. Definitions of intellectual capital statement

Organization	ICS definition
Actell	"In line with our belief that intellectual capital is the source of competitiveness and future value, we not only assist our client companies with IC-based management, but also practice what we preach, by implementing and executing this methodology on ourselves as we strive to maximize our own corporate value. We created a report called "Intellectual Capital (IC) Report" in order to present the results of our own implementations "(2005, p. 4).
Center for Molecular Medicine-Karolinska University Hospital	"CMM aims to use intellectual capital reporting to benchmark against similar distinguished international institutions to evaluate and improve its performance. This will also increase the visibility of Swedish research abroad and help attract talent to Sweden. Furthermore the annual analysis and report will help control the knowledge-based.value creation process and help increase transparency for the public" (2003, p. 9).
Danish Agency for Trade and Industry	It is "an integrated part of company knowledge management. It identifies the company's knowledge management strategy, which includes the identification of its objectives, initiatives and results in the composition, application and development of the company's knowledge resources. It also communicates this strategy to the company and the world at large" (2003, p. 7).
Intercos	"The intellectual capital statement represents "an important communication means to promote the results relating to corporate performance towards clients and all main interest groups […] a powerful tool for internal management […] a system to control the vitality of the organization whereby ensuring company's global evolution excellence and future" (2003, p. 2).
RICARDIS	"IC statements are primarily about internal reporting, management and control of the business but this internal focus is an essential pre requisite for the ability of management to communicate what they are doing to external audiences which is of particular importance when the organisation needs to seek finance from banks or equity from investors [...] It is complementary to a financial statement as it provides insight into important resources that are not found on the balance sheet including knowledge, access to networks, and human resources" (2006, p. 7).
Systematic	The report "gives a broad, comprehensive picture of Systematic and illustrates our vision, mission, values and objectives. In this way, the intellectual capital report functions as a window to the world - a kind of business card. The target group is current and future customers, employees and cooperation partners (2004).
Tolvumidlun	"Our IC report cover the threee aspects of IC: human capital, relational capital and structural capital and is an addition to our finacial report, describing our intangible assets" (2005, p. 3).

Intellectual capital statements represent all the value creating resources in an organization that are not captured in traditional financial statements but are of critical importance to a firm's long-term competitive advantage.

Based on the analysis of intellectual capital statements published by 38 firms (Actell, ARCS, Balrampur Chini Mills, Bankinter, BBVA, Brembo, BSCH, Caja Madrid, Carl Bro, Celemi, Center for Molecular Medicine (Karolinska University Hospital), Coloplast, Cowi, Creadesign Oy, Dieu, DLR, EES Group, Experimentarium, Genetrix, Intercos, Kronsberg, Mekalki, NANONET-Styria, Navneet, OENB, Plastal, Reinisch, Reliance, Shree Cement Limited, Sentencia, Skandia, Systematic, Telia, TM Software, Tölvumidlun, Union Fenosa, and 24-Seven Office) from 9 countries (Austria, Germany, Iceland, India, Italy, Japan, Spain, Sweden, and UK) during the period of 1992-2006, the intellectual capital statement can be defined as an innovative corporate report that basically covers information on knowledge-based resources not covered in traditional annual reports. It also presents information on knowledge management strategies, activities, and results. Why do organizations build the intellectual capital statement? The opinions of some firms and organizations committed with the building of the intellectual capital statement are summarized in Table 2.

Table 2. The goals of the intellectual capital statement

Firm/Organization	ICS Goal
Actcell	"The goal of this report is to share the current progress of our IC-based management efforts with our shareholders, as well as those associated with us in the business community. We believe that disclosing a current assessment on our IC and our management style based on the IC concept will help us build long-term relationships with shareholders, thereby solidifying our overall Intellectual Capital" (2005, p. 4).
Center for Molecular Medicine-Karolinska University Hospital	"CMM aims to use intellectual capital reporting to benchmark against similar distinguished international institutions to evaluate and improve its performance. This will also increase the visibility of Swedish research abroad and help attract talent to Sweden. Furthermore the annual analysis and report will help control the knowledge-based.value creation process and help increase transparency for the public" (2003, p. 9).
Creadesign Oy	"The aim is to monitor the initiatives and goals and show results of how the company develops its resources and cares for its values using IC monitoring as a management tool" (2005, p. 3).
Danish Agency for Trade and Industry	This statement "informs about organizational efforts to achieve, develop, share and institutionalize knowledge-based resources which are necessary to create value for the company by means of improving their growth, flexibility and innovation" (2001, p. 13).

continued on following page

Table 2. continued

Firm/Organization	ICS Goal
Experimentarium	With the intellectual capital statement, "we can ensure quality and renewal and strengthen the company's ability to reach its goals. At the same time, the intellectual capital statements enable the surrounding world to gain an insight into Experimentarium status and development" (2004, p. 20).
Nanonet	"[...] is to provide a transparent, verifiable overview of the effects of the research funds invested in nanotechnology [...] it provides a modern communication and control instrument for knowledge-intesive issues" (2003, pp. 2-3).
OENB	The OENB's intellectual capital statement "makes transparent the stock of knowledge-based capital as well as internal and external knowledge flows. It thus helps document the OENB's intangible assets, which the Annual Statement fails to capture in a comprehensive way" (2003, p. 8).
RICARDIS	"A good IC report will improve an organisations internal processes for managing its overall resources, both tangible and intangible and more importantly it will provide a sound basis for improving the quality of the dialogue with financiers by explaining why the organisation does what it does and how it is building the resources and capabilities necessary to succeed in the future. IC statements help to clarify the way in which competitive advantage is being built by providing a narrative which explains both value chain positioning and the business model which is to be used to create value" (2006, p. 7).
TM Software	"In the last four annual reports we have included a detailed IC chapter that formally tries to shed light on development of the company's assets that are not registered in the annual accounts" (2004, p. 12).
Tolvumidlun	"Our IC report [...] is an addition to our financial report [...] Combined the two reportss are a fuller and more complete account of the real assets and future potential of an IT company" (2005, p. 3).
Sentencia	"IC report is to give a holistic view of the company, based on well-defined indicators on the basis of the company vision, strategy, basic values and goals" (2005, p. 2).
24 Seven Office	"We will in this report try to give our stakeholders a better insight in our company then the financial report can give alone. Since most of our assets are intangible assets, we feel this is our most important report" (2004, p. 3).
Skandia	"To increase the visibility of hidden value for better management as well as renewal to gain truly sustainable earnings" (1994, p. 3)

The Most Frequent Weaknesses and Errors when Doing the Intellectual Capital Report

1. Not including an intellectual capital model that links these strategic resources with the company's overall vision, mission, and strategy in the one hand and with the organizational results on the other.

2. Reducing the intellectual capital statement to a series of simple tables with indicators, without explaining either why these indicators were chosen or the knowledge flows that exist between the intellectual capital components.

3. Once the intellectual capital statement has been published, this corporate report is not really used in the decision-making process.

4. Not stating specific objectives for each intellectual capital indicator to get a benchmark.

5. The use of new intellectual capital indicators and/or elimination of previously used indicators without any justification as to why.

6. Not seeing the systemized interdependencies.

Content of the Intellectual Capital Statement

The analysis carried out on the intellectual capital statements highlights the lack of standardization with respect to the structure and content of the information presented. Generally speaking, what the majority of companies include fundamentally boils down to a company profile, namely basic details (i.e., number of employees, sales volume, andprofitability) and the indicators chosen for measuring some of the intellectual capital.

However, it is our belief that this information is insufficient and that more intelligence should be included, especially that related with knowledge management activities and the systematized generating of intellectual capital. On the one hand, in its intellectual capital statement the company should include the activities it carries out and the investments it makes with respect to knowledge management and provide an analysis of its objectives and performance in these fields, how they were developed and the degree to which they were achieved. On the other hand, with respect to intellectual capital, the company should clearly define what it understands by intellectual capital and what it sees the component parts thereof as being. The company should then incorporate the actions it has carried out as well as the indicators it has used to measure each component of its intellectual capital, making mention of the significant factors related with these components. Likewise, the company should analyze the methodology used to quantify its intellectual capital, the incorporation of new indicators, and the elimination of others, plus the dynamics and interdependencies of the critical IC components.

Structure of the Intellectual Capital Statement

Next, we shall analyze the categories of indicators and the indicators that we recommend companies use to measure their intellectual capital. It is important to point out this is a general recommendation of categories and indicators that each company shall have to adapt, taking its particular sector of activity into account and relate it to the process flow. Below we present a list of tentative IC indicators that might lead up to an emerging standard for benchmark. However they have to be relevant for its context.

Table 3. Structure of the ICR

INTELLECTUAL CAPITAL REPORT						
HUMAN CAPITAL	**Year t**	**Year t-1**	**Assesment B=Bad N= Normal G= Good**	**Short term goal**	**Medium term goal**	**Long term goal**
Indicators						
RELATIONAL CAPITAL	**Year t**	**Year t-1**	**Assesment B=Bad N= Normal G= Good**	**Short term goal**	**Medium term goal**	**Long term goal**
Indicators						
STRUCTURAL CAPITAL	**Year t**	**Year t-1**	**Assesment B=Bad N= Normal G= Good**	**Short term goal**	**Medium term goal**	**Long term goal**
Indicators						

Human Capital

The principal indicator categories that should be used for quantifying the knowledge, skills, experience, and competence of the company's employees—in other words, its human capital—are the following:

Employee Profile

- Total number of staff
- Distribution of staff (production, distribution, IT department, etc.)
- Gender distribution (male, female)
- Age distribution
- Average age of employees
- Number of managers
- Percent of research staff
- Number of full time employees

Adaptability Capacity

- Number of employees who permanently work abroad
- Number of employees who have participated in international projects during the year

Staff Turnover

- Circulation percentage of personnel
- Beginners
- Resigned
- Percent of unwanted personnel circulation

Educational Capital

- Unskilled personnel
- Skilled personnel
- Length of education
- Number of employees fluent in English
- Number of awards

- Professional publications per employee
- International experience (traveling activities)

Educational Renewal
- Number of competence development plans
- Number of carrier development plans

Commitment and Motivation
- Average seniority
- Permanent contracts
- Percent of individual goal achievement
- Percent of staff with variable retribution/total staff
- Employees with shares and convertible bonus programs
- Number of award-winning employees
- Suggestions systems (money prizes, point prizes)
- Percent of promoted staff/total staff
- Percent of staff feeling explicit recognition
- Percent of staff feeling their opinion is taken into account

Knowledge Transfer
- Percent of applicants who share knowledge for maximum value creation
- Percent of employees that find their knowledge appreciated and useful on the job

Permanent Training
- Percent of employees who received training during the year
- Training
    - Training days per employee
    - Average number of training hours per employee/year
    - Ratio training hours/working hours (annual)
    - Training investment (employee/year)
    - Ratio training cost/wages (annual)
    - Satisfaction index about training

    ◦   Average index of application of the training received in daily tasks

    ◦   Mentoring pairs

- Permanent learning through external agent relations

    ◦   Number of alliances and collaborations with academic institutions and research centers

Human Capital Results

- Employee satisfaction index
- Employee satisfaction
- Satisfaction with the opportunity for on-the-job skills development
- Total satisfaction with the opportunity for on-the-job skill development
- Personal injury with loss of working hours
- Costs attributable to external faults
- Absence due to sickness (days/employee)
- Number of dissertations completed in the group
- Number of published papers in referred international journals in the current year
- Value adding per head count

Relational Capital

The main indicator categories recommended for visualizing the value of the relationships the company has with other economic agents (customers, suppliers, stakeholders, partners, etc.)—that is to say, its relational capital—are the following:

Client Profile

- Number of private clients
- Number of public clients
- Number of semipublic clients
- Number of clients abroad

Customers' Portfolio

- Contract portfolio

    ◦   Number of contracts

- ○   First-time customers
- ○   Points of sale
- New stakeholders
- Brand
  - ○   National/international market share
  - ○   Market share of closet's competitor (both national and international)
  - ○   Clients' impression of the firm
  - ○   Customer loyalty index
  - ○   Number of customer suggestions
  - ○   Number of offices with customer satisfaction measuring systems
  - ○   Customer satisfaction index
- Strategic portfolio
  - ○   Five largest customers during the year
  - ○   Duration of existing customer relationships
  - ○   Percent of customers who would recommend our firm
  - ○   New strategic customers during the year
  - ○   Investment on relational marketing
- Number of clients from the same business sector
- Contract rookie rate
- Contract turnover

Client Satisfaction
- Customer perception of service rendered
- Customer satisfaction with flow of information

Public Image
- Spontaneous notoriety index
- Exposure to the media
- Number of unsolicited applications

Connectivity Capital
- Number of countries in which the firm operates
- Number of alliances with business schools

- Number of commercial alliances
- Number of distribution channels
- Number of business conferences attended
- Lectures at scientific conferences
- Sponsorship agreements
- Professional networks
- Employees involved in boards (business, political, scientific)

Investor Capital
- Number of favorable recommendations from analysts
- Number of contacts with investors and analysts
- Number of solved consultations from shareholder's information office

Structural Capital

The main indicator categories recommended for measuring the value of the knowledge embedded in organizational structures, processes, routines, and policies are the following:

Knowledge-Based Infrastructure
- Number of best practices on the Intranet
- Number of employees with Intranet access/total staff
- Shared documents on the Intranet
- Percent of updated knowledge documents on the Intranet
- Number of databases to which the firm has access
- Database searches
- Number of employees with Internet access/total staff
- Number of shared knowledge databases
- Number of participants in best practices processes
- Number of knowledge management projects

Innovation Capital
- Innovation investment
  - Number of shared ideas and experiences

    ○ Average number of ideas per employee

    ○ Investment in I+D+I projects

    ○ Investment in product development

    ○ Investment in process improvement

    ○ Centers of excellence

    ○ Ongoing projects

- Innovation results

    ○ Number of products/services

    ○ Number of new products/services

    ○ Volume of sells linked to new products/services introduced last year

    ○ Total innovation

    ○ Percent of group turnover

    ○ Average turnover project

Intangible Assets

- Number of new patents in the year
- Investment in intellectual property protection
- Number of patents and its life length of partner portfolio
- Number of other intellectual property rights

Infrastructure

- Number of employees connected via e-mail
- Reliability of hardware and software
- Employees with the option of teleworking
- Employees with corporate mobile phone
- Employees with corporate laptop
- Investment

    ○ Investment in premises and office equipment

    ○ Investment in computer equipment

    ○ IT expenses per employee

- Servers

    ○ Number of servers per worker

    ○ Number of hits on the Web site per day

    ○ Average number of homepage hits per month

- Office
  - ○ PCs per office

Customer Support
- Number of national offices
- Number of offices abroad

Administrative Processes
- Average response time for calls to switchboards
- Percent of inquiries handled within the same day

Quality
- Employee participation in internal improvement and technological innovation projects
- Accreditations and certifications
- Number of ISO-9000 certifications
- Number of quality committees
- Number of employees with formation on total quality

Organizational Management Model
- Maximizing benefits of leadership and cohesion
  - ○ Average experience of executive team
- Shared organizational values
  - ○ Shared organizational values
- Business and advanced management models
  - ○ Investment in management models
  - ○ Number of own business models
- Shared strategic management
  - ○ Number of users of strategic-planning system
  - ○ Number of employees who participated in the building of the organizational strategic plans
- How often are strategy and goals reviewed?
- Customer relation management

Social and Environmental Commitment

- Investment in cultural support and solidarity projects
- Environmental investment in the business
- Number of labor audits to installations of the firm

Midterm and Longitude Results

- Number of patents approved during this year
- Number of spin-off companies created
- Long-term impact on key stake holders
- Other sustainability proxies

The intellectual capital report will have to complement and explain the information contained in the intellectual capital flow reports and intellectual capital memo.

The intellectual capital flows account will reflect both the increases and the reductions of intellectual capital that occurred during the financial year, with the difference between these being the result. This information will be compiled for each indicator, indicator category, and intellectual capital component, as well as at an aggregated level (intellectual capital). Likewise, the objectives for each on the indicators, indicator categories, and intellectual capital components will be specified (Ordóñez de Pablos, 2004b).

In line with traditional accounting plans, the report will include information regarding the company's activity or activities, the standards used to evaluate intellectual capital, as well as events occurring after the closure of the accounts that do not affect these, but knowledge of which will be useful to the users of the intellectual capital accounts.

Figure 2. Intellectual capital statements

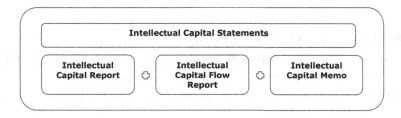

Table 4. Intellectual capital flow report

INTELLECTUAL CAPITAL FLOW REPORT					
CATEGORY	SUB-CATEGORIES AND INDICATORS	YEAR			
		VARIATIONS		GOAL	
		△	▽	SHORT TERM	LONG TERM

Major Steps to Get Started

First, the companies should define a holistic model that shows the input-output relationships and that enables the status of the company's knowledge stocks and flow and how these contribute towards its competitive positioning to be explained.

The company must clearly define what it understands by intellectual capital and what the major components of its intellectual capital actually are. In the literature on intellectual capital a number of different types have been developed, but the most commonly accepted proposals for taxonomy consider that intellectual capital consists of human capital, relational capital, and structural capital.

The indicators will be presented in tables, which will include information about the value of the indicator with respect to the current financial year, the previous financial year, as well as the short-, medium- and long-term objectives for a structured intelligence as a supplement to the traditional financial reporting.

The indicators shall have to present certain properties, thereby making them:

1.   **Reliable:** In other words, objective and verifiable.
2.   **Objective:** The value of the indicator should not include biases derived from the interests of the parties involved in the quantification thereof.
3.   **Verifiable:** It should be possible to evaluate the reliability of the information provided.

4.   **Comparable:** The indicators should be quantified and presented in line with recommended standards and criteria in such a way that users can make comparisons both in time and between companies.

5.   **Truthful:** The information they show shall reflect the real situation of the company with respect to the question it is dealing with.

Following the recommendations of the directives regarding the preparation of intellectual capital statements, the indicators can be divided up into three types:

1.   **General:** Those that can be used comparatively across companies and industries.

2.   **Specific to a certain industry:** In these cases, comparison will only be viable within a single industry.

3.   **Specific to a particular company:** In this case comparisons are extremely difficult to make and can even be considered as useless as the definition of the indicator varies from company to company.

The indicators of each intellectual capital component will be accompanied by an explanation of the most relevant aspects related to and of the activities and projects

Figure 3. Intellectual capital flows

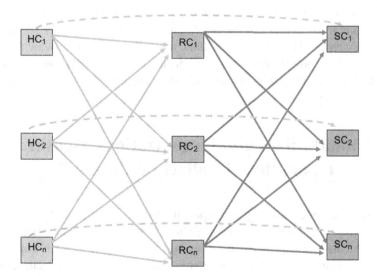

linked with each category of the intellectual capital in order to achieve the desired objectives.

The intellectual capital statement should be accompanied by the flow report and the intellectual capital report in line with the ideas proposed by the 3R model. The intellectual capital flow report should include an analysis into the interdependencies that exist between the intellectual capital indicators.

It is also important to identify the strongest relationships between the intellectual capital indicators, both positive and negative, in order to subsequently take decisions regarding organizational policies and projects. In the German approach there is also a distinction on how strong influence management might have on the key components as well as the manageability. This is resulting in a decision template for further IA investments.

On the other hand, the importance of transparency in the presentation of these reports must be highlighted. It is essential to show information regarding the processes and procedures implemented and the suppositions made when preparing the report if, that is, the aim is to produce a credible report.

It is important that the publication of this statement coincides with that of the other corporate reports in order to thereby strengthen the links between the company's financial results and its knowledge-based resources.

Intellectual capital statements have a dual utility. From an internal point of view, they act as a support mechanism for the taking of management decisions as well as serving to communicate knowledge management objectives to employees. From an external viewpoint, these reports keep the stakeholders informed and constitute a useful marketing tool. For example, Novo Nordisk, a Danish firm that manufactures and markets pharmaceutical products and services, has been awarded for their outstanding work on stakeholder reporting. As a medical company, they have not put the product in the center, but the patient, and then built a network perspective on which they report. The report is also done in the Danish context, which was the first country to start protototyping based on the learnings from Skandia in Sweden, as well as the first country to pass a law on the IC reporting.

Why Should Firms and Organizations Measure and Report their Intellectual Capital?

Why should companies quantify and report their intellectual capital? Our experience with those companies who pioneered the quantification of intellectual capital shows that the main benefits that companies can gain if they measure this intangible resource: (1) attaining a competitive advantage; (2) developing new products/services;

(3) identifying new markets; (4) increasing revenue; (5) improving market share; (6) reusing their knowledge base; (7) less redundancies; (8) reducing mistakes and increasing productivity; (9) raising the quality of their products/services; and (10) expanding what they know about their customers.

Alternatively:

- To increase understanding of the holistic dynamics
- To increase the intelligence and transparency of hidden value
- To increase the process efficiency
- To increase the renewal and innovation
- To increase the security or, in other words, to address the risk of IA and IC

Conclusion

The wave of intellectual capital is increasing. It is evolving within universities, accounting standards groups, and political and business communities. The message is that we need to deeper understand and follow the wave of intangibles and knowledge economics. The alternative is perishing by riding the downward life cycle curve of industrial economics. It is a leadership liability not to address the potential or intellectual capital in waiting.

The corporate longitude is focusing on the lateral dimensions, as well as time to the future. This calls for another type of leadership role than traditional management. The book *Corporate Longitude* describes Leif Edvinsson's approach to the corporate challenges and three-dimensional issues, also called the longitude problem. It links the value of human and intellectual capital into measurement, cultivation, and valuation of organizational performance. It suggests that current valuation models are flawed and present only a small part of the reality. As a result, accountants and analysts alike are sailing the seas with latitude data (financial data) but no longitude data. Much more refined processes and flow approaches for management and measuring are now in growing practice in Europe as well as Japan; more refined measuring approaches as described by Roos, Pike, and Fernstrom (2005) are also in practice. A firm's intellectual capital is in waiting for generating new value. This is calling for a new regime based on more intelligence and cultivation of the intangibles.

References

Alwert, K. (2006). Wissensbilanzen fur Mittelstandische Organisationen. PhD thesis, Stuttgart.

Andriessen, D. (2004). *Making sense of intellectual capital.* Butterworth-Heinemann.

Blair, M., & Wallman, S. (2001). *The unseen wealth.* Brookings Institution Press.

BMWA- Bundes Ministerium fur Wirtschaft unt Arbeit. *Guidelines for wissesnkapital.* Retrieved January 14, 2008, from www.akwissenskapital.info

Bounfour, A., & Edvinsson, L. (2005). *Intellectual capital for communities – nations, regions, and cities.* Oxford: Butterworth- Heinemann.

Bueno, E. (2003). *Modelo intellectus: Medición y gestión del capital intelectual* [Intellectus model: Model for the measurement and management of intellectual capital]. *Documento Intellectus, 5.* Madrid: CIC-IADE (UAM).

Bueno, C. E., & Ordóñez de Pablos, P. (in press). The intellectual capital statement: New challenges for managers. In J. Luiz (Ed.), *Strategies for information technology and intellectual capital: Challenges and opportunities.* Hershey, PA: IGI Global Inc.

Danish Agency for Development of Trade and Industry (DATI). (2000). *Intellectual capital statement-Towards a guideline.* Retrieved January 14, 2008, from www.efs.dk/icaccounts

Danish Agency for Development of Trade and Industry (DATI). (2001). *A guideline for intellectual capital statements: A key to knowledge management.* Retrieved January 14, 2008, from www.ebst.dk/publikationer/rapporter/guidelineICS/ren.htm

Danish Agency for Development of Trade and Industry (DATI). (2003). *Intellectual capital statements: The new guideline.* Retrieved January 14, 2008, from http://videnskabsministeriet.dk/site/forside/publikationer/2003/intellectual-capital-statements—the-new-guideline

Edvinsson, L. (1994). Developing intellectual capital at Skandia. *Long Range Planning, 30*(3), 366-373.

Edvinsson, L. (2002). *Corporate longitude: Discover your true position in the knowledge economy.* Financial Times Prentice Hall.

Edvinsson, L. (Ed.). (2004). *Intellectual capital reporting in health care centers: The development of a prototype framework.* Sweden: University of Lund.

Edvinsson, L., & Kovikas, M. (2007). IC or Wissesnbilanz process. *Journal of IC, 3.*

Edvinsson, L., & Malone, M. S. (1997). *Intellectual capital. Realizing your company's true value by finding its hidden brainpower* (1st ed). Harper Collins Publishers.

European Commission. (2006). *RICARDIS (Reporting Intellectual Capital to augment research, development and innovation in SME's)*. Retrieved January 14, 2008, from http:// europa.euint/comm./research/rtdinfo/index_en.html

Federal Ministry of Education, Science and Culture of Austria. (2002). *University organisation and studies act: University act 2002* (No. 120). Author.

Lev, B. (2001). *INTANGIBLES: Management, measurement, and reporting*. Brookings Institution Press.

MERITUM Project. (2002). *Guidelines for managing and statementing on intangibles* (intellectual capital statement). Madrid: Airtel-Vodafone Foundation. Retrieved January 14, 2008, from www.eu-know.net

Mouritsen, J., Larsen, H. T., & Bukh, P. N. D. (2001a). Intellectual capital and the 'capable firm': Narrating, visualising and numbering for managing knowledge. *Accounting, Organizations and Society, 26*(7/8), 735-762.

Mouritsen, J., Larsen, H. T., & Bukh, P. N. (2001b). Reading intellectual capital statements: Describing and prescribing knowledge management strategies. *Journal of Intellectual Capital, 2*(4), 359-383.

Nakamura, L. (2006, June 20). *The rise of us intellectual capital: A trillion dollars of intangible investment annually*. Paper presented at the Conference on Intellectual Capital for Communities (Nations, Regions, Cities), World Bank Office, Paris. Federal Reserve Bank of Philadelphia.

Nordika Project. (2002). *Intellectual capital: Managing and statement*. Oslo: Nordic Industrial Fund.

Ordóñez de Pablos, P. (2004a). A guideline for building the intellectual capital statement: The 3R model. *International Journal of Learning and Intellectual Capital, 1*(1), 3-18.

Ordóñez de Pablos, P. (2004b). Measuring and reporting structural capital: Lessons from European learning firms. *Journal of Intellectual Capital, 5*(4), 629-647. ISSN: 1469-1930.

Ordóñez de Pablos, P. (2005). Intellectual capital reports in India: Lessons from a case study. *Journal of Intellectual Capital, 6*(1), 141-149.

PRISM. (2003). Retrieved January 14, 2008, from www.euintagibles.net

RICARDIS. (2006). *"Ricardis" (reporting intellectual capital to augment research, development and innovation in SMEs)*. European Commission.

Roos, G., & Burgman, R. (2007). The importance of IC reporting. Evidence and implications. *Journal of IC, 1*.

Roos, G., Pike, S., & Fernstrom, L. (2005). *Managing intellectual capital in practice*. Butterworth-Heinemann.

Society for Knowledge Economics. (2005). *Australian guiding principles on extended performance management: A guide to better managing, measuring and reporting knowledge intensive organisational resources*. Author.

Subcommittee on Management & Intellectual Assets. (2005). *Interim report by subcommittee on management & intellectual assets*. New Growth Policy Committee, Industrial Structure Council, Japan. Retrieved January 14, 2008, from www.meti.go.jp/policy/intellectual_assets/english.htm

University Organisation and Studies Act. (Universities Act 2002). (2002, August 9). *University organisation amendment act and universities of the arts organisation amendment act* (No. 120). National Council of the Republic of Austria.

Viedma, J. M. (2004). CICBS: A methodology and a framework for measuring and managing intellectual capital of cities. A practical application in the city of Mataró. *Knowledge Management Research & Practice (KMRP), 2*(1), 13-23.

Wissenskapital. (2003), *Future culture and earnings capabilities of Celle Technology Center*. Oberreichenbach: Wissenskapital Edvinsson & Kivikas Entwicklungsunternehmen.

Chapter III

Modeling Techniques for Knowledge Management

Hanno Schauer, University Duisburg-Essen, Germany

Carola Schauer, University Duisburg-Essen, Germany

Abstract

Knowledge management is an umbrella concept for different management tasks and activities. Various modeling abstractions and techniques have been developed providing specialized support for different knowledge management tasks. This article gives an overview of modeling abstractions that are frequently discussed in the knowledge management literature as well as some promising techniques in a mature research state. Six groups of modeling techniques are presented and additionally evaluated with respect to their suitability for different fields of applications within the knowledge management domain.

Introduction

Knowledge management (KM) is a collective concept for a variety of management tasks and embraces different management functions. The term knowledge management covers strategic as well as operational activities that are dedicated to the

- Management—that is, analysis, planning, control, and leadership—of the knowledge base of a company
- Personnel management of knowledge workers
- Organization of knowledge work
- Management of information systems supporting knowledge work

Each of the four management areas of knowledge management embraces a multiplicity of possible tasks and management instruments. Knowledge management is additionally complicated by the fact that the different management areas are interdependent and connected. Hence, knowledge management is often faced with sociotechnical as well as socioeconomical challenges.

The complexity of the domain and the multiplicity of possible management instruments require watchful analysis of the problem domain and careful strategy development as well as planning of knowledge management measures. In order to support (systems) analysis, discussion of strategic knowledge management issues, and knowledge management planning, academic literature and business practice suggest a number of modeling techniques and methods. They promise to foster the explication and collaborative reflection of strategic issues, the understanding of operational challenges, as well as the planning and documentation of specific measures for knowledge management in a particular enterprise.

This article gives an overview of modeling abstractions for knowledge management and compares the techniques according to their relevance for different fields of application within the knowledge management domain. Our discussion covers modeling abstractions frequently discussed in knowledge management literature as well as some promising techniques that are in a mature research state. Section 2 examines mapping techniques typically used in early planning stages of knowledge management initiatives. Section 3 presents different types of conceptual modeling techniques for knowledge management. Section 4 is dedicated to formal modeling techniques for knowledge management, focusing on ontologies. A comparative evaluation of the different modeling techniques is provided in Section 5. The article closes with concluding remarks.

Mapping Techniques

Knowledge work and knowledge management activities frequently entail collaboration and communication. Hence, it is no surprise that specific forms of creativity and group work techniques, mainly mapping techniques, are discussed in the knowledge management literature as well as used in practice for knowledge management purposes. In the following, typical mapping techniques for knowledge management are discussed. The presentation systematizes two groups of mapping techniques: semantic networks and knowledge maps.

Semantic Networks

A common language is a basic prerequisite and foundation for communication and collaboration. More specifically, successful collaboration and cooperation require a common understanding of relevant terms in the area of interest, that is, in a specific knowledge domain.

Modeling Concepts

Semantic networks (semantic nets, not to be confused with Semantic Web) are an easy to understand form of visualization representing natural language terms and their interrelation. Semantic networks are usually displayed in a graph structure including terms as nodes and relationships between terms as edges. Usually, the types of relationships between terms are not restricted and can be determined by the users, for example, is-a-special-type-of or is-included-in. While semantic networks use a basal grammatical structure allowing for tool support to a limited extent, they do not provide any formal description of terms and are, thus, not intended to be machine-readable.

There are different forms of semantic networks that mainly differ in the symbols used for modeling terms and the types of relationship that are already built in the

Figure 1. Mind map of the modeling techniques discussed in this article

language. Topic maps, mind maps, or concept maps are popular examples of semantic networks. Figure 1 displays an example of a mind map structuring the modeling techniques discussed in this article.

Intended Fields of Application

Semantic networks are a visual aid for structuring natural language terms in a domain. They are frequently used to support creativity and group work activities. They can help to find a consensus within the collaborating group of people on the meaning and relationships of relevant terms in a domain.

In scenarios of knowledge work and knowledge management semantic networks are usually used in early planning stages (e.g., in kick-off or brainstorming meetings). Hence, they are intended to support the process of establishing a common terminology in a certain field of knowledge. For example, the mind map in Figure 1 can serve as a basis for finding a consensus on the fundamental terms in the knowledge domain "Modeling Techniques for Knowledge Management."

Preliminary Assessment

Semantic networks offer primarily visual support for group work. The concepts provided are rather simple (terms and relationships). Hence, they are easy to learn and to understand. Also, they can be applied flexibly and are not bound to any certain domain of interest. The high level of flexibility and independence from a specific domain, however, comes along with the need to derive more formal terminological structures (e.g., an ontology) if the developed terminological structure is to be used by software tools.

Knowledge Maps

Knowledge sources or resources[1], knowledge consumers, and their relationship are of obvious interest and also a suitable starting point for detailed systems analysis for knowledge management. Hence, there is a frequent need to relate possible sources and relevant consumers of certain types of knowledge.

Modeling Concepts

Knowledge maps[2] are largely informal visualizations of knowledge sources or resources (e.g., human experts or data warehouse systems) and, optionally, of

Figure 2. Knowledge map in accordance with Gentsch (2000, p. 36)

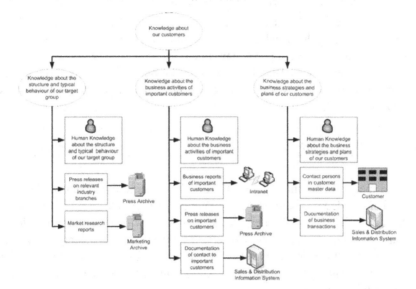

knowledge consumers (e.g., decision makers) for particular fields of knowledge. Knowledge maps model fields of knowledge by topics. In knowledge maps, topics, subtopics, as well as knowledge sources and knowledge consumers are related in a graph like structure. The edges of knowledge maps usually do not have any formal semantics and require interpretation by the observer.

A typical knowledge map is displayed in Figure 2. As opposed to semantic networks, knowledge maps embrace additional graphical elements which are supplemented by textual annotations and support the differentiation of different concepts.

Intended Fields of Application

Similarly to semantic networks in general, knowledge maps are primarily a visual aid for collaborative settings. They can be used in early stages of collaborative enterprise analysis and planning. During the drawing and refinement process of knowledge maps, a common understanding of possible knowledge flows (i.e., conceptual paths of knowledge between knowledge sources and its consumers) is developed. The understanding of existing and possible flows of knowledge is a suitable basis for the discussion of knowledge barriers and potentials for improvement in daily knowledge work and for the preliminary design of possible knowledge management initiatives (Davenport & Prusak, 1998; Eppler, 2001; Gentsch, 2000). The suggestions can be used as a starting point for more detailed enterprise analysis using more specialized methods, such as methods for conceptual modeling and business redesign.

Knowledge maps can also be used for staff information and staff participation. They can be applied as a simple visual aid to support members of an enterprise in locating information or in finding a particular contact person. Furthermore, knowledge maps can be used as a visual interface to information systems that allow access to information sources or assist in finding the right contact person (Davenport & Prusak, 1998).

Preliminary Assessment

Knowledge maps can be interpreted as a domain specific extension of semantic networks. Knowledge maps are also easy to understand and to use. They are well-suited for giving members of an enterprise an overview of important knowledge sources and consumers. They can also serve as a basis for discussing knowledge flows and possible knowledge barriers. However, because the concepts provided lack common domain-specific semantics, knowledge maps are a rather weak tool for a more detailed analysis.

Conceptual Modeling

The mapping techniques described above are primarily directed at supporting communication. They do not provide specific concepts or support for detailed analysis and planning of the knowledge base or the knowledge work within a company. Conceptual modeling languages are the prevailing form of modeling techniques for enterprise analysis and planning. Conceptual modeling is a general term for different forms of domain-specific and semiformal modeling concepts. A domain specific modeling language (technique) for knowledge management typically includes abstractions of the management domain in general and of knowledge management in particular, thus reflecting the technical terminology of the people responsible for the analysis. For the context of knowledge management it seems appropriate to require semiformal language concepts. Semiformal means that, on the one hand, the language concepts have to adhere to specific rules, typically defined in a metamodel (e.g., a database schema). On the other hand, the concepts provided are not completely formal and leave room for human interpretation of the models.

Popular conceptual modeling techniques for the management domain include models of business processes, organizational structure, or market matrices. In principle, all modeling abstractions from the management domain are relevant for knowledge management purposes, but not all of them are discussed frequently in the knowledge management literature. In the following we will focus on three vital techniques that offer concepts along with specific analysis guidelines for knowledge management purposes: Section 3.1 examines modeling techniques for (knowledge intensive) business processes; Section 3.2 discusses techniques for task modeling; And Section 3.3 gives an outlook on an upcoming method for multiperspective modeling for knowledge management.

Business Process Models

Processes and a process oriented perspective, respectively, are a central paradigm of thinking about organizations. The appeal and potential of a process oriented perspective is based on the following two aspects:

1. **Focus:** Process models focus on the way resources are allocated and used, and how goods and services are created. In particular, process models abstract to a large extent from the organizational circumstances in which the creation takes place.

2. **Opportunity for comparison:** Humans and machines, as well as automatic, partly automatic, and human work are treated within the same perspective and are modelled with similar concepts.

The large amount of knowledge management literature dealing with business process analysis for knowledge management indicates the prominent role of business process analysis for the analysis and design of knowledge work. The reason for this can directly be derived from the above mentioned general advantages: models of knowledge intensive processes allow (i) focusing on knowledge work and (ii) modeling and analysis of different forms of knowledge (i.e., human knowledge and skills, explicit knowledge, data and information) and knowledge sources (i.e., humans and data sources) within the same model and with comparable concepts.

Modeling Concepts

Business processes are sets of activities which are structured in their timely and logical order (Becker & Schütte, 2004; Hammer & Champy, 1993). Business process models are semiformal, graphical illustrations of the activities of a process, events that can occur during the process, and the timely order of activities and events. Most techniques additionally annotate the organizational unit responsible for each activity. A sample business process is depicted in Figure 3. The process of

Figure 3. Model of a business process

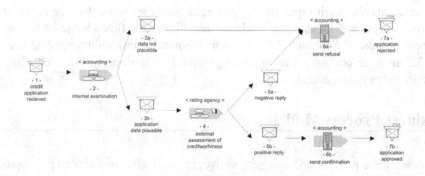

examining loan applications takes place at a credit institution. It involves various subprocesses and events. The process finishes with a rejection or an acceptance of the loan application depending on the results (events) created by the subprocesses (internal examination and external assessment).

Typical models of knowledge intensive processes are furthermore enriched with information about data, knowledge, or skills that are required to carry out an activity as well as information about the way specific knowledge is changed or produced during an activity.

Intended Fields of Application

Process models applied as tools in systems analysis can support the identification of information relevant for the detailed analysis of knowledge work. Different kinds of information are revealed in different stages of the systems analysis. Business process analysis for knowledge management can be systematized in three steps, which are briefly described in the subsequent paragraphs. The order of the three steps or stages can be adapted to specific circumstances and requirements of each individual analysis case.

Step 1: Modeling and Analysis of Subprocesses
The first step comprises the modeling of the processes and the initial analysis of individual processes. Issues of interest from the view point of knowledge management are

- The human skills, information, and knowledge needed to carry out a process.

- Communication and collaboration activities within a process.

- The data, information, or knowledge produced or changed within a process.

Identifying this kind of information helps to reveal communication and knowledge, possible resource conflicts between different activities in a process (e.g., overstraining competent knowledge workers), as well as barriers of communication and knowledge work, such as media clashes.

Step 2: Conflicts and Synergies

The second step aims at revealing knowledge related synergies, resource conflicts, or communication demands between activities of different processes. Therefore, activities and subprocesses have to be identified that are similar either in terms of the skills needed, resources used, or knowledge applied.

Connecting process steps, that occur in different business processes, with organizational units or roles carrying out this activity, can provide further important information on knowledge work. Such an analysis can identify communication needs, potential barriers of communication due to organisational borders, potential for synergies through intensified collaboration, as well as competence or knowledge monopolies.

Step 3: Communication and Knowledge Chains (optional)

Business process models typically focus on the creation of a good or service. However, there are a number of communication processes that are not represented

Figure 4. Annotated model of a business process

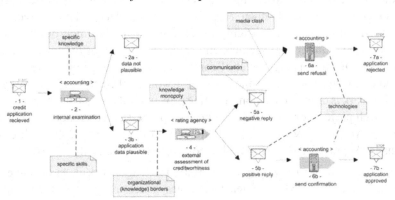

by typical business process models. Hence, the third step focuses on the modeling and analysis of process models depicting the communication chains and knowledge evolution for particular fields of knowledge. Models of the knowledge flow can serve to answer questions such as: Is the right knowledge delivered to the business processes? Is newly created knowledge stored and distributed reasonably? Is critical knowledge appropriately secured?

Figure 4 displays the loan application examination process annotated by different aspects that are of interest for knowledge management.

Preliminary Assessment

Methods of business process analysis have proven to be an effective and efficient tool for the detailed analysis of knowledge intensive business processes and the knowledge flow within a company. Moreover, business process models are a fundamental perspective for business planning and control; hence, the models used for knowledge management purposes have high prospects for reuse in the context of other management tasks.

Additionally, business process models are an easy to understand and suitable instrument for communication within the management domain. Only a relatively short training period is necessary to become familiar with the notation and graphical elements of a business process modeling language. However, while business process models are relatively easy to learn and understand by those educated and experienced in the management domain, they are often not intuitively understood by functionally specialized staff. Hence, dedicated training is needed when business process models are to be used as instrument for staff participation.

Task Models

Often knowledge work includes a high variety of possible activities to be carried out and the outcome is frequently open. Many forms of knowledge intensive work are characterised as ill-structured and highly dynamic in terms of the timely order. Typical examples can be found in management and leadership functions or in research and development. Due to this high level of contingency, knowledge intensive work is often autonomously controlled by the knowledge workers themselves. In many cases knowledge work is organized in nonrepetitive projects and carried out in team work (e.g., research projects or software development processes) (Davenport & Prusak, 1998; Kock, McQueen, & Corner, 1997; Maier, Hädrich, & Peinl, 2005; Schreiber, Akkermans, Anjewierden, de Hoog, Shadbolt, Van de Velde et al., 1999).

The unsettled character of weakly structured knowledge work is an obstacle for planning and controlling. Management techniques, which are appropriate for routine business, are often not well-suited for the management of knowledge-intensive work. Especially methods of business process modeling, which rely fundamentally on a targeted control-flow structure, lack appropriate abstractions for describing the ill-structured and open-ended elements of (knowledge) work (Remus, 2002; Schauer, 2007). Hence, specialized concepts are needed to effectively model, analyze, plan, and control knowledge intensive work.

Modeling Concepts

Tasks are the prevailing modeling abstraction for planning and controlling weakly or ill-structured processes. The typical form of modeling ill-structured work is to start with one major task, which fulfils the primary (project) objective, and then to gradually subdivide the task(s) and responsibilities in a tree structure, a so called task breakdown structure. The best-known examples for task breakdown structures are the well-known instruments for project planning: object breakdown structure and work breakdown structure.

Despite the obvious suitability of the task concept for knowledge management and despite its everyday use in planning knowledge management projects, so far, only one specialized modeling technique for task modeling for knowledge management has been developed. The modeling technique is part of *Knowledge-MEMO*, a multiperspective enterprise modeling method for knowledge management (Schauer, 2007). Figure 5 applies the *Knowledge-MEMO* notation to depict the task breakdown structure of the "Building Blocks of Knowledge Management" (Probst, Raub, & Romhardt, 2000), a widely known and often cited knowledge management framework. Beside the tasks and their division in subtasks or super-tasks, the Knowledge-MEMO notation also describes the kind of contribution of a subtask to a super-task (e.g., operational, administrative, supporting, exception handling), which is vital information for the analysis of task breakdown structures.

Intended Fields of Application

So far, task models have not been discussed explicitly as a tool for business analysis in knowledge management literature. However, models of task breakdown structures can be used for knowledge management purposes in a way similar to business process models. The analysis of the task decomposition structure can provide information analogue to business processes. The steps described above for systems analysis of models of knowledge intensive business processes can be applied to task breakdown structures as follows (Schauer, 2007):

- **Step 1:** Modeling and analysis of subtasks uncovers (1) skill, information, and knowledge demands, (2) communication and collaboration activities, and (3) the data, information, or knowledge produced or changed. This kind of information helps to reveal possible resource conflicts between different tasks, barriers of collaboration and knowledge work, or communication demands.

- **Step 2:** The relation of similar tasks and the assessment of the organizational distribution of responsibilities for similar tasks reveals indications for knowledge related synergies, resource conflicts, or communication demands.

- **Step 3:** An optional analysis of communication tasks related to a certain field of knowledge (e.g., communication tasks prescribed by the chain of command) may reveal further information on the appropriateness and effectiveness of the knowledge treatment.

Since the suggested steps for the analysis of task breakdown structures and business process models are very similar and the respective modeling abstractions are comparable, a joint analysis of task breakdown structures and business process models is possible and, generally, advisable.

Figure 5. Task breakdown structure in Knowledge-MEMO notation

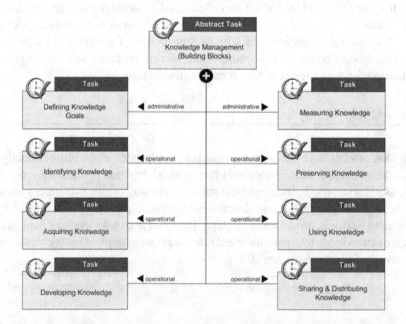

Preliminary Assessment

Task breakdown structures are the prevailing instrument for modeling ill-structured or weakly structured work. Since knowledge work often is ill-structured and open in its outcomes, task breakdown structures are particularly suitable for modeling knowledge work. While task breakdown structures and business process models can be analyzed following the same principle steps, the analysis results differ in two respects. First, a task-based analysis cannot yield outcomes, which directly result from the sequence in which tasks/processes are carried out (e.g., media clashes). Second, since task breakdown structures are used to model ill-structured knowledge work, the task models developed in business practice are necessarily less precise than business process models.

Enterprise Models

Knowledge management is a diverse management task and relates to various aspects of business planning. Among others, the following business functions are related: strategic planning, human resource management, organization, information systems management, and managerial accounting. The complexity and diversity of the knowledge management task suggests a holistic approach to knowledge management.

Modeling Concepts

Methodical support for holistic knowledge management requires supporting different planning languages for different, relevant views on a company. Conceptual views for knowledge management should at least include models of goals and strategies of an enterprise, of its organizational structure, of the knowledge work (tasks and processes), of skills and competencies of its personnel, as well as models of the IT infrastructure. A holistic knowledge management approach should include not only a set of model types (modeling languages) for the different perspectives. Due to the interdependencies between the different aspects and perspectives in knowledge management aforementioned, it is necessary to also provide for compatible concepts and abstractions in the different views and model types. Modeling methods fulfilling those requirements are subsumed under the term enterprise modeling.

Although the need for multiperspective enterprise modeling approaches for knowledge management and multiperspective reference models for knowledge management, respectively, have been discussed by several authors (e.g., Frank, 2002; Fettke & Loos, 2002; Loucopoulos & Kavakli, 1999), so far no dedicated multiperspective method for knowledge management is available in practice. Hence, we want to introduce Knowledge-MEMO (Schauer, 2007), a multiperspective modeling method

Figure 6. Knowledge-MEMO framework

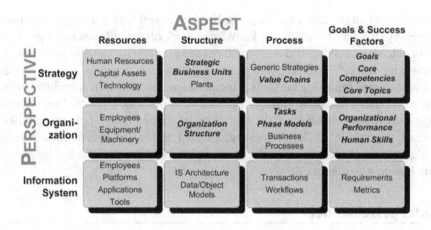

for knowledge management, which is still in a research state. Knowledge-MEMO is a domain specific extension of the enterprise modeling *multiperspective enterprise modeling (MEMO)* method (Frank, 1994, 1999, 2002a). Knowledge-MEMO provides integrated modeling languages and guidelines for knowledge management and puts a particular emphasis on the perspectives mentioned above: goals and strategies of an enterprise, the organizational structure, skills and competencies of its personnel, and IT infrastructure. Figure 6 shows the Knowledge-MEMO framework, comprising the views MEMO and Knowledge-MEMO offer specialized modeling languages for.

Most information on Knowledge-MEMO is currently available in German language only. However, an Internet portal on Knowledge-MEMO will be made available in English language at www.knowledge-memo.org, providing language concepts, process models, guides for applying the method, and experience reports.

Intended Fields of Application

Holistic knowledge management does not only require specialized modeling abstractions but also particularly dedicated modeling guidelines (process models) for analysis and planning. Knowledge-MEMO encompasses several interrelated process models for analysis of knowledge work and the design of knowledge management measures. The previously presented steps for the analysis of business process models and task breakdown structures, including models of the organizational structure, provide a compact overview of one Knowledge-MEMO process model.

Preliminary Assessment

A methodical approach to holistic knowledge management requires analysing and relating several different conceptual views on a company. Hence, using a multiperspective enterprise modeling method is particularly suitable and strongly recommended for holistic knowledge management. However, methods of multiperspective enterprise modeling for knowledge management are still in a—albeit mature—research state. Thus, in contrast to all other presented modeling paradigms, tool support is not yet available. Furthermore, while thorough evaluations of the language concepts in practice are still under way, it is expected that understanding and using the various modeling languages does require certain training in advance, in particular for those users who are not educated in management and not experienced in conceptual management instruments.

Formal Specifications (Ontologies)

Formalization is a prerequisite for computer support and automated reasoning. The modeling abstractions discussed above are only informal or semiformal and, therefore, only partly machine-readable. In order to specify computer behaviour and automated knowledge processing the use of formal modeling languages is required.

Different forms of formal specifications can be relevant for knowledge management, including database schemas, programming languages, or mathematical concepts used in Operations Research. Despite the multiplicity of formal modeling concepts relevant for knowledge management in principle, the knowledge management literature discusses mainly, more or less *pars pro toto*, ontologies. Hence, this section focuses on ontologies. Nevertheless, most of the remarks can be applied to other kinds of formal specifications for knowledge management as well.

Modeling Concepts

An ontology is a formally specified system of terms and relationships between terms. Ontologies are intended to make terms (e.g., natural language terms) machine-readable. They are, thus, not primarily aimed at providing persons with an understanding of a domain of interest. In contrast to semantic networks, which are also structures (i.e., graphs) of terms and relationships, ontologies are formal specifications. The meaning of a term described in an ontology is defined exclusively by the attributes of the term's specification and its—also formal—relationships to other terms.

Figure 7. Graphical specification of a person's contact data in RDF (Manola & Miller, 2004)

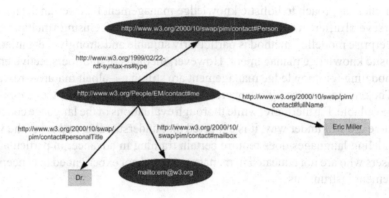

Figure 8. XML-based specification of a person's contact data in RDF (Manola & Miller, 2004)

```
<?xml version="1.0"?>
<rdf:RDF xmlns:rdf="http://www.w3.org/1999/02/22-rdf-syntax-ns#"
 xmlns:contact="http://www.w3.org/2000/10/swap/pim/contact#">

 <contact:Person rdf:about="http://www.w3.org/People/EM/contact#me">
 <contact:fullName>Eric Miller</contact:fullName>
 <contact:mailbox rdf:resource="mailto:em@w3.org"/>
 <contact:personalTitle>Dr.</contact:personalTitle>
 </contact:Person>

</rdf:RDF>
```

There are different types of specification languages that can be used to describe ontologies (e.g.. RDF, DAML+OIL, F-Logic, OWL, WSML, KIF). These languages differ in terms of the level of expressiveness and the abilities for automated reasoning. Typical ontology specification languages used for knowledge management purposes do not offer concepts to model dynamic behaviour; their semantic expressiveness is similar to database schemas.

Ontologies can be visualized as graphs. Figure 7 shows an example of the specification of the contact data of a person displayed as a tree structure and in RDF-syntax, respectively.

Ontologies are often of substantial size. Graphical models, as displayed in Figure 7, quickly become too large to handle if several hundreds of terms are modelled. Figure 8 shows a representation of the model drawn in Figure 7 in a formally equivalent XML-based notation.

Intended Fields of Application

In today's practice successful business applications of ontologies are to a large extent aimed at integrating different data sources. Within companies, for example, ontologies are often used to specify interfaces for not-integrated information systems or heterogeneous data sources (Fensel, 2001; Sure, Staab, & Studer, 2002). Ontologies are the formal basis of the Semantic Web. In the Semantic Web, formal ontology-based specifications, for example, structures to describe contact information on persons or biographical data, allow a standardized description of Web sites in a machine-readable format. Search engines can take advantage of this more formal description and, thus, return more precise results on user queries.

Preliminary Assessment

Formalization (e.g., via an ontology) includes significant advantages for knowledge management. It allows computer support and automated reasoning on the models. However, not every domain or problem is suitable for formalization. There are two basic barriers to formalization to be thoroughly considered. (1) Formalization of natural language terms is usually accompanied with simplification, disguising ambiguities, or inaccuracies. Thus, the meaning of the original term is possibly obscured in the reconstruction. For example, enterprise ontologies are aimed at reconstructing terms of the technical language of the management domain. However, enterprise ontology projects (e.g., Stader, 1996; Schreiber et al., 1999) have so far only been successful if specifically trained researchers were involved. (2) Technical languages tend to change over time, in particular, if technological innovations occur. In order to be accepted by the users, the ontology has to be kept correct over time. However, due to the detailed level of description building up and maintaining an ontology is a very costly effort, in particular compared to the modeling techniques discussed above.

Comparison and Evaluation

While the presented modeling techniques propose different concepts and abstractions, the notations used to display the models are quite similar. Most techniques suggest a graphical and net-like structure. In this way, the models are more intuitive and faster to grasp than lengthy written text documents. All modeling techniques for knowledge management are adaptations or extensions of general modeling techniques from the management domain and—to a large extent—well known in business practice. Such a close alignment with classic planning approaches seems beneficial, because knowledge management can relatively easily be integrated in existing enterprise planning processes.

Selecting suitable modeling techniques is an essential part in preparing for a knowledge management initiative. The multiplicity of possible modeling abstractions, however, makes this task a challenge on its own. In order to provide support for the selection decision, we suggest a framework which includes evaluation criteria related to concepts, fields of application, and modeling efforts and benefits. Table 1 provides an overview of the evaluation framework with a brief description of each criterion.

The evaluation results for mapping techniques (semantic networks and knowledge maps), conceptual models (business process models, task models, and enterprise models), and ontologies are displayed in Table 2 and Table 3, respectively.

The modeling techniques are considerably different in terms of the concepts and abstractions provided. Semantic networks and ontologies are not restricted to a particular domain while all other modeling techniques are more or less restricted (e.g., to knowledge sources and consumers or to well-structured processes).

The evaluation indicates that the level of formalization directly corresponds to the required training effort; semantic networks and knowledge maps provide only informal concepts, so that no specific user training is necessary. The conceptual modeling techniques use semiformal abstractions and, thus, imply a moderate effort for training (usually depending on the users' experience with business management terminology). Ontologies provide formal concepts. Hence, considerable training effort is required for users to understand the abstractions and formal syntax of ontology languages.

The analysis of the fields of application shows significant differences in terms of typical objectives and usage scenarios. Semantic networks and ontologies primarily aim at structuring terms of a domain. Knowledge maps, business process models, task models, and enterprise models are more closely related to the specific processes and tasks in business practice. While knowledge maps provide relatively simple concepts, the conceptual modeling techniques support more complex abstractions.

Table 1. Framework for comparing modeling techniques

aspect	criterion	description
concepts	domain	areas of interest or domains that can be modelled with the concepts provided
	level of formalization	possible values: formal, semiformal, informal
fields of application	typical objectives and results	results that can be achieved by applying this technique, for example, structure of terms in a domain
	usage in business practice	KM planning and analysis stages or tasks supported by this technique
	tool support	possibility of and/or need for tool support based on the concepts availability of tools for business practice
modeling efforts and benefits	training effort	training effort required to learn the language concepts and application guidelines possible values: none, moderate, considerable
	effort for maintenance	effort required to adapt the developed models to changes, for example, in terminology, over time possible values: moderate, considerable, high
	chances for reuse	possibilities to use parts or adaptations of existing models for other purposes or in other contexts possible values: high level of reuse, low level of reuse

Of the three conceptual modeling techniques, enterprise models offer the most complex and integrated abstractions and modeling languages. Hence, according modeling techniques are best suited for holistically analysing an organization and planning knowledge management measures. Because of their low level of formalization, semantic networks and knowledge maps are suited for supporting group work and staff participation in early stages of a knowledge management initiative. The high level of formalization allows for using ontologies for formal specifications of information systems.

Generally, tool support is possible for all modeling techniques. For most techniques—all except enterprise models—there are software tools available for usage in business practice. The level of formalization and the complexity of the modeling concepts directly relate to the recommendation of using dedicated modeling tools. Structuring terms in semantic networks or developing a knowledge map can be done

Table 2. Comparison of modeling abstractions for knowledge management (part 1)

	Semantic Networks	Knowledge Maps	Business Process Models
Concepts			
domain	not restricted to any fixed domain	knowledge sources and knowledge consumers	well-structured business processes
level of formalization	informal	informal	semiformal
Fields of application			
typical objectives and results	structuring terms in an area of interest	informal overview of knowledge sources and consumers	analysis and (re)design of processes
usage in business practice	support for group work in early planning stages	staff participation in early stages of a KM initiative	analysis and (re)design of knowledge intensive (business) processes
tool support and usage	possible but not necessary	possible but not necessary	possible and recommended
	tools available for specific types, for example, mind maps and concept maps	common graphical tools are suitable	several tools for business process analysis available (not specifically for KM)
Modeling efforts and benefits			
training effort	none	none	moderate effort
effort for maintenance	moderate effort	moderate effort	moderate to high effort, depending on how extensive processes are modelled
chances for reuse	low level of reuse	low level of reuse	high level of reuse

with common graphical tools and does not require specific software. Conceptual modeling techniques should be applied using a specialized tool that supports users by providing graphical elements, by checking for model validity, and by allowing for automated analysis. The high level of formalization requires the use of dedicated software for developing and maintaining ontologies.

Structures and models developed with any modeling technique require a certain effort for maintenance. This effort increases with a higher level of formalization and with a higher level of complexity and integration of the modeling concepts. Thus, of the conceptual modeling techniques, enterprise models require a relatively high effort

Table 3. Comparison of modeling abstractions for knowledge management (part 2)

	Task Models	Enterprise Models	Ontologies
Concepts			
domain	weakly or ill-structured forms of labor	different aspects of businesses	domain-neutral modeling concepts
level of formalization	semiformal	semiformal	formal
Fields of application			
typical objectives and results	task decomposition and task allocation	modeling businesses from different perspectives	formal specification of terms
usage in business practice	analysis and (re)design of knowledge intensive work	holistic KM	specifying interfaces for heterogeneous information systems and/or data sources
tool support and usage	possible and recommended project management task tools available (no specific KM task tools)	possible and recommended, specific KM-tools not yet available	possible and highly recommended several tools available
Modeling efforts and benefits			
training effort	moderate effort	moderate effort	considerable effort
effort for maintenance	moderate to high effort, depending on how extensive tasks are modelled	considerable to high effort	high effort
chances for reuse	high level of reuse	high level of reuse	high level of reuse

for maintenance. As discussed above, formal ontologies entail significant cost for maintaining the terminological structure. The effort for updating and maintaining enterprise models and ontologies depends to a certain extent on the quality of the supporting tools.

The meaning and interpretation of semantic networks and knowledge maps is only to a very limited extent defined by the respective language concepts. Hence, the meaning of such models highly depends on the specific development context, that is, the interpretations and objectives of the respective group of participants. So, the chances for reusing semantic networks or knowledge maps in a different context or for different purposes are very limited. Because the modeling concepts of conceptual modeling techniques and ontologies are more clearly defined, such models can be reused for different analysis and planning purposes or for the development of further information systems.

Concluding Remarks

Knowledge management differs significantly from many other management functions, that is, knowledge management is not a management task with a clear and unambiguous goal, a well-bound domain, and a given process model. Knowledge management embraces a variety of management activities and intersects with different standard management functions, including strategic management, human resources, organizational planning, and information systems management.

This chapter presented a number of modeling techniques that are intended to support planning and documentation of strategic issues and operational measures for knowledge management in different ways. Among other aspects, the techniques vary in terms of the conceptual foundation, the level of formalization, and the domain specificity. The comparative evaluation showed that the different modeling concepts and guidelines are suited for different knowledge management tasks and help to address different knowledge management challenges.

In practice, knowledge management might be implemented through individual initiatives and measures that can be supported, depending on the specific conditions and requirements of each case, by one of the modeling techniques discussed. However, establishing long-term and comprehensive knowledge management in a company requires an integrated and holistic approach to modeling for knowledge management. Hence, for any holistic knowledge management approach, multiperspective modeling techniques that provide integrated language concepts for all views and aspects relevant for knowledge work are recommended.

References

Becker, J., & Schütte, R. (2004). *Handelsinformationssysteme: Domänenorientierte Einführung in die Wirtschaftsinformatik*. Landsberg/Lech: Verlag Moderne Industrie.

Brosch C. (2003). *Einsatz von Self-Organizing Maps im Wissensmanagement*. Duisburg, Köln: Wiku.

Davenport, T. H., & Prusak, L. (1998). *Working knowledge: How organizations manage what they know.* Boston: Harvard Business School Press.

Eppler, M. (2001). Making knowledge visible through Intranet knowledge maps: Concepts, elements, cases. In *Proceedings of the 34th Hawaii International Conference on System Sciences (HICSS-34)* (p. 10).

Fensel, D. (2001). *Ontologies: A silver bullet for knowledge management and electronic commerce.* Berlin/Heidelberg/ New York: Springer.

Fettke, P., & Loos, P. (2002). Der Referenzmodellkatalog als Instrument des Wissensmanagements: Methodik und Anwendung. In J. Becker & R. Knackstedt (Eds.), *Wissensmanagement mit Referenzmodellen: Konzepte für die Anwendungssystem- und Organisationsgestaltung* (pp. 3-24). Heidelberg: Physica.

Frank, U. (1994). *Multiperspektivische Unternehmensmodellierung: Theoretischer Hintergrund und Entwurf einer objektorientierten Entwicklungsumgebung.* München: Oldenbourg.

Frank, U. (1999). *MEMO: Visual languages for enterprise modeling* (Research Rep. No. 18). University Koblenz-Landau, Institute for Informations Systems.

Frank, U. (2002a). A multi-layer architecture for knowledge management systems. In S. Barnes (Ed.), *Knowledge management systems* (pp. 97-111). Thomson.

Frank, U. (2002b). Multi-perspective enterprise modeling (MEMO): Conceptual framework and modeling languages. In *Proceedings of the 35th Hawaii International Conference on System Sciences (HICSS-35).*

Gentsch, P. (2000). *Wissen managen mit innovativer Informationstechnologie: Strategien - Werkzeuge - Praxisbeispiele.* Wiesbaden: Gabler Verlag.

Hammer, M., & Champy, J. (1993). *Re-engineering the corporation.* New York: Harper Business.

Kock, N. F., McQueen, R. J., & Corner, J. L. (1997). The nature of data, information and knowledge exchanges in business processes: Implications for process improvement and organizational learning. *The Learning Organisation 4*(2), 70-80.

Loucopoulos, P., & Kavakli, V. (1999). Enterprise knowledge management and conceptual modeling. In P. P. Chen, J. Akoka, H. Kangassalo, & B. Thalheim (Eds.), *Conceptual modeling: Current issues and future directions* (pp. 123-143). London/Berlin/Heidelberg: Springer.

Maier, R., Hädrich, T., & Peinl, R. (2005). *Enterprise knowledge infrastructures.* Berlin/Heidelberg/New York: Springer.

Manola, F., & Miller, E. (Eds.). (2004). *RDF primer: W3C recommendation 10 February 2004.* Retrieved February 12, 2007, from http://www.w3.org/TR/2004/REC-rdf-primer-20040210/

Probst, G., Raub, S., & Romhardt, K. (2000). *Managing knowledge: Building blocks for success*. New York/ Weinheim: Wiley & Sons.

Remus, U. (2002). *Prozessorientiertes Wissensmanagement. Konzepte und Modellierung*. Unpublished dissertation thesis, University of Regensburg.

Schauer, H. (2007). *Multiperspektivische Unternehmensmodellierung für das Wissensmanagement: Theoretischer Hintergrund und Entwurf einer Methode*. Submitted as dissertation thesis, University Duisburg-Essen.

Schreiber, G., Akkermans, H., Anjewierden, A., de Hoog, R., Shadbolt, N., Van de Velde, W., et al. (1999). *Knowledge engineering and management: The CommonKADS methodology*. Cambridge/London: MIT Press.

Stader, J. (1996, December). Results of the enterprise project. In *Proceedings of Expert Systems '96, the 16th Annual Conference of the British Computer Society Specialist Group on Expert Systems*, Cambridge, UK.

Sure, Y., Staab, S., & Studer, R. (2002). Methodology for development and employment of ontology based knowledge management applications. *SIGMOD Record, 31*(4), 18-23.

Useful URLs

MEMO: A brief overview of the enterprise modeling method. *MEMO: Multi-perspective enterprise modeling*. Retrieved January 4, 2008, from http://www.icb.uni-due.de/um/MEMO

Mind Map. (2007, February 12). *Wikipedia, the free dncyclopedia*. Retrieved February 12, 2007, from http://en.wikipedia.org/w/index.php?title=Mind_map&oldid=107456741

Ontology (computer science). (2007, February 4). *Wikipedia, the free encyclopedia*. Retrieved February 12, 2007, from http://en.wikipedia.org/ w/ index.php?title=Ontology_%28computer_science%29&oldid=105655781

Special Interest Group on Conceptual Modeling of the German Informatics Society (GI). Retrieved January 4, 2008, from http://www.gi-modellierung.de/

The Semantic Web. Retrieved January 4, 2008, from http://www.w3.org/2001/sw/

Topic Map. (2007, January 19). *Wikipedia, the free encyclopedia*. Retrieved February 12, 2007, from http://en.wikipedia.org/w/index.php?title=Topic_map&oldid=101775738

Further Readings

For further readings please see references section, too.

Fensel, D. (2001). *Ontologies: A silver bullet for knowledge management and electronic commerce.* Berlin/Heidelberg/New York: Springer.

Frank U. (2001). Informatik und Wirtschaftsinformatik – Grenzziehungen und Ansätze zur gegenseitigen Befruchtung. In J. Desel (Ed.), *Das ist Informatik.* Berlin/Heidelberg: Springer.

Gronau, N., & Weber, E. (2004). Modeling of knowledge intensive business processes with the declaration language KMDL. In M. Khosrow-Pour (Ed.), *Innovations Through Information Technology: 2004 Information Resources Management Association International Conference*, New Orleans, (pp. 284-287). Hershey, PA: IGI Global Inc.

Hirschheim, R., Klein, H. K., & Lyytinen, K. (1995). *Information systems development and data modeling: Conceptual and philosophical foundations.* Cambridge: Cambridge University Press.

Maier, R. (2002). *Knowledge management systems: Information and communication technologies for knowledge management.* Berlin/Heidelberg/New York: Springer.

Maier, R., Hädrich, T., & Peinl, R. (2005). *Enterprise knowledge infrastructures.* Berlin/Heidelberg/New York: Springer.

Mylopoulos, J. (2001). *Conceptual modeling for knowledge Mmnagement: A tutorial.* Hong Kong: City University of Hong Kong. Retrieved February 13, 2007, from http://www.comp.polyu.edu.hk/ds9/john.pdf

Endnotes

[1]   The notions of knowledge sources and knowledge resources differ in a subtle way. Both terms are largely identical. However, organizational knowledge sources, such as knowledge supplying companies, are usually not interpreted as knowledge resources; parts of knowledge resources, such as a single document in a document base, are usually not seen as knowledge sources.

[2]   The term knowledge map is differently used. In a broader, fairly contingent meaning knowledge maps are equal to semantic networks. In this article the term knowledge map is only used in its stricter sense.

Chapter IV

Classifying Knowledge Maps:
Typologies and Application Examples

Martin J. Eppler, University of Lugano (USI), Switzerland

Abstract

This chapter looks at graphic strategies to reference knowledge and how to make it more accessible through interactive knowledge maps. It discusses pragmatic ways of classifying knowledge maps to give an overview of their application contexts and formats. In the chapter, we show where and how the term knowledge map has been previously used and which criteria must be met in a sound and useful knowledge map classification that can support knowledge management (KM) processes and strategies. Various classification principles are presented and discussed. A table then matches map formats to knowledge management purposes and knowledge-related contents in order to serve as a selection and organizing framework. Examples of some of the main types of knowledge maps are presented to illustrate the variety of knowledge mapping present in the classification. The article concludes by discussing its limitations and future research questions in the area of knowledge mapping.

Introduction: Benefits of a Knowledge Map Classification

An early step toward understanding any set of phenomena is to learn what kinds of things there are in the set – to develop a taxonomy.

Herbert A. Simon

The main goal of this chapter is to provide an overview on the possible formats that exist to reference knowledge graphically or in other words to map it. In the chapter we assess knowledge maps as a useful tool for knowledge management (KM) and discuss various application parameters, benefits, and risks of using knowledge maps. We develop a systematic classification and show examples of various types of knowledge maps. This can help in assessing the potential of knowledge maps as useful elements of a comprehensive knowledge strategy. The following figure outlines the key components of this chapter and highlights its main contributions, namely eliciting quality criteria of a good classification, applying this approach to structure the realm of knowledge maps, and structuring implementation aspects of using knowledge mapping in knowledge management.

The advantages of visual representations for the field of knowledge management have long been recognized and discussed (Eppler, 2002, 2003; Newbern & Dansereau, 1995; Sparrow, 1998; Vail, 1999; Wexler, 2001; Wurman, 2001) and include a better *overview*, a faster *access,* and a more efficient and *memorable* representation and

Figure 1. Outline of the main topics of this chapter

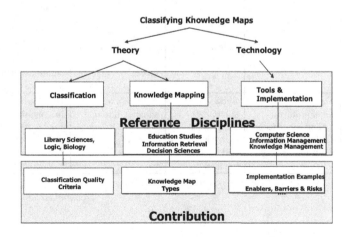

communication of knowledge assets (such as experts, practice documents, communities, patents, etc.). Visual representations have also proved particularly useful in *eliciting* (Hodgkinson, Maule, & Bown, 2004) or *referencing* implicit knowledge (Meyer, 1991; Sparrow, 1998) and thus can help to make knowledge more widely and easily available. The terms knowledge map (Eppler, 2002; Sparrow, 1998) or knowledge mapping (Wexler, 2001) have been used to designate a wide variety of approaches to organize and structure knowledge sources, knowledge application steps, insightful concepts, expert networks, or communities of practice (Vail, 1999). These varieties of knowledge maps have so far never been systematically classified

Table 1. An overview of four typical visualization genres

Format: Parameters:	Concept Map (A. Novak)	Mind Map (T. Buzan)	Conceptual Diagram (i.e., UML)	Visual Metaphor (i.e., nature, objects, sports, stories)
Sample thumbnail representation				
Definition	A concept map is a top-down diagram showing the relation-ships between concepts, including cross connections among concepts, and their manifestations (examples).	A mind map is a multicolored and image centred radial diagram that represents semantic or other connections between portions of learned material.	A conceptual diagram is systematic depiction of a situation, concept, process, or application in typified boxes with specified relationships, typically based on a theory, visual language, or model.	A visual metaphor is a graphic structure that uses the shape and elements of a familiar natural or human-made artefact or of an easily recognizable activity or story to organize content meaningfully and use the associations with the metaphor to convey additional meaning about the content.
Main function or benefit	Show systematic relationships among subconcepts relating to one main concept.	Show subtopics of a domain in a creative and seamless manner.	Analyze a topic or situation through a proven analytic framework.	Organize content meaningfully and convey main message about it.

continued on following page

Table 1. continued

Format: Parameters:	Concept Map (A. Novak)	Mind Map (T. Buzan)	Conceptual Diagram (i.e., UML)	Visual Metaphor (i.e., nature, objects, sports, stories)
Disadvantage	Difficult to represent procedural knowledge.	Bound to hierarchic structures.	Can be highly complex both in creation and in use.	May be misinterpreted.
Typical application context	Classroom teaching, self study and revision	Personal note taking and reviewing	Slide presentations, text illustration, student exercises	Text book illustration, student summary
Application Guidelines	Use it as a learning support tool for students, that is, to summarize key course topics or to clarify the elements and examples of an abstract concept.	Use it for preanalytic idea jostles or rapid note-taking, or to structure the main contents of a course or topic hierarchically.	Use it to structure a complex topic with the help of predefined categories.	Use it to memorize the key elements of a method or concept by placing them meaningfully within a fitting graphic metaphor that shares one or more properties with the topic.
Employed graphic elements	Boxes/bubbles with text and labelled connector arrows	Central topic bubble and colored (sub)branches with text above branches, pictograms	Labelled boxes and arrows with embedded text (if needed: icons)	Text within visual structure, sometimes connected through arrows
Core design rules or guidelines	Start with main concept (at the top), and end with examples (bottom, without circles); boxes/bubbles designate concepts, arrows represent relationships; include cross-links among elements	Start with main topic (center) and branch out to subtopics, employ pictograms and colors to add additional meaning. Write text above the branches.	Label all boxes. Fill all boxes with corresponding text. Larger boxes designate more important information.	Employ a visual metaphor that has a strong and clear main association that is related to the conceptual domain that is mapped. Use a metaphor with clearly detectable areas.
Typical software package supporting the visualization format	www.inspiration.com	www.mindmanager.com	www.visio.com	www.lets-focus.com

and compared in terms of their characteristics, unique features, or application parameters (for a first tentative classification see Eppler, 2002). So far, only the employed visualization techniques have been classified and this is regardless of their use in knowledge management. In Table 1, we give a sample overview of four frequently used visualization technique genres that have already been applied in knowledge management contexts, though not always as tools to reference or map knowledge areas, carriers, assets, or sources.

There are numerous benefits that can be achieved through a classification of knowledge maps. First, it can provide a descriptive overview of the domain (Bailey, 1994, p. 12) and can function as an inventory or repository (ibid., p.13) like a structured toolbox. In this way a classification can also become a problem solving heuristic (Dherbey, 2005, p. 68) that relates possible mapping solutions to knowledge management challenges. Thus, a classification reduces the complexity inherent in choosing a knowledge map format for a particular application context. As a further benefit, a map classification helps to recognize the similarities and differences among different types of knowledge maps. It helps to compare different types of knowledge maps along pertinent criteria. This can help in choosing a format of knowledge map for a given knowledge strategy (i.e., a diagrammatic, hyperlinked knowledge source map for a personalisation strategy). As a side-benefit of developing a classification, one has to develop an exhaustive description of the variables that define a knowledge map's application context. Finally, a classification of knowledge maps may also reveal new forms of knowledge maps that so far have not been applied. The classification may systematically go beyond the current state-of-the-art practice of knowledge mapping and show potential future formats.

Having listed the benefits that can be expected from a systematic classification of knowledge maps, one should also note the potential *disadvantages* of this research approach. Such disadvantages are the focus on description, rather than explanation. Classification may lead to reification (Bailey, 1994, p. 15); that is to say to pretend that an ideal archetype does exist, when it is merely hypothetical. Tied to this criticism is the fact—relevant in many knowledge management application contexts—that classifications tend to be rather static and difficult to adjust as a domain changes and evolves.

These disadvantages lead to the recommendation that a classification system should not just rely on one classification principle, but should propose various, alternative classification criteria. Thus, we will propose different useful classification principles to structure the domain of knowledge mapping. These principles can also be used to analyze one's knowledge strategy and see which map best fits the chosen approach.

Background: Criteria for
High-Quality Classifications

Classification lies at the heart of every scientific field. Classifications structure domains of systematic inquiry and provide concepts for developing theories to identify anomalies and to predict future research needs.

Lohse et al., 1994

Before examining existing classifications of knowledge maps and proposing our own set of categories, we should briefly examine the general rules or criteria that lead to valid and useful classifications. In this section we thus review the key requirements discussed in classification and categorization literature (Bailey, 1994; Bowker & Star, 1999; Dherbey, 2005; Lakoff, 1987; Minto, 1995; Wurman, 2001) in order to apply this research method adequately. As a side-benefit, the resulting quality criteria for classifications may also help knowledge managers in developing consistent and useful taxonomies for use in other areas (as in structuring the contents of an intranet).

A classification, according to Bailey (1994), is the ordering of entities into groups or classes on the basis of their similarity. Classifications minimize within-group variance, and maximize between-group variance (Bowker & Star, 1999). In other words, a classification should maximize the homogeneity within a group, as well as the heterogeneity among groups, thus facilitating analysis, organization, and assessment (Bailey, 1994). According to Bowker and Star (1999) classification can also be described as a spatial-temporal segmentation of the world (or one aspect of it). Taxonomies, as a special kind of classification, are tied to a purpose, and in the context of this chapter, allocate the right type of knowledge map to the right type of knowledge management problem. Bailey points out the difference between taxonomy and typology: whereas a typology is conceptual, deductive and based on reasoning, a taxonomy is empirical, inductive, and based on large sets that are examined and grouped (Bailey, 1994, p. v). The classification proposed in this chapter is partly a taxonomy derived from existing real life knowledge maps. In part, it is a typology, as it aims to point out other possible forms of knowledge mapping that may not yet have been applied in real-life contexts. A high-quality classification system that is fit for use should be both consistent and manageable. Consequently it should meet at least two sets of criteria, namely logic criteria and pragmatic criteria. In terms of the logic or formal criteria that make a classification sound, the classification has to have unique classificatory principles in operation which are not mixed at each level of abstraction or hierarchy (Bailey, 1994; Minto, 1995; Wurman 2001). This will ideally guarantee that the resulting categories are mutually exclusive (nonoverlapping) (Minto, 1995), and that the classification system is complete (the categories are collectively exhaustive), meaning that there are no items in the domain that cannot be assigned to a category (the classification is comprehensive). A classification should capture the totality of phenomena supposedly contained within it. In our case, there should not be knowledge maps that cannot be classified within the proposed system. Furthermore, a good classification assigns items to groups based on objective and stable attributes, so that there are no unclear category fits of particular items. The labels for different groups (on a particular hierarchic level) are on the same level of abstraction (ibid.); the classification should not mix specific (sub)groups with very general ones. It should also be made explicit what lies beyond the categorization scope and the boundaries of the classified domain or area should be clear (i.e., one should give inclusion or exclusion criteria). With regard to the pragmatic criteria that make a classification more ergonomic to use, one must pay attention to self-explanatory informative category names, as well as take into account the total number of categories that should not result in an overly heavy cognitive load for the targeted users. The process of item attribution to a category is made easier if each category has a typical representative, a so-called prototype member that can act as a mnemonic device for the category and thus makes it more memorable (Lakoff, 1987). The granularity of the classification should be in line with its intended use requirements (not more specific than actually needed). In summary, we can state that an ideal (sound and useful) classification should have the following properties, of which the first six are formal (or soundness) criteria and the subsequent four are pragmatic (or usability) ones:

1.   It consists of mutually exclusive categories (groups that do not overlap).

2.   That are collectively exhaustive (i.e., together the groups cover the entire classified domain).

3.   That are based on stable and objective grouping criteria (in order to unequivocally assign an item to a category in a classification).

4.   That have category names on a consistent level of abstraction (per hierarchic level).

5.   Based on one explicit, consistent, and informative classification principle per level of hierarchy.

6.   For a clearly specified and delineated topic area or domain.

7.   Where the categories have self-explanatory, informative category names or labels.

8.   And contain typical, representative (prototype) members for each group in the classification.

9.   Resulting in a well-organized system that does not overload the users as it contains an adequate amount of groups that can still be managed by short-term

memory (the granularity of the distinction does not exceed the level of detail necessary for the envisioned task that the classification supports).

10. A system that is hence understandable and usable by the envisioned user groups.

The ten criteria compiled above can provide guidelines for the assessment of current knowledge map classifications and for the development of new classifications. The former is presented in the next section, the latter in the subsequent section.

Prior Definitions and Typologies of Knowledge Maps

The map is the territory if people treat it as such.

Karl Weick

In this section, we review prior definitions and classifications of knowledge maps and point out their limitations and the resulting need for new classifications. The term knowledge map has so far been used in at least seven different scientific communities: in *education studies* or in researching instructional methods, such as mind maps, concept maps, and related graphic learning tools (Tergan & Keller, 2005); in organization studies (Huff, 1999; Huff & Jenkins, 2002) and *in requirements engineering* (Browne & Ramesh, 2002) where the term designates the elicited, visualized mental models of managers or IT users; in *decision analysis* to elicit crucial information (Bowne, Curley, & Benson, 1997); in *information retrieval* to designate interactive search result displays and search result browsing interfaces (Coyne, 1995); in *decision support systems* to designate, among other things, the informative graphic rendering of decision variables (Smelcer & Carmel, 1997); in *artificial intelligence* where it can designate the conceptual representation of an expert domain (Gordon, 2000); and in the *knowledge management* community (Burnett, Illingworth, & Webster, 2004; Vail, 1999). In the context of knowledge management, a knowledge map generally designates an overview on a collection of knowledge-related contents. A knowledge map typically consists of two main parts: a ground or background layer which represents the context for the mapping, and the individual elements that are mapped within this context. The elements which are mapped onto such a shared context range from experts, project teams, or communities of practice, to more explicit and codified forms of knowledge such as white papers or articles, patents, lessons learned (e.g., after action reviews or project debriefings), events (i.e., trainings), databases, or similar IT applications such as expert systems or simulations. Knowledge maps group these elements to show their relationships, locations, or other attributes. Knowledge maps answer questions such as: How do I find relevant knowledge? How can I judge its quality? How can I make sense of its structure? How do I go about applying or developing it? Definitions of knowledge maps that we have found in the literature follow this logic. Vail (1999), for example, defines a knowledge map as follows:

A knowledge map is a visual display of captured information and relationships, which enables the efficient communication and learning of knowledge by observers with differing backgrounds at multiple levels of detail. The individual items of knowledge included in such a map can be text, stories, graphics, models, or numbers. [...] Knowledge mapping is defined as the process of associating items of information or knowledge (preferably visually) in such a way that the mapping itself also creates additional knowledge. (p. 10)

A more recent definition by Renukappa and Egbu (2004) also stresses relationships, but adds the important element of maps referring also to tacit knowledge. It also highlights the important notion of knowledge dynamics, next to knowledge stores or repositories: "A knowledge map is a navigation aid to both explicit and tacit knowledge, showing the importance and the relationships between knowledge 'stores' and the dynamics."

According to Ernst and Young (Novins, 1997), to take a practitioner's definition, a knowledge map is a place to find the source of answers, a method and format for collecting and communicating where knowledge resides and is lacking, typically within an organization, a visual representation of the knowledge content areas. Based on these typical definitions we can conclude that the minimal criteria for a knowledge map are that it is a graphic overview and reference of knowledge-related content that serves a knowledge management related purpose.

Let us next look at how this domain has been structured so far, that is, to say which types of knowledge maps have already been distinguished. In knowledge management, the classical cartographic map types (aimed at representing information about a geographic territory) are less fruitful (Peterson, 1995). Eppler (2002) proposes a simple knowledge map typology based on knowledge management tasks, namely knowledge creation and development maps, knowledge identification maps, knowledge assessment maps, and knowledge application maps. The main problem with this classification is that it is not comprehensive, versatile, or precise enough to be of general use in knowledge management.

A different, more abstract set of map categories is used by Anne S. Huff in her anthologies on the topic of mapping strategic thought and knowledge (Huff, 1999; Huff & Jenkins, 2002). In her mapping typology, she focuses on cognitive maps and distinguishes the following map types: text and language analysis maps, classification maps, network maps, conclusive maps, and schematic maps of cognitive structures (Huff & Jenkins, 2002). The problem with this classification is that it is not based on one consistent classification principle and not always applicable to knowledge management.

Novins (1997) distinguishes among three types of knowledge maps, namely pointer models (pointing to the correct source, usually a person), linkage models (adding some metainformation on the sources), and solution models (relating knowledge areas to business problems). Pointer models are knowledge source maps that typically map experts. They can be geographic or organized by topic. Linkage models provide more visual context on how the referenced knowledge can be used, for example, by linking knowledge to a visualized business process. Still more metainformation on the referenced knowledge is represented in solution models. In this type of dense and informative map, descriptive and prescriptive elements are mixed. While this is a useful categorization, its groups are not fully mutually exclusive and the classification only focuses on the main functions and content types of knowledge maps and neglects other application parameters such as graphic format, scope, medium, creation mode, or required skill level.

These existing classifications and distinctions are relevant, but they may be limiting the potential of knowledge maps to too few areas. It may be beneficial to explore new, alternative, and concurrent ways of classifying knowledge maps in order to explore and extend their application potential beyond the currently implemented or envisioned solutions. Developing multiple classification schemes may also improve our understanding of the application parameters of different forms of knowledge maps. Such new classifications—that strive to meet the ten categorization criteria listed previously—are explored in the next section.

Classification Principles and Typologies for Knowledge Maps

You do not understand anything, until you understand it in more than one way.

Marvin Minsky

In the study of taxonomies, there is a general rule that a classification should always be based on key characteristics of its items, but—according to Bailey (1994)—there is no proven rule to find these attributes (p. 2). Nevertheless, cognitive linguist George Lakoff provides insightful directions in his theory of categorization. A classification according to Lakoff (1998) can be one of four types. These types are:

1.   **Purposive:** Categorizing by intended use; in our context, classifying maps by the knowledge management purpose they serve.

2.   **Perceptual:** Categorizing by common format/look; in our case, by the graphic format of a knowledge map.

3.   **Functional:** Categorizing by personal use or type of the content of the knowledge map.

4.   **Motor-activity:** Based on physical interaction with the content; in our case, the medium or application context of a knowledge map.

These classification principles can also be found in seminal taxonomies of visual representations. Shneiderman's (1996) task by type taxonomy of visual representation formats suggests both application purpose or *functionality* (task) and *content* (type) as classification principles. Lohse, Biolsi, Walker, and Rueter (1994) conclude that extant taxonomies of graphs and images in general are either functional, that is, by purpose, or structural, that is, by *graphic form*, although there are also model-based taxonomies (Chi, 2000; Tory & Möller, 2002), as well as other possible classification criteria, such as social *context*, or cognitive process (Blackwell & Engelhardt, 2002). An example of a functional taxonomy has been developed by Tufte (1990) and structural classifications have been developed by Bertin (1994), Horn (1999), and Rankin (1990). From these prior approaches we derive our primary knowledge map classification principles, which are by *purpose*, by *graphic form*, by *content*, by application *level*, and by *creation* mode. We believe that these classification principles are relevant for a pragmatic taxonomy of knowledge maps as they all relate to the actual application of knowledge maps. The pragmatic logic of these classification principles can be illustrated (Wexler, 2001) by converting them into questions or interrogatives. Choosing a particular type of knowledge map necessitates answering a number of key questions, namely:

1.   Which knowledge management **purpose** do I want to achieve with the map? (the "why?" of the map)

2.   Which kind of **content** about knowledge do I want to represent in the map? (the "what?" of the map)

3.   Who should **use** the map in which **context** or situation and at what **level** (the "for whom?" and "when?" of the map)

4.   Which graphic **form** should be used and who can **create** the map in what way? (the "how?" and "who?" of the map)

While the purpose describes the knowledge management task supported by the map (frequently tied to an application context), the content dimension describes the elements that are contained and referenced in a knowledge map. Usually, a knowledge map contains only one kind of content, although there are maps that contain information on experts, documents, communities, and databases in parallel. Table 1 shows sample knowledge map types based on these primary classification principles. The items in the open lists are intended to serve as illustrative examples and not as exhaustive options.

Table 2. Knowledge map classifications

A. Classifying knowledge maps by intended **purpose or KM process (why?)**:

1. Knowledge creation maps: Illustrate the planned steps to develop a certain (organizational) competence or create new knowledge (i.e., a technology road map).

2. Knowledge assessment or audit maps: Illustrate the evaluation of certain knowledge assets graphically for example by a 2x2 matrix (axes: current ability and future importance).

3. Knowledge identification maps: Provide a graphic overview on knowledge assets (experts, patents, practices) and points to their locations/coordinates.

4. Knowledge development or acquisition maps/learning maps:

    a) Learning overview and learning path maps

    b) Learning content structure maps

    c) Learning reviewing/repetition maps

5. Knowledge transfer, sharing, or communication maps: Show who transfers knowledge to whom.

6. Knowledge application maps: Show which knowledge is necessary for carrying out certain processes or steps in a single process.

7. Knowledge marketing maps: Can be used to signal competence to the public in a certain domain.

B. Classifying maps by their **content (what?)**:

I. By (digital and analogue) content formats:

1. Web sites (including blogs, portals, homepages)

2. Documents (including books)

3. Databases or repositories

4. Learning objects or online courses (or modules)

5. Other file formats (e.g., sketches, drawings)

II. By content types:

1. Methods

2. Processes

continued on following page

Table 2. continued

3. Experts (including groups)

4. Organizations/departments/institutions

5. Lessons learned/experiences

6. Skills and competencies

7. Concepts

8. Events

9. Patents

10. Knowledge or communication flows or relationships

11. Interests or knowledge needs

C. Classifying maps by the application **level (who?)**:

1. Personal knowledge maps (visualizing one's own skills or expert contacts [Burnett et al., 2004; Eppler & Sukowski, 2000])

2. Dyadic knowledge map (to support knowledge creation, transfer, or assessment between two people)

3. Team knowledge maps (visualize the skills present or needed in a project team, like the T-matrix [Eppler and Sukowski, 2000])

4. Departmental knowledge maps

5. Community knowledge maps

6. Organizational knowledge maps

7. Interorganizational/network knowledge maps

D. Classifying knowledge maps by graphic **form (how?)**:

I. Table-based format (e.g., Heng, 2001):

1. Person by skills table

2. Skill area by people table

3. People by documents

4. Team by project experience table

II. Diagrammatic format:

1. *Structure diagrams*

   a) Venn diagram

   b) Concentric circles (with or without segments)

   c) Matrix (i.e., 2 by 2)

   d) Network diagram

   e) Mind map

   f) Concept map (Tergan & Keller, 2005)

continued on following page

Table 2. continued

g) Cognitive map (Huff & Jenkins, 2002)

h) Strategy map

i) Fishbone

2.   *Process diagrams* (Galloway, 1994)

a) Timeline

b) Swim lane chart

c) Flow chart

d) Event chain

e) Critical path method

f) Gantt chart

g) Cycle chart

h) Decision Tree

i) Value chain

j) Flight plan (Eppler & Sukowski, 2000)

III Cartographic format:

1.   Geographic map: globe/continent/land/island/region

2.   Informational map: park

3.   Tube/metro (Burkhard & Meier, 2005) map

4.   Galaxy/stars

5.   Sea/ocean

6.   Building/architectural map

IV. Metaphoric format:

a)   From the natural realm:

1. tree

2. iceberg

3. canyon

4. mountain

5. river

b)   Man-made artefacts:

1. house

2. temple structure

3. radar screen

4. bridge

5. race track

continued on following page

Table 2. continued

E. Classifying maps by their **creation method (how? and who?)**

1.   Maps that are automatically and dynamically generated by the computer (such as self-organizing maps [Kohonen, 2001]).

2.   Maps that are semiautomatically generated (automatically assembled and then optimized by analysts).

3.   Maps that are designed once by domain and mapping experts and then used in the same way by all users.

4.   Maps that are iteratively created, modified, or extended by the map user(s) themselves (community generated maps).

Other possible, but potentially less useful, stable, or objective classification principles include the managerial *application domain* or functional area (e.g., maps for project management, strategy, quality management, procurement, risk management, finance, production, etc.), the *amount of resources (time, money)* associated with generating, updating, or using a map, the required *skill level* of map users (from novice maps to expert maps), the *size of the map* (10 entries vs. 10,000 entries), and the *medium* of the map (i.e., paper, poster, or digital).

Having presented different possible classification principles and resulting typologies, we can now combine the most relevant ones into a *matching matrix* that can serve as a first, generic selection guide for knowledge maps (that evidently requires adaptation for specific application contexts). For this matrix, we chose the *use* of the knowledge map in knowledge management (the knowledge management process) as the dominant feature, as well as the *format* of the map and the *level* and *content type* of the map (the former two as table axes, the later two as table entries). These are considered to be the most relevant dimensions as they guide the actual implementation process; knowledge content needs to be adequately represented in a graphic format for a particular knowledge management process at a certain level. In this sense, the following matrix can serve as a starting point and *discussion template* for a deliberation on which kind of knowledge map may be useful for a given knowledge management process or challenge.

The table represents the following reasoning (along seven KM processes). For the *creation* of new knowledge, knowledge maps can help in the generation of new concepts by representing emerging topics in cartographic maps, in diagrams, or through visual metaphors (as well as through sketching not included in this classification). While tables could be used in this phase, they might not represent a rich enough structure to uncover new insights or elaborate concepts; they could, however, be used to highlight the possible combination of skills or concepts. To *assess* the knowledge of experts, groups, or departments, one can employ (as in one example listed in this article) simple tables. Cartographic maps cannot (because of their loose structure) be easily used for ratings. Diagrams, such as matrices, however, can provide visual ratings easily. Visual metaphors, finally, may be too playful and open for the task of rating knowledge assets. To easily *identify* knowledge, tables usually do not provide a concise overview. Cartographic, diagrammatic, or metaphoric maps can provide richer means of overview in this case. In order to *develop* new knowledge or acquire new knowledge through learning, one can rely on the didactic power of cartographic learning maps (such as trail maps outlining learning steps), diagrams (such as concept

Table 3. A possible matching matrix for knowledge map parameters

K Map Format Knowledge Management Process/Purpose:	I Table Format	II Diagrammatic Format	III Cartographic Format	IV Metaphoric Format
1. Creation of Knowledge		m,l,c 1-3	m,l,c 1-3	m,l,c 1-3
2. Assessment or Audit of Knowledge	e, f, s 1-5	e, f, s 1-5		
3. Identification of Knowledge	m, e 1-4	m, e, f 1-7	f, e, f 1-7	m, e, f 1-7
4. Development of Knowledge		M,S, C 1-7	m, s, c 1-7	m, s, c 1-7
5. Sharing, Transferring, Communication of Knowledge	m 2-7	m, l, c, s, f 2-7	m, l, c, s 2-7	m, l, c, s 2-7
6. Application of Knowledge	m, l, s 1-7	m, l, s 1-7	m, l, s 1-7	m, l, s 1-7
7. Marketing of Knowledge		m, e, c, s 4-7	m, e, c, s 4-7	m, e, c, s 4-7

Note. Knowledge Map Content Types:

m = methods (procedural knowledge, know-how)

e = experts, organizations, groups, institutions and so forth. (know-who, knowledge carriers or sources)

l = lessons learned, and experiences (know-why)

c = concepts (declarative knowledge, know-what)

f = flows or relationships (i.e., communication flows, collaboration relations)

s = skills and competencies (i.e., capability maturity levels, expertise levels, core competencies, etc.)

Application Levels: 1= personal = dyadic, 3= team, 4= dept., 5. = community, 6 = org., 7. network maps or mind maps), or metaphoric maps that convey additional insights about the content, or relate what is new to what is already known. This reasoning is equally applicable to knowledge sharing maps, although in this case, tables may provide a simple format to *share* or communicate the main steps of a method. The *use* or *application* of knowledge can be supported by any of the above means: through tables outlining sequential action steps and corresponding documents, concepts or experts, as well as through cartographic trail maps, diagrammatic process maps, or metaphoric depictions (i.e., a ladder or a road) that show how to accomplish a goal by referencing concepts, documents, or experts. For the final knowledge management task examined in this chapter, namely knowledge *marketing*, the attention of the target group is a crucial element. In order to draw the attention of potential clients to an organization's methods, experts, concepts, or skills, novel, original, and even surprising ways of representing the offered knowledge need to be employed. Hence the table format may prove not to be attractive enough. There is, however, a trade-off between map novelty and clarity that has to be managed.[1]

In this way the application parameters for a specific knowledge map can be systematically gathered for a specific application context. The reasoning outlined above may, however, have to be adapted for specific application contexts. Depending on the parameters defined in a knowledge strategy (such as knowledge management processes, levels, or types of knowledge), the classification attributes may be adapted accordingly.

Application Examples

To illustrate key types from these classifications, we provide real-life, interactive online knowledge map examples in this section. In terms of purposes, the examples include knowledge assessment, application, identification, marketing, and acquisition maps. In terms of *content*, they refer to experts, tools and methods, documents, institutions, concepts, applications, and Web sites.

The maps range from the departmental to the interorganizational *level*. None of the examples are *automatically generated* maps. As mentioned by Vail (1999), employing automatic mapping techniques (such as e-mail traffic or questionnaire-based social network analysis software) foregoes the chance of using the *collaborative mapping process itself* as a communicative sense-making and identity- or consensus-building process for the involved communities of practice. The knowledge maps that are depicted in Figures 3, 4, and 7 can be viewed and explored interactively at http://www.unisi.ch/knowledgedomainmap.htm.

Table 4 compares these seven examples in terms of their main parameters in order to illustrate the represented spectrum of knowledge maps applied in our projects.

The table reveals that several of the combinations from the matching table have been implemented, but that there may be many other feasible combinations that are still left to explore and that may provide tangible benefits for current and future knowledge management challenges. Some of these challenges are discussed in the following conclusion.

Figure 2. A table-based departmental knowledge assessment map of an IT consultancy

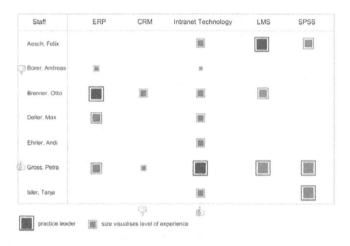

Figure 3. A diagrammatic, knowledge application map of medium-sized market research firm (Eppler, 2003)

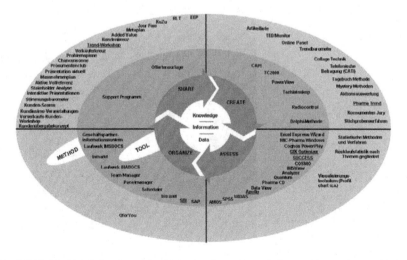

Figure 4. An institution-centred diagrammatic knowledge identification map visualizing researchers in the area of e-learning

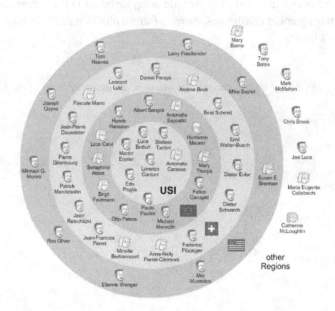

Figure 5. A Venn diagram-based knowledge identification map listing and structuring institutions that have expertise in the area of health communication

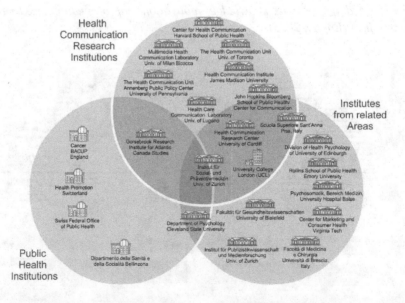

Figure 6. A metro-style knowledge identification map documenting the experiences, experts, and documents of a three year project (Eppler, 2003)

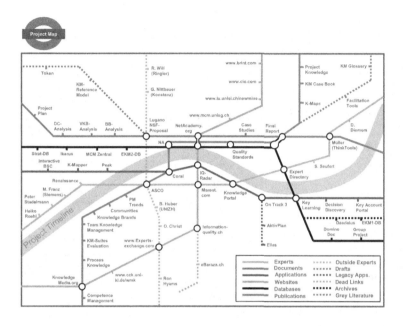

Figure 7. An animated, cartographic knowledge development map (learning path or file rouge map) from the www.swissling.ch project (Armani & Rocci, 2003)

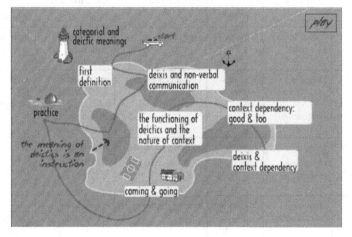

Figure 8. A metaphoric knowledge identification map of a European Research Center (EJO = European Journalism Observatory)

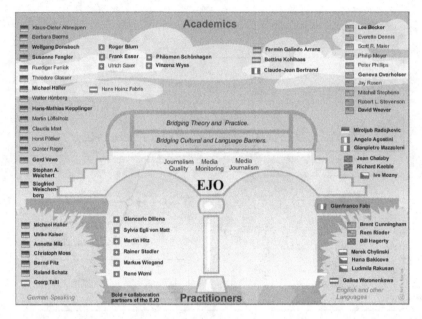

Table 4. A comparison among the seven maps using the parameters of the classification

KM Process	Map Format	Map Content	Mapping Level	Main Benefits	Industry Context
1. Knowledge Assessment	Table: domain by expert	Experts	Department	Training planning, staff allocation	Telecom
2. Knowledge Application and Knowledge Marketing	Diagram: cycle chart	Methods	Organization	Allocation of methods and tools along a business process, documentation	Market Research & Consulting
3. Knowledge Identification	Diagram: concentric circles	Experts	Interorganizational	Highlighting experts and contacts	University/ Research & Development
4. Knowledge Identification	Diagram: Venn diagram	Institutions	Interorganizational	Highlighting experts and contacts, fostering domain understanding	University/ Research & Development

continued on following page

Table 4. continued

KM Process	Map Format	Map Content	Mapping Level	Main Benefits	Industry Context
5.Knowledge Identification	Carto-graphic: under-ground map	Experts, documents, applications, Web sites, databases, publications	Inter-organizational	documentation of knowledge during a project	Corporate-University Collaboration
6. Knowledge Development	Carto-graphic: island map	Concepts, learning content/ modules	Inter-organizational	Building knowledge about linguistic theories through an overview and sequence	University/ e-learning
7. Knowledge Identification	Metaphor: bridge	Experts	Inter-organizational	Identifying experts and contacts in a research domain	University-Practice Collaboration

Conclusion

Sapientis est ordinare. It is the function of the wise man to order.

ARISTOTLE

In this chapter, we have made first steps towards a pragmatic—that is to say consistent and useful—taxonomy of knowledge maps that can be used in devising knowledge management solutions. Our approach has been based on rules and guidelines of high quality classifications. As a main contribution, we have shown various ways in which knowledge maps can be classified. The benefit of such *multiple classification principles* lies in sensitizing managers and researchers for the application parameters and requirements of different knowledge maps formats. We have proposed a tentative *matching table* that suggests how different map formats can be used for different purposes and contents. The lack of empirical validation of this matching is a weakness of this chapter, although the template was presented as a generic starting point for application discussions, rather than a final result. Subsequent research should nevertheless demonstrate through *evaluation studies* whether this matching is indeed correct and under what circumstances.

A further open research question regards the development of *prototypes* for some of the stipulated map types in different industry settings, including follow-up evaluations. Related to this question is another research endeavour, namely to match knowledge map types with adequate information technology applications.[2] A final open research route in this rich domain of inquiry concerns *trade-offs* among map types present in the classification. While some knowledge map formats (such as manually developed metaphoric expert identification maps or diagrammatic knowledge structure maps) may be useful for communication purposes, they may not be highly scaleable or easily maintainable. Identifying and analyzing such application trade-offs in knowledge map types seems like a highly relevant future research area, particularly in order to match generic *knowledge strategies* with fitting knowledge map formats.

In conclusion, it thus seems that we have only begun to chart this intriguing research territory in the knowledge management domain. There are many other feasible visual strategies to improve the creation, transfer, application, or codification of knowledge in organizations that are still to be discovered, developed, tried out, and implemented.

References

Armani, J., & Rocci, A. (2003). Conceptual maps in e-learning. How map based interfaces help the contextualization of information and the structuring of knowledge. *Information Design Journal + Document Design, 11*(2/3), 171-184.

Bailey, K. D. (1994). *Typologies and taxonomies: An introduction to classification techniques.* Thousand Oakes: Sage.

Bertin, J. (1973). *Sémiologie graphique.* Paris: Mouton.

Blackwell, A. F., & Engelhardt, Y. (2002). A meta taxonomy for diagram research. In M. Anderson, B. Meyer, & P. Olivier (Eds.), *Diagrammatic representation and reasoning.* Berlin: Springer.

Bowker, G., & Star, S. L. (1999). *Sorting things out: Classification and its consequences.* Cambridge: MIT Press.

Browne, G. J., Curley, S. P., & Benson, P. G. (1997). Evoking information in probability assessment: Knowledge maps and reasoning-based directed questions. *Management Science, 43*(1), 1-13.

Browne, G. J., & Ramesh, V. (2002). Improving information requirements determination: A cognitive perspective. *Information & Management, 39*, 625-645.

Burkhard, R., & Meier, M. (2005). Tube map visualization: Evaluation of a novel knowledge visualization application for the transfer of knowledge in long-term projects. *Journal of Universal Computer Science, 11*(4), 473-494.

Burnett, S., Illingworth, L., & Webster, L. (2004). Knowledge auditing and mapping: A pragmatic approach. *Knowledge and Process Management, 11*(1), 25-37.

Chi, E. H. (2000). A taxonomy of visualization techniques using the data state reference model. In *Proceedings of the IEEE Symposium on Information Visualization* (pp. 69-75).

Coyne, R. (1995). *Designing information technology in the postmodern age, from method to metaphor*. Cambridge: MIT Press.

Dherbey, G. R. (2005). Connaissance des choses naturelles et des affaires humaines chez Aristotle. In G. Samana (Ed.), *La connaissance des choses* (pp. 55-70). Paris: Ellipses.

Eppler, M. (2002). Making knowledge visible through knowledge maps. In C.W. Holsapple (Ed.), *Handbook on knowledge management* (pp. 189-206). Springer.

Eppler, M. (2003). *Managing information quality: Increasing the value of information in knowledge-intensive products and processes*. Berlin: Springer.

Eppler, M., & Sukowksi, O. (2000, June). Managing team knowledge: Core processes, tools and enabling factors. *European Management Journal*, 334-341.

Galloway, D. (1994). *Mapping work processes*. Milwaukee: ASQC Quality Press.

Gordon, J. L. (2000). Creating knowledge maps by exploiting dependent relationships. *Knowledge-Based Systems, 13*, 71-79.

Hellstrom, T., & Husted, K. (2004). Mapping knowledge and intellectual capital in academic environments: A focus group study. *Journal of Intellectual Capital, 5*(1), 165-180.

Heng, M. S. H. (2001). Mapping intellectual capital in a small manufacturing enterprise. *Journal of Intellectual Capital, 2*(1), 53-60.

Hodgkinson, G. P., Maule, A. J., & Bown, N. J. (2004). Causal cognitive mapping in the organizational strategy field: A comparison of alternative elicitation procedures. *Organizational Research Methods, 7*(1), 3-26.

Horn, R. E. (1999). *Visual language*. Lexington: MacroVue.

Huff, A. (Ed.). (1990). *Mapping strategic thought*. New York: Wiley.

Huff, A., & Jenkins, M. (Eds.). (2002). *Mapping strategic knowledge*. London: Sage Publications.

Kohonen, T. (2001). *Self-organizing maps*. New York: Springer.

Lakoff, G. (1987). *Women, fire, and dangerous things. What categories reveal about the mind*. Chicago: University of Chicago Press.

Lohse, G., Biolsi, K., Walker, N., & Rueter, H. (1994, December). A classification of visual representations. *Communications of the ACM*, 36-49.

Meyer, A. D. (1991). Visual data in organizational research. *Organization Science, 2*(2), 218-236.

Minto, B. (1995). *The pyramid principle, logic in writing and thinking*. London: Pitman Publishing.

Newbern, D., & Dansereau, F. D. (1995). Knowledge maps for knowledge management. In K. Wiig (Ed.), *Knowledge management methods: Practical approaches to managing knowledge*. Arlington: Schema Press.

Novins, P. (1997, September 8). *Knowledge representation*. Paper presented at the MKO Semi-Annual Conference.

Peterson, M. P. (1995). *Interactive and animated cartography*. New Jersey: Prentice Hall.

Rankin, R. A. (1990). A taxonomy of graph types. *Information Design Journal, 6*(2), 147-159.

Renukappa, S. H., & Egbu, C. O. (2004, September 1-3). Knowledge mapping: Concepts and benefits for a sustainable urban environment. In *Proceedings of the 20th Annual Conference Association of Researchers in Construction Management (ARCOM)* (pp. 905-914). Farzad Khosrowshahi, University of Herriot-Watt, Edinburgh, UK.

Shneiderman, B. (1996). The eyes have it: A task by data type taxonomy for information visualizations. In *Proceedings of 1996 IEEE Visual Languages*, Los Alamos, CA, (pp. 336-343). IEEE

Smelcer, J. B., & Carmel, E. (1997). The effectiveness of different representations for managerial problem solving: Comparing tables and maps. *Decision Sciences, 28*(2), 391-420.

Sparrow, J. (1998). The role of physical representations in knowledge elicitation. In J. Sparrow (Ed.), *Knowledge in organizations* (pp. 51-78). Thousand Oaks: Sage.

Tergan, S. O., & Keller, T. (Eds.). (2005). *Knowledge and information visualization*. Berlin: Springer.

Tory, M., & Möller, T. (2002). *A model-based visualization taxonomy* (working paper). Simon Fraser University, School of Computing Science.

Tufte, E. R. (1990). *Envisioning information*. Cheshire: Graphics Press.

Vail, E. F. (1999, May-June). Mapping organizational knowledge. *Knowledge Management Review, 8*, 10-15.

Wexler, M. (2001). The who, what, why of knowledge mapping. *Journal of Knowledge Management, 5*(3), 249-263.

Wurman, R. S. (2001). *Information anxiety 2*. Indiana: Macmillan Publishing.

Internet Session: Visual-literacy.org – An Interactive Course on Knowledge Visualization

http://www.visual-literacy.org

This site offers an interactive overview on more than a hundred visual methods that can be used to represent knowledge graphically. It also hosts two demo tutorials on visualization for knowledge management.

Interaction:

Correctly allocate visual formats to their application context. Rate examples of knowledge maps. Explore a periodic table of visualization methods. Find other real-life examples of the discussed formats online using Google or Alltheweb image search.

Useful URLs

1. Let's Focus: A Tool to Generate Knowledge Maps , http://www.lets-focus.com

2. Inspiration: A Tool to Create Lively Knowledge Maps: http://www.inspiration.com

3. Examples of Academic Knowledge Maps: http://www.unisi.ch/knowledgedomainmap.htm

4. A Large Term-Oriented Knowledge Map Example: http://www.cognitiveoverload.com/kmap.php

Further Readings

Eppler, M. (2006). *Managing information quality* (2nd ed.). Springer.

Sparrow, J. (1998). The role of physical representations in knowledge elicitation. *Knowledge in organizations* (pp. 51-78). Thousand Oaks: Sage.

Wurman, R.S. (1996). *Information architects*. Graphis Press. (includes a great procedural knowledge map from Roche's new product approval process)

Endnotes

[1]   Chillimind (www.chillimind.de), a mobile commerce company, has marketed its skills through an imaginative cartographic map of mobile commerce concepts. Upon first glance, the map seems to depict an island. Only upon close observation can one detect that it is actually a jostle of key technologies, business models, and technical terms from the realm of mobile business. The same holds true for KLM's map for its alliance partners, outlining its partnering strategy.

[2]   So far, we have used the following IT applications to manually create (which implies maintainability issues) online interactive knowledge maps: www.lets-focus.com, www.inspiration.com, www.visio.com, and www.mindmanager.com. There are, however, also tools available that can automatically generate knowledge maps, such as the solutions of Aurigin, Autonomy, or Semio, to name but three suppliers.

Chapter V

Knowledge Engines for Critical Decision Support

Richard M. Adler, DecisionPath, Inc., USA

Abstract

Current knowledge capture and retention techniques tend to codify "what-is" and "who knows" more effectively than "how-to." Unfortunately, "how-to" knowledge is more directly actionable and indispensable for critical organizational activities such as strategic analysis and decision making. Knowledge management (KM) theorists often despair over "how-to" expertise as a form of tacit knowledge that is difficult to articulate, much less transfer. We argue that tacit strategic performance-based knowledge can often be captured and deployed effectively via frameworks that combine scenario planning methods with "what-if" simulation. The key challenges are two-fold: (1) modeling complex situational contexts, including known behavioral dynamics; and (2) enabling knowledge workers to manipulate such models interactively, to safely practice situational analysis and decision making, and learn from virtual rather real mistakes. We illustrate our approach with example knowledge-based decision support solutions and provide pointers to related literature.

Introduction

Knowledge management (KM) targets the capture, codification, and dissemination of knowledge across organizations to enhance value. In effect, KM aims to productize and distribute knowledge as an explicit asset.

Knowledge capture and transfer across organizations can be accomplished by direct person-to-person interactions. Examples include training, mentoring, discussions, and other meetings. Knowledge can also be transferred indirectly, mediated by software applications and communication technologies. Examples include passive systems such as knowledge repositories, interactive applications such as expert systems and intelligent search engines, and systems that coordinate collective interaction such as collaborative workgroup spaces.

Within the framework of this book, these two approaches— call them *personaliza-tion* and *codification*—delineate a spectrum of strategies for managing knowledge. Organizations generally favor one strategy or the other to manage knowledge, driven by affinities with their overall business model and competitive strategy, although they often use the other in supporting roles (Hansen, Nohria, & Tierney, 1999).

This chapter introduces a methodology and supporting knowledge "engine" for productizing and distributing *performance-based knowledge*. We specifically target bodies of expertise required to perform strategic analysis and decision making as exemplified by the following kinds of critical questions: What products and services should we offer? With whom should we partner and how? How can we best defend against adversaries and prepare for disasters? Where should we invest to improve our strategic positioning for the future?

The knowledge that enables strategic reasoning is widely viewed, correctly, as tacit content that is difficult to articulate, codify, and transfer. KM literature pays relatively little attention to this kind of high-level, open-ended knowledge, despite its obvious importance to organizational performance, growth, and security over the long term. Consequently, strategic performance knowledge is often omitted from formal knowledge strategies, or "managed," at best, by defaulting to ad hoc personalization transfer methods, since its capture in documents or less inert digital forms seems problematic.

Contrary to this conventional wisdom, this chapter argues for a codification strat-egy for explicitly managing organizational knowledge about strategic analysis and decision making. We describe a generalized methodology and architecture for capturing and packaging knowledge about strategic reasoning in rich interactive software engines. These engines enable retention *and* sharing/dissemination of critical strategic performance knowledge at levels that are not possible from direct person-to-person transfer strategies.

Our knowledge engine architecture consists of a software platform that supports interactive modeling, "what-if" simulation, and analysis of complex situations and decisions. This platform provides tools for capturing and deploying strategic knowledge tailored to specific domains (e.g., the pharmaceutical industry, homeland security) and types of critical problems (e.g., competitive marketing strategy, change management, critical infrastructure preparedness). We describe a supporting modeling and decision-making methodology derived from scenario planning to help users apply the codified domain knowledge to solve their strategic problems.

We call the resulting knowledge-based solutions virtual decision environments (VDEs). VDE essentially provide low risk virtual "test drives," helping knowledge workers frame, explore, and compare alternate analyses, policies, strategies, or plans involving complex environments and extended time frames. The benefits of performance-based knowledge systems for strategic decision support include:

- Codifying, retaining, and maintaining best practices decision-making expertise
- Providing organization-wide availability to this expertise in actionable form
- Reducing exposure to risk (from unintended consequences)
- Improving uniformity, confidence, and consistency in critical decisions
- Establishing baselines to drive continuous improvement in decision processes

This chapter addresses the following objectives:

1. Define performance-based knowledge systems for critical decision support (VDEs)
2. Illustrate VDE concepts via example decision support solutions in the disparate domains of competitive marketing strategy and change management
3. Compare and contrast VDEs with other types of knowledge products, such as knowledge repositories, expert, and case-based reasoning systems
4. Describe the methodology and architecture of a generalized software platform for domain-specific VDEs

Figure 1 depicts a summary topical framework for understanding this chapter.

Figure 1. Summary framework for chapter

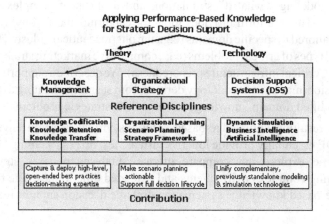

Background

The KM literature has long distinguished between explicit and tacit knowledge (Davenport & Prusak, 1998, Gherardi, 2006; HBR, 1998, Sackman, 1992; Zack, 1999). Broadly speaking, tacit knowledge encompasses open-ended "how-to" skills that workers learn over extended periods of time though experience and practice. Tacit knowledge tends to be complex and difficult to articulate, document, and teach. In contrast, explicit knowledge, which broadly encompasses "what-is" and "who knows," tends to be simpler and easier to capture and transfer.

Moving beyond definitions, consensus breaks down on what can and should be done to manage tacit knowledge. Some authors (e.g., Polyani, 1962; Tsoukas, 2005) take the pessimistic stance that tacit knowledge is inherently "situated" and "ineffable" and hence, not overtly manageable; at best, it can be observed in the process of being applied to specific work tasks. More optimistic KM writers suggest various ways that tacit knowledge can be converted to explicit knowledge (Nonaka, 1991; Nonaka & Takeuchi, 1995) or otherwise transferred across individuals within an organization (Ambrosini, 2003; Brown & Duguid, 1998; Bukowitz & Williams, 1999; Choo, 2006; Dixon, 2000; Roth & Kleiner, 1998; Wieck, 1995). The most plausible transfer models include variations on narrative storytelling and immersion (i.e., extended contact with experts).

One must look to the field of artificial intelligence (AI) for concerted development of generalized methodologies and software frameworks for capturing and packaging tacit knowledge. The most relevant approaches here include expert systems (Baets, 1998; Gupta, Forgionne, & Mora 2006; Hayes-Roth, Waterman, & Lenat, 1983; Turban, 1988) and case-based reasoning (CBR) systems (Kolodner, 1993), which will be discussed later.

Equally important, AI researchers developed a rich set of techniques, tools, and representation scheme for extracting and codifying tacit knowledge and tools (Brachman & Levesque, 1985; Ford & Bradshaw, 1993; Shapiro, 1992). Most notably, protocol analysis employs structured interviews to elicit "compiled" knowledge from experts as they work through specific problems (Ericsson & Simon, 1984). AI knowledge acquisition techniques were adapted, in turn, from methods developed for field sociology and linguistics (Egan, 1983; Samarin, 1967).

The literature on strategic decision making is voluminous. We restrict mention here to several representative frameworks for managing long-term uncertainty across business and military domains (Courtenay, Kirkland, & Viguerie, 1997; Davis, 2001; Day & Reibstein, 1997; De Geus, 1988; Gilad, 2006; Porter, 1980; Russo & Schoemaker, 2001; Schoemaker, 2002).

Our VDE platform synthesizes work from three research areas. Our primary inspiration derives from organic, experience-based theories of organizational learning (De Geus, 1997; Senge, 1990). Second, we adopted—and extended—scenario planning as a disciplined methodology for characterizing complex situations over strategic time frames (Schwartz, 1991; Schoemaker, 2002; van der Heiden, 1996). Third, we heavily exploited established modeling and simulation techniques for decision support (Schoemaker, 2002; Legna et al., 2006, Wagner, 2006). Specific sources here include rule- and case-based reasoning systems (Hayes-Roth et al., 1983), system dynamics (Senge, 1990; Sterman, 2000), stochastic (Monte Carlo) methods (Fishman, 1996); game theory (Axelrod, 1997), and agent-based and complex adaptive systems (Auyang, 1998; Epstein & Axtell, 1996; Holland, 1995; Langton, 1995; Waldrop, 1992).

Finally, we distinguish VDEs from so-called electronic performance support systems (Brown, 1996; Gery, 1991). These systems focus largely on workflow automation and enabling work that is much less knowledge and skill intensive than strategic problem solving. An advanced variant, just-in-time knowledge delivery (Davenport & Glaser, 2002) proposes a more intelligent infrastructure, but a much less interactive application of knowledge to perform work than VDEs.

Virtual Decision Environments (VDEs)

A test drive offers consumers a simple and effective means of experiencing what it is like to own and operate vehicles prior to purchasing them. As such, a test drive reduces risks (of errors and unhappiness), thereby facilitating considered purchase decisions. Analogously, a VDE helps organizations experience the consequences of prospective critical decisions before executing them. In essence, a VDE helps organizations *practice* making decisions safely and learn from inevitable mistakes such as unintended consequences. VDEs reduce exposure to risk through more thoroughly considered decisions and smoother execution.

Specifically, a VDE provides a framework for characterizing complex strategic situations, framing prospective interventions, and evaluating the relative strengths and weaknesses of those candidate strategies. Evaluations are driven by "what-if" simulations: given an assumed plausible future in which the world evolves along path X, VDEs project the likely outcome for an organization (and other relevant parties) of executing candidate strategy Y. VDEs also incorporate analytic tools for exploring projected outcomes: users compare projected values of domain-specific performance metrics to assess the relative strengths and weaknesses of alternate strategies.

VDEs are quintessential knowledge-based products. They provide users with actionable frameworks for modeling and analyzing complex situations and decisions. Such frameworks embody previously tacit knowledge of expert strategists in specific domains, such as the pharmaceutical industry, or cross-domain types of decisions, such as managing organizational change or portfolios (e.g., of information technology or security assets and investments).

The domain metamodel grounding a VDE embodies prescriptive knowledge; it identifies what kinds of information must be collected in order to characterize complex situations and decisions effectively, and how best to represent those data. VDE metamodels also dictate (implicitly, by omission), what information is *not* necessary. In today's data saturated world of vast repositories and the World Wide Web, such exclusions are highly valuable; they save substantial time, cost, and effort to identify, gather, validate, maintain, and apply information that is not germane or critical to a decision outcome (as per expert opinion).

Building upon situational models, VDE simulation frameworks provide an explicit actionable methodology for decision support. Once users characterize their situational context for a pending decision, the VDE supports the following sequences of tasks:

- Framing a set of plausible futures (i.e., assumptions that define alternate paths along which current situations are expected to evolve).

- Formulating candidate strategies for intervening to shape those futures to better align with organizational goals and objectives.

- Projecting the likely outcomes of alternate strategies across the possible futures.

- Analyzing and comparing projected outcomes to identify the candidate strategy that produces the best outcomes across target scenarios.

This heuristic methodology leads to robust decisions in real world strategic situations where exact knowledge, closed-form analytic methods and "optimal" solutions are seldom available. Robustness in this context means that a strategy leaves the organization well-situated despite imperfect knowledge of, and control over, both the present and future.

In short, VDEs provide *true* knowledge-based decision support, which we define as methods that actively enable and enhance decision-making processes. In this respect, VDEs stand in clear contrast with business intelligence (BI) tools such as data warehouses and executive dashboards. BI systems deliver, at best, timely access to current status, historical performance, and possibly limited trending (assuming limited kinds of change). That is, BI drives *situational awareness*. While situational awareness is clearly a critical prerequisite, it constitutes a passive input rather than an active enabler to sound decision-making processes.

Finally, the world is rarely static after strategic decisions have been made. Environments continue their inexorable change, while interested parties, both internal and external, react to those changes and to the results of one's strategy as it is executed. VDEs support active monitoring and management of these latter phases of strategic decision "lifecycles;" organizations can periodically update initial scenarios to reflect currently available knowledge, and apply VDEs to reproject and reassess the chosen decision. In this sense-and-response mode, a VDE revalidates the chosen decision if it continues to produce attractive outcomes across updated scenarios. If outcomes are not favorable, the VDE serves as an early warning system, helping users to isolate divergences from earlier assumptions and to adapt (or replace) strategies to address emerging problems.

Example VDE Solutions

To illustrate the concept of a VDE, we describe two representative decision support systems (DSS). Each description highlights four features of a VDE:

1. The strategic problem of interest and deficiencies of existing approaches
2. The ontology of the domain decision model
3. The dominant situational dynamics
4. Analytic outputs-key performance metrics

Both systems were implemented using our VDE platform, using knowledge acquisition techniques noted in the second section, along with design methods specific to our platform. Principals from two management consulting firms, Strategic Decisions Group and D.J. Koehn Consulting, supplied relevant domain expertise for competitive drug marketing strategy (CDMS) and change, adaptation, and learning model (CALM) VDEs, respectively.

Competitive Drug Marketing Strategy (CDMS)

After development costs, the second largest expense for pharmaceutical companies is marketing and selling new drugs. Challenges include competition, declining returns on marketing to doctors, uncertain returns from consumer advertising, price resistance, and the shifting roles of consumers and physicians in buying decisions.

Many mathematical techniques exist for "optimizing" the mix of investments across marketing channels to grow market share. Unfortunately, these methods generally assume that strategies are executed in a world that is either static or dynamic, but not adaptive. In reality, competitors quickly detect your strategy's success and modify their spending to counter your initiatives. Failing to anticipate the realities of dynamic competition and adaptive counter-moves exposes organizations to serious risks such as wasted spending or destructive price wars.

Figure 2. CDMS VDE ontology

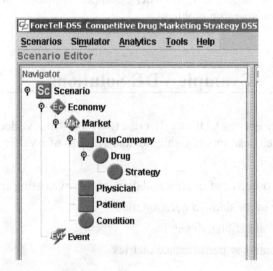

Our CDMS VDE allows companies to model their drug (or drugs), the market in which it competes, and prospective marketing mixes. It also exploits a drug company's available business intelligence about how competitors respond to perceived market changes.

The domain model for the CDMS VDE includes the following entity types: scenario, economy, market, drug company, drug, strategy, and event. Markets depict the current and potential target population for a class of drugs used to treat one or more medical conditions. An example would be the U.S. market for proton pump inhibitor drugs (e.g., Prevacid and Nexium), which are used to treat gastrointestinal disorders such as acid reflux disease. Key attributes for drugs include order of market entry, time on the market, price per prescription, branded vs. generic, number of adverse side effects, and costs to produce. This ontology is depicted in Figure 2. Indents can be interpreted as "contains" or "owns."

Users specify candidate drug marketing strategies by specifying current drug prices and spend rates in marketing channels (in $MM/month), and planned schedules for changing prices and spend rates. Channels include direct to consumer (DTC) ads, detailing and sampling to physicians, and payer rebates. Next, adaptive behaviors of competitors are captured via declarative stimulus response rules. A simple example follows: If Company-X's market-share declines by Y% over N months, THEN (expect them) to increase DTC spending by Z% over 3 months. Users can also inject potential disruptive events into scenarios, such as mergers of competitors or changes in government drug payment policies 6 months hence.

The CDMS VDE simulates the likely outcomes of prospective marketing strategies under different scenarios of market growth and competitor responses in two phases. First, it projects market growth and changes in market share from market, drug, and drug strategy inputs using a predictive model derived from historical market data (Berndt, Bui, Reiley, & Urban, 1994). Next it applies the drug strategy decision rules to model anticipated responses from competitors, the company of interest's counter-responses, and so on. These (meta)rules modify drug strategies for future cycles and so on in a nondeterministic game theoretic simulation. Key performance metrics include market share and complete drug financial projections, including total revenue, net income before taxes, and net present value.

The CDMS VDE helps brand managers plan responses to market shifts expected from drugs going off patent and the introduction of new branded or generic drugs or events such as changes in regulation or government reimbursements. It can be also be used to monitor and tune strategies on an ongoing basis as market conditions change. Its unique contribution is to incorporate adaptive competitive behaviors routinely observed in real world markets into strategic spend planning.

Change, Adaptation, and Learning Model (CALM) VDE

Organizations often face transformational changes due to mergers, redesigned business processes, or new enterprise software systems (Kotter, 1995). Such transformations upset the status quo, causing employee uncertainty, fear, resistance, and reduced focus and performance. Change management (CM) attempts to forestall such disruptions through initiatives such as improving communications, modifying workforce structures, and changing compensation schemes. Businesses spend $50B on CM consulting annually, but report failure rates of over 70% (Pascale, Millemann, & Gioja, 2000)!

Conventional CM methods focus tactically on specific impending changes, rather than preparing strategically to face change on a continual basis. Standard CM practices also prescribe the kinds of mechanistic techniques used to manage projects such as product development or systems integration. However, helping employees cope with major work changes involves more than simply allocating resources and careful scheduling; qualitative factors such as psychological, social, and cultural dynamics must be addressed explicitly to ensure success.

Our CALM VDE for CM treats readiness to change as a persistent strategic issue that requires an organic understanding of organizational dynamics and cognitive

Figure 3. CALM VDE ontology

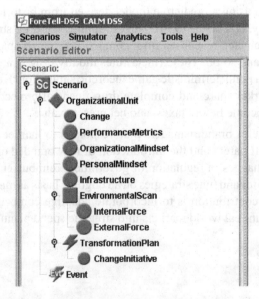

psychology to address effectively (Koehn & Adler, 2006). CALM allows users to develop and test drive CM strategies. It does this by helping users to assess an organization's readiness to respond to change, identify a target readiness state likely to ensure a successful transformation, define prospective transformation plans, and project progress from the initial state towards that goal state under different scenarios about future conditions and alternate change enablement plans.

The CALM VDE's ontology includes scenarios, organizational units, changes, internal and external forces, transformation plans, change initiatives, and events (cf. Figure 3). Change Initiatives depict the individual activities making up an organizational strategy, such as targeted communication or training programs. Readiness to change is assessed via a three-dimensional state space, whose axes measure infrastructure capability, organizational and personal mindsets. Each dimension decomposes into four to six metrics drawn from management theory, organizational, and cognitive psychology. Example metrics include business process re-engineering capability, infrastructure flexibility, leadership capacity to change, cultural alignment and teaming, employee self-confidence, and emotional intelligence. These baselines were selected for their coverage of change risk factors. Estimated values range from 1 to 100.

CALM's situational dynamics project the evolution of organizational readiness over time under the influence of internal forces such as leadership and resources, external forces such as economic conditions and competition, and a set of proposed change initiatives making up a transformation plan. CALM's goal is to help users systematically devise and validate cost effective transformation plans that address all of the metrics comprising the dimensions of change. Competing CM theories have focused (until very recently) predominantly on metrics relating to infrastructure, which we believe accounts for the high failure rates for CM efforts. Key performance metrics in CALM include the measures comprising the three change dimensions plus standard business metrics such as profitability and competitiveness.

CALM dynamics are based predominantly on system dynamics principles, which are implemented using declarative causal "rules." Environmental forces have a magnitude. Rules trigger on magnitude changes, inducing induce proportional changes to readiness components on a scale of -5 to +5. For example, improved leadership causes incremental improvements to organizational mindset factors (e.g., +1 to + 3). Change initiatives within a proposed transformation plan have projected schedules, costs, and similar causal effects on readiness metrics. The scale allows users to explore not only the impacts of carrying out initiatives successfully (i.e., positive effect values), but also the consequences of failures. CALM's causal rules incorporate latencies and durations of effects, and feedback effects typical of system dynamics, along with relative weights for tuning purposes.

CALM provides a library of predefined forces and change initiatives to expedite scenario and transformation plan construction. CM practitioners using CALM can alter library entities' predefined assignments of causal influences by experts to fit their particular organization, industry, and transformation. In addition, users can add custom metrics to the dimensions of change and assign them causal effects. Finally, as with the CMDS VDE, CALM can be used not simply to define and validate change strategies in advance, but also through the execution lifecycle of that plan, to monitor results and adapt chosen strategies as necessary. This is obviously important given that organizational environments inevitably evolve and stakeholders change their behaviors after the point of decision.

To the best of our knowledge, CALM is the first VDE/DSS to explicitly explore the dynamics of organizations using organic "new science" paradigms.

VDEs Compared with Other (Intelligent) Decision Support Systems

VDEs package strategic analytic expertise as a shareable best practices knowledge product. How does VDE packaging compare with alternate knowledge products such as repositories, expert, and CBR systems?

Repositories capture knowledge products that can be shared across organizations to improve productivity of knowledge workers and quality and consistency of their outputs. Organizational repositories include, variously: templates, in-progress, and completed work products (e.g., proposals, case studies, reports, designs, and software components); competitive intelligence; work instructions and process recipes; decision or practice guidelines; and lessons learned from after action reviews.

Repository products may be annotated with metadata to facilitate search. They may be coupled with a community of practice (COP) through groupware systems to facilitate discussion and capture dialog of common interest. A repository containing a single knowledge product, such as a documented best practice, can deliver substantial value to users (Wenger, 1998).

Knowledge repositories are largely passive and inert, in that users must take full initiative to search for content, evaluate it for their purposes, and apply it to meet their needs. For example, lessons learned for military decision support report on what did and did not work (and why) in particular situations, recommend courses of action, and perhaps supply context-dependent dos and don'ts. However, user judgment is required to determine which lessons are relevant and how to adapt them to the present situation.

Repositories may be enhanced via workflow engines, which automate standardized processes that facilitate and guide the production, refinement, annotation, and certification of knowledge products. Repository engines primarily perform search as they help locate relevant resources based on keywords specifying needs or interests.

Expert systems, in contrast, are more highly engineered and automated knowledge products. They typically consist of a collection of conditional (if-then) rules that codify specialized bodies of performance expertise such as medical diagnosis or configuration planning for complex systems. Decision making is automated by a rules engine, which prompts users for situational data via a series of questions, which are determined dynamically by data-driven algorithms traversing the rule base. Upon completing its interrogation and reasoning, the expert system produces an answer, such as a diagnosis or recommended plan. Conclusions are typically justified or explained via a trace of the sequence of rules that were fired during the session. Expert systems require a critical mass of rules to deliver value.

Despite their promise and often impressive performance, expert systems never achieved widespread adoption, hampered by the high costs and level of effort required to build, validate, and maintain them. Rule-based systems are used most commonly today in tactical rather than strategic settings to maintain and automatically apply operational business logic such as criteria or constraints. Examples include approving loans or insurance policies, configuring equipment, or avoiding adverse interactions from combining prescription drugs.

CBR systems essentially retrieve solutions from a repository of previously encountered problems and proven strategies for resolving them. CBR knowledge architectures revolve around defining salient sets of attributes for precedent situations and solutions (i.e., past cases or "frames") and populating a knowledge base with a suitably rich set of precedent situations and responses. CBR systems incorporate two kinds of knowledge engines: (a) interactive intelligent search facilities to identify cases and strategies that resemble the user's present problem; and (b) automated logic to adapt selected solutions to reflect material differences between the user's situation and the selected case(s). Common CBE applications include intelligent assistance for call center personnel, design, and planning.

VDEs differ from expert or CBR systems primarily with respect to target problems and how they allocate knowledge and reasoning responsibilities between system and user. Like CBR systems, VDEs capture expert knowledge in the form of predefined frameworks (i.e., domain-specific "metamodels") designed to capture available knowledge about target situational contexts and candidate decisions. Also, much as expert and CBR systems codify and automate tacit reasoning such as diagnosing problems or adapting plans, VDEs codify situational dynamics and apply them to project the evolution of situations given assumptions about the future and prospective intervention strategies.

However, expert and CBR systems generally target problems that are either static or involve time only weakly (e.g., manipulating constraints for sequencing a set of

actions). In contrast, the automated reasoning performed by VDEs focuses predominantly on projecting situational changes over time, driven, variously, by interacting
environmental forces, trends, and events. Most importantly, advanced VDEs explicitly
reason about adaptive (and goal-driven) behaviors of key actors as they sense and
respond to their evolving environment and to each other's actions.

Strategic decision making is, for the most part, sufficiently open-ended and complex
to preclude closed-form analytic solutions or automated intelligent-constructive
problem solving. Accordingly, current VDEs do not aim to devise and validate solutions autonomously as do expert and CBR systems; rather, they enable and enhance
strategic decision-making processes. As such, they offer knowledge-based decision
support rather than decision making.

Thus, VDEs presuppose end-users that are competent but likely nonexpert practitioners in the chosen domain. Users must be able to characterize complex situations
and devise strategies, albeit supported by domain metamodels and libraries of predefined and validated building blocks. They must also possess judgment and analytic
capabilities to interpret and evaluate outcomes by VDE simulation engines (or be
capable of being trained to do so). The potential user bases for VDEs are typically
much smaller than those for expert and CBR systems, but one would anticipate this
on a priori grounds given the innate complexity of strategic thinking.

In short, current VDEs package and deploy best practices strategic expertise in a
highly interactive format; they enhance and standardize performance by qualified
knowledge workers in highly complex tasks, rather than automating less complex
tasks.

Architecture of a VDE (Platform)

ForeTell® is a generalized platform for rapidly developing and deploying domain-
specific VDEs such as the two examples described above. We describe ForeTell's
decision-support methodology and then briefly review the modeling, simulation,
and analysis frameworks and supporting graphical user interfaces (GUIs) it supplies
for domain-specific VDEs. The details of ForeTell's tools for developing new VDEs
lie beyond the scope of this discussion.

ForeTell embodies and extends scenario planning, the leading methodology for
thinking strategically about the future. Scenario planning helps organizations prepare
for critical decisions in highly uncertain and risk-intensive environments, typically
over years or decades. The technique was developed to support U.S. nuclear defense strategists during the Cold War, and later refined for commercial use by oil
industry strategists.

Traditional scenario planning employs facilitated discussions among leaders and experts to identify the major forces driving the evolution of a target market (or society). These forces are divided into relatively predictable trends and more volatile uncertainties. The dominant uncertainties are projected to extremes (e.g., intensive vs. limited regulation) and combined to frame alternate futures. The resulting schematic futures are fleshed out using the remaining trends and uncertainties into vivid scenarios that depict key actors, their strategic positions, and the prevailing situational dynamics. Decision makers can then use these results as baselines or targets for developing strategies to influence or respond to those scenarios for their organizations' advantage.

For example, oil companies use scenario planning to anticipate future energy needs, price structures, and sociopolitical environments. They then plan long-term investments in energy assets, production technologies, and business models in order to increase their likelihood of continued growth. Scenario planners at Royal Dutch Shell actually anticipated the emergence of a Middle-East oil cartel, and positioned their company successfully for the upheavals caused by OPEC. Similarly, military strategists use scenario planning to help envisage future threats and alliances, and then plan force structures and weapons and logistics systems to respond appropriately. Despite its recognized value, scenario planning is not applied very broadly, for two key reasons: difficulty and generality.

First, developing effective scenarios requires considerable knowledge and experience to focus on the issues of direct relevance while maintaining receptivity to the unexpected. Because scenarios are so difficult to craft, organizations typically bring in outside consultants to drive these exercises. Equally important, organizations rarely revisit and update scenarios more frequently than every five years because the process is costly, time consuming, and arduous.

Second scenarios paint possible futures rather broadly; they tend to focus on general populations of market players rather than specific ones, except the most prominent actors (e.g., America, the FDA, industry giants). In addition, the dynamics of scenarios are depicted with coarse granularity for obvious reasons. Imagine playing extended chess games that involve hundreds of distinct pieces, positions, and allowable moves. Human beings are not very adept at thinking about combinations of complex forces and player behaviors over time, a cognitive limitation that contributes strongly to the law of unintended consequences.

Serious drawbacks result from scenario planning's "50,000 foot" perspective. First, scenarios are not "personalized": they generally cannot answer the first obvious question that decision makers ask, which is, "What will WE (and our stakeholders) look like in this possible future?"

Second, scenarios are passive: they do not help assess HOW proposed interventions such as plans, investments, or strategies will perform. (This follows, in part, from the first problem: if actors of interest are not depicted explicitly, their prospective actions cannot be either.) However, anticipating outcomes of prospective strategies is *precisely* what is required to answer decision makers' second key question, namely, "What can we do to position ourselves for success in this future?"

In short, traditional scenario planning focuses on envisaging alternate futures rather than defining and weighing strategic responses to them. While this produces a valuable front-end framework for decision making, it provides little support for the process of formulating actionable strategies and validating them across scenarios.

ForeTell extends scenario planning with modeling, "what-if" simulation, and analysis software tools. In essence, ForeTell's domain modeling framework personalizes traditional scenarios by allowing users to populate them with specific actors of interest, including their own organization and key stakeholders. It makes scenario planning actionable by allowing users to explore and compare detailed projected outcomes of prospective strategies across alternate plausible futures.

ForeTell mitigates the difficulties of developing scenarios in two ways. First, it supports metamodels that codify experts' domain-specific frameworks—static *and* dynamic—for characterizing strategic situations. Second, it supports domain-specific libraries of predefined building blocks which users can select and populate or adapt to rapidly construct desired scenarios. These building blocks consist of templates and specific (reusable) entities of interest. Templates consist of object classes that depict relevant entity types, such as locations or other environmental "containers," goal-driven actors (individual and organizational), forces and events, and prospective strategies or actions. Entity templates define relevant descriptive attributes and relationships, including performance metrics whose values enable users to evaluate projected outcomes with respect to strengths and weaknesses.

For example, consider a manufacturer facing strategic production capacity decisions. Entity types include markets, manufacturers (including competitors), customers, products, and suppliers. Situational forces include: internal and industry-wide capacity, cost structures, and productivity rates; demand; regulatory and trade policies; and general economic conditions. Key metrics might include capital investment, production capacity, turnaround time, cost per unit, operating costs, return on investment, and net present value. Candidate strategies might include expanding (or closing) existing plants, building new plants, acquisitions, outsourcing, or time-phased combinations of these alternatives. Actor behaviors would include possible responses by competitors to expansion (or contraction) strategies.

ForeTell's *Scenario Editor* provides a GUI for creating, editing, browsing, and maintaining scenarios. Users create scenarios by "snapping together" and editing instances of desired entity types. Entities can be created from scratch, copied from libraries, or imported from data files or external databases. Users inspect and edit attribute values via standard GUI controls such as text boxes, sliders, lists, and tables. Users can also annotate individual attribute values with metadata to facilitate scenario maintenance, sharing, and "sense-making." Metadata includes comments, sources, and tags indicating fact vs. assumption and certainty level. To facilitate "what-if" analyses, complete scenarios can be copied in their entirety; copies of a baseline version can then be edited selectively to quickly define variant strategies or alternate assumptions about forces, trends, events, and actor behaviors.

ForeTell's *Simulation Engine* projects the evolution of situations described in scenarios, using domain-specific dynamics. Typically, dynamics are a mixture of "hard-wired" and user-defined behaviors tailored for particular VDEs and decision domains. Users can customize dynamics by adding entities with relevant dynamics into their scenarios, such as forces, events, or strategies, and by editing exposed parameters on such entities (e.g., magnitudes and rates of trends, relative importance of factors to a decision rule). ForeTell supports the following types of situational dynamics:

- **Trends:** Slowly varying, predictable changes in entity attributes such as rates of population or economic growth.

- **Events:** Disruptive changes tied to specific points in (simulated) time. Events can alter one or more attribute values for any entity type, reflecting spontaneous, exogenous changes; for example, Israel launches attacks on Palestinian terrorists in Gaza in Month 7.

- **Causality (hard-coded):** Causal (system dynamic) rules that transparently propagate effects from changes in entity attributes; for example, increases in demand for oil increases its price, which increases income for oil-producing nations.

- **Causality (soft-coded):** Causal rules defined on entity types such as forces. These rules expose causal parameters, which users can tailor to fit their situation (e.g., latency, duration, feedback, and magnitudes of effects); for example, an increase in anti-Western sentiment (force) causes increases in recruitment rates by terrorist group.

- **Actor behaviors:** Process-oriented activities such as terrorist groups planning, funding, and preparing to stage attacks. Activities typically involve schedules, resources, and constraints.

- **Actor decision-rules:** Production rules which, which, when triggered, can modify actor behaviors as well as attributes. Examples of such "metabehaviors" include switching current tactics or targeting priorities in response to changing conditions.

- **Statistical variation:** A Monte Carlo utility allows users to specify value distributions for selected entity attributes (inputs) and then run a specified number of scenario "trials" in a batch simulation mode. Users can also generate populations of entities within scenarios and assign them attributes based on statistical distributions of values.

The ForeTell VDE platform employs a novel hybrid discrete event simulator to exercise these situational dynamics. The core engine uses a complex adaptive system (or agent-based) simulation paradigm, which is extended with event, system dynamics, and Monte Carlo overlays. At each simulated interval, the engine invokes the model's entities in a uniform order. Each such entity runs its type-specific behaviors, which include updating trends, carrying out processes, and executing decision rules. These actions potentially involve sensing internal and external state and responding according to their (intentional) patterns. The engine then propagates causal influences from productions triggered in the current cycle.

VDE users monitor and control executing scenarios through ForeTell's "dashboard" style GUI, made up of controls, gauges, and time series graphs. Users can suspend simulations to monitor situational metrics (e.g., cumulative sales and profits) and to inspect specific entities.

As the VDE simulator runs, it logs all changes in scenario entity state to the database. ForeTell's *analytics engine* helps users access and reduce this mass of data to explore projected outcomes of individual scenarios. More importantly, users can compare outcomes across scenarios involving competing strategies and/or alternate assumptions. Such differential analyses are vital for isolating relative strengths and weaknesses, uncovering unintended consequences, refining analyses or strategies, and identifying resilient strategies. Users can quickly generate summary analytics via a menu-driven, including tabular reports, time series and radar plots, and frequency histograms. ForeTell's analytics engine embeds open source math, graphics, and statistics libraries, allowing rapid extension to satisfy new analytic requirements.

The ForeTell platform integrates diverse support tools. An online help facility presents documentation on VDE entity types and attributes. Scenarios and simulation logs can be imported and exported via open systems data exchange formats such as XML, CSV, and SQL. Curve fitting and liner interpolation utilities convert observational data into executable specifications for entity behaviors. Finally, ForeTell exposes descriptions of VDE dynamics to users on demand via behavior viewers and influence diagrams; given the number of "moving parts" such "transparency" of behavioral logic is critical for user acceptance.

Future Trends

We anticipate growing attention to performance-based knowledge and VDEs in the near future, driven by several converging trends: demographic, management, and technological. Collectively, these trends will elevate the priority for managing tacit (strategic) knowledge on organizations' knowledge-strategy agendas.

First, government agencies and businesses are starting to recognize the urgency for retaining critical knowledge that will otherwise be lost as workers from the baby-boom generation retire in increasing numbers (De Long, 2004). Current strategies and techniques are clearly inadequate for retaining the complex "how-to" strategic–level knowledge and skills discussed in this chapter.

Second, organizational needs for systematic support for critical decision making grow as the world becomes more complex and unforgiving. Pervasive forces such as globalization, hyper-competition, regulation, terrorism, and technology advances drive change across diverse markets and entire societies. Stakeholder tolerance for errors declines in both financial markets and political arenas. Failure to correctly anticipate downstream consequences of prospective decisions can be catastrophic.

Third, ongoing advances in simulation and processor technologies continually enhance levels of decision model sophistication, ease-of-use, and affordability. This enabling trend will facilitate adoption of VDEs to meet the needs raised by the first two trends.

As VDEs become more common, they will evolve. We anticipate advancements in several directions, including integration, intelligence, and ease-of-use. First, interfaces between VDEs and other enterprise systems will become more standardized and transparent. Obvious integration targets include executive dashboards, business process monitors, business intelligence and military command, and control systems. These systems provide situational awareness, highlighting problems, threats, and opportunities. Integrating BI tools with VDEs could automate scenario generation. Users could then apply VDEs to explore responses to long term strategic issues as they emerge, and potentially develop and validate short-term tactical courses of action as well.

Second, VDEs can become more intelligent in several respects. We deferred adding learning components to our own VDE platform because of validation and verification problems. (Users can modify domain-specific behavioural dynamics, but only manually.) However, adding modules to monitor VDE simulations and analysis activities and to modify decision models autonomously is technically feasible: models can become more accurate based on experience and feedback. Second, our VDE does not formulate new strategies; it only provides a library of reusable building blocks. Adding CBR modules would allow the VDE to suggest (or critique user) scenarios and strategies

Finally, ease-of-use can be improved through more intuitive end-user GUIs and more transparent development tools. Our VDE platform requires explicit programming (in Java) and compilation to create and deploy domain-specific solutions. The next generation of VDEs should support scripting languages or purely declarative tools to construct domain models and behavioural dynamics.

Conclusion

Superior strategies constitute the sole sources of *sustainable* competitive advantage in business (Porter, 1980). Cogent strategies are no less indispensable in the government sector to ensure effective policies and long-term investments for national defense, economic security, public safety, and social well-being.

Unfortunately, relatively little attention has been paid in the KM literature in *actively* codifying, retaining, and leveraging the kinds of tacit knowledge that enable strategic analysis and decision making. Instead, the focus of technology-driven organizational strategies to date has been on more tractable tactical and operational kinds of knowledge, such as functional competencies and processes.

Thus, strategic knowledge has generally been managed, if at all, via direct person-to-person knowledge strategies, such as recruiting workers with documented strategic expertise, obtaining formal (academic) training for workers, and ad hoc mentoring by senior leaders. These nonautomated approaches limit uniformity, tailoring to organization-specific domains and decisions, opportunities for continuous improvement, and leveraging of scare expertise in these critical areas.

We argue for a more aggressive strategy based on explicit codification, sharing, and on-going management of strategic performance-based knowledge. In particular, this chapter has argued that critical strategic knowledge can, in fact, be articulated, captured, and disseminated effectively in rich, interactive computer-based forms called knowledge engines.

We described a novel methodology and its embodiment in a knowledge engine software architecture (VDE) to enable best practice knowledge-based critical decision support. We then illustrated the utility of VDEs across two disparate domains: competitive marketing strategy and organizational change management. (We have developed other VDEs that support strategic decision making for counter-terrorism preparedness and critical infrastructure risk mitigation, IT portfolio management, and dynamic social network analysis.)

We have learned several lessons from deploying VDE solutions to date. First, the economics required to develop and maintain VDEs appear to be more attractive than those for correspondingly complex expert and CBR systems. We have developed useful VDEs in several person weeks, including validation testing. We believe that VDEs require less knowledge and engineering, particularly in the areas of common sense and automated inferences, because (a) they support rather than automate decision making and (b) they presuppose domain practitioners as users, who contribute knowledge and reasoning to VDE mixed initiative processes of decision formulation and analysis. Thus, we believe that VDEs finesse the problem of brittleness and high lifecycle costs that impeded widespread adoption of AI solutions.

Secondly, users report that the front-end exercise of populating scenarios provides equal, if not greater value than back-end "what-if" simulations and outcomes analysis. This confirms the importance of thorough framing in decision making (Russo, 2001). As a corollary, users appreciate that VDE decision models implicitly exclude factors that experts deem to be of secondary importance. Perceived value here consists of substantial savings in time, cost, and effort to collect, validate, maintain, and apply information that is likely to prove noncritical and defocusing.

Finally, we have received unexpected interest in VDEs for training applications, particularly in continuing education settings. Our VDE, like traditional simulations, enables decision methodologies to be taught via predefined case studies. Feedback indicates that our platform goes further by allowing students to build scenarios for imminent decisions that they face, obtain critiques from instructors, and then to take the methodology with them in software and apply it on the job.

VDEs make several contributions to the practice of KM. First, our approach extends proven scenario planning techniques, rendering them actionable rather than passive precursors to decision-making processes. The knowledge embodied in domain-specific VDE decision models prescribes how to think systematically about critical situations, delineating what actors, environmental factors, *and* dynamics should be considered and how to represent that information. VDEs also broaden the scope, consistency, detail, and speed of scenario thinking, emphasizing detailed "what-if" projections of complex situational dynamics.

Second, our framework prescribes an intuitive, empirically-oriented methodology that actively *supports* decision-making processes: define plausible futures; project candidate strategies; and compare them to identify a robust strategy that produces attractive outcomes across those possible futures. Equally important, this methodology can be applied subsequent to the point of decision for monitoring execution results (and environmental changes), detecting problems, and responding promptly. (In contrast, other simulators provide methodologies for applying their particular technique, not for making decisions directly.)

Third, our VDE unifies previously standalone simulation techniques, reflecting the fact the real-world situations are driven by diverse dynamic drivers of change. In particular, our VDE embodies the "new science" theories developed expressly to model causality in complex environments, intentional actors, and the interactions between the two (e.g., systems thinking, complex adaptive systems, Monte Carlo, etc.). VDEs support higher fidelity, more intuitive models because they distort or exclude relevant dynamic factors less than "unimodal" simulators.

Fourth, VDEs advance the packaging of explicit and tacit knowledge via interactive systems that embody theories that promote organizational learning by "doing" (De Geus, 1997). Specifically, VDEs help knowledge workers practice critical decisions, thereby developing instincts and intuitions about (adaptive) situational dynamics and the likely consequences of prospective interventions. They also provide a tangible dynamic platform for sharing best practices decision-support knowledge across the organization.

Finally, VDEs generate organizational audit trails which provide baselines for continuous improvement, both of VDE knowledge and of decision-making processes. VDE scenarios also convey compelling stories about organizations, how their leaders view the world, and their possible futures. Such products facilitate alignment, training, communication, and sense making across organizations.

References

Ambrosini, V. (2003). *Tacit and ambiguous resources as sources of competitive advantage.* New York: Palgrave Macmillan.

Auyang, S. Y. (1998). *Foundations of complex-system theories.* New York: Cambridge University Press.

Axelrod, A. (1997). *The complexity of cooperation: Agent-based models of competition and collaboration.* Princeton University Press.

Baets, W. J. (1998). *Organizational learning and knowledge technologies in a dynamic environment.* Dordrecht: Kluewer.

Berndt, E. R., Bui, L. T., Reiley, D. H., & Urban, G. L. (1994). *The roles of marketing product quality and price competition in the growth and composition of the U.S. anti-ulcer drug industry* (working paper 19-94). Cambridge, MA: MIT Sloan School Program on the Pharmaceutical Industry.

Brachman, R. J., & Levesque, H. J. (Eds.). (1985). *Readings in knowledge representation.* Los Altos, CA: Morgan-Kaufmann.

Brown, L. A. (1996). *Designing and developing electronic performance support systems.* Boston: Elsevier Butterworth-Heinemann.

Brown, J. S., & Duguid, P. (1998). Organizing knowledge. *California Management Review, 40*(3), 90-111.

Bukowitz, W. R., & Williams, R. L. (1999). *The knowledge management fieldbook*. London: Prentice Hall.

Choo, C. W. (2006). *The knowing organization: How organizations use information to construct meaning, create knowledge, and make decisions.* New York: Oxford University Press.

Courtney, H., Kirkland, J., & Viguerie, P. (1997, November-December). Strategy under uncertainty. *Harvard Business Review*, 67-79.

Davenport, T. H., & Glaser, J. (2002, July). Just in time delivery comes to knowledge management. *Harvard Business Review*, 107-111.

Davenport, T. H., & Prusak, L. (1998). *Working knowledge: How organizations manage what they know*. Boston: Harvard Business School Press.

Davis, P. K. (2001). Effects-based operations: A grand challenge for the analytical community. *RAND Corporation (MR-1477-USJFCOM/AF)*. Retrieved January 7, 2008, from http://www.rand.org/publications/MR/MR1477/

Day, G.S ., & Reibstein, D. J. (1997). *Wharton on dynamic competitive strategy.* New York: Wiley.

De Geus, A. P. (1988, March-April). Planning as learning. *Harvard Business Review, 2*, 70-74.

De Geus, A. P. (1997). *The living company: Habits for survival in a turbulent business environment*. Boston: Harvard Business School Press.

De Long, D. W. (2004). *Lost knowledge: Confronting the threat of an aging workforce.* New York: Oxford University Press.

Dixon, N. M. (2000). *Common knowledge: How companies thrive by sharing what they know*. Boston: Harvard Business School Press.

Egan, D. E. (1983). Retrospective reports reveal differences in people's reasoning. *Bell System Technical Journal, 62*(6), 1675-1697.

Epstein, J. M., & Axtell, R. (1996). *Growing artificial societies: Social science from the bottom up*. Washington D.C.: Brookings Institution Press.

Ericsson, K. A., & Simon, H. A. (1984). *Protocol analysis: Verbal reports as data.* Cambridge, MA: MIT Press.

Fishman, G. S. (1996). *Monte Carlo: Concepts, algorithms, and applications*. New York: Springer.

Ford, K. M., & Bradshaw, J. M. (Eds.). (1993). *Knowledge acquisition as modeling.* New York: Wiley & Sons.

Gery, G. (1991). *Electronic performance support systems: How and why to remake the workplace through the strategic application of technology.* Boston: Weingarten Publications.

Gherardi, S. (2006). *Organizational knowledge: The texture of workplace learning.* Malden, MA: Blackwell.

Gilad, B. (2006). *Early warning.* New York: AMACOM.

Gupta, J. N., Forgionne, G. A., & Mora, M. (Eds.). (2006). *Intelligent decision-making support systems: Foundations, applications and challenges.* New York: Springer.

Hansen, M. T., Nohria, N., & Tierney, T. (1999, March-April). What's your strategy for managing knowledge. *Harvard Business Review*, 106-116.

Harvard Business Review (HBR). (1998). *On knowledge management.* Boston: Harvard Business School Press.

Hayes-Roth, F., Waterman, D., & Lenat, D. B. (1983). *Building expert systems reading.* MA: Addison-Wesley.

Holland, J. H. (1995). *Hidden order: How adaptation builds complexity.* Reading, MA: Addison-Wesley.

Koehn, D. J., & Adler, R. M. (2006). Change adaptation learning model. *American Society for Training and Development (ASTD) OD-Leadership Network Newsletter, 4*(9). Retrieved January 7, 2008, from http://www.astd.org/astd/Publications/Newsletters/OD_Leadership_News/2006/Oct/October+ODL+Koehn

Kolodner, J. (1993). *Case-based reasoning.* San Mateo: Morgan Kaufmann.

Kotter, J. P. (1995, March-April). Leading change: Eight ways organizational transformations fail. *Harvard Business Review,* 59-67.

Langton, C. (1995). *Artificial life: An overview.* Cambridge, MA: MIT Press.

Legna, C. A., & Gonzalez, C. S. (2006). *Using system dynamics and case-based reasoning (CBR) to build an intelligent decision-making support system that improves strategic public decisions.* In Gupta et al.

Nonaka, I. (1991, November-December). The knowledge-creating company. *Harvard Business Review*, 96-104.

Nonaka, I., & Takeuchi, H. (1995). *The knowledge-creating company: How Japanese companies create the dynamics of innovation.* New York: Oxford University Press.

Pascale, R. T., Millemann, M., & Gioja, L. (2000). *Surfing the edge of chaos: The laws of nature and the new laws of business.* New York: Three Rivers Press.

Polyani, M. (1962). *Personal knowledge.* Chicago: University of Chicago Press.

Porter, M.E. (1980). *Competitive strategy: Techniques for analyzing industries and competitors.* New York: The Free Press.

Roth, G., & Kleiner, A. (1998). *Field manual for the learning historian.* Retrieved January 7, 2008, from The Learning History Research Project Web site: http://ccs.mit.edu/lh

Russo, J. E., & Schoemaker, P. J. H. (2001).*Winning decisions: Getting it right the first time.* New York: Doubleday Currency.

Sackman, S. (1992). Culture and subcultures: An analysis of organizational knowledge. *Adminstrative Science Quarterly, 37*, 140-161.

Samarin, W. (1967). *Field linguistics.* New York: Holt, Rinehart & Winston.

Schwartz, P. (1991). *The art of the long view.* New York: Doubleday Currency.

Schoemaker, P. J. H. (2002). *Profiting from uncertainty: Strategies for succeeding no matter what the future brings.* New York: The Free Press.

Senge, P. M. (1990). *The fifth discipline: The art & practice of the learning organization.* New York: Doubleday Currency.

Shapiro, S. C. (1992). *Encyclopedia of artificial intelligence.* New York: Wiley.

Sterman, J. D. (2000). *Business dynamics: Systems thinking and modeling for a complex world.* Boston: Irwin/McGraw-Hill.

Tsoukas, H. (2005). *Complex knowledge: Studies in organizational epistemology.* New York: Oxford University Press.

Turban, E. (1988). *Decision support and expert systems: Managerial perspectives.* New York: Macmillan.

van der Heijden, K. (1996). *Scenarios: The art of strategic conversation.* New York: John L. Wiley & Sons.

Wagner, G., Pardice, D., & Courtney, J. (2006). *A software laboratory for advancing decision support simulation.* In Gupta et al.

Waldrop, M. (1992). *Complexity: The emerging science at the edge of order and chaos.* New York: Simon & Schuster.

Wenger, E. (1998). *Communities of practice: Learning, meaning, and identity.* New York: Cambridge University Press.

Weick, K. (1995). *Sensemaking in organizations.* Thousand Oaks, CA: Sage.

Zack, M. H. (1999). Managing codified knowledge. *Sloan Management Review, 40*, 45-57.

Internet Session: Decision Strategies International

http://www.thinkdsi.com

Decision Strategies International is a consultancy that specializes in scenario planning and other strategic consulting services. It provides a library of videotaped lectures and numerous publications by Dr. Paul Schoemaker, the DSI founder and one of the early practitioners of Scenario Planning at Royal Dutch Shell.

Interaction:

For example: View the videotapes or download an industry report (e.g. Scenario Planning for the credit union industry) or other publication and prepare a presentation on the subject

Case Study

A. Title of Case

Using scenario planning to capturing knowledge for making strategic decisions

Questions:

1. What kinds of strategic decisions are made by an organization you work for or are familiar with? Who makes these decisions and what kinds of knowledge do they need to analyze their situation and make decisions?

2. What kinds of futures can you envisage for this organization? Who are the key players (competitors, customers, regulators)? What are the effects of their behaviors? Of dominant environmental forces?

3. How would you go about capturing this kind of knowledge for others? What kinds of modeling techniques and software tools are relevant?

Useful URLs

1. DecisionPath, Inc. case studies of VDE solutions and download resources: http:/www.decpath.com

2. Decision Strategies, International – scenario planning consultancy: http://www. thinkdsi.com/leadership/media.asp

3. Global Business Network – scenario planning consultancy: http://www.gbn. com/

4. Scenario planning resources: http://www.well.com/~mb/scenario/

5. Strategy network: http://www.strategynet.org.uk/portal/portal.htm

6. John Sterman, MIT Systems Dynamics guru: http://web.mit.edu/jsterman/ www/

7. Knowledge Management Network: http://www.brint.com/

8. Knowledge Board – KM discussion group: http://www.knowledgeboard. com/

9. Knowledge Management Advantage: http://www.providersedge.com/kma/

10. CIO library, Special Issue: Knowledge Management: Big Challenges, Big Rewards: http://www.cio.com/sponsors/091599_km_1.html

11. Society for Organizational Learning (SOL): http://www.solonline.org/organizational_overview/

12. CBEL, Knowledge Management links: http://www.cbel.com/knowledge_management/

13. KMTool, search engine for KM: http://www.kmtool.net/

14. Steve Denning: http://www.stevedenning.com/knowledge_management.htm

Further Readings

Bonabeau, E., & Meyer, C. (2001, May). Swarm intelligence: A whole new way to think about business. *Harvard Business Review,* 107-114.

Bonabeau, E., & Meyer, C. (2002, March). Predicting the unpredictable. *Harvard Business Review,* 109-116.

Ford, D. N., & Sterman, J. D. *Expert knowledge elicitation to improve mental and formal models* (MIT Tech. Rep. D-4686). Retrieved January 7, 2008, from http://web.mit.edu/jsterman/www/ford_sterman_elicit_1.pdf

Hanset, M. T., Nohria, N., & Tierney, T. (1999, March-April). What's your strategy for managing knowledge? *Harvard Business Review,* 106-116.

Rogers, E. W. *Introducing the pause and learn process: Adapting the army after action review to the NASA project world at the Goddard Space Flight Center.* Retrieved January 7, 2008, from http://missionsuccess.gsfc.nasa.gov/files/PaLwhitepaperV3.pdf

Chapter VI

Knowledge Management Strategy for Web 2.0 Integration

R. Todd Stephens, AT&T Corporation, USA

Abstract

This chapter examines the elements of the new Web 2.0 technology base and discusses a framework for implementing it into the typical knowledge store. The collaborative environment opens the door to move away from the traditional command and control of information that exists throughout an organization to a more collaborative environment based on trust. The rapid growth of information and the advancements in knowledge store technology has created an environment where organizations can expand the value and utility generated by integrating the Web 2.0 technologies. While the definition of Web 2.0 varies, the basic idea of user-contributed content dynamically alters the lifecycle of knowledge itself. This analysis should present the reader with several different integration techniques including component integration and complete application replacement.

Introduction

The vast majority of **information workers** are not familiar with collaborative solutions and need guidance on how to best utilize and integrate this technology into there day-to-day operations. A company's ability to manage information effectively over the life cycle, including sensing, collecting, organizing, processing, and maintaining information, is crucial to the long-term success in a global economy. The business community is increasingly interested in knowledge management and **knowledge stores** as a differentiation technology which allows for cost transformation, risk mitigation, and ongoing maturity progression. Despite the rich history of publications around knowledge management, very little has been focused on the new Web 2.0 technologies. In particular, there is very little literature available around the concept of knowledge store integration.

In this chapter, the author will establish a foundation of technologies and introduce various methods of collaborative integration. Figure 1 depicts the model for transformation whereby a static knowledge store is transformed into a dynamic cocreated environment based on **Web 2.0** technologies. The author will either bring in the internal case study or an outside organization to provide insight and lessons learned. The setting for the internal case study is a Fortune 500 organization within the telecommunications industry with a customer base exceeding 44 million. The following background will serve to orient the reader to the basic concepts and frameworks of knowledge management and the knowledge management store (i.e., repository application). Additionally, the background section will describe the Web 1.0 environment and define the foundation for Web 2.0 technologies.

Figure 1. Web 2.0 transformation framework

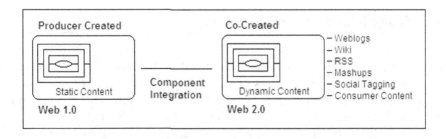

Background

Knowledge Management

Knowledge management continues to be one of the most critical aspects of doing business in today's environment. Organizations are beginning to realize the importance of managing organizational knowledge in order to deliver innovation and competitive products. Sewry and Sunassee (2003) indicate that the only true source of competitive advantage is knowledge. Managing this intangible asset requires a change in mindset from a command and control to a collaborative perspective for sharing information. Knowledge management is central to improving the overall effectiveness of the organization where the growing complexity of the distributed work environment requires better utilization of knowledge. Applehans, Globe, and Laugero (1999) define knowledge as the ability to turn information and data into action. Knowledge and content management emerged as disciplines due to the needs of businesses to ease the partnering aspects of the organization, manage expertise turnover, and decentralize decision making. Knowledge management includes acquiring or creating knowledge, transforming it into a reusable form, retaining it, and finding it and reusing it (Grudin, 2006). Finally, knowledge can be defined as a fluid mix of framed experiences, values, contextual information, and expert insight that provides a framework for evaluating and incorporating new experiences and information (Davenport & Prusak, 1997).

Researchers divide knowledge into two main categories: explicit and tacit. Explicit knowledge is knowledge that can be articulated, codified, and stored in various types of media. This media may be in the form of manuals, presentations, documents, spreadsheets, or database systems. Tacit knowledge is often transmitted through a combination of demonstration, illustration, annotation, stories, experiences, and discussion. This type of knowledge is usually not openly expressed or taught. This does not imply that tacit knowledge is inaccessible to conscious awareness, unspeakable, or unteachable, but merely that it is not taught directly in the normal course of business (Wagner & Sternberg, 1985).

Knowledge Management Systems

The base requirement of knowledge management is the knowledge management system (KMS). The KMS is a class of information system applied to managing organizational knowledge (Bock & Qian, 2005). For the purpose of this research chapter, a closer review of the natural evolution of knowledge repositories is required. Information systems that only take into account **structured information** are considered registries. The current Web service registry is an example, where metadata information is captured without any unstructured information. Many traditional data and information stores start out containing only structured information but soon realize that the vast majority of knowledge is embedded in the unstructured associated content. The Web service registry can be transformed into a Web service repository by adding **unstructured information** sources like design diagrams, integration instructions, user guides, and data domains.

Both the traditional repository and registry can be defined as passive knowledge stores; passive in the sense that information can be reviewed or pushed to the end user vs. integration into the business process or automated with workflow. In order to transform the repository into an active application, organizations need to add automated business and application processes. Business processes may include functions like automated scanning, asset submission, asset consumption, versioning, and subscription services. Application automation focuses on the utilization of the actual information of the repository like metrics, impact analysis, product comparison, and personalization. These services transform the passive repository into an active one. Ruggles (1997) describes tools that generate knowledge as active applications where data mining can be used to discover new patterns. Active tools can notify users when it is likely that users require some kind of knowledge. Passive tools require a user to actively seek knowledge without any system support (Dingsoyr & Royrvik, 2003).

This transformation from registry to repository to active application leads one to believe that knowledge stores naturally evolve over time. Considering this fact along with the gaps and friction in the process of collecting, storing, and disseminating knowledge, we should expect another transformation to occur. This evolutionary next step is integrating Web 2.0 technologies into the knowledge store.

Web 1.0

The term Web 1.0 emerged from the research around Web 2.0. Basically, Web 1.0 focused on a read-only Web interface while Web 2.0 focuses on a read-write interface where value emerges from the contribution of a large volume of users. The Internet as well as the Intranet initially focused on the command and control of the information itself. Information was controlled by a relatively small number of resources but distributed to a large number which spawned the massive growth of the Web itself. Like television, the Web allowed for the broadcasting of information to a large number of users.

Inside the organization, the Intranet has changed the way organizations structure and operate their business. Specifically, the Intranet has centralized communications and corporate information as well as built a sense of community across organizational boundaries (McNay, 2000). Typical organizations will have office-based employees in various locations, telecommuting, and off-shoring staff. The traditional day-by-day communication landscape has changed from personal to electronic. The migration to electronic communications emerged as standards, technology, and infrastructure matured. This allowed more information sharing and community building to occur without a requirement of physical location. Over the past several years Intranets have emerged as the key delivery mechanism for application and business information. Intranets may be thought of as providing the infrastructure for intraorganizational electronic commerce (Chellappa & Gupta, 2002). This allows organizations to utilize the technology to achieve their organizational goals and objectives. Web 1.0 allowed the organization to govern the information flow and focus on achieving the business goals.

Unfortunately, most technologies fail to deliver competitive advantages over an extended period of time. Investments in information technology, while profoundly important, are less and less likely to deliver a competitive edge to an individual company (Carr, 2003). This is especially true in the world of the Web 1.0 since much of the knowledge and information is disseminated all over the world as quickly as it gets published. Organizations are beginning to see that the command and control model is no longer effective at developing a high performance work force which opens the door for the next evolution in technologies as described by the Web 2.0 framework.

Web 2.0

While Web 2.0 has been debated by researchers as to who and when the concepts emerged, little argument exists that the technology and demand has arrived. Unlike Web 1.0, this new technology encourages user participation and derives its greatest value when large communities contribute content. User-generated metadata, information, and designs enable a much richer environment where the value is generated by the volume of employees. Sometimes referred to as sharing, **collaboration**, aggregate knowledge, or community-driven content, social software creates the foundation of collective intelligence (Weiss, 2005). Much of the Web 2.0 technology is difficult to nail down an exact definition; the basic truth is that Web 2.0 emphasizes employee interaction, community, and openness (Millard & Ross, 2006). Along with these characteristics, Smith and Valdes (2005) add simple and lightweight technologies and decentralized processing to the mix. O'Reilly (2005) defines Web 2.0 as a platform, spanning all connected devices. Web 2.0 applications are those that make the most of the intrinsic advantages of that platform: delivering software as a continually-updated service that gets better the more people use it; consuming and remixing data from multiple sources, including individual users, while providing their own data and services in a form that allows remixing by others; creating network effects through an "architecture of participation"; and going beyond the page metaphor of Web 1.0 to deliver rich user experiences. While Web 2.0 has many and often confusing definitions, most include the concepts of Weblogs, wikis, really simple syndication (RSS) functionality, social tagging, mashups, and user defined content.

Weblogs or Blogs

Weblogs or blogs have become so ubiquitous that many people use the term synonymously for a "personal Web site" (Blood, 2004). Unlike traditional hypertext markup language (HTML) Web pages, blogs offer the ability for the nonprogrammer to communicate on a regular basis. Traditional HTML style pages required knowledge of style, coding, and design in order to publish content that was basically read-only from the consumer's point of view. Weblogs remove much of the constraints by providing a standard user interface that does not require customization. Weblogs originally emerged as a repository for linking but soon evolved to the ability to publish content and allow readers to become content providers. The essence of a blog can be defined by the format which includes small chunks of content referred to as posts, date stamped, reverse chronological order, and content expanded to include links, text, and images (Baoill, 2004). The biggest advancement made with Weblogs is the permanence of the content which has a unique universal resource locator (URL). This allows the content to be posted and, along with the comments, to define a permanent record of information. This is critical in that having a collaborative record that can be indexed by search engines will increase the utility and spread the information to a larger audience. With the advent of software like Wordpress and Typepad, along with blog service companies like blogger.com, the Weblog is fast becoming the communication medium of the new Web.

Sample Weblog URL's

* Tom Peters Business Blog (http://www.tompeters.com)
* Randy Basler's Boeing Blog (http://boeingblogs.com/randy/)
* Jonathan Schwartz's Sun Blog (http://blogs.sun.com/jonathan/)
* Rough Type by Nicholas Carr (http://www.roughtype.com)

Wikis

A Wiki is a Web site that promotes the collaborative creation of content. Wiki pages can be edited by anyone at anytime. Informational content can be created and easily organized within the wiki environment and then reorganized as required (O'Neill, 2005). Wikis are currently in high demand in a large variety of fields, due to their simplicity and flexibility nature. Documentation, reporting, project management, online glossaries and dictionaries, discussion groups, or general information applications are just a few examples of where the end user can provide value (Reinhold, 2006). The major difference between a wiki and blog is that the wiki user can alter the original content while the blog user can only add information in the form of comments. While stating that anyone can alter content, some large scale wiki environments have extensive role definitions which define who can perform functions of update, restore, delete, and creation. Wikipedia, like many wiki type projects, have readers, editors, administrators, patrollers, policy makers, subject matter experts, content maintainers, software developers, and system operators (Riehle, 2006). All create an environment open to sharing information and knowledge to a large group of users.

Sample Wiki URL's

- Wikipedia (http://www.wikipedia.org/)
- Reuters Financial Glossary (http://glossary.reuters.com/)
- Internet 2 (https://wiki.internet2.edu/confluence/dashboard.action)

RSS Technologies

Originally developed by Netscape, RSS was intended to publish news type information based upon a subscription framework (Lerner, 2006). Many Internet users have experienced the frustration of searching Internet sites for hours at a time to find relevant information. RSS is an XML based content-syndication protocol that allows Web sites to share information as well as aggregate information based upon the users needs (Cold, 2006). In the simplest form, RSS shares the metadata about the content without actually delivering the entire information source. An author might publish the title, description, publish date, and copyrights to anyone that subscribes to the feed. The end user is required to have an application called an aggregator in order to receive the information. By having the RSS aggregator application, end users are not required to visit each site in order to obtain information. From an end user perspective, the RSS technology changes the communication method from a search-and-discover to a notification model. Users can locate content that is pertinent to their job and subscribe to the communication.

Sample RSS URL's

- Newsgator (http://www.newsgator.com/)
- FeedBurner (http://www.feedburner.com/)
- Pluck (http://www.pluck.com/)
- Blog Lines (http://www.bloglines.com/)

Social Tagging

Social tagging describes the collaborative activity of marking shared online content with keywords or tags as a way to organize content for future navigation, filtering, or search (Gibson, Teasley, & Yew, 2006). Traditional information architecture utilized a central taxonomy or classification scheme in order to place information into specific predefined bucket or category. The assumption was that trained librarians understood more about information content and context than the average user. While this might have been true for the local library with the utilization of the Dewey decimal system, the enormous amount of content on the Internet makes this type of system unmanageable. Tagging offers a number of benefits to the end-user community. Perhaps the most important feature to the individual is to be able to bookmark the information in a way that is easier for the user to recall at a later date. The benefit of this ability on a personal basis is obvious, but what about the impact to the community at large? The idea of social tagging is allowing multiple users to tag content in a way that makes sense to them; by combining these tags, users create an environment where the opinions of the majority define the appropriateness of the tags themselves. The act of creating a collection of popular tags is referred to as a folksonomy, which is defined as a folk taxonomy of important and emerging content within the user community (Ahn, Davis, Fake, Fox, Furnas, Golder, et al., 2006). The vocabulary problem is defined by the fact that different users define content in different ways. The disagreement can lead to missed information or inefficient user interactions (Boyd, Davis, Marlow, & Naaman, 2006). One of the best examples of social tagging is Flickr, which allows user to upload images and "tag" them with appropriate metadata keywords. Other users, who view your images, can also tag them with their concept of appropriate keywords. After a critical mass has been reached, the resulting tag collection will identify images correctly and without bias.

Sample Social Tagging URL's
_____

- Flickr (http://www.flickr.com/)
- YouTube (http://www.youtube.com/)
- Del.icio.us (http://del.icio.us/)
- Technorati (http://technorati.com/)

Mashups: Integrating Information

The final Web 2.0 technology describes the efforts around information integration or sometimes referred to as "mashups." These applications can be combined to deliver additional value that the individual parts could do not on their own. One example is HousingMaps.com that combines the Google mapping application with a real estate listing service on Craiglists.com (Jhingran, 2006). Other examples include Chicagocrime.org who overlays local crime statistics onto Google Maps so end users can see what crimes were committed recently in the neighborhood. Another site synchronizes Yahoo! Inc.'s real-time traffic data with Google Maps. Much of the work with Web services will enable greater extensions of mashups and combine many different businesses and business models. Organizations, like Amazon and Microsoft are embracing the mashup movement by offering developers easier access to their data and services. Moreover, they are programming their services so that more computing tasks, such as displaying maps onscreen, are done on the users' personal computers rather than on their far-flung servers (Hof, 2005)

Sample Mashup URL's
_____

- Housing Maps: (http://www.housingmaps.com/)
- Chicago Crime (http://www.chicagocrime.org)
- Healthcare Product (http://www.vimo.com/)
- Global Disease Map (http://healthmap.org/)

User Contributed Content

One of the basic themes of Web 2.0 is user contributed information. The value derived from the contributed content comes not from a subject matter expert, but rather from individuals whose small contributions add up. One example of user contributed content is the product review systems like Amazon.com and reputation systems used with ebay.com. A common practice of online merchants is to enable their customers to review or to express opinions on the products they have purchased (Hu & Liu, 2004). Online reviews are a major source of information for consumers and demonstrated enormous implications for a wide range of management activities, such as brand building, customer acquisition and retention, product development, and quality assurance (Hu, Pavlou, & Zhang, 2006). A person's reputation is a valuable piece of information that can be used when deciding whether or not to interact or do business with that person. A reputation system is a bidirectional medium where buyers post feedback on sellers and vice versa. For example, eBay buyers voluntarily comment on the quality of service, their satisfaction with the item traded, and promptness of shipping. Sellers comment about the prompt payment from buyers, or respond to comments left by the buyer (Christodorescu, Ganapathy, Giffin, Kruger, Rubin, & Wang, 2005). Reputation systems may be categorized in three basic types: ranking, rating, and collaborative. Ranking systems use quantifiable measures of users' behavior to generate and rating. Rating systems use explicit evaluations given by users in order to define a measure of interest or trust. Finally, collaborative filtering systems determine the level of relationship between the two individuals before placing a weight on the information. For example, if a user has reviewed similar items in the past then the relevancy of a new rating will be higher (Davis, Farnham, & Jensen, 2002).

Sample User Contributed Content URL's

- Amazon.com (http://www.amazon.com)
- Ebay (http://www.ebay.com)
- Trip Advisor (http://www.tripadvisor.com/)
- Review Centre (http://www.reviewcentre.com/)

Web 1.0 Compared to Web 2.0

While the differences between Web 1.0 and Web 2.0 are grey at best, we can attempt to draw some segmentation by reviewing the high level characteristics. Table 1 provides a side-by-side comparison of these technologies.

Table 1. Characteristics of Web 1.0 and Web 2.0

Web 1.0 Characteristics	Web 2.0 Characteristics
Static Content	Dynamic Content
Producer Based Information	Participatory Based Information
Messages Pushed to Consumer	Messages Pulled by Consumer
Institutional Control	Individual Enabled
Top Down Implementation	Bottom Up Implementation
Users Search and Browse	Users Publish and Subscribe
Transactional Based Interactions	Relationship Based Interactions
Goal of Mass Adoption	Goal of Niche Adoption
Taxonomy	Folksonomy

In the Web 1.0 environment, information was largely static and controlled by a few resources. Specifically, the individual or organization that produced this information pushed information to the end user by either controlling the access or limiting the feedback options. Web 2.0 turns that model around and creates a far greater dynamic environment where each consumer has the ability to contribute to the overall value of the information itself. Instead of searching and browsing topics, Web 2.0 users are allowed to publish and subscribe to the content which results in a more bottom-up implementation. The following section will review how these new technologies can be integrated into the current knowledge environments that have traditionally followed the command and control model of information.

Integration of Collaborative Solutions

The prior section established a foundation for the knowledge store and the emerging Web 2.0 technologies. The question remains on the best approach to integrate these technologies inside the organization. Specifically, how can Web 2.0 technologies be integrated into the various knowledge stores within the enterprise? The first step in integrating these technologies is to break down the structure of the knowledge store itself. Figure 2 provides a framework for the typical environment.

At the heart of any knowledge store is the core **asset** being described. The asset may be a document within a content management system, an entity within a metadata repository, a book within an electronic commerce system, or shared software in an open source registry. As the knowledge stores evolve, each area will obtain some

Figure 2. Knowledge store framework

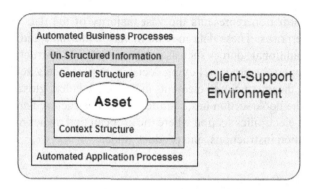

level maturity: structured information, unstructured information, automated business processes, automated application processes, and a client-support environment.

Structured Information

Structured information may be characterized as information whose intended meaning is unambiguous and explicitly represented in the structure or format of the data. This information may be placed into a database structure where metadata can describe the content, meaning, and domain of the information. Focusing on the book area of Amazon.com, two structured information classifications can be observed. The first is a general structure used to describe the book which includes the title, description, keywords, author, and price. Irregardless of asset type, general information provides a consistent convention for describing the asset. The Dublin Core standard is one such generic standard that can be applied across asset types. The second classification of structured information is specific to the asset itself. That is to say that while general metadata applies across to all asset types, context metadata varies depending on the asset being described. Examples of context metadata models include object management group (OMG), common warehouse model (CWM), reusable asset specification (RAS), and Web service definition language (WSDL). At Amazon.com, book specific information includes the publisher, page count, weight, language, and product international standard book number (ISBN).

Unstructured Information

Unstructured information represents the vast majority of the data collected and accessible to enterprises. These data may be in various formats and may lack the organization of traditional sources such as database records. Unstructured information is used to support the product, buying decision, or place the asset into context. On Amazon.com, the unstructured elements included the index, glossary, and book excerpts. While the book section has a limited set of unstructured artifacts, this is not true under the electronics section where the user can find owner manuals, setup guides, configuration instructions, and product guides.

Business Processes

Within a knowledge store, automated business processes act upon the various elements of described information to create value for the end user. These may include full text search, product availability, shopping cart functionality, product ordering, order status, and order tracking. The essence of electronic commerce is to automate the business transactions in a way that creates a frictionless environment. Additional business processes may include product bundling which combines various assets in a way to create value above and beyond the value created from the individual asset. Related products are products that are predefined by the asset owner as an information source that is directly related, such as relating a monitor with a computer in order to create an additional sale.

Application Processes

Application processes act upon the core information or end user behavior in order to deliver value. For example, many knowledge stores will publish the "most viewed" or "most popular" item. This is an application processes since the system is generating the data by monitoring the end-user traffic then providing value based upon the usage metrics. Other application processes may include displaying similar purchases and product comparisons. In and of themselves, these automated functions do not create business value as do business process automation. Additional application functions may include "hot" items, most downloaded, or impact analysis.

Client-Support

Client-support functions include information and processes that support the end user with the application itself. These may include online help, account management, recent orders, password management, and personalization. Each of these contribute to the overall success of the application and business functions. Client-support functions answer five basic questions of the knowledge store:

- What products and services are available to me?
- How can I utilize these products and services within my environment?
- Who can help me in case I need some professional guidance?
- Are the collaborative applications ready for enterprise usage?
- How am I doing in comparison to others or against best practices?

In order to address these questions, organizations should look toward developing a support group that can enable the end user rather than hindering the end user's understanding of a collaborative environment. Meeting the needs of the customer may vary depending on the level of knowledge the user brings to the environment. Customers who are new to technology expect a high level of reliability and support in order to gain the greatest value possible (Johnston & Supra, 1997). Customer service should not be homogeneous and both the online and physical support environments need to take into account the experience level of the end user (Dutta & Roy, 2006).

Integrating Web 2.0 Components

Many organizations are taking a look at the Web 2.0 or collaborative technologies and adding them to the information framework, as depicted in Figure 3.

Figure 3. Update knowledge framework

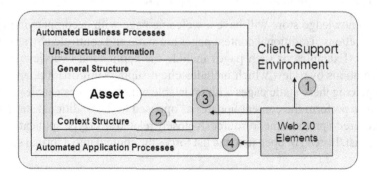

Collaborative technologies can be integrated into the four areas associated with the components of the knowledge store (Labels 1-4). Collaborative component-based integration keeps the basic knowledge store intact but looks to add value through the addition or replacement of collaborative tools.

In the studied organization, the knowledge store is the internal procurement system for all technology related products. The ordering system acts as a product catalog and electronic commerce system for the entire organization including external partners. Products like printers, personal computers, software, and peripherals are included as well as back-end accounting integration. This system replaced the original document-based application which requires 4-6 weeks of the delivery time for an average order. As discussed in the prior section, this system evolved from a knowledge registry to an active application for knowledge management. Some of the business processes include account management, history, order status, bundling of products, inventory management, and business-to-business (B2B) transactions. The system has been in production for 4 years and has processed over $41 million in orders. The essence of this system is to govern the technology standards of the organization to ensure consistency and accountability thoughout the organization. This knowledge store was selected for transformation specifically for it level of maturity in all of the areas described in Figure 3.

Client-Support Integration

Component based integration takes a look at some of the static informational type client-support elements (Label 1 in Figure 3) and replaces them with collaborative components. The key to this type of strategy is to keep the core business processing and workflow intact while replacing the other elements. One question that may emerge is why focus on the client-support area is the first step in component integration? The idea is at the core of Web 2.0 technology; users want to feel in perceived control of their information and environment. The client-support elements are there to help the end user gain the highest level of utility from the technology. By replacing these components first, the end user can be eased into the environment as well as gain that feeling of belonging to the community.

A mature knowledge store will have a welcome page with accompanying client-support functions. Traditional content pages are static and controlled by a very few individuals. Examples of such pages include the application overview or about page, operations overview which includes client support information, and online help. Replacing these static pages with updatable wiki type pages enables multiple resources to perform the content updates as opposed to the traditional static pages which required a programmer resource. A closely related wiki type application is the updatable list. Instead of open text, the list forces the content into a formal structure, similar to a spreadsheet. Examples of this type of content include frequently asked questions (FAQ), contact information, and product announcements.

One of the most frequently used support functions is the discussion thread in which users can discuss the benefits and issues around the various products. A Weblog is the perfect tool replacement in that much of the functionality is already built in. The Weblog also provides a method for the product owners to communicate with the user community on various issues like software upgrades, replacement parts such as the Dell battery replacement, or "out of support" products. While current corporate implementations of Weblogs are focused around corporate strategy, enormous opportunities exist in the client-support area.

The current application has a built-in service which notifies an end user when a product is updated or additional documentation has been added. This is a prime replacement for the RSS feed and the document library. As with any knowledge store, users want to be notified when changes have occurred in the product offering or support information. Unfortunately, the primary mechanism for this type of communication is e-mail. The average user gets inundated with hundreds of e-mails per day and critical business information can easily be lost. The RSS technology will allow the user to utilize the news reader in order to subscribe to important information throughout the enterprise.

Structured Information Integration

The core content of any knowledge store is the structured information (Label 2 in Figure 3) that supports the object contained in the store. In the studied organization, the base objects are technology products. The structured information for each product includes manufacturer, description, images, keywords, order constraints, price, product number, and associated parts. This information can be presented to the end user in the form of a structured table. Traditionally, structured and unstructured information have been stored in relation databases and content management systems. With the advent of wiki type systems, structured lists can replace the functionality of the database. A list is basically an editable collection of fields than can be defined and altered by the owner. The basic foundation of a list is the idea of a collection of facts, or pieces of knowledge, that are related to one another. The list is simply a record of these facts structured in a simple horizontal model, similar to an Excel spreadsheet. The benefits of utilizing the wiki list include the ability to sort, filter, and group various data fields which could provide greater utility or show the end user similar products. Additionally, lists can easily be exported to spreadsheets for further analysis.

Unstructured Information Integration

The associated unstructured content management application could be replaced with a simple document library that allows anonymous update to the knowledge store. Associated unstructured information (Labeled 4 in Figure 3) for technology products might include user guides, technical specifications, setup, and configuration instructions. While not specifically designated as a wiki utility, the document library allows users to post and publish documentation which provides a great deal of value for the organization. Consider the original method of publishing: the product owner would receive the updated documentation which would then be sent to the support group along with specific instructions. When the content was updated in the test system, the product owner would then recommend additional changes required as well as sign off of the final version. Once complete, then the updates would be moved into production. With the collaborative document library utility, the product owner can simply update document as well as associated content changes required. This enables much faster turn around and a higher quality of information since the effort is relatively small. Web 2.0 environments are fundamentally changing the way in which we think about published information. Traditionally, information or knowledge had to be perfected, reviewed, and approved before making it to the forefront of the organization. Collaborative technologies allow the organization to publish information at the right time, to the right people, in the right context. Without the friction of governance, the organization can become much more agile and responsive to the competitive forces of business.

Business and Application Automation Integration

Knowledge stores that have matured beyond the passive storage of information will have automated many of the application and business functions associated with the store itself. Early versions of enterprise collaborative tools were weak on workflow and process automation. While integrated tools are available, consumers want built-in and easy-to-use workflow engines. One traditional workflow that permeates throughout the organization is approvals. Most organizations have a huge collection of small workflow applications including purchase approvals, access approvals, or content promotion approvals. Current solutions require high-end consulting and expensive tools in order to deliver this functionality which creates physical and cultural barriers, similar to how the Weblog and wiki solutions have simplified the Web design and update functions in order to expand the content and usage in the environment. Simplified workflow would enable more automation and remove the friction associated with business processes like approvals.

Summary of Changes

Table 2 provides a review of each of the components replaced or planned replacement in the near future for the studied application.

Complete Replacement

While this chapter focused on integrating Web 2.0 technologies, the next step would be a complete replacement of infrastructure and functionality. With the new versions and future releases of collaborative software, the power will shift from the centralized information technology organization to the end user. This fundamental shift will create enormous value and movement toward dynamic knowledge stores. There will still be requirements of governance, findability, and usability within the knowledge store but as technology progresses the ability to deliver value will shift to the end user. The addition of user-contributed content and removal of the barriers between knowledge producer and consumer will create that elusive frictionless environment that most organizations are moving toward. Complete replacement of

Table 2. Component replacement

Area	Category	Web 2.0 Component
FAQ	Client-Support	Wiki-List
Events	Client-Support	Wiki-List
Announcements	Client-Support	Wiki-List
Operations	Client-Support	Wiki-Standard
Document Library	Client-Support	Wiki-Document Library
Contact Us	Client-Support	Wiki-List
About Us	Client-Support	Wiki-Standard
Online Help	Client-Support	Wiki-Standard
Notifications	Client-Support	RSS Feed
Discussion Thread	Client-Support	Weblog
How Do I...	Client-Support	Wiki-List
Product Information	Structured Information	Wiki-Standard
Support Documentation	Un-Structured Information	Wiki-Document Library
Order Approval	Business Workflow	Planned
Order Notification	Business Workflow	Planned
Product Feedback	Application Workflow	Planned
Product Classification	Structured Information	Planned
Customer Registration	Business Workflow	Planned

knowledge stores based on Web 1.0 standards will take time, both from a culture perspective as well as technology evolution.

In the studied organization, one knowledge store was introduced as a proof of concept (POC) for complete replacement. The passive repository held both structured and unstructured information around common service components. The components were highly reusable service programs that operate at the enterprise tier. The POC setup to demonstrate that the repository could be completely rebuilt utilizing Microsoft's SharePoint Services and Portal Server. Based on the lessons learned from the component replacement, the complete replacement was simple and straight forward. The only automated application automation required was notification of changes, which was accomplished by the built in "Alert Me" and RSS part which was included in the current release of the application (Microsoft's SharePoint). The POC proved that a complete replacement was not only possible but allowed for greater control by the owning organization. We are still in the infancy of Web 2.0 technologies and the full impact within the organizational walls remains undefined. The following section will look toward the future and conclude by defining the impact of this knowledge management strategy.

The Future of Collaboration and Knowledge Stores

Overview

The base problem organizations will have in integrating Web 2.0 technologies is the culture. In 1968, Mel Conway (1968) devised the "Conway Law" which states that the structure of systems will reflect the structure of the organization that develops it. Since the majority of organizations are built under the command and control, centralized, and authoritative model, the ability to incorporate collaborative technologies will be limited at best. Integrating these technologies into established knowledge stores approaches the problem, not from the top down but rather from the bottom up. **Collaboration** and decentralization require a significant transformation which most companies are not prepared to make the sacrifices required.

Removing the Barriers of Communication

Knowledge stores, by their very nature, create friction between those that create knowledge and those that consume it. In the studied organization, the producer of the knowledge is the product owner or architect. This person is responsible for selecting the standard products as well as collecting the product information for the online knowledge store. The consumers of this information are the employees throughout the organization which is spread across a nine state region. Clearly, the ability for the end user to communicate with the product owner and disseminate that information is limited to e-mail or phone conversations. Integrating the collaborative components fundamentally changes the communication medium of the application itself. No longer is the application acting as a one-way or even a two-way communication tool but rather allows for multiple paths of interaction. This collaborative communication does more than bring the producer closer to the single consumer, rather, collaboration brings the entire market closer to the product architecture. The product is no longer just the physical device of the order but the community of knowledge that surrounds the product.

Knowledge Store Integration

One area that will need to be researched in the future is the ability to integrate the information across all knowledge stores. Today, most knowledge stores are a segregated collection of technologies, standards, and applications. By integrating and adding collaborative technologies, the amount of information will expand exponentially. With the integration of collaborative technologies, governance of the information will be an issue that needs to be addressed. Information technology governance specifies accountabilities of technology related business outcomes and helps companies align their technology investments with their business priorities (Ross & Weill, 2004). This idea of integrated knowledge store will become a realization when organizations integrate knowledge stores with collaborative solutions.

Conclusion

Much of this chapter was devoted to the integration of the collaborative technology with little attention paid to the end user and the culture transformation that needs to actually happen. The knowledge store itself can act as a barrier between those that create knowledge assets and those that consume them. This barrier works well in a command and control environment where the producer and consumer play well defined roles. However in a collaborative world, the producer and consumer work together to create new value as many electronic commerce sites have done with customer reviews and ratings. The corporate knowledge store is evolving and will continue to change as new technology and cultural traditions emerge. This chapter attempted to demonstrate how Web 2.0 technologies could be integrated into and replace knowledge stores. As collaborative products mature, this type of effort will become common place and set the stage for a truly collaborative experience. Knowledge management can no longer be static or producer of generated activity. In order to deliver value, new strategies are needed in utilizing the Web 2.0 technologies. Old strategies of knowledge management ensured that information was delivered to people when they needed it. Collaborative knowledge management enables the cocreation whereby information is emergent and integrated from the beginning.

References

Ahn, L., Davis, M., Fake, C., Fox, K., Furnas, G., Golder, S., et al. (2006). Why do tagging systems work? In *Proceedings of the SIGCHI Conference on Human Factors in computing systems*. Montreal, Canada: The Association of Computing Machinery.

Applehans, W., Globe, A., & Laugero, G. (1999). *Managing knowledge: A practical Web-based approach*. Boston: Addison-Wesley.

Baoill, A. (2004). Conceptualizing the Weblog: Understanding what it is in order to imagine what it can be. *Interfacings: Journal of Contemporary Media Studies, 5*(2), 1-8.

Blood, R. (2004). How blogging software reshapes the online community. *Communications of the ACM, 47*(12), 53-55.

Bock, G., & Qian, Z. (2005). An empirical study on measuring the success of knowledge repository systems. In *Proceedings of the 39th Annual Hawaii International Conference on System Sciences*. Kona, HI: Institute of Electrical and Electronics Engineers, Inc.

Boyd, D., Davis, M., Marlow, C., & Naaman, M. (2006). Social networks, networking & virtual communities: HT06, tagging paper, taxonomy, Flickr, academic article, to read. In *Proceedings of the Seventeenth Conference on Hypertext and Hypermedia*. Odense, Denmark: The Association of Computing Machinery.

Carr, N. (2003). *Does IT matter? Information technology and the corrosion of competitive advantage*. Boston: Harvard Business School Press.

Chellappa, R., & Gupta, A. (2002). Managing computing resources in active intranets. *International Journal of Network Management, 12*(2), 117-128.

Christodorescu, M., Ganapathy, V., Giffin, J., Kruger, L., Rubin, S., & Wang, H. (2005). An auctioning reputation system based on anomaly detection. In *Proceedings of the 12th ACM Conference on Computer and Communications Security*. Alexandria, VA: The Association of Computing Machinery.

Cold, S. (2006). Using really simple syndication (RSS) to enhance student research. *ACM SIGITE Newsletter, 3*(1), 6-9.

Conway, M. (1968). How do committees invent? *Datamation*, *14*(4), 28-31.

Davenport, T., & Prusak, L. (1997). *Information ecology: Mastering the information and knowledge environment*. New York: Oxford University Press.

Davis, J., Farnham, S., & Jensen, C. (2002). Finding others online: Reputation systems for social online spaces. In *Proceedings of the SIGCHI Conference on Human Factors in Computing Systems: Changing our World, Changing Ourselves*. Minneapolis, MN: The Association of Computing Machinery.

Dingsoyr, T., & Royrvik, E. (2003). An empirical study of an informal knowledge repository in a medium-sized software consulting company. In *Proceedings of the International Conference on Software Engineering*. Portland, OR: Institute of Electrical and Electronics Engineers, Inc.

Dutta, A., & Roy, R. (2006). Managing customer service levels and sustainable growth: A model for decision support. In *Proceedings of the 39th Annual Hawaii International Conference on System Sciences*. Kona, HI: Institute of Electrical and Electronics Engineers, Inc.

Gibson, F., Teasley, S., & Yew, J. (2006). Learning by tagging: Group knowledge formation in a self-organizing learning community. In *Proceedings of the 7th International Conference on Learning Sciences*. Bloomington, IA: The Association of Computing Machinery.

Grudin, J. (2006). Enterprise knowledge management and emerging technologies. In *Proceedings of the 39th Annual Hawaii International Conference on System Sciences*. Kona, HI: Institute of Electrical and Electronics Engineers, Inc.

Hof, R. (2005). Mix, match, and mutate. *Businessweek online*. Retrieved October 1, 2006, from http://www.businessweek.com/@@76IH*ocQ34AvyQMA/magazine/content/05_30/b3944108_mz063.htm

Hu, M., & Liu, B. (2004). Mining and summarizing customer reviews. In *Proceedings of the 10th Conference on Knowledge Discovery and Data Mining*. Seattle: The Association of Computing Machinery.

Hu, N., Pavlou, P., & Zhang, J. (2006). Can online reviews reveal a product's true quality?: Empirical findings and analytical modeling of online word-of-mouth communication. In *Proceedings of the 7th ACM Conference on Electronic Commerce*. Ann Arbor, MI: The Association of Computing Machinery.

Jhingran, A. (2006). Enterprise information mashups: Integrating information simply. In *Proceedings of the 32nd International Conference on Very Large Data Bases*. Seoul, Korea: The Association of Computing Machinery.

Johnston, B., & Supra, J. (1997). Toward an integrated approach to information services support. In *Proceedings of the 25th Annual ACM SIGUCCS Conference on User Services*. Monterey, CA: The Association of Computing Machinery.

Lerner, R. (2006). At the forge: Creating mashups. *Linux Journal, 147*, 10.

McNay, H. E. (2000). Corporate Intranets: Building communities with data. *IEEE Technology & Teamwork*, 197-201.

Millard, D., & Ross, M. (2006). Blogs, wikis & RSS: Web 2.0: hypertext by any other name? In *Proceedings of the Seventeenth Conference on Hypertext and Hypermedia*. Odense, Denmark: The Association of Computing Machinery.

O'Neill, M. (2005). Automated use of a wiki for collaborative lecture notes. In *Proceedings of the 36th SIGCSE Technical Symposium on Computer Science Education SIGCSE '05*. St. Louis, MO: The Association of Computing Machinery.

O'Reilly, T. (2005). *What Is Web 2.0: Design patterns and business models for the next generation of software*. Retrieved July 17, 2006, from http://www.oreillynet.com/pub/a/oreilly/tim/news/2005/09/30/what-is-Web-20.html

Reinhold, S. (2006). Wikitrails: Augmenting wiki structure for collaborative, interdisciplinary learning. In *Proceedings of the 2006 International Symposium on Wikis WikiSym '06*. Odense, Denmark: The Association of Computing Machinery.

Riehle, D. (2006). How and why wikipedia works: An interview with Angela Beesley, Elisabeth Bauer, and Kizu Naoko. In *Proceedings of the 2006 International Symposium on Wikis WikiSym '06*. Odense, Denmark: The Association of Computing Machinery.

Ross, J., & Weill, P. (2004). *IT governance: How top performers manage IT decision rights for superior results*. Watertown, MA: Harvard Business School Press.

Ruggles, R. (1997). *Knowledge management tools*. Boston: Butterworth-Heinemann.

Sewry, D., & Sunassee, N. (2003). A theoretical framework for knowledge management implementation. In *Proceedings of the 2002 Annual Research Conference of the South African Institute of Computer Scientists and Information Technologists on Enablement Through Technology*. Port Elizabeth, South Africa: The Association of Computing Machinery.

Smith, D., & Valdes, R. (2005). *Web 2.0: Get ready for the next old thing* (Gartner research paper). Stamford, CT.

Wagner, R., & Sternberg, R. (1985). Practical intelligence in real-world pursuits: The role of tacit knowledge. *Journal of Personality and Social Psychology, 49*(2), 436-58.

Weiss, A. (2005). The power of collective intelligence. *netWorker, 9*(3), 16-23.

Further Readings

Bughin, J., & Manyika, J. (2007). *How businesses are using Web 2.0: A McKinsey global survey*. Retrieved May 5, 2007, from http://www.mckinseyquarterly. com/article_page.aspx?ar=1913&L2=16&L3=16&srid=27&gp=0

Coyne, K., Schwartz, M., & Nielsen, J. (2006). *Intranet design annual 2007*. Fremont, CA: Nielson Norman Group.

Mangelsdorf, M. (2007). Beyond enterprise 2.0. *MIT Sloan Review, 48*(3), 50-55.

Mayfield, R. (2006). *Dresdner Kleinwort Wasserstein case study*. Retrieved April 19, 2007, from http://www.socialtext.com/files/DrKW%20Case%20Study.pdf

McAfee, A. (2006). Enterprise 2.0: The dawn of emergent collaboration. *MIT Sloan Review, 47*(3), 21-28.

Chapter VII

Knowledge Management and Organization Security Issues

James A. Sena, California Polytechnic State University, USA

Abstract

This chapter focuses on organization security issues in knowledge management. Security has always been a major corporate consideration. It must be ingrained in the firm's core processes. An organization's ability to learn from experience and translate ideas into action is key to sustaining competitive advantage. Under this context and prescribed purpose, technology and communication tools are the glue that allows the people to operate under the company's structure. The social impact of physical space, technology adjustment, and the change to the business environment is dictated by security restrictions and innovations in communication. This chapter addresses security by looking at technology tools, resource utilizers, and communication tools.

Introduction

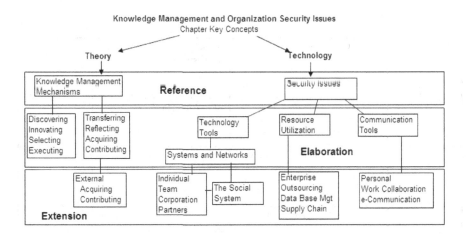

Background

Table 1 presents the primary literature references for this chapter.

Strategy and the Company's Environment

Business strategy has historically focused on the analysis of the company's industrial environment and its competitive positioning. Recently, the emphasis has shifted to the interface between strategy and the company's internal environment. Capabilities are key requisites for companies to make this shift. At the business level, development and organizing capabilities can be a source for competitive advantage. A key emerging issue is to match the company's capabilities with those opportunities that arise in the external environment. A company can use the business context, its current strategy, and capabilities to find better ways to develop internal mechanisms which ensure the continuity of these successful practices.

Foremost though is the deployment of security measures. These measures are threaded in the processes and fiber of the organization. Knowledge lives in the company through its employees (knowledge workers), as interwoven teams, and collectively across the organization. Figure 1 depicts the channels where knowledge is acquired, used, and disseminated. Security considerations arbitrate the management of knowledge

Table 1. Primary sources for literature review

Issue	Reference	Contribution
Organizational Learning	Chen (2005)	model containing nine organizational subsystems
	Christensen (1997)	examples of companies and the recognition of novel technologies
	Tushman and O'Reilly (1996).	coping in an external environment
	Van de Ven (1986)	difficulties in motivating people to attend to new ideas, needs and opportunities
	Morgan (1996)	consideration of external and internal environment as warning signals
Knowledge Management	Prahalad and Hamel (1990)	need to focus on core systems
	Nonaka and Takeuchi (1995)	companies should be knowledge-creating—becoming innovation factories—breakthrough innovation projects require a commitment of financial and human resources
Security Issues	Bell (2003)	businesses that have tried to introduce complicated global matrix management structures—where employees formally have several lines of reporting—team-based benefits have failed to fully materialize
	Jensen and Xiao (2001)	peer-to-peer networking might not automatically maintain accountability when false or misleading information is spread
	Friedman (2005)	few companies can afford to develop and support a complex global supply chain

throughout the organization. Communication tools are the facilitators and potential sources of security compromise.

Figure 1. Knowledge channels

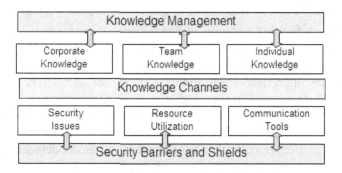

Knowledge Management Mechanisms

Recent studies on organizational learning and organizational learning mechanisms have sharpened the focus on design principles and processes. Learning mechanisms for knowledge management are core concepts for designing and sustaining knowledge management processes and performance. Knowledge management mechanisms are formal configurations: structures, processes, procedures, rules, tools, methods, and physical and technological-based for developing, enhancing, and sustaining knowledge creation, knowledge management, and enhancing the company's performance.

Much progress has been made in the organizational learning field, including pioneering work (e.g., Argyris & Schon, 1978; Argyris & Schon, 1996; Cyert & March, 1963; DeGeus, 1997; Garvin, 1993; Garvin, 2000; Huber, 1991; Levitt & March, 1988; Senge, 1990). Enhancing organizational learning capability is a difficult and challenging task. Practical methods (such as models and corresponding practices/tools) are needed to support an organization's learning capabilities (Chen, 2005).

Writers in innovation management and organizational learning have identified many problems that established organizations face in recognizing breakthrough opportunities. Christensen (1997) provides some examples of leading companies that have been unable to recognize novel *technologies* developed in or external to their organizations, for the future of their own industries and markets. Van de Ven (1986) notes that the more successful an organization is, the more difficult it is to *motivate* people to attend to new ideas, needs, and opportunities. Tushman and O'Reilly (1996) note the need to *manage current operations* and simultaneously develop dramatically new and different ones to cope with turbulent environments.

These writings focus on the dual importance of the individual and the organizational context, that is, the role of the creative individual in seeing and championing an opportunity, and the role of organizational context to ease and support creativity.

An organization's learning system is embedded in its human resources, structure, process, policy, and culture. The greater an organization's learning capability, the greater the possibility that it will maintain sustainable existence and development. Based on this definition, nine organizational learning subsystems were proposed by Chen (2005). These subsystems are (1) "discovering," (2) "innovating," (3) "selecting," (4) "executing," (5) "transferring," (6) "reflecting," (7) "acquiring knowledge from the environment," (8) "contributing knowledge to the environment," and (9) "building organizational memory." In this chapter the system model was modified to include *acquiring* and *contributing* knowledge *to* and *from* the company's business partners along its supply chain and customer interface (CRM). Figure 2 depicts the steps in this model. The various data banks, depicted as cylinders, show deployment and subsets about and from the enterprise information system. The steps contribute to the building of organizational memory. The databases are the repository of this memory. The demilitarized zone (DMZ) is the secure database available to the firm's partners but separate from the internal systems of the organization.

Changes in the firm's external and internal environment drive organizational learning. Organization members may not be aware of these changes. The organization needs to

Figure 2. Organizational learning model

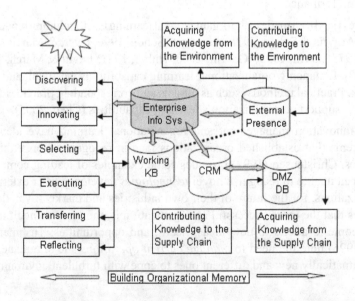

build a **discovering subsystem** enabling it to sense and monitor changes, problems, challenges, and opportunities in its internal and external environment, and to provide early warning signals of shifting trends (Morgan, 1996). Only through conscious and systematic monitoring and analysis can an organization retain its sensitivity to environmental changes. From a security perspective this discovery system needs to be shielded from outside forces that could compromise the organization.

In order for an organization to develop and thrive, it must focus on its core competencies and develop new products and services. This is accomplished by improving management process and systems (Prahalad & Hamel, 1990). According to Nonaka and Takeuchi (1995), companies should be knowledge-creating by becoming innovation factories. Introducing breakthrough innovation projects require a commitment of financial and human resources. Investment is often staged, rather than committed for the entire development path. Higher-level technical and business managers along with external partners frequently engage in opportunity recognition as a triggering mechanism for the opportunity evaluation process leading to decision making about commitment of resources. The research manager, as the first to identify the opportunity, acts as the catalyst to set off this chain reaction in which technical and business managers engage in the opportunity recognition process.

Discovering and innovating, an organization must construct a system enabling it to make the right choices among innovative ideas. An organization should develop sound **selecting** methodologies, processes, activities, and capabilities so that a better business decision can be made and more qualified and suitable people recruited and promoted.

Electronic information seeking can be a highly complex and ill-defined decision process. Information seekers are faced with a wide array of information sources and options which they must access, reject, or interrogate during their selection of information sources. Cues drawn from these information sources, and from other motivational sources, such as self-regulatory responses, performance feedback, and environmental influences, may all lead to changing strategies as the task is continued.

Organizational learning not only includes changes of perception and thinking (such as discovering, innovating, and selecting), but also changes of behavior. No action means no real learning. Executing new ideas is not easy. The "**executing**" subsystem is important for organizational learning. The successful organization is the one that can make things happen and use knowledge learned to make a difference. Individuals and team learnings best ideas, practices, and experience achieved by individuals, teams, or departments should be **transferred** to the rest of the organization. From a security perspective the social network needs to be managed to filter these transfers.

The reason to build a "**reflecting**" subsystem is for an organization to learn from past experience. It does not matter whether the experience was successful or unsuccessful; the organization can use the formal reflecting subsystem to make a better decision for the future. Reflecting is derived from "learning from failure" and "learning from success." To survive, an organization should be an open system with a continuous exchange of energy, information, and knowledge within its environment. This **acquiring** system is crucial for an organization's ability to learn faster and build competitive advantage, especially in a new environment.

An organization should build its own **knowledge base** where documents, work reports, academic journals, magazine, books, and newspapers are stored electronically and mechanically. An organization should design its Intranet system to accommodate individual and organizational knowledge. Not only should an organization **acquire knowledge from outside**, but also **contribute to the outside**, especially sharing and exchanging information with its business partners along its supply chain. For some organizations, such as universities, schools, consulting companies, and so on, providing knowledge service is the reason for their existence. Other organizations such as manufacturing companies do this as well. Contributing knowledge can improve an organization's reputation, and, from the perspective of learning, can give the organization feedback opportunities about its management and performance.

With the growing complexity of the environment, **organizational memory** is increasingly needed for continuous learning. When knowledge generated by the other subsystems is stored in organizational memory, the stored knowledge also affects these subsystems. If an organization fails to set up organizational memory to retain knowledge, the loss means that great-organizational learning cannot be constantly upgraded and further learning cannot occur. Good experience cannot be exploited and failure may be repeated.

The Impact of Security Issues on Knowledge Management

Most organizational knowledge is stored in digital form "somewhere" as depicted in the data banks in Figure 2. Beyond these formal corporate mechanisms are data stored in a wide variety of places and media. A company often has data stored on the workstations of all workers in and beyond the boundaries of the company. Work group and collaboration teams have data stored on local and virtual networks. Communication occurs in a wide variety of modes such as e-mail, messaging, voice mail, the telephone, and direct contact. Most of these data sources can also be saved in digital form, the company's digital assets. Without the knowledge to defend its digital assets, the company is lost, and these potential losses can grow everyday as employees, suppliers, and customers continue to pour the contents of their personal and business lives into databases, PDAs, personal computers, and

Web servers through routers, hubs, switches, cell phones, gateways, copper, coax, and the air itself. The paradigm has shifted in recent years to the seemingly ever expanding distributed Internet and the World Wide Web (WWW).

Recent events have led companies to regard security, especially information security, as a significant focus in the way they conduct their business. Most businesses today have at least a rudimentary security program in place, and many programs are growing in maturity. As these programs mature there is a need to move beyond the view that security is just a technical issue. *Security* today should be part of the fabric of a business. In doing so, information security programs need to move from tactical implementations of technology to strategic partners in business. Although many companies have committed to developing information security program they may not have integrated them into the framework of their businesses. Security is a *barrier and a protective shield* for the company.

Given the variety of knowledge flow and the need for security, organizations face a daunting task to manage their knowledge in today's work place. In this chapter, security issues are addressed through looking at technology tools, resource "utilizers," and communication tools.

Technology Tools

Technology tools are the instruments, models, techniques, and processes that transform and support the business products and service. These tools are embedded in all business levels. Not only are they part of the business but they emanate externally through social networks, the customer, and supply chain interfaces to the outside world. Figure 3 relates the technology tools to the knowledge management system as they operate in the organization and interfaces to the external environment.

Figure 3. Security and technology tools

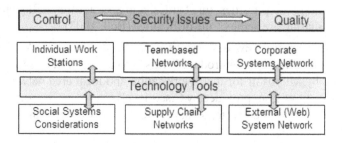

The Individual Work Station

The first line of defense is the individual worker. Most companies have an in-place security system for the desktop and its interface to the corporate system either directly or through some form of local area network. The typical organization has a PC-based workstations, most of which use Microsoft products. Microsoft, and other end-user software products, provides the means to control the deployment of each workstation through user identification, rights and permissions, and access control lists. These controls are extended to the local and corporate environment in which the workstations are housed.

There is no substitute for employee awareness, *the social aspect,* and commitment to adhere and support the company's security policy. Over two-thirds of all security breaches occur from inside the organization. Attackers' motivation emanate from a variety of reasons. One reason may be employee resentment where an employee harbors feelings of mistreatment by the company and that the company "owes" the employee in some way. There are instances of the internal hacker curiously testing personal skills by trying to gain unauthorized access not for revenge but just to experiment. Many workers have the ability to bypass the physical and logical controls put in place to protect the perimeter of the company's network and have obtained credentials to access a significant part of its infrastructure. As no company can exist without employees, it is inevitable reality that some individuals are potential security risks. People will always be susceptible to manipulation, but it is possible to combat this to an extent with proper training and awareness along with other security measures.

The Team-Based Network

Team working is vital to the success of the organization. Even for those that work in the same office, it can be challenging at times. With an organization's employees working across different continents and time zones, a friendly face-to-face chat around the water cooler is not always an option. In businesses that have tried to introduce complicated global matrix management structures—where employees formally have several lines of reporting—team-based benefits have failed to fully materialize. Conflicting priorities, turf battles, a loss of accountability, and a lack of knowledge-sharing are some of the difficulties (Bell, 2003).

Security assumes several new dimensions when local area networks (LANs) or wide area network (WANs) are introduced. This second line of defense includes the tools provided by Microsoft for their workstation and local area network and the network security provisions provided by Cisco-level measures (Cisco Inc. being the primary provider of WAN and Internet hardware and software). As the workstation is connected to routers and switches, each interface can be individually controlled to allow access based on the user, the type of protocol being used, and, the network or subnetwork of origin or destination. It is more difficult to compromise such measures.

Workgroups use common databases and other software tools to develop and conduct the work product for the company. These databases can and should be protected from illegitimate access and modification. As with the individual workstation, each database (e.g., from the basic Microsoft Access to the Corporate Level Oracle database management system) has provisions to define users and groups with rights and permissions. It is important that there be coordination among the security providers for the workstation, network, and data management to insure consistent and synchronized management.

Corporate System Network

As companies adopt business-critical enterprise applications such as customer relationship management (CRM), enterprise resource planning (ERP), collaboration applications, and electronic workflows, eavesdropping on the internal network traffic could become a lucrative option to would-be hackers. Security breaches could exploit the vulnerabilities in information. When introducing technical countermeasures to manage risks to unprotected business application communications, the main security services that the information security solution should bring are: *confidentiality* of communications to prevent eavesdropping of sensitive information; *data integrity* to prevent the undetected access and change of information in transit; *authentication* to ease reliable verification of user identity before providing access to business applications; and authorization for information users.

Social System Considerations

By recognizing threats the company established its second line of defense: supplementing the first line of defense of network security. It is up to the employee to choose to exercise security precautions. It is also important to set up a clear reporting process for security problems. Proper education and reinforcement help establish a culture of safety. Security training classes check lists; new employee training, security audits, and random test calls are steps to address this need. A good security policy should include instructions on user network access control and approval, setting up new user accounts, and account password changes. Others include Intranet security procedures, locks, IDs, shredding of important company documents, storage of important company documents, and most importantly, after-hours or weekend company policies.

The Corporate Network Infrastructure

There are three logical (and possibly physical) parts to the corporate network infrastructure: including the Intranet, Extranet, and the Internet. Each of these parts are separated/isolated/ protected by/from some form of firewall. The Intranet is the secure layer where the internal operations of the company are conducted. The Extranet is the less secure layer where the company conducts its commerce with its partners along the supply chain. The Internet is the unsecured environment where the company communicates with the business world and the general consumer.

With Internet use, information, sometimes including security information, becomes accessible to the general public. Because the Internet is a public network, anyone on the Net could potentially "see" other systems. At first this was not a major issue because sensitive information was not easily accessible. As use of the Internet grew, companies permitted access to information and networks over the Internet.

Peer-to-peer network software adds new problems since monitoring distributed network files is like monitoring millions of telephone conversations every minute of every day. There are also concerns over copyrights, privacy, repudiation, and data integrity and credibility. First, copyrights might be violated as the provider might not be acknowledged when information is consumed by users. Second, as users access data on others' computers on the network, there is a great danger that the provider's privacy might be invaded. Peer-to-peer networking might not automatically maintain accountability when false or misleading information is spread. This also damages the credibility and integrity of the shared information. (Jensen & Xiao, 2001).

As information security awareness and incursions emerged companies invested more extensively to protect corporate networks against various external threats such as hackers, e-mail viruses, and network worms coming from the public Internet. The corresponding security techniques, antivirus solutions, firewall, and virtual private networks (VPNs), collectively called perimeter security, provided protection between the nontrusted Internet and the trusted internal network. This perimeter security provided adequate network security when the internal network could be assumed to be trusted.

Resource Utilization

Business and environmental complexity is one reason that few companies have established close connections between their strategy, sustainability, and learning. An essential element in creating business sustainability is the establishment of flexible organizational learning mechanisms. The strategist(s) and the designer(s) have the responsibility to create effective learning mechanisms. A company may require a few years to turn its economy around, while a technology shift may take longer.

It can take even longer to develop new key competencies, not only in individual companies but more specifically at the industry level. Developing the competence to handle a new technology can take much longer in an entire industry than in the individual leading companies.

Companies need to develop a strategy to deploy and protect their resources. Since each company is a unique collection of highly differentiated resources and capabilities the choices about the ways to deploy and protect them will drive profitability and sustainability (see Figure 4). Much of the managers' work is likely to shift away from structure and planning to create flexible learning mechanisms. An organization's internal ability to learn from experience, assimilate new ideas, and translate them into action is key in sustaining competitive advantage. Some argue that the company's ability to learn faster than its competition is a critical source for competitive advantage. Outsourcing by American companies has become a way of doing business. Outsourcing and strategic sourcing are means for companies to compete strategically in the global marketplace. Through collaboration, joint venture, or strategic alliance, an organization can acquire knowledge from and contribute knowledge to its partners. More Western and Eastern companies collaborate to do business in the global market (Chen, 2005). An organizational Web site open to the public is one of the important windows through which outside people view the firm.

Supply Chain Interface

Supply chain management supports the information flow among the stages in a supply chain. The interface consists of four components: the strategy for managing resources to meet customer demand for all products and services; the partners chosen to deliver finished products, raw materials, and services (includes pricing, delivery, and payment process along with partner relationship monitoring); scheduling for

Figure 4. Security and resource utilization

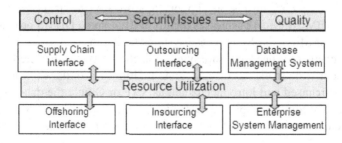

production activities (includes testing, packaging, and preparation for delivery); and the product delivery processes and elements (includes orders, warehouses, carriers, returns, and invoicing.)

There are many approaches to the management of the supply chain. Foremost is an Extranet to insure the secure communication with the firm's business partners. There are extremes such as Wal-Mart where their major suppliers adopt a specific information system structure as a requirement to do business with them. Most banks share a common interface to credit card system providers. Department stores have similar, but less secure, interfaces to either the banks or the credit card system providers. Some companies contract with another firm such as UPS to handle their supply line including transportation, repair service, warehousing, and scheduling.

Outsourcing Interface

It is unlikely that a company is an expert in every aspect of their business (Overrell, 2004). Core competence is the goal. Technology has cut sharply the costs of communication to the extent that outsourcing of many information technology activities is becoming increasingly standard. So strong is this trend that outsourcing specialists also tend to outsource several further specialized aspects of a task to others. The result, in practical terms, is that organizations are maintaining many more relationships. These companies are in the age of the "middleman."

A major concern is protecting intellectual property (IP) and security. Companies often are more focused on cost savings and gaining productivity without taking into account security issues. Although countries such as India have patent, copyright, and IP protection laws, these laws are often difficult to enforce. IBM has expanded their business model to provide information technology, facilities management, and contract services. EDS and IBM provide these services to many U.S.-based firms. The companies go to great lengths to insure stable linkages and transparency for the contracted firms.

Database Management System

The information systems core is the supporting software (the data base management system [DBMS]). Most businesses deploy and use some DBMS product such as Oracle SQL or Microsoft SQL. These systems tend to have a life of their own. Earlier in this chapter the need to insure synchronization between the heterogeneous parts of the security network was discussed. As multimillion dollar enterprise-wide products are purchased and introduced such as SAP or Oracle the database management system becomes complex. Transaction processing systems and integrated business systems are assumed. Data warehouses, data mining, business intelligence, and knowledge discovery systems are widely used and contribute to the firm's competitive position. The DBMS is the foundation for these information systems. Proper security to control and enable these suprasystems may be beyond the role of the firm's data base administration group. Formal on-going communication and coordination needs to be established with the existent information systems support, the ERP provider, and the firm's corporate security officer (CSO).

Offshoring Interface

Technology has enabled companies to construct virtual teams with members from different locations. There are various ways to communicate when offshore companies perform company tasks. One is through e-mail, or online discussions. In this method the sender and receiver can communicate at their own pace. Compared to real-time communication such as video and audio conferencing where people can see and hear each other, gestures and voice tones can be misinterpreted. One side of the conferencing may be speaking in a foreign language; their slowness in speech could be misinterpreted as lower intelligence or lack of attention or enthusiasm. In this case using e-mail would be a better method of communication. Another issue with offshore interaction is the time differences. Because the time of day affects fatigue, hunger, and attitudes about finishing early and starting a weekend, one may run into different attitudes from remote team members.

Insourcing Interface

Insourcing is a common approach using the professional knowledge in an organization to develop and maintain the organization's information technology and knowledge management systems. It has been instrumental in creating a supply of knowledge management professionals and a better quality workforce by enabling learning mechanisms through enhanced technical and business skills. Insourcing not only takes advantage of its internal knowledge management resource for the company's business but extends the business of the company to include knowledge and information technology management services for other companies. It (Friedman, 2005) is a whole new form of collaboration and creating value horizontally. Few companies can afford to develop and support a complex global supply chain such as that developed by Wal-Mart. Insourcing by large companies is a phenomenon that allows small companies to be transparent in size by outsourcing some of their business processes to other companies that specialize in selected areas. IBM is the leading provider of outsourced information technology management and UPS went into the business of "synchronized commerce solutions" spending $1 billion to buy 25 different global logistics and freight-forwarding companies that could service many supply chains worldwide. Through these intense collaborations, IBM and UPS provide trust and intimacy to their clients and the client's customers.

IBM's IT outsourcing capabilities have helped corporations address business risks. When information technology departments are not centralized the threats of in-house system failures, outages, and security breaches are lessened. IBM's business transformation services have also helped companies become more productive by outsourcing technical support centers. As an example, the employees of a financial investment company can call the company's overseas technical support desk for departmental computer problems cutting the need for in-house IT tech support.

Enterprise System Management

Enterprise resource planning (ERP) integrates all departments and business functions into an IT system to support company-wide decisions. At this level managers and knowledge workers have access to all business operations-related information. Throughout the organization computer hardware, software and telecommunications provide the underlying foundation to support the organization's goals. ERP provides a unified approach to manage these separate pieces. Several integration tools are needed for enterprise system management. These tools include Intranets and enterprise/company-wide information portals. An Intranet is the internalized part of the system. The portals are the knowledge workers' interface to the supply chain, company's partners (DMZ), and the Internet.

The Companies Communication Tools

Organizational processes, such as work design, creativity and innovation, culture, learning, and change are considered in organizational design. The way the organization is designed and coordinated affects the achievement of its goals. Many factors influence the behavior and performance of the organization, including the context, purpose, people, and structure as they interface with the core transformation and management support processes to set up the organization's performance level. The glue that brings these together is the company's *communication tool,* as depicted in Figure 5.

The social impact of physical space, technology adjustment, and the change to the business environment are a result of innovations in communication. Behavioral changes in human interaction and behavior need to be addressed. The impact of the enablement of e-mail on the organization is an opportunity and a threat. The attacker can use several sources of communication to create some type of relation-

Figure 5. Security and communication tools

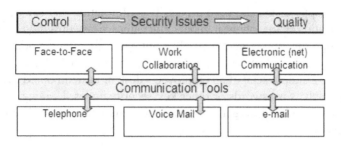

ship with the victim. The attacker may combine methods of communication to fool the victim into divulging sensitive information. Just as anyone would keep in touch with their friends, the attacker communicates with the employee. The normal communication medium are telephone, e-mail, trash/dumpster, and over the shoulder (face-to-face).

At first the Internet served as a communication platform connecting end users and computers. Today, the Internet provides a broad range of business functionality, including marketing, sales and transactions, customer service, and other business applications. As a result, building and maintaining e-business infrastructure has become more complex, time-consuming, and expensive. Current e-business implementations involve integration and management of many components, including server hardware, networking elements, software, storage, security, and system monitoring.

The *telephone* is the most popular method of communication. An attacker could call a strategically chosen employee at a specific time. The attacker would strike during the times when people are most vulnerable, such as on a Friday afternoon or just before the end of the day when people rush to get out of the office. In the right circumstances employees will divulge information when normally they might not.

The *e-mail* method is not as popular because the success rate is not as great as the telephone. The attacker can ask for the same information in an e-mail as the attacker would ask on the telephone, and may get a response. The attacker can also include a backdoor virus, which an employee could inadvertently click open. This can be done using instant messaging as well, where an attacker sends a convincing message along with an attachment.

In the *dumpster* case there is no direct communication between the attacker and employees. Because people are usually careless about what they throw away, attackers can physically get this information by searching through someone's trash. Trash can contain paper print outs, old hardware, and discarded memory such as DVDs, CDs, floppy disks, and flash drives. The information that can be found includes organization charts, phone numbers, full names, passwords, notes, and so on. The information found may seem unusable, but when the offender collects all the needed pieces and uses it to their advantage it can become detrimental. Even over the shoulder or a simple scan of an employee's desk or bulletin board can provide information, such as passwords or other key security codes. Leaving a computer unattended to take a break or get a cup of coffee could be a potential opportunity for the attacker.

To coax the employee the attacker may take roles, including posing as an authority figure, a technician, an end user, or a new employee. An employee will trust a relevant authority figure such as an IT administrator. Authority is normally not questioned out of respect or fear. This includes other figures; similar to authority are telecom technicians or individuals who would have physical access to the company's data systems. Attackers can also play the role of a partner organization because it seems relevant for them to ask for financial information to perform needed business tasks.

Conclusion

Adding to the complexity of information security is that organizations must enable employees, customers, and partners to access information electronically to be successful in this electronic world, enabling learning. Doing business electronically automatically creates tremendous information security risks and, simultaneously, opportunities for enhanced corporate knowledge. The main issue surrounding information technology and the deployment of learning mechanisms is not technical but people.

Insiders—employees (knowledge workers), suppliers, and partners—can purposely or accidentally misuse their access to the corporate system and its surrounding knowledge environment. The company needs to identify rules and specify an information security plan that details how to implement their information security policy. The next step is to communicate this policy to all employees and stakeholders by setting clear expectations. On the positive side these communications extend learning and provide rich sources for learning and new methods of acquisition and discovery.

The second line of defense for security is technology. Once an organization has protected its intellectual capital by arming its people with a detailed security plan, it can start to focus its effort on deploying technologies to authenticate and authorize, for prevention and resistance, and detection and response. By design the company needs to establish a network framework encompassed by firewall hardware and software to guard its private networks, to filter information to and from its partners, suppliers, and customers, and to securely interface to the Internet world. The establishment of a secure environment between the companies supply chain, partners, and customers not only safeguards the company's knowledge base but ensures opportunities to extend and share working knowledge.

References

Argyris, C., & Schon, D. A. (1978). *Organizational learning: A theory of action perspective*. Reading, MA: Addison-Wesley.

Argyris, C., & Schon, D. A. (1996). *Organizational learning II: Theory, method and practice*. Reading, MA: Addison-Wesley.

Bell, S. (2003). Remote control: Global team working promises huge benefits for organizations. *Human Resources, 44*.

Chen, G. (2005). Management practices and tools for enhancing learning capabilities. *SAM Advanced Management Journal, 70*.

Christensen, C. M. (1997). *The innovator's dilemma: When new technologies cause great companies to fail*. Boston: Harvard Business School Press.

Cyert, R. M., & March, J. (1963). *A behavioral theory of the company*. Englewood Cliffs, NJ: Prentice-Hall.

DeGeus, A. (1997). *The living company*. Boston: Harvard Business School Press.

Friedman, T. L. (2005). *The world is flat: A brief history of the twenty-first century*. New York: Farrar, Straus, and Giroux.

Garvin (1993). Building a learning organization. *Harvard Business Review*, 78-91.

Garvin (2000). *Learning in action: A guide to putting the learning organization to work*. Boston: Harvard Business School Press.

Huber, G. P. (1991). Organizational learning: The contributing process and the literature. *Organizational Science, 2*, 88-115.

Jensen, R., & Xiao, J. (2001). Customizing financial reporting, networked databases, and distributed file sharing. *Accounting Horizons, 15*(3), 209-222.

Levitt, B., & March, J. G. (1988). Organizational learning. *Annual Review of Sociology, 14*, 319-340.

Morgan, G. (1996). *Images of organizations*. Newbury Park: Sage.

Nonaka, L., & Takeuchi, H. (1995). *The knowledge creating company: How Japanese companies create dynamic innovation*. New York: Oxford University Press.

Overrell, S. (2004). Knowledge that gets to the business core. *Financial Times Management.*

Prahalad, C. K., & Hamel, G. (1990). The core competence of the organization. *Harvard Business Review, 68,* 181-196.

Senge, P. M. (1990). *The fifth discipline: The art and practice of the learning organization.* New York: Doubleday Currency.

Tushman, M. L., & O'Reilly, C. A. (1996). Ambidextrous organizations: Managing evolutionary and revolutionary change. *California Management Review, 38*(4), 8-30.

Van de Ven, A. H. (1986). Central problems in the management of innovation. *Management Science, 32*(5), 590-607.

Case: Reality Check on Organization Security: What is Happening

The major part of this case was taken directly from an article in *CIO* written by Alan Holmes (Sep 15, 2006.Vol.19, Iss. 23) entitled "The Global State of Information Security 2006 ; Some things are getting better, slowly, but security practices are still immature and, in some cases, regressing."

Introduction

According to the "The Global State of Information Security 2006," survey information executives, still relatively new to security's disciplines, are learning and improving but are still prone to risky behaviors, behaviors that could have devastating consequences. The study by CIO, CSO, and Price-waterhouse-Coopers (PwC), with 7,791 respondents in 50 countries, indicates that an increasing number of executives (CEOs, CFOs, CIOs, CSOs, and VPs and directors of IT and information security) across all industries and in private- and public-sector organizations continue to make incremental improvements in deploying information security policies and technologies, although the rate of improvement is slower than in previous years.

The survey shows us that most executives with security responsibilities have made little or no progress in implementing strategic security measures that could have prevented many of the security mishaps reported this year. Only 37% of respondents said they have an overall security strategy and that they are planning to focus more on tactical fixes than on strategic initiatives, ensuring that in the coming year they will be more reactive than proactive.

One of the most unsettling findings in this year's study is the sad state of security in India, by a wide margin, the world's primary locus for IT outsourcing. The problem is less with the outsourcing companies themselves than with the dangerous waters they swim in. Many respondents from India admit to not adhering to the most routine security practices.

Harder to ignore is the news of large organizations losing laptops packed with unencrypted personal data on millions of customers. Such incidents should motivate companies to tighten security, but every year the survey indicates that is not happening. Similarly, even after Hurricane Katrina, which hit the Gulf Coast, a majority of companies still did not have a business continuity/disaster recovery plans in place; plans to complete one this year have become less important to security officials than in previous years.

There is evidence that organizations that comply with security laws are more likely to be integrating and aligning security with their enterprise's business strategy and processes, which in turn reduces the number of successful attacks and the financial losses that result from them. In short, security can create value if it is part of an organization's business plan and if the executive in charge is part of the executive team making those strategic spending and policy decisions.

Strategic Concerns

The 2006 survey shows that a few more companies than last year are thinking about security strategically, at least in some areas. A larger percentage of companies are aligning security objectives with business objectives (20% of respondents said they align all security spending with their business objectives, up from 15% in 2004) and are prioritizing data sets based on the sensitivity of the information contained in each application. They are then protecting those sets with the appropriate amount of security (25% in 2006, up from 21% in 2004).

More companies are integrating physical and information security. The percentage of organizations that reported having some form of integration between physical and information security has grown rapidly from 29% in 2003 to 75% in 2006. A similar spike occurred in the percentage of respondents saying their physical and information security chiefs report to the same executive leader (40% from 11% in 2003).

Why is that Important?

To answer that, one needs look no further than the daily newspaper stories about lost and stolen laptops containing private customer information. Just ask the U.S.

Department of Veterans Affairs and AIG, both of which were involved this spring in high-profile cases of stolen laptops. With physical and information security combined, fewer laptops may be lost. And if they are lost or stolen, that combination should make gaining access to the data stored in them nearly impossible.

Outsourcing Concerns

India lags far behind the rest of the world in instituting even the most basic information security practices and tools, with the subcontinent claiming status as the outsourcing partner of choice for the biggest IT powerhouses in the world (49% of all offshore outsourcing implementations are located in India, with up to 90% of worldwide outsourcing revenue going to India).

The widespread absence of even the most routine security tools has left many Indian companies vulnerable to serious attacks and the inevitable financial losses that follow. Extortion, fraud, and intellectual property theft occurred last year at 1 in every 5 or 6 Indian companies, rates that are double and even quadruple those of the rest of the world. Nearly 1 in 3 Indian organizations suffered some financial loss because of a cyber attack last year, compared with 1 out of 5 worldwide and 1 out of 8 in the United States.

What Steps Might a Firm take if they Contemplate Outsourcing Information Services to India?

1. *Suggest taking a cautious tack before jumping into an outsourcing relationship. The first step companies should take when considering outsourcing work to India is to verify that an Indian-based unit's security processes and policies are of the same caliber as its U.S. unit.*

2. *Conduct a risk assessment of the Indian unit's security practices. Even if an Indian organization says that it follows a familiar, specific security practice, do not presume the organization defines the practice the same way; conducting background checks may mean something entirely different in India than it does in the U.S.*

The Strategy Gap

From the top dozen items on the 2006 security to-do list, seven can be described as a technological fix. Among the top 5 are some of the more routine and easy security measures, including data backup, network firewalls, application firewalls, and instituting user passwords. The percent of companies reporting they have an overall strategic plan in place was unchanged at 37%.

At the very least, some of the shifts are perplexing. Dropping from the top spot in 2005 to 4th place this year is the development of a business continuity and disaster recovery plan. That is a surprising result given Hurricane Katrina's reminder of the importance of such plans. But news coverage about disasters and security breaches may not be a driver for security investments. Our prediction that last year's 10th item on the information security to-do list—spending on IP protection—would move up because of the sharp increase in high-profile identity thefts and the increase in the amount of digitized content (such as iTunes) did not occur. IP protection did not even make the 2006 top 10 list. Even some of the simpler and less costly strategic security practices dropped. Conducting employee awareness training dropped from 2nd to a tie for 10th on the priority list.

What's Happening? Why has Strategic Planning for Security become an Afterthought?

One answer may be that in an information vacuum (information security executives report that they are unsure of their budgets, where attacks have come from and where they will find people with the skills they need), short-term solutions seem more prudent than long-range ones. Information security managers may speak geek; a bridge is needed between the technology and the risk that firm faces to help them make decisions.

What is Needed for Information Security to be most Effective?

For information security to be most effective, aligning the technological processes with the organization's strategic plan is critical. Companies should make security part of their strategic plan,

Compliance-Is it Taking Place

A surprising portion of survey respondents admitted that they are not in compliance with the information security laws and regulations that govern their industries. Noncompliance runs broad and deep in all industries, and ignorance of applicable law is a big factor. Nearly 1 in 5 U.S. survey respondents said they should be but are not in compliance with California's 2002 security breach law, which requires companies to notify individuals if an unauthorized person obtains access to their private information (such as credit card numbers). But only 22% of all U.S. respondents said the law applies to them. However, given that the law applies to any organization that has even one California resident as a customer, student, or client (more than in 10 Americans) a good portion of the 78% of enterprises that think the law does not apply to them are likely wrong.

What is at the Root of this Noncompliance Problem?

At the root of this may be a lack of enforcement. To date, the cost of noncompliance is not as high as the expense of complying (i.e., the price of labor, hardware and software). In the absence of penalties, security executives have not been able to mount a business case for compliance. Add to that the fact that despite high profile security breaches and lost laptops over the past year, the actual damages and ID thefts that can be directly tied to the incidents are small, as they used to be," he says, and so not complying with laws is perceived as less risky.

Organizations should assign penalties for not complying with their own security policies; the penalty needs to match the infraction

Is the Security Plan Working?

A large percentage of security leaders worldwide have no idea if their security plans are working because they do not know any of these numbers. Attacks can be hard to identify, and networks can be extensive. What is less comprehensible is that a significant portion of respondents said they have not installed some of the most rudimentary network safeguards. More than 20% of respondents do not even have a network firewall.

How do you Calculate the loss of Intellectual Property or the Damage to a Corporate Reputation?

Until the security department can put a credible dollar figure on what the company is losing because of poor security, the boardroom is not going to listen to security executives asking for more money to spend on technology or on skilled security workers (cited as the top resources needed to improve security). The CEO wants to know how security affects shareholder value. Answering that would require a strategic overview but security professionals, by and large, do not have one.

Useful URLs

www.WindowsSecurity.com

www.Searchsecurity.techtarget.com

www.itworld.com

For a comprehensive review/portal of information systems literature including publications, books, whitepapers, and magazines see www.brint.com

Further Readings

Belsis, P., & Kokolakis, S. (2005). Information systems security from a knowledge management perspective. *Information Management & Computer Security, 13*(3).

Davis, B. J. (2005). PREPARE: Seeking systemic solutions for technological crisis management. *Knowledge and Process Management, 12*(2), 123-131. Retrieved January 10, 2008, from www.interscience.wiley.com

Hong, K.-S., Chi, Y.-P., Cho, L. R., & Tang, J.-H. (2003). An integrated systems theory of information security management. *Information Management and Security, 11*(5).

Kokolakis, S. A., Demopoulos, A. J., & Kiountouzis, E. A. (2000). The use of business process modelling in information systems security analysis and design. *Information Management & Computer Security, 8*(3).

Kwok, L., & Longley, D. (1999). Information security management and modeling. *Information Management & Computer Security, 7*(1).

Peter, R. J. (2005). Trim: Managing computer security issues: Preventing and limiting future threats and disasters. *Disaster Prevention and Management, 14*(4).

Chapter VIII

Enterprise Knowledge Management for Emergent Organizations:
An Ontology-Driven Approach

Mariel Alejandra Ale, CIDISI, UTN – FRSF, Argentina

Omar Chiotti, INGAR, CONICET, Argentina

Maria Rosa Galli, INGAR, CONICET, Argentina

Abstract

Lately, some knowledge management (KM) solutions suggest strategies to identify and acquire the invaluable organizational knowledge. These statements seem especially true in the case of emergent organizational forms for which the beginning of the new century has brought about a paradigm change in which capital and work are no longer the only fundamental bases for successful management. Although this has caught the attention of both the industrialists and researchers, an important gap exists between these two domains, mainly due to the lack of understanding of the KM concept and the activities that it implies by organizational managers.

Several KM models have appeared in the research field, but none of them includes all the necessary aspects for an effective KM. This chapter presents a distributed knowledge management conceptual model that encompasses the key factors for KM in emergent organizations and proposes the means to implement them. Moreover, to address heterogeneity, documentation overload and lack of context, we propose onto-DOM, a question-answering ontology-based strategy within a distributed organizational memory (DOM).

Introduction

Nowadays, few would question the validity of the assertion that we currently live in a knowledge-based society. Organizational experts agree that knowledge is one of the most important resources that contribute to the competitive advantage of an organization but, at the same time, is a multifaceted concept with multilayered meanings. It has also been argued that only those organizations that can develop best practices for managing this complex concept of knowledge will be the ones to ride today's "competitive wave" (Sarker, Sarker, Nicholson, & Joshi, 2005).

These statements seem especially true in the case of emergent organizational forms for which the beginning of the new century has brought about a paradigm change in which capital and work are no longer the only fundamental bases for successful management. Globalization is another factor that has significant implications for organizational knowledge management. In this global scenario, the trend towards knowledge-intensive products makes critical an efficient knowledge management (KM) to bundle knowledge in the design, production, and delivery of goods and services.

Now, organizations strongly depend on their skill to identify and adequately use the knowledge they possess and, over the past two decades, KM has captured enterprises' attention as one of the most promising ways to reach success in this information era. In this context, companies are beginning to understand the importance of knowledge as an organizational asset that makes it possible to obtain a sustainable competitive advantage (Bolloju, Khalifa, & Turban, 2002). For this reason, KM is no longer just an idea in industry leaders' minds, it has become a requirement to survive in today's competitive environment (Desouza, 2003).

There are already a large number of KM activities implemented in organizations, which often lack a strategic perspective. KM seems to "absorb" all kinds of theoretical approaches as well as practical activities, measures, and technologies without very much deep consideration as to its strategic or business value. There are also a number of authors who pragmatically suggest a series of KM activities, efforts, or strategies without very much differentiation between these concepts. Most of these authors base their findings on empirical studies investigating KM initiatives in organizations (Maier & Remus, 2001).

Moreover, although there is a growing recognition of the importance of organizational knowledge, often managers cannot identify where knowledge value resides or how to use it as competitive advantage. The organizational knowledge—embedded in people and communities formed inside the organization—is rarely detailed enough to be especially valuable and it is often lost when people leave the organization.

On the other side, some organizations have not yet approached KM activities in a structured way and this is because companies are still struggling to understand the KM concept and which activities it implies. The reason for this is the lack of clarity in identifying the main characteristics of the KM process. Moreover, there is an important gap between the academic research and the practical KM initiatives and, as a consequence, many organizations still have no explicit, consolidated knowledge strategy to steward the required knowledge. Instead, many attempts at KM have been simply based on new information systems technologies to capture all the possible knowledge of an organization into databases that would make it easily accessible to all employees (King, 1999; Levine, 2001). This philosophy of regarding knowledge as a "thing" that can be managed like other physical assets has not been quite successful for several reasons. One is the apparent difficulty concerned with knowledge capture and the issue of tacit-to-explicit transformation. Another is the question of intellectual asset management. Third is the narrow interpretation of KM in terms of information management, which involves breaking information into smaller pieces that can be detected throughout the organization, stored for later use, manipulated by being combined with other pieces, and transferred where they are needed. The ultimate goal of such KM efforts is to get the right information to the right people at the right place with the right information technologies (Nonaka & Takeuchi, 1995; Vat, 2004).

In the academic field, researchers have proposed a variety of KM frameworks, models, and perspectives to help understand this emerging phenomenon. Two kinds of KM frameworks can be identified (Holsapple & Joshi, 1999): descriptive and prescriptive. The descriptive frameworks try to characterize the nature of the KM phenomena, whereas prescriptive frameworks present methodologies to follow in conducting KM. Among the descriptive frameworks are those mentioned by Wiig, Leonard-Barton, Arthur Andersen & APQC, Choo, and Van der Spek-Spijkervet. Wiig's (1993) framework focus is on management and identifies the main necessary functions to manage knowledge. Leonard-Barton's (1995) framework centers on the interaction of the technological capacities of the organization and the activities of knowledge development. The Arthur Andersen & APQC's (1996) model provides the bases for the conduction of a benchmarking process of KM between organizations and also within the same organization. According Choo's (1996) framework an organization uses information in a strategic way for sensemaking, knowledge creation, and decision making. Finally, Van der Spek and Spijkerver's (1997) framework characterizes the cycle that governs the conduction of KM (conceptualize, reflect, act, and retrospect).

Among the prescriptive frameworks, the ones proposed by Sveiby, Petrash, Nonaka, Szulanski, and Alavi are presented. Sveiby's (1997) framework focuses on the characterization and measurement of organizational intangible assets (particularly knowledge). Petrash's (1996) model centers on the characterization and measurement of the organizational "intellectual capital," that is to say, it is oriented to the identification of knowledge resources. Nonaka's (1994) model presents the knowledge creation process as the interaction between two types of knowledge (tacit and explicit). Szulanski's (1996) model focuses on the identification of barriers that exist for knowledge transfer within the organization. Finally, Alavi's (1997) model centers on the use of technology for KM accomplishment.

As it has been described, the focus of each model and framework reveals KM dimensions or aspects emphasized or contemplated. Each of them addresses certain KM elements. However, none of them appears to subsume all the others. We believe that a successful KM strategy must be based on a comprehensive understanding of what the knowledge challenge implies. The essence of this challenge is presented in this chapter as a series of key factors combined in a more comprehensive and unified conceptual model for describing the nature of distributed KM. In the next section, we discuss the nature of organizational knowledge and the activities it implies. We present the foundations along with our vision of each process. We relate knowledge creation with teaching, learning, coaching, and mentoring processes and the generation of individual and collective knowledge. Regarding knowledge sharing we argue that this process must be fostered between knowledge domains within the organization and that a knowledge network should support it. For knowledge representation and information retrieval we propose a distributed organizational memory (DOM) system based on domain ontologies.

In the third section, we present a distributed knowledge management conceptual model that encompasses all the necessary key factors—described in the previous section—for a successful KM implementation. In the following section, we analyze the implications of this model in today's organizations. More specifically, we argue that a new emergent type of organization exists that can be seen as an evolution of other organizational types that arise from partial KM implementations. Finally, in the last section, we present conclusions.

Organizational Knowledge

Despite the recognized importance of KM, there exists no consensus on what KM means. Moreover, as Spiegler (2003) concludes, KM suffers from a lack of agreement on the definition of knowledge itself, mistaking it for data or information. In order to clarify these terms, Spiegler suggests a recursive and spiral model that relates the three concepts (i.e., data, information, and knowledge). In this model, yesterday's data are today's information and tomorrow's knowledge, and the latter one will serve like feedback for future data and information. As it can be seen in Figure 1, for Bellinger, Castro, and Mills (2006), data represent a fact or statement of event without relation to other things. Information embodies the understanding of a relationship of some sort among data, possibly a cause and effect relationship. Finally, knowledge represents a pattern that connects and generally provides a high level of predictability.

A diametrically opposed vision is proposed by Tuomi (2000) who argues that data emerge last, only after there is knowledge and information available. Knowledge is needed before collecting data because this previous knowledge will determine which data must be collected.

Another necessary distinction is between information management and KM. In information management, information is stored, usually in databases, sorted, and retrieved. Knowledge, on the other hand, requires a system that not only can store the existing knowledge as information, but it also can retrieve and use that information as knowledge when needed. In this manner, new knowledge can be created from existing knowledge in combination with new information (Hall, Paradice, & Courtney, 2001).

Knowledge has, as an organizational asset, its own characteristics that distinguish it from the rest of manageable resources (Wiig, de Hoog, & Van der Spek, 1997). Knowledge is intangible, and therefore difficult to measure. It is volatile. Most of the times it is embodied in people. It is not consumed in the process and sometimes it is even increased with the use, having as well, a high organizational impact. It is more and more evident that sharing and integrating organizational knowledge brings a number of benefits. In addition, sharing and integrating knowledge enables

Figure 1. Data, information, and knowledge

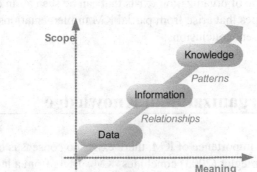

people to understand the widespread effect of their actions, improving coordination and fostering synergy (Lubit, 2001).

The discussion of knowledge classification is important because different types of knowledge have different KM implications and require different elements in a KM model. It is possible to distinguish between two types of knowledge; information processing in the mind of an individual produces what Polanyi (1962) calls tacit knowledge. Tacit knowledge is highly personal and difficult to formalize, making it difficult to communicate or share with others. Tacit knowledge is deeply rooted in an individual's actions and experience as well as in ideals, values, or emotions the individual embraces. When it is articulated and communicated, this tacit knowledge becomes information or what Nonaka (1994) calls, explicit knowledge. Explicit knowledge can be expressed in words and numbers and shared in the form of data, specifications, manuals, product descriptions, and alike. This kind of knowledge can be transmitted formally and systematically between individuals.

As organizational knowledge is derived from individual knowledge, KM must support the acquisition, organization, and communication of both tacit and explicit employees' knowledge. Tacit knowledge is acquired by experience. In this context, tacit knowledge includes beliefs, perspectives, and mental models so embodied in people's minds that they are taken for granted (Nonaka & Takeuchi, 1995). Explicit knowledge is knowledge that has been captured in a code, or a language that facilitates communication. In its most advanced state, explicit knowledge is contained in codified theories (Hall & Andreani, 2003).

Organizational knowledge is the collective sum of tacit and explicit knowledge within an organization. Organizational knowledge is processed information embedded in routines and processes that enable action. It is also knowledge captured by the organization's systems, processes, products, rules, and culture. These definitions are good conceptual notions about what organizational knowledge is, but they offer little guidance as how to acquire, manage, and transfer it among entities within the organization.

Despite the growing recognition of its importance, often it is not clear what KM implies and this is the reason why we found many definitions of KM (Hlupic, Pouloudi, & Rzevski, 2002; Snyder & Wilson, 2002). According to O'Leary (2002), KM can be defined as the efforts made by organizations to capture knowledge, convert personal knowledge (tacit) into groupware available knowledge (explicit), connect people to people, people to knowledge, knowledge to knowledge, and measure knowledge to facilitate resource management and to help to understand its evolution. KM is also defined as the application of knowledge activities operating on the knowledge resources. These activities are constrained and facilitated by factors influencing KM (Joshi, 2001).

Polenis and Fair-Wessels (1998) view KM as a new dimension of strategic information management. Smith and Farquhar (2000) describe the goal of KM to be the improvement of organizational performance by enabling individuals to capture, share, and apply their collective knowledge to make optimal decisions in real time. Thomas, Kellogg, and Erickson (2001) call the need to augment the typical view of KM as a problem of capturing, organizing, and retrieving information with a perspective that also acknowledges the role of human cognition in knowledge situated in social work contexts. King, Marks, and McCoy (2002) recognize the strong role information technology plays in KM and identify key applications in this area which are based on existing information technology infrastructures: knowledge repositories, best-practices and lessons-learned systems, expert networks, and communities of practice (Hackbarth & Grover, 1999; McDermott, 1999; Zack, 1999). Skyrme (2003) suggests that KM is the purposeful and systematic management of vital knowledge along with its associated processes of creating, gathering, organizing, diffusing, using, and exploiting that knowledge.

In our proposed model, the building blocks will be the necessary activities involved in a KM process. These knowledge activities are knowledge creation, knowledge representation, knowledge retrieval, and knowledge sharing.

Knowledge creation refers to the activity that alters organizational knowledge resources through knowledge socialization, internalization, externalization, and combination. Knowledge representation refers to the activity that facilitates knowledge retrieval by offering a common representation of knowledge objects. Knowledge retrieval is an activity of applying existing knowledge to daily tasks and, at the same time, generates new knowledge. Knowledge sharing refers to dissemination and distribution of knowledge. In others words, KM is the practice of adding actionable value to information by capturing tacit knowledge and converting it to explicit knowledge by filtering, storing, retrieving, and disseminating knowledge and by creating and testing new knowledge (Nemati, Steiger, Iyer, & Herschel, 2002).

Although it is important to describe organizational knowledge in a comprehensive way, it is also important to understand how this knowledge is developed and maintained. Any KM model has to contemplate all these aspects to perform a successful integration of organizational knowledge. Each of these activities will be an important part of the proposed model.

Knowledge Creation

Seufert (2000) states that organizational learning requires individual learning and, at the same time, individual learning has to interact in a dynamic social environment in order to contribute to organizational learning. This relationship between individual and organizational learning can be conceptualized as a spiral of knowledge creation where companies can turn into continuously learning organizations by enabling and managing the dynamic knowledge conversion processes between the individual and the organization, and between tacit and explicit knowledge. There are two main dimensions of knowledge, which are decisive for knowledge creation. The first dimension describes the levels of knowledge distinguishing who holds the knowledge: individual level, group level, organizational, as well as interorganizational level. The second dimension is the type of knowledge that we have already mentioned: tacit and explicit. There are two dimensions of tacit knowledge. On the one hand, the technical dimension which means the kind of informal personal skills or crafts often referred to as "know how." On the other hand, the cognitive dimension. It consists of beliefs, ideals, values, schemata, and mental models which we often taken for granted. While difficult to articulate, this cognitive dimension of tacit knowledge shapes the way we perceive the world. These types of knowledge do not exist independently but can be converted into one another. Following Nonaka and Takeuchi there are four conversion modes that can be distinguish: socialization, externalization, combination, and internalization.

Nonaka (1994) proposes that new organizational knowledge can be created through four conversion processes that involve tacit and explicit knowledge: socialization, externalization, combination, and internalization. We argue that these conversion processes are tightly relate with learning, teaching, coaching, and mentoring capabilities within the organization.

As is it shown in Figure 2, knowledge externalization refers to the conversion of tacit knowledge into explicit knowledge. In this process, individuals try to articulate their tacit knowledge eliciting their experiences and beliefs. Externalization describes transformation processes. On the one hand, this means the conversion of implicit into explicit knowledge, and on the other hand, the exchange of knowledge

Figure 2. Knowledge creation

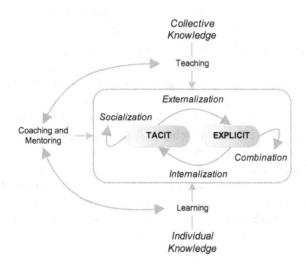

between individuals and a group. Since implicit knowledge is difficult to express, the conversion process is often supported by the use of metaphors, analogies, language rich in imagery, or stories, as well as visualization aids like models, diagrams, or prototypes. In a sense, it could be seen as a teaching process.

The second type of knowledge conversion, socialization, refers to the creation of new tacit knowledge from shared tacit knowledge. Individuals acquire new knowledge through a coaching process where expert workers guide trainees in their learning process. Socialization comprises the exchange of tacit knowledge between individuals in order to convey personal knowledge and experience. Joint experience results in new shared implicit knowledge, such as technical skills. In practice, this could mean, for instance, gaining intuitive and personal knowledge through physical proximity and attaining direct communication with customers or a supplier.

Knowledge combination refers to the creation of new knowledge through the combination and exchange of explicit knowledge in the organization. We believe that this process should be supported by the notion of a distributed organizational memory, described in the next section, that led workers to sort, reuse, add, and recontextualize explicit knowledge. The acquired tacit knowledge undergoes a crystallization process during which it is assessed and validated by experts and practitioners, and finally made available for downstream knowledge sharing and utilization. Tacit knowledge acquisition is broadly defined as the transfer of problem solving expertise from a knowledge source—a domain expert for example—to a computational formalism (Abidi, Cheah, & Curran, 2005).

The fourth type of knowledge conversion, internalization, takes place when explicit knowledge becomes tacit. In this learning process individuals embody new knowledge, updating their mental models. Internalization comprises the conversion of organization-wide, explicit knowledge into the implicit knowledge of the individual. This tacit knowledge and the experience gained on an individual level can be shared again (socialized) with others to become organizational knowledge, so that the knowledge spiral may be set in motion once more.

Acquisition of tacit knowledge is a challenging task because it demands the capture and structuring of an expert's mental model—where the mental model may comprise an unstructured collection of beliefs, assumptions, feelings, biases, intuitions, memories, and so forth. (Malhotra, 1999)—that is configured in response to an expert's individual experiences and problem-solving strategies. Besides, not everything we know can be codified as documents or tools. Sharing tacit knowledge requires interaction and informal learning processes such as storytelling, conversation, coaching, and apprenticeship. The tacit aspects of knowledge often consist of embodied expertise, such as a deep understanding of complex, interdependent elements that enables dynamic responses to context-specific problems. This type of knowledge is very difficult to replicate. This is not to say that it is not useful to document such knowledge in whatever manner serves the needs of practitioners. But, even explicit knowledge is dependant on tacit knowledge to be applied (Vat, 2004).

Learning at an individual level serves to provide training and education for individuals through the institution of workshops, apprenticeship programs, and the establishment of informal mentoring programs. Learning at an organizational level focuses on the use of communities of practice approach, leading to the formation of collaborative groups composed of professionals who share experience, knowledge, and best practices for the purposes of collective growth. According to several authors, the interplay between the individual and collective knowledge is an important aspect of organizational knowledge creation, amplification, and sharing.

Knowledge Sharing

As knowledge is an important asset that allows obtaining and retaining competitive advantage knowledge, sharing has become a strategic priority for most organizations. Alavi (2000) suggests that one of the biggest reasons for focusing on knowledge sharing is that knowledge creation by itself cannot lead to superior performance for the organization. Rather, companies have to create value by using that knowledge, and knowledge can only be utilized if it is shared successfully. Therefore, organizations have to effectively manage the knowledge transfer process to obtain success.

One of the prerequisites for enabling collaboration among individuals with diverse backgrounds in terms of domains and levels of expertise is the team's ability to create a sense of mutuality and thus a shared frame of reference (Sarker et al., 2005).

Knowledge sharing occurs when knowledge is diffused from one entity (e.g., an individual) to others. This process can unfold through processes of coaching, teaching, and learning. Knowledge may be purposefully shared or it may occur as an outcome of another activity.

Knowledge sharing may be challenging due to a number of factors, including the type of knowledge and an inability to locate and access the required knowledge source (Abidi et al., 2005).

On the other hand, the increased globalization causes knowledge transfer to take place among entities that are not necessarily located in the same place, but separated geographically and culturally (Von Krogh, Ichijo, & Nonaka, 2000). For example, knowledge transfer across space and time could be problematic due to the "localness of knowledge." Davenport and Prusak (1998) explain the implications of localness of knowledge suggesting that people usually get knowledge from their organizational neighbors. The knowledge market depends on trust, and individuals usually trust people they know. Face-to-face meetings are often the best way to get knowledge or reliable information about more distant knowledge sources. Also, mechanisms for getting access to distant knowledge tend to be weak or nonexistent.

Leading KM researchers suggest that one of the most important aspects of KM is the transfer of knowledge from one set of individuals to another. In the literature, knowledge transfer is characterized as the process where a complex, causally ambiguous set of routines, is recreated and maintained in a new setting (Szulanski, 2000). Knowledge transfer is also seen as a process through which one unit (e.g., group, department, or division) is affected by the experience of another (Argote & Ingram, 2000). Knowledge transfer can occur among entities spanning multiple levels, that is, among individuals, groups, and organizations. It has been argue that with the increase in globalization, knowledge transfer may also occur among entities that are not necessarily colocated, but separated by geographic distances and national cultures.

We argue that this sharing process must be fostered between knowledge domains (KD) within the organization. A KD is the area of knowledge one community agrees to learn about. It is negotiated among participants, especially the community's experts. KD exists both internally and externally to the organization (Malone, 2002).

Each individual within an organization ultimately obtains the needed knowledge, either directly or indirectly, from the various KD. The filtering of knowledge from these KD into the organization's core processes is done by knowledge communities (KC) and communities of practice (CoP). These kinds of learning communities provide support to higher levels of learning in organizations. A CoP is a social-technical system that can provide the means to develop and share knowledge among professionals, particularly when they are not colocated. A CoP is capable of providing individuals and organizations with a single-source solution for education, training, and performance support (LaContora & Mendoca, 2003).

Although both CoP and KC are communities formed within the organization, there are two principal characteristics that distinguish KC from CoP. The first is that the firm takes responsibility for identifying likely areas of interest and establishing KC. Contrarily, CoP are organic in nature, that is, they form spontaneously in response to professional interests that lie within the firm. The second quality is that while the organization actively establishes and supports KC, they do not typically have well-defined goals, other than to expand thinking along common areas of interest. Direction and objectives of KC tend to be less well defined. Unlike KC, which are organized by the firm for the purpose of filtering knowledge for potential value, a CoP is a community whose main goal is learning.

The importance of these communities stems from the fact that knowledge cannot be separated from its context. In all types of knowledge activities, even where technology is very helpful, knowledge contributors as well as seekers require a common community to share general conversation, experimentation, and experiences with other people who do what they do. While they are inside the community, knowledge workers are informally as well as contextually bound by a shared interest in knowledge sharing and in applying common practices (Pan & Leidner, 2003).

A challenge encountered in KM initiatives is how to connect these communities (CoP and KC) to enable sharing across, not just within, communities. A possible solution,

Figure 3. Knowledge network

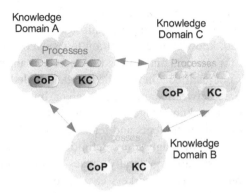

as shown in Figure 3, is the establishment of a knowledge network (KN) among these communities. A KN is an informal network of communities between KD. A KN facilitates knowledge transfer and sharing between KD and helps to channel worker's efforts. KN are vehicles through which knowledge may be communicated and shared. Essentially, KN are the media by which knowledge (as well as information and data) is conveyed. In our case, we will give support to a KN through a distributed organizational memory as is described in the following section.

Knowledge Representation and Information Retrieval

Knowledge acquisition techniques go hand in hand with knowledge representational issues as the manipulation of the acquired knowledge largely depends on how the knowledge is represented to reflect the expert's mental model (Abidi et al., 2005). Remembering what an organization has learned in reusing its relevant knowledge (generated internally or acquired externally) is an important aspect of effective KM. Like individuals, organizations may lose track of their knowledge and forget. Thus, organizations codify their knowledge in order to preserve and reuse it.

Since organizations are continuously engaged in the process of knowledge generation and application, it would be useless to attempt to codify and store all organizational knowledge. Besides, the approach to codification of knowledge depends on its type (tacit or explicit).

A great deal of effort has gone into the creation of electronic media necessary to capture and store information and improve communications. Nevertheless, this is not enough for an effective KM implementation. Experience shows that few workers contribute to knowledge repositories (case bases, knowledge bases, etc.) or search knowledge in them, and in this way, knowledge generated through the normal execution of daily tasks is lost (Nemati et al., 2002). Three key factors can be mentioned as possible causes of not using knowledge repositories (Kwan & Balasubramanian, 2003). On the one hand, knowledge contribution to repositories requires an extra documentation effort for workers and unless they perceive an immediate benefit, the additional work is not justified. On the other hand, knowledge sharing requires a common mental frame between source and receiver, but people from different backgrounds have different knowledge structures and perspectives. Moreover, repositories design focuses on contents and tends to provide little context of the knowledge they contain. Knowledge is, by definition, highly context dependent while every explicit representation generally causes context elimination. Without contextual information, knowledge workers cannot fully understand or trust the knowledge source and therefore adopt it (Ackerman, 1994). Finally, in most cases, a culture does not exist that fosters knowledge exchange within organizations.

To face these drawbacks it is necessary to develop knowledge enabler information systems that provide a common framework to capture, increase, store, organize, analyze, and share not only information and data but also knowledge. Currently, organizational memories (OMs) are proposed as support for effectively using, handling, and preserving knowledge over time and space—as much as possible—without human intervention (Abecker Bernardi, Hinkelmann, Kühn, & Sintek, 1998). From the organizational perspective, an OM can act as a tool for KM and gives support to three types of learning in organizations: individual learning, learning through direct communication, and learning using a knowledge repository (Heijst, Spek, & Kruizinga, 1997). An OM comprises a variety of knowledge sources where information elements of different kinds, structures, contents, and media types are available and should be able to control and access heterogeneous knowledge sources according to the user's information needs.

Although the previous definition seems to suggest a centralized approach, the centralization of an OM presents some disadvantages related to the distributed nature of organizational knowledge and the high maintenance cost of a centralized structure. These reasons lead to consider a distributed organizational memory approach (Ale, Chiotti, & Galli, 2004). As is shown in Figure 4, we propose to associate each KD with their own OM, adding an interface that allows the recovery of knowledge from other MOs if is necessary, creating in this way, a KN (Ale, Chiotti, & Galli, 2005).

Additionally, in today organizations, many knowledge intensive tasks (KITs), such as dealing with complexity, uncertainty, and abstractions, must be performed. These tasks involve an effective combination of corporative competencies and constant knowledge object availability. These organizations, therefore, have to efficiently manage their capabilities, create mechanisms to elicit innovation, and collect ideas and other knowledge sources to cope with KITs (Vasconcelos, Gouveia, & Kimble,

2002). Many authors have proposed explicit business process modeling as a means to represent context and facilitate the treatment of specific situations anticipating knowledge objects requirements (Abecker et al., 1998). However, knowledge intensive processes tend to be characterized for dynamic changes in their objectives, context, and restrictions. These kind of processes often presents collaboration patterns and highly ad hoc communications that make the detailed and previous planning of the KITs difficult and, at the same time, make this proactive approach unsuitable to give support to the dynamic information needs that are very common in KITs performance. For these cases, a reactive approach is necessary. In this chapter we present a DOM with a reactive behavior, which let users ask for the needed information at any point of their daily activity.

We propose a strategy for semantic representation of knowledge sources (more precisely, documents) with a domain ontology overcoming this way two major problems already mentioned: documentation overload and lack of context.

In this particular type of OM, the characteristics, attributes, and semantics of the knowledge objects, as well as the relationships among them are represented through

Figure 4. Knowledge representation and information retrieval through a DOM

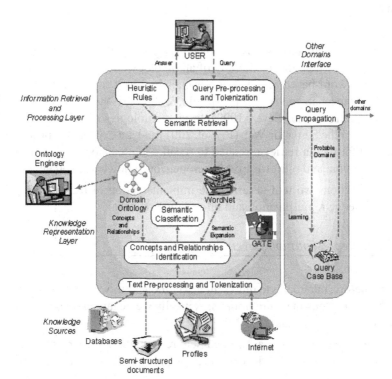

a domain ontology. Ontologies aim to capture domain knowledge in a generic way and provide a commonly agreed understanding of a domain, which may be reused, shared, and operationalized across applications and groups (Fensel, 2001).

An additional benefit of ontology modeling is the context representation. Ontologies provide a domain model that allows knowledge objects to be seen in their context and this can be crucial for subsequent reinterpretation or use in a new task or project. As is shown in Figure 4, our onto-DOM architecture has three main components:

1. **Information retrieval and processing layer:** It is responsible for user query analysis, query transformation to a matching format, and information retrieval.

2. **Knowledge representation layer:** This component is responsible for the knowledge extraction and representation from heterogeneous sources. It implements an ontology-based automatic classification strategy of knowledge sources, addressing documentation overload problem (Ale, Chiotti, & Galli, 2006).

3. **Other domains interface:** It is responsible for propagating the user query to other domains that can provide an answer. In order to accomplish this task the module implements a learning mechanism to propose possible target domains.

Another important advantage provided by ontologies can be seen in the information retrieval area, where the availability of an ontology allows the replacing of the traditional keyword-based retrieval approaches by more sophisticated ontology-based retrieval mechanisms (Guarino, Masolo, & Vetere, 1999; Richard-Benjamins, Fensel, Decker, & Gómez-Pérez, 1999). In fact, ontologies are often presented as silver bullets for the Semantic Web (Fensel, 2001) and are expected to bring several benefits to information retrieval related to recall and precision, user assistance in query formulation, and retrieval from heterogeneous knowledge sources.

In the next sections we will describe the implementation of the most important layers: knowledge representation and information retrieval.

Knowledge Representation Layer

As we said before, our goal is to represent in a homogenous way knowledge sources that are heterogeneous in nature (more specifically we began our experiments with natural language documents).

We propose a strategy for semantic document representation where ontologies are used as the main structure for the classification process. Our proposal relies on the hypothesis that domain ontologies contain all the relevant concepts and relationships in a given domain even though the way in which ontologies are built up in the domain is out of the scope of this chapter. To illustrate our strategy, we present an example using an extended version of the Travel[1] ontology that contains more than 120 concepts from the tourism area and an extract of a Web page[2] of the same domain that is shown in Figure 5.

Tokenization and Lexical-Morphological Analysis for Concepts Identification

This task is divided into two main phases: the tokenization of the text and the lexical-morphological analysis of each token. Tokenization consists of dividing the text into single lexical tokens and involves activities such as sentence boundary detection, simple white space identification, and proper name recognition, among others. After tokenization, a lexical-morphological analysis has to be done using a part-of-speech (POS) tool. In our case, we use the POS tagger provided by general architecture for text engineering (GATE[3]), which specifies if a term is a verb, an adjective, an adverb, or a noun.

Usually, the decision on whether a particular word will be used as a representative term is related to the syntactic nature of the word. In fact, nouns frequently carry more semantics than adjectives, adverbs, and verbs (Baeza-Yates & Ribeiro-Neto, 1999). As, in our case, representative terms will be determined by ontological concepts, which are nouns; we will focus on this syntactic category within the tagged text.

In this sense, ontological concepts can be seen as possible classifying categories. At this stage, if the noun is not directly found in the ontology, using the synonyms set and hyperonymic/hyponymic structure provided by WordNet[4], we semantically expand every noun identified in the text and perform a new search in the domain ontology.

Figure 5. Example document

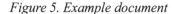

By doing this, we do not only identify exact ontological concepts occurrences but also derivations of the same word or even a synonym. Up to this point, we are not interested in the meaning of each possible concept and that is why the presence of more than one sense for each noun in WordNet is not a problem.

For example, the concept "food" has been found with WordNet assistance. In this particular case, by using WorldNet's hypernym relationship we found out that "meal" (a concept present in the text) is a kind of "food," which is a concept in the ontology. In other cases, this tool helps us to mark, as ontological concept occurrences, the presence of synonyms; in this way, if the noun is not found directly in the ontology, WordNet allows us to expand the matching possibilities, taking advantage of related concepts (synonyms, hypernyms, etc.).

Semantic Document Representation

At this point, we navigate through the domain ontology using the properties structure in order to find relationships among previously identified concepts. By doing this, we expand the possible document descriptors using intermediate ontology levels and contextualizing those concepts that, in another way, could not be related to other concepts among those that were identified in the previous step.

We take advantage of ontological relationships and knowledge contained in the domain ontology in order to perform a more accurate and contextualize representation of the document. As a result, we finally obtain the subset of the domain ontology that best models the document semantic content (Figure 6). Figure 7 shows the knowledge representation prototype from where ontology engineers obtained the

Figure 6. Ontology representation

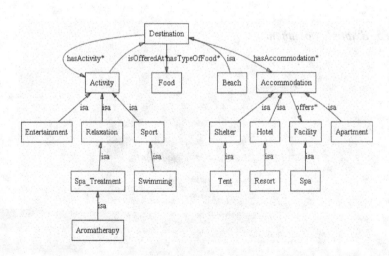

Figure 7. Knowledge representation prototype

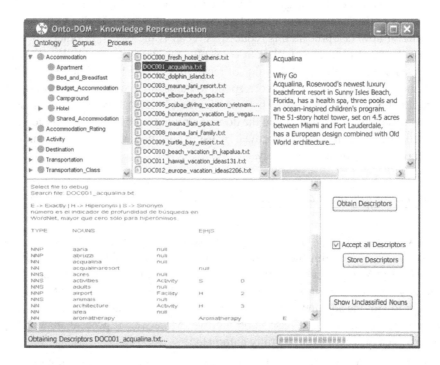

descriptors for each document along with the methodology to be used (straight finding, synonyms, hypernyms, etc.). This semantic document classification will enable new, semantically enhanced access methods.

Representation Evaluation

As a first step in the implementation process, we estimate the representation strategy performance applying the following metrics according to Yang's (1999) definitions: recall, precision, fallout, and accuracy[5].

Recall	Precision	Fallout	Accuracy
87%	70%	14%	86%

Recall is a measure of strategy performance in finding relevant concepts. Recall is 100% when every relevant concept is annotated. In theory, it is easy to achieve good recall simply annotating every noun in the text. Therefore, recall for itself is not a good measure of strategy quality. Precision, on the other hand, is a measure of strategy performance in not annotating nonrelevant nouns. Finally, fallout is the measure of how fast precision is reduced as recall is increased; in other words, it represents the portion of nonrelevant concepts that were annotated. We analyzed the reason for the relatively low value of recall measure and found that 82% of the not annotated relevant concepts correspond to names of vacation destinations that were either places not recognized by WordNet (i.e., Caicos) or types of destinations that were not taken into account in the domain ontology (i.e., islands, archipelago). We believe that recall can be improved by using common vocabulary domain lists and enriching the domain ontology.

Information Retrieval and Processing Layer

Most works on ontology-based question-answering tends to focus on simple query expansion or on exploiting the availability of a knowledge base linked to the ontology to provide a precise answer. In the first case, we believe that this is a limited use of ontology potential and, in the second case, a vast knowledge base must be learned in order to provide adequate answers. The effort required to feed all organizational knowledge in a knowledge base is prohibitive. Moreover, if precise answers are required this process cannot be fully automated.

Ontologies ensure an efficient retrieval of knowledge resources by enabling infe-rences based on domain knowledge. This vision relies on the assumption that an ontology designed to describe a domain can both annotate and retrieve knowledge sources. In fact, this is not always the case because domain specialists usually build the ontologies and users do not always share or understand their viewpoints. Users might not use the right concepts—from an ontologist´s viewpoint—when writing a query, leading to missed answers. For example, a user might use "student lodging" instead of "hostel." Or, perhaps a user asking for a "hotel" might also ap-preciate the retrieval of documents about "resorts." Consequently, we partially use the same strategy applied to document descriptors determination in the semantic query treatment.

In this case, onto-DOM accepts natural language queries and, using the domain onto-logy, transforms the query by eliminating natural language ambiguity and recovering those knowledge objects that are most likely to contain the answer. In a sense, this layer tries to find similarity between the query and the ontological concepts.

Our strategy to determine similarity includes both conceptual and relationship similarity. The first step is to transform the query in a format that facilitates ulte-rior evaluations and, to this aim, we apply part of the same strategy for document representation. After this stage, we have not only nouns that match ontological concepts but we also keep the verbs in order to evaluate relationship similarity and wh-words that give us an idea of the type of answer expected (e.g., time, location, person, etc.).

We go beyond taxonomic relationships (is-a) making use of semantic relationships to sharpen query comprehension. Essentially, we are trying to "understand" the question lying on the codified knowledge in the domain ontology, lexical resources as WordNet and GATE, and the heuristics associated to the treatments of wh-words. For example, after the first analysis of the query "Where can I eat Vegetarian dishes?" we obtain the following useful information:

eat(Vegetarian, Food) (where, location)

In this case, the concept food is derived from dishes with the help of WordNet's hyperonymy structure. Nevertheless, as we said before, our main objective is to go beyond a keyword search or the use of the domain ontology as a query expansion tool. To this aim, on the one hand, we will use the verbs detected in the query to look for semantic similarity related to relationships, and on the other hand, we will analyze the concepts related to those relationships to see if they belong to the expected type according to the wh-word.

Following the previous example we recover the ontological concepts identified in the query along with their neighbors, restaurant and chef (Figure 5). To decide if one of these neighbors is useful to represent the query (and not search only by food and vegetarian) we evaluate similarity between the verb in the query (eat) and the verbs in the relationships attached to the identified concepts (serve, specialize) using the synonym and correlate sets of WordNet.

Figure 8. Ontological concepts identified in the query (with their neighbors)

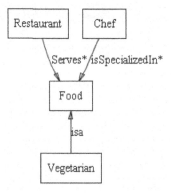

As it can be seen in Figure 9 "serve" has a higher semantic similarity with "eat" than "specialize."

To confirm this result, or as an alternative in case we are not able to obtain a conclusive result in the verbs comparison, we analyze the concepts at each end of the relationships (restaurant, chef) to see if they match with the expected type according to the wh-word. In this particular case, WordNet tells us that restaurant is a location (expected type according to the wh-word "where" in the query) and chef is a person confirming that the portion of the domain ontology that best represents the query contains the concepts: food, vegetarian, and restaurant.

As regards to query evaluation the same results as those for document annotation are expected since the strategy being used is almost the same, adding in this particular case verbs treatment and the use of the ontological relationships. In this sense, our analyses have demonstrated that the queries, due to their short length, are much more sensible to the errors of the strategy. In these cases, a concept detection error attributable to the POS-tagging tool or the annotation strategy has a much greater impact than the same error in a document. To address this problem we are working in a domain independent heuristics set to improve query treatment.

Distributed Knowledge Management Conceptual Model

KM requires a suitable infrastructure for creating and managing tacit and explicit knowledge. Although conventional enterprise information systems typically support explicit knowledge, few of them support tacit knowledge. Providing pathways,

Figure 9. Relationship similarity analysis

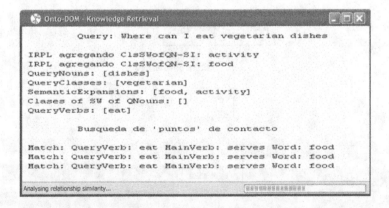

channels, and mechanisms for sharing, distributing, and locating tacit knowledge sources is therefore a challenge.

KM systems integrate existing components at both infrastructural and content levels, bringing together people and information systems associated with collaborative, knowledge intensive tasks. Tools that handle explicit content, as well as components that enable sharing and distributing tacit content, must be temporally and spatially integrated. In order to promote a common understanding of KM, it is essential to organize and consolidate knowledge manipulation activities in a way that not only describes each activity clearly and completely, but also identifies their interrelationships.

There are two tendencies related to KM modeling focus: the repository model and the network model (Abidi et al., 2005). The repository model aims at codification of knowledge (i.e., creation and maintenance of stocks of explicit knowledge). In this model, knowledge is seen as an object that can be gathered, stored, organized, and distributed. As such, these systems are focused on explicit knowledge management and primarily in the creation and storage/retrieval aspects of the organizational KM. The network model aims at using the power of information and communications technologies to support the flow of knowledge in organizational settings and among networks of KD. We argue that both approaches (repository and network models) are needed for a successful KM implementation.

In Figure 10, we present a distributed knowledge management conceptual model that encompasses all the necessary—previously described—key activities for a successful KM implementation. In this model we distinguish between an organizational memory system (OMS) and a knowledge management system (KMS).

OMS consists of the processes and information systems components used to capture, store, search, retrieve, display, and manipulate an OM. A KMS consists of the tools and processes used by knowledge workers to identify and transmit knowledge to the knowledge base contained in the OM (Croasdell, Jennex, Yu, & Christianson, 2003). That is, the knowledge creation process is carried out through four conversion processes. The knowledge combination process refers to the creation of new knowledge through the combination and exchange of explicit knowledge in the organization. This process requires the knowledge transfer and sharing among organizational memories from different knowledge domains, which is allowed by the knowledge network that helps to channel the worker's efforts.

From Learning to Emergent Organizations

Successful organizations are often described as knowledge organizations composed of knowledge workers who continually perform knowledge intensive tasks using

Figure 10. Distributed knowledge management conceptual model

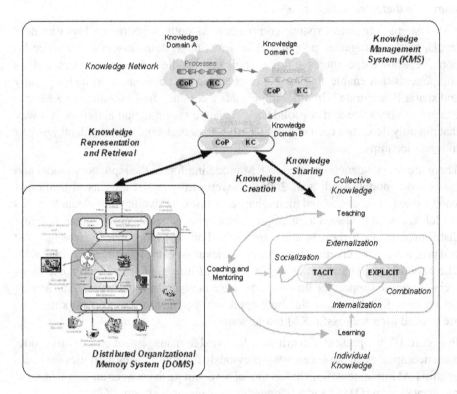

and creating new knowledge. To become a knowledge organization it is necessary to manage organizational knowledge in a holistic manner. Many authors (Fowler, 2000; Nonaka & Takeuchi, 1995) have analyzed the concept of knowledge organization and its role in the knowledge creation process. These successful companies create new knowledge, share and spread this knowledge through the entire organization, and quickly embody it in new products and technologies. This is important because knowledge that cannot be shared within an organization remains the property of a few people, rather than of the organization, and will have a limited impact on the organization's ability to create value.

There are other organizational classifications that arise from partial KM implementations. The learning organization (LO) is an organization that facilitates the learning of its members and continuously transforms itself. A LO is an organization that is continually expanding its capacity to create its future. It is a place where people continually expand their capacity to create the results they truly desire, where new and expansive patterns of thinking are nurtured, where collective aspiration is set free, and where people are continually learning how to learn (Senge, 1994). A learning organization could be considered as an organization, which focuses on developing and using its information and knowledge capabilities in order to create higher-value information and knowledge, to modify behaviors to reflect new knowledge and insights, and to improve bottom-line results (Vat, 2004). The key to obtaining long-term competitive advantage is increasingly found by modern organizations in the ability to continuously learn from experiences, to generate new knowledge, and to move on to new products and services. Organizational learning is visible as activities that go on in a learning organization, which is a type of organization whose internal structure and process is marked by imaginative flexibility of style in its leadership and by empowered contributions from its membership. Its members engage in a continuous process of discovery and experimentation. In such organizations, learning becomes a way of life. Members feel free to challenge the governing values of their practice. In a LO the company does not force the employees to learn, but creates a context in which they will want to learn. Organizational learning is often divided into two types, which are called single loop and double loop learning, or adaptive and generative learning. In single loop learning, new knowledge is applied for routine, to improve the quality and efficiency of existing operations. Double loop learning leads to new practices and to innovation within the organization.

It is widely recognized that running an organization requires learning support for knowledge acquisition and creation and to reinforce the relationship between individual and organizational goals. In a LO, everyone, and the organization as well, is engaged in a continuous learning process. There is a knowledge feedback between the organization, which is more than the sum of the individuals, and its components that emerge from this learning process.

Organizational learning focuses on activities that promote information exchange and knowledge sharing. Whereas incremental process innovations, as they take place within a stable organization, can be created through single loop learning, turbulent environments required for continuous learning in a double loop mode. As we said before, knowledge is increasingly recognized by modern organizations as their most important source of lasting competitive advantage. However, the key for obtaining long-term competitive advantage is not to be found in the administration of existing knowledge, but in the ability to constantly generate new knowledge, and to move on to new products and services. Rather than viewing firms as devices for processing information, making decisions, and solving problems, one should realize that they are based increasingly on knowledge-seeking and knowledge-creation.

A teaching organization (TO) is one in which everyone is a teacher, everyone is a learner, and reciprocal teaching and learning are embodied into everyday activities. In this kind of organization the teaching process is fostered inside the organization and strategic knowledge is systematically taught to everyone. The teachers belong to the organization and the teaching process is completely developed with organizational resources.

A coaching organization (CO) is an organization that creates an environment where the behaviors and practices involved in continuous learning exchange both explicit and tacit knowledge; reciprocal coaching and self-leadership development are actively encouraged and facilitated. Coaches play a more proactive role in orienting a person to the realities of the organization, helping the individual to remove barriers to optimum performance while maintaining personal and professional integrity. The coaching relationship with a trainee involves mutual commitment, trust, and respect. It encourages freedom of expression, is pragmatic in employing useful models, and is reciprocal with both coach and trainee learning.

In this chapter, the term "coach" refers to a leadership approach or technique that helps others to recognize their own potential to solve problems. It must not be confused with the initial training of a new employee. During the learning process, the coach articulates emotional, corporal, and psychological elements tying them to the trainee experiences. The main objective is to get rid of acquired knowledge preconceptions and to enter in the zone of effort and arduous training. Some important ties found in this process are mental models that prevent the incorporation of new concepts. In this sense, the coach that leads the learning process will impel the other to learn and to be a different observer and to identify the goal towards which he or she goes.

Finally, knowledge organizations (KO) obtain a competitive advantage from continuous learning, both individual and collective. In organizations with a well-established knowledge management system, learning by the people within an organization becomes learning by the organization itself. This type of organizations fosters KC and CoP formation. These communities that are organized around the principles of entrepreneurship have the best chance of success. Members of these communities would act less like followers and more like empowered founders and builders of a new organizational value. To become a knowledge organization it is necessary not only to give support to learning, teaching, and coaching processes, but also to go beyond the implementation of these processes in isolation. In a way, as it is shown in Figure 11, a knowledge organization could be seen as an evolution of the other types of organizations.

We argue that any organization can become a knowledge organization through the systematic application of the entire key activities presented in our distributed knowledge management conceptual model.

Final Remarks

As we have established, few would question the validity of the assertion that we currently live in a knowledge-based society. Now, organizations strongly depend on

Figure 11. Emergent organization

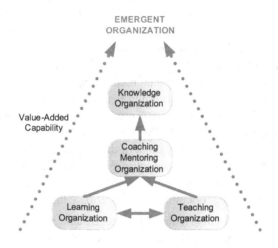

their skills to identify and adequately use the knowledge they possess and, over the past two decades, knowledge management (KM) has captured enterprises' attentions as one of the most promising ways to reach success in this information era. In this context, companies are beginning to understand the importance of knowledge as an organizational asset that makes it possible to obtain a sustainable competitive advantage. Nevertheless, there is an important gap between the academic research and the practical KM initiatives and, as a consequence, many organizations still have no explicit, consolidated knowledge strategy to steward the required knowledge. In the academic field, researchers have proposed a variety of KM frameworks, models, and perspectives to help understand this emerging phenomenon. The focus of each model and framework reveals KM dimensions or aspects, emphasized or contemplated. Each of them addresses certain KM elements. However, none of them appears to subsume all the others. We believe that a successful KM strategy must be based on a comprehensive understanding of what the knowledge challenge implies. The essence of this challenge was presented in this chapter as a series of key factors combined in a more comprehensive and unified conceptual model for describing the nature of distributed KM. We presented the foundations along with our vision of each process. We related knowledge creation with teaching, learning, coaching, and mentoring processes and the generation of individual and collective knowledge. Regarding knowledge sharing we argue that this process must be fostered between knowledge domains within the organization and that a knowledge network should support it. For knowledge representation and information retrieval we have proposed a distributed organizational memory system based on domain ontologies.

Historically, experience shows that few workers contribute to knowledge repositories (case bases, knowledge bases, etc.) or search knowledge in them, and in this way, knowledge generated through the normal execution of daily tasks is lost. To address this problem it was necessary to develop a knowledge-enabler information system that provides a common framework to capture, increase, store, organize, analyze, and share not only information and data but also knowledge. These reasons lead us to consider a distributed organizational memory approach where we propose to associate each KD with their own OM adding an interface that allows the recovery of knowledge from other MOs if is necessary, creating this way a knowledge network. In this chapter we have presented a DOM with a reactive behavior, which let users ask for the needed information at any point of their daily activity. Within the DOM we have implemented a strategy for semantic representation of knowledge sources (more precisely, documents) with a domain ontology addressing this way two major problems already mentioned: documentation overload and lack of context.

Finally, we have presented a distributed knowledge management conceptual model that encompasses all the necessary key factors—described in the previous section—for a successful KM implementation. We have analyzed the implications of this model in today's organizations. We have found that to become a knowledge organization it is necessary not only to give support to learning, teaching, and coaching processes, but also to go beyond the implementation of these processes in isolation. More specifically, we argue that this new emergent type of organization can be seen as an evolution of other organizational types that arise from partial KM implementations. We believe that any organization can become a knowledge organization through the systematic application of the entire key activities presented in our distributed knowledge management conceptual model.

References

Abecker, A., Bernardi, A., Hinkelmann, K., Kühn, O., & Sintek, M. (1998). Towards a well-founded technology for organizational memories. *IEEE Intelligent Systems and their Applications, 13*(3), 40-48.

Abidi, S., Cheah, Y., & Curran, J. (2005). A knowledge creation info-structure to acquire and crystallize the tacit knowledge of health-care experts. *IEEE Transactions on Information Technology in Biomedicine, 9*(2).

Ackerman, M. S. (1994). Definitional and contextual issues in organizational and group memories. In *Proceedings of Twenty-Seventh IEEE Hawaii International Conference of System Sciences (HICSS 94)* (pp. 191-200).

Alavi, M. (1997). KPMG Peat Marwick U.S.: One giant brain. *Harvard Business School* (case), 9-297-108.

Alavi, M. (2000). Managing organizational knowledge. In R.W. Zmud (Ed.), *Framing the domains of IT management*. Cincinnati, OH: Pinnaflex Educational Resources, Inc.

Ale, M., Chiotti, O., & Galli, M.R. (2004). Agent-supported ontology-based knowledge management system. In *Proceedings of ASIS 2004 (Simposio Argentino de Sistemas de Información) and JAIIO 2004 (33° Jornadas Argentinas de Informática e Investigación Operativa)*, Argentina, (p. 11).

Ale, M., Chiotti, O., & Galli, M. R. (2005, December). A distributed knowledge management conceptual model for knowledge organizations. *ICFAI Journal of Knowledge Management*, 27-39. ICFAI University Press.

Ale, M., Chiotti, O., & Galli, M. R. (2006). Semantic document representation in an ontology-driven distributed organizational memory. In *Proceedings of JIISIC 2006*, Puebla, México, (pp. 191-198). ISBN 970-94770-0-5.

Argote, L., & Ingram, P. (2000). Knowledge transfer: A basis for competitive advantage in firms. *Org. Behav. Human Decision Process, 82*(1), 150-169.

Arthur Anderson and The American Productivity and Quality Center. (1996). The Knowledge Management Assessment Tool: External Benchmarking Version.

Baeza-Yates, R., & Ribeiro-Neto, B. (1999). *Modern information retrieval*. Wokingham, UK: Addison-Wesley.

Bellinger, G., Castro, D., & Mills, A. (2006). *Data, information, knowledge and wisdom*. Retrieved January 12, 2008, from http://www.systems-thinking. org/dikw/dikw.htm

Bolloju, N., Khalifa, M., & Turban, E. (2002). Integrating knowledge management into enterprise environments for the next generation decision support. *Decision Support Systems, 33*(2), 163-176.

Choo, C. (1996). *An integrated information model of the organizations: The knowing organization*. http://www.fis.utoronto.ca/people/faculty/choo/FIS/KO/ KO.html1

Croasdell, D., Jennex, M., Yu, Z., & Christianson, T. (2003). *A meta-analysis of methodologies for research in knowledge management, organizational learning and organizational memory: Five years at HICSS*. Paper presented at the 36th Annual Hawaii International Conference on System Sciences (HICSS 03) (p. 110).

Davenport, T. H., & Prusak, L. (1998). *Working knowledge: How organizations manage what they know*. Cambridge: Harvard Business School Press.

Desouza, K. (2003). Knowledge management barriers: Why the technology imperative seldom works. *Business Horizons, 46*(1), 25-29.

Fensel, D. (2001). *Silver bullet for knowledge management and electronic commerce.* Berlín: Springer Verlag.

Fowler, A. (2000) The role of AI-based technology in support of the knowledge management value activity cycle. *The Journal of Strategic Information Systems, 9*(2-3), 107-128.

Guarino, N., Masolo, C., & Vetere, G. (1999). Ontoseek: Content-based access to the Web. *IEEE Intelligent Systems, 14*(3), 70-80.

Hackbarth, G., & Grover, V. (1999). The knowledge repository: Organizational memory information systems. *Information Systems Management, 16*(3), 21-30.

Hall, R., & Andriani, P. (2003). Managing knowledge associated with innovation. *Journal of Business Research, 56*(2), 145-152.

Hall, D., Paradice, D., & Courtney, J. (2001). Creating feedback loops to support organizational learning and knowledge management in inquiring qrganizations. In *Proceedings of the 34th Hawaii International Conference on System Sciences (HICSS-34)* (p. 10).

Heijst, G., Spek, R., & Kruizinga, E. (1997). Corporate memories as a tool for knowledge management. *Expert Systems with Applications, 13*(1), 41-54.

Hlupic, V., Pouloudi, A., & Rzevski, G. (2002). Towards an integrated approach to knowledge management: Hard, soft, and abstract issues. *Knowledge and Process Management, 9*(2), 90-102.

Holsapple, C., & Joshi, K. (1999). Descriptions and analysis of existing knowledge management frameworks. In *Proceedings of the 32nd Annual Hawaii International Conference on System Sciences (HICSS-32)* (Vol.1, p. 15).

Joshi, K. (2001). A framework to study knowledge management behaviors during decision making. In *Proceedings of the 34th Hawaii International Conference on System Sciences (HICSS-34)* (Vol. 4, p. 4024).

King, W. R. (1999). Integrating knowledge management into IS strategy. *Information Systems Management, 16*(4), 70-72.

King, W. R., Marks, P. V., & McCoy, S. (2002). The most important issues in knowledge management. *Communications of the ACM, 45*(9), 93-97.

Kwan, M., & Balasubramanian, P. (2003). KnowledgeScope: Managing knowledge in context. *Decision Support Systems, 35*(4), 467-486.

LaContora, J., & Mendonca, D. (2003) Communities of practice as learning and performance support systems. In *Proceedings International Conference on Information Technology: Research and Education (ITRE2003)* (pp. 395-398).

Leonard-Barton, D. (1995). *Wellsprings of knowledge.* Boston: Harvard Business School Press.

Levine, L. (2001). Integrating knowledge and processes in a learning organization. *Information System Management*, 21-32.

Lubit, R. (2001). The keys to sustainable competitive advantage: Tacit knowledge and knowledge management. *Organizational Dynamics, 29*(3), 164-178.

Maier, R., & Remus, U. (2001). Towards a framework for knowledge management strategies: Process orientation as strategic starting point. In *Proceedings of the 34th Hawaii International Conference on System Sciences*.

Malhotra, Y. (1999). Knowledge management for organizational white-waters: An ecological framework. *Knowledge Management*, 18-21.

Malone, D. (2002). Knowledge management: A model for organizational Learning. *International Journal of Accounting Information Systems, 3*(2), 111-123.

McDermott, R. (1999). Why information technology inspired but cannot deliver knowledge management. *California Management Review, 41*(4), 103-117.

Nemati, N., Steiger, D., Iyer, L., & Herschel, R. (2002). Knowledge warehouse: An architectural integration of knowledge management, decision support, artificial intelligence and data warehousing. *Decision Support Systems, 33*(2), 143-161.

Nonaka, I. (1994). A dynamic theory of organizational knowledge creation. *Organization Science, 5*(1), 14-37.

Nonaka, I., & Takeuchi, H. (1995). *The knowledge-creating company: How Japanese companies create the dynamics of innovation*. New York: Oxford University Press.

O'Leary, D. (2002) Chapter 13: Knowledge management in accounting and professional services. In V. Arnold & S. Sutton (Eds.), *Researching accounting as an information systems discipline*. Sarasota, FL: American Accounting Association.

Pan, S., & Leidner, D. (2003). Bridging communities of practice with information technology in pursuit of global knowledge sharing. *Journal of Strategic Information Systems, 12*(1), 71-88.

Petrash, G. (1996). Dows journey to a knowledge value management culture. *European Management Journal, 14*(4), 365-373.

Polanyi, M. (1962). *Personal knowledge: Toward a post-critical philosophy*. New York: Harper Torchbooks.

Ponelis, S., & Fair-Wessels, F. (1998). Knowledge management: A literature overview. *South Africa Journal of Library Information Science, 66*(1), 1-10.

Richard-Benjamins, V., Fensel, D., Decker, S., & Gómez-Pérez, A. (1999). (KA)2: Building ontologies for the Internet: A mid-term report. *International Journal of Human-Computer Studies, 51*(3), 687-712.

Sarker, S., Sarker, S., Nicholson, D., & Joshi, K. (2005). Knowledge transfer in virtual systems development teams: An exploratory study of four key enablers. *IEEE Transactions on Professional Communications, 48*(2).

Senge, P. (1994). *The fifth discipline* (1st ed.). Doubleday Books.

Seufert, S. (2000). Work-based learning and knowledge management: An integrated concept of organizational learning. In H. R. Hansen, M. Bichler, & H. Mahrer (Eds.), *Proceedings of the Eighth European Conference on Information Systems*, Vienna, (pp. 1413-1420).

Skyrme, D. (2003). Knowledge management: Making sense of an oxymoron. *Management Insight, 22*. Retrieved January 12, 2008, from http://www.skyrme.com/insights/22km.htm

Smith, R. G., & Farquhar, A. (2000). The road ahead for knowledge management: An AI perspective. *AI Magazine*, 17-40.

Snyder, C.A., & Wilson, L.T. (2002). Implementing knowledge management: Issues for managers. In D. White (Ed.), *Knowledge mapping and management* (pp. 154-165). Hershey, PA: IGI Global, Inc.

Spiegler, I. (2003, July). Technology and knowledge: Bridging a "generating" gap. *Information & Management, 40*(6), 533-539.

Sveiby, K. (1997). *The new organizational wealth.* San Francisco: Berret-Koehler.

Szulanski, G. (1996). Exploring internal stickiness: Impediments to the transfer of best practice within the firm. *Strategic Management Journal, 17*(Winter), 27-43.

Szulanski, G. (2000). The process of knowledge transfer: A diachronic analysis of stickiness. *Org. Behav. Human Decision Process, 82*(1), 9-27.

Thomas, J. C., Kellogg, W. A., & Erickson ,T. (2001). The knowledge management puzzle: Human and social factors in knowledge management. *IBM Systems Journal, 40*(4), 863-884.

Tuomi, I. (2000). Data is more than knowledge: Implications of the reversed knowledge hierarchy for knowledge management and organizational memories. *Journal of Management Information Systems, 16*(3), 103-117.

Van der Spek, R., & Spijkervet, A. (1997). Knowledge management: Dealing intelligently with knowledge. In J. Liebowitz & L. Wilcox (Eds.), *Knowledge management and its integrative elements.* New York: CRC Press.

Vasconcelos, J., Gouveia, F., & Kimble, C. (2002). An organizational memory information system using ontologies. In *Proceedings of the 3rd Conference of the Associação Portuguesa de Sistemas de Informação*, University of Coimbra, Portugal.

Vat, K. (2004). *Conceiving a learning organization model for sustainable development: The IS manager's perspective based on soft systems methodology*. Paper presented at the International Engineering Management Conference.

Von Krogh, G., Ichijo, K., & Nonaka, I. (2000). *Enabling knowledge creation*. New York: Oxford University Press.

Wiig, K. (1993). *Knowledge management foundations.* Arlington: Schema Press.

Wiig, K., de Hoog, R., & Van der Spek, R. (1997). Supporting knowledge management: A selection of methods and techniques. *Expert Systems with Applications, 13*(1), 15-27.

Yang, Y. (1999). An evaluation of statistical approaches to text categorization. *Journal of Information Retrieval*. Retrieved January 12, 2008, from http://citeseer.ist.psu.edu/yang97evaluation.html

Zack, M. (1999). Managing codified knowledge. *Sloan Management Review, 40*(4), 45-58.

Endnotes

[1]   Available at http://protege.stanford.edu/plugins/owl/owl-library/index.html (for the extended version send a request to male@frsf.utn.edu.ar)

[2]   Available at http://www.vacationidea.com/hotels/ acqualina.html

[3]   Available at http://gate.ac.uk/

[4]   Available at http://wordnet.princeton.edu/index.shtml

[5]   Perform over 150 documents with 35.091 words

Chapter IX

Implementing Communities of Practice to Manage Knowledge and Drive Innovation

Nicole M. Radziwill, National Radio Astronomy Observatory, USA

Abstract

A community of practice (CoP) unites individuals with shared interests and shared or complementary competencies to interact on a regular basis, advancing communal learning and knowledge. By facilitating increased, relevant interactions between people, CoPs often improve organizational effectiveness. They can be initiated as a performance-improvement intervention at the individual, group, and organizational levels. After describing the theoretical background of CoPs as discussed in the organizational theory and knowledge management literature, this chapter classifies the results of research in the knowledge management domain, dating from 1991, into an actionable plan-do-check-act (PDCA) model. Future trends in CoP development, including e-science and digital ecosystems, are then discussed.

Introduction

A "community of practice" (CoP) is a "group of people who share a concern or a passion for something they do and learn how to do it better as they interact regularly" (Lave & Wenger, 1991). According to Lesser and Storck (2001), a CoP is equivalently defined as a group "whose members regularly engage in sharing and learning, based on common interests." Members share competencies that distinguish them from nonmembers, and "engage in joint activities and discussions, help each other, and share information... develop[ing] a shared repertoire of resources: experiences, stories, tools, ways of addressing recurrent problems" (Wenger, 2006). According to these researchers, there are four requirements for a CoP to exist: there must be people, shared interests, shared competencies, and shared activities performed on a regular basis that advance learning and knowledge. The latter two requirements exclude, for example, interest groups that do not qualify its members based on skill, social clubs in which members share experiences in the absence of advancing a communal body of knowledge, or the typical professional or academic conference for which the core group of attendees varies.

Though the term "community of practice" was first coined in the 1991 study by Lave and Wenger, the concept was not new even at that time. Their research, focusing on the theory underlying community-based learning, was initiated as a study in anthropology. It examined the learning processes in traditional apprenticeship settings, such as medieval tradesmen's guilds, and provided a descriptive framework for the characteristics of these communities and their knowledge generation and dissemination processes. The authors determined that the learning process followed the pattern of *legitimate peripheral participation*, in which members initially joined the community as limited participants, but as their competence strengthened, they became more central to the community and adopted apprentices of their own. At the turn of the 20th century, Schloss (1898) attributed the mechanisms for accomplishing team-based work in factories to a similar process he described as employee self-organization.

A comprehensive review of the literature describing CoPs and the theories underlying them, particularly organizational theory, was performed to construct a conceptual model for the practical implementation of a CoP. The primary limitation for this study is that it represents a collection of recommendations from the research literature which has not been validated empirically and collectively as a methodology for implementing CoPs in the context of a quality improvement culture. Nonetheless, the presentation of results from theory development and empirical studies in an operational context is novel and provides substantiated guidance for implementing CoPs.

The following sections describe the background as provided by supporting literature, the outcomes from the research organized for actionable implementation and quality improvement, a summary of the enabling technologies for CoPs, a description of future trends and possibilities, and a summary of the findings.

The objectives of this chapter are to:

- Familiarize the reader with the evolution of the CoP concept, from medieval times to the present
- Provide a synopsis of the literature describing the theoretical foundations for this concept
- Relate CoP deployment to targeted performance-improvement interventions
- Describe an actionable process for developing and launching a new CoP using a quality management approach
- Familiarize the reader with new horizons for applying the CoP concept to advance science, technology, and society

Background

Theoretical Foundations

Theoretical and empirically motivated research into CoPs has been based on foundations in organizational theory, social learning, and more recently, the knowledge management literature. Davenport and Prusak (1998) advocate creating the repository of "structured knowledge." Schultze and Leidner (2002) claim that most of the research in knowledge management is focused on this limited area, codification of explicit knowledge. But this neglects the criticality of tacit (or experiential) knowledge sharing, which is the aim of the CoP. However, according to Nonaka (1991), explicit and tacit aspects of knowledge sharing are not mutually exclusive; from either perspective, the CoP provides a rich platform for investigating the complementary nature of the two.

The CoP as a Performance-Improvement Intervention

An intervention is activity undertaken for the express purpose of improving something. When "something" refers to performance improvement at the individual, group, or organizational levels, the activities are called performance-improvement interventions. These may be noninstructional interventions (such as workplace design, knowledge management, communities of practice, multimedia/technology solutions, culture change management, and process reengineering) or instructional (e-learning, classroom training, on the job training, games, and simulations).

CoPs are often affected as a performance-improvement intervention at any or all of the levels of performance (i.e., individual, group, and organization). The typically desired benefits, as discovered in a survey of 60 CoP leaders by Millen, Fontaine, and Muller (2002), are promoting collaboration, improving social interactions, increasing productivity, and improving organizational performance. Note that the first two "benefits" are merely means to achieving the real benefits, productivity and performance, which are directly tied to business results.

Social Capital and Innovation through CoPs

The CoP has also been cited numerous times as a mechanism to support and drive innovation. Nahapiet and Ghoshal (1998) provide conceptual evidence by tracing the development of theory through family and urban development studies dating from the 1960s. They define social capital as "the sum of the actual and potential resources embedded within, available through, and derived from the network of relationships possessed by an individual or social unit," and establish that it is the synergistic effect of the network as well as the assets and resources that are made accessible as a result of that network. Social capital, they assert, is a necessary ingredient in the dynamics of innovation and value creation.

Innovation is described in the same study as the effect of exchanging information from different domains and combining it in new ways. It involves the three steps of generating new ideas and inventions, exploiting them for value creation (and competitive advantage, in some situations), and diffusing the knowledge appropriately. CoPs emerge or are instituted to be a vehicle for building social capital through interactions and catalyzing new idea generation, thus creating value and simultaneously serve as both a formal and informal channel for disseminating results (Cox, 2005).

Enabling Technologies

Many networking and software applications are available to support and facilitate improved communication and collaboration. The following enabling technologies, from the areas of communications, knowledge networks, and organizational network analysis, are representative of the tools that are available at the time of writing. This section is intended to give a brief overview of the classes of technologies, with some names of products within those spaces.

Asynchronous and Synchronous Communication

Members of a community may wish to involve one another through message or document-based, asynchronous means, or by communicating in real time. Examples of these types of facilitating technologies include instant messaging, e-mail, discussion boards, project workspaces such as Communispace (http://www.communispace.com), e-learning workspaces such as Blackboard (http://www.blackboard.com), and wiki environments such as TWiki (http://twiki.org). The wiki is a Web-based document structuring environment in which groups of people can collaborate to produce shared documents. It is a particularly useful construct because version control and change tracking is handled automatically.

Knowledge Networks and Groupware

The applications that integrate functions such as e-mail, discussions, and point-to-point messaging are collectively referred to as knowledge networks, which grew out of the groupware applications of the 1990s. As an example, Microsoft Share-Point and its add-on product, Knowledge Network (http://www.microsoft.com/kn), provide an online environment in which communications, document sharing, and business intelligence metrics are integrated. The add-on augments the system with user profiling and skill set matching so that members of the organization can more easily find others with certain skill sets. The key limitation of these systems is that they are intended for codifying and disseminating explicit knowledge, which is important, but does not eliminate the need for managing tacit knowledge.

Organizational Network Analysis Systems

Primarily through surveys, the technique of organizational network analysis (ONA) maps the key relationships between individuals in an organization. This is done to identify the weaknesses and strengths of the interactions, and the relative roles of the individuals, in order to recommend appropriate interventions. Software (e.g., UCINET) can be applied to improve CoPs by graphical analysis of the network. (Cross, Laseter, Parker, & Velasquez, 2005)

A PDCA Framework for CoP Implementation

The plan-do-check-act (PDCA) quality-improvement approach developed by Shewhart (1939) was popularized by W. Edwards Deming as a quality-improvement approach. The "plan" stage involves understanding the goals and objectives of the proposed change. The "do" step involves executing according to the plan. "Check" means that objective metrics are collected and data-driven recommendations for improvement are made, and at the "act" stage, those improvements are realized and the cycle begins again.

In the following sections, outcomes from theoretical and empirical research from the past two decades are presented and organized according to stages of the PDCA cycle. The main contribution of this presentation is to communicate the results from research studies in a way where they may effectively and readily be used in practice.

PLAN

PLAN – Step 1: Establish the Business Case and Charter

The bulk of the empirical research on the subject of CoPs has been carried out by the American Productivity and Quality Center (APQC; http://www.apqc.org). In their 2001 benchmarking report, they studied CoPs and nested CoPs using surveys, including one company that managed nearly a hundred CoPs (APQC, 2001). From their investigation, they outlined nine critical success factors for forming and sustaining a CoP. The first was to develop a clear, compelling business case for all participants in a community. Two questions were provided to guide in the development of this business case: "What value does belonging and participating in a CoP have for an individual?" and "What value does it bring a department if one staff member takes time to participate?" Vestal (2006) further articulates this concept when he asserts that a community must have a mission and a vision, be aligned with the goals of a business, and be continually revisited and audited to maintain its relevance.

Additionally, APQC identified that while enabling technology is not a requirement for a CoP to exist, "best practice organizations typically create an information technology tool to support CoPs." For this reason, the remainder of the discussion will assume that the CoP implementation includes technology as one of its aspects.

PLAN – Step 2: Conduct Readiness Self-Assessment

According to Callahan (1997), there are six steps that are common to all models for the performance-improvement process, and these can also be applied to a readiness

Table 1. Callahan's summary of the performance improvement process

---

1. Identify business needs linked to performance gaps.
2. Establish measurable performance goals that can be linked to the overall organizational strategy.
3. Determine the performance needed to accomplish the goals.
4. Outline obstacles and barriers to success.
5. Identify interventions to close the gap, taking into consideration the pertinent obstacles.
6. Conduct an evaluation to ensure the gaps are closed.

---

assessment when a CoP is chosen to be the desired performance-improvement intervention. The six steps are summarized in Table 1, and represent the general process that is followed when a performance-improvement intervention is done.

Additional forms and questionnaires to guide the self-assessment process have been made available by the Full Circle Associates consulting group, and could be employed as planning for a CoP is underway. (White, n.d.)

PLAN – Step 3: Benchmarking and Best Practices

By examining the practices of companies that had implemented CoPs, Vestal (2003), through qualitative interviews, uncovered ten characteristics of successful CoP initiatives. These are: a compelling, clear business value proposition; a dedicated, skilled facilitator; a coherent, comprehensive knowledge map; an outlined, easy-to-follow knowledge sharing process; an appropriate technology mechanism; communication and training plans for both internal and external members; an updated roster of members and relationships between members; key metrics displayed to reflect business success; a recognition plan; and an agenda of critical discussion topics for the first 3 to 6 months of the community's existence.

In 2005, the APQC conducted an empirical study of 700 community members in organized CoPs at 22 sponsor sites which confirmed these findings. One of the key findings of the APQC study, as summarized by Vestal (2006), was that effectively motivating workers to participate in the community was essential for the success of the initiative. From qualitative interviews, the recommendation was made that a CoP be externally facing to increase its viability. For example, a knowledge management community would serve not only the internal employees, but also the customers or markets the company sponsoring the CoP wished to reach.

PLAN – Step 4: Technology & Environmental Analysis

Many CoPs integrate software systems to provide a virtual platform for communication, but this is not a requirement. While investigating the factors contributing to successful technology implementations in virtual communities, Wenger (2001) notes that several approaches are valid, ranging from simple and low cost to complex and expensive. These approaches are: a) use technologies such as e-mail and discussion lists which are already available to most organizations; b) start with a simple base system (including discussion groups, project-oriented workspaces, and document sharing), and be ready to expand as the community grows; c) deploy a community-based software system such as Communispace or ArsDigita; or d) implement an enterprise class collaboration system (e.g., LiveLink). Wenger recommends that a full technology evaluation be considered according to the same process a company would use for evaluating any significant information technology investment, and notes that an organization must "devise a strategy appropriate to each unique situation."

PLAN – Step 5: Budgeting and Metrics

Millen et al. (2002) conducted semistructured interviews with the leaders of 60 communities to determine typical costs and benefits of CoPs to quantify the financial impact of implementation. They found that cost estimates were not limited to deployed technologies, but included the salaries of community leaders, publication costs, and event costs for face-to-face gatherings. A complete list of costs and benefits identified by their surveys is presented in Table 2. This is not an exhaustive list, but represents the typical costs that may be incurred and benefits that may be derived from a CoP implementation. Benefits are more easily quantifiable if there are tangible assets that are produced by the CoP which can be financially valued.

The authors also surveyed the cost breakdowns for actual CoP implementations of the communities represented by the 60 leaders, and found that only a small fraction supported the development of the enabling technologies. They advised that if the total cost of ownership (TCO) was calculated using only technology costs, as commonly done by technology implementers, the actual TCO would be significantly underestimated. The average cost data from their survey is charted in Figure 1.

Table 2. Typical costs and benefits of CoPs

Costs	Benefits
Technology investments	Increased idea creation
Cost of participation	Increased quality of knowledge
Meeting/conference expenses	Creating a common context
Content publishing	Creating sense of shared goals
Promotional expenses	Improving communication to enhance successful project completion, new business acquisition
Cost of community support	Increasing speed to generate ideas
	Increasing speed of making value decisions
Permanent staff	Creating new tangible assets

Figure 1.Cost data from CoP implementations (adapted from Millen et al. 2002)

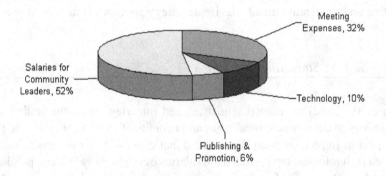

PLAN – Step 6: Create Form and Function (Quality Management System)

Results from APQC studies involving structured surveys of CoP implementers, as described by Vestal (2006), support the establishment of "form and function" for the CoP. This would include providing a knowledge map for the system, enabling an "easy to follow knowledge sharing process," and keeping a dynamic roster of community members. The implication is that the processes used to understand, conduct, and grow the operations of the CoP should be articulated and well understood. This can be accomplished by instituting a quality management system for the CoP, which documents the processes and provides a mechanism for auditing and continually improving those processes. The knowledge transformation spiral (internalization, socialization, combination, externalization) popularized by Nonaka and Takeuchi (1995) can be used to guide the process identification.

DO

DO – Step 1: Establish the Community Leadership Team

APQC recommends that a "dedicated, skilled facilitator or leader" be instituted to manage the activities and the direction of the community. This person should assist the core team as it develops and grows the business case for the community, and must "have the skills to facilitate an organic, outside-of-line responsibility group." Millen et al. (2002) extend this by outlining several roles that should constitute a CoP team that has critical mass; in addition to the community leader, these are community member, subject matter expert, sponsor, mentor, facilitator, content coordinator, events coordinator, technologist, and journalist. These individuals must collectively identify catalysts for participation.

DO – Step 2: Implement Supporting Technologies, Conduct Launch Event, Sustain Community through Relevant Activities

A key finding of many CoP researchers was that face-to-face activities were necessary but not sufficient for CoP success. Kimball and Ladd (2004) recommend, on the basis of developing virtual communities for large organizations such as the U.S. Department of Agriculture and Fannie Mae, that a face-to-face "launch event" be held to provide the initial foundations for trust and impetus for online communication. They also recommend activities to reinforce participation, such as simple acknowledgement of others' contributions, and summarizing discussions.

DO – Step 3: Cultivate the Membership

Incentives for community membership must be must be ever-present for the community to be both viable and sustainable. Evangelou and Karacapilidis (2005), leveraging social-technical systems theory, identify individual and organizational behaviors that contribute to CoP performance. These included intelligence, cognition, ambition, reciprocity, communication skills, motivation, and expertise on the individual level; at the organizational level, a knowledge culture, shared codes and values, a technological infrastructure, and team coherence were cited as fac-

Table 3. Examples of negative and positive reinforcement

Negative Reinforcement	Positive Reinforcement
"Knowledge is Power" dilemma; hoarding	Constructive relationships formed
Negative criticism, loss of reputation or respect	Enhanced respect for social and individual identities
Manipulation of shared knowledge	Assignment of tasks based on shared interests
Lack of intellectual absorptive capacity	Measurement and reward of cooperation

tors. Furthermore, they formulated negative and positive modes of reinforcement substantiated by the theory, which are presented in Table 3. The implication is that the community leaders should promote the behaviors that contribute to CoP success, and do so using the recommendations for positive reinforcement guided by the theory.

CHECK

CHECK – Step 1: Community Effectiveness Metrics

The effectiveness of a CoP can be assessed in terms of indicators that describe the degree of collaboration that is occurring and the value that is being generated from collaboration, typically expressed in financial terms. To evaluate the effectiveness of the collaborations, the most significant work to date has come from the highly successful Macuarium CoP (a Spanish language support group for Mac computer users, based in Madrid). The community leader has identified a four-quadrant model to manage the value derived from a CoP, which maps value delivered to the user on the vertical axis, and value to the organization on the horizontal axis (Castro, 2006). Value to the user is subjectively assessed on a scale that progresses from "subjective" to "objective," and organizational value from "indirect" to "direct." Using this conceptualization, the authors discovered that community leaders should seek to continually improve their activities so that for each element of the CoP, the evaluations fall in the upper right quadrant. This indicates direct benefits to the organization and objective benefits for the user.

CHECK – Step 2: Tools Evaluation

At this stage, the utility of the enabling technologies that have been selected to help the CoP achieve its goals should be revisited. Tools that are outdated should be replaced, new tools that would advance the goals of the community should be recommended, and the technological environment should be scanned for new tools or tools under development.

CHECK – Step 3: Costs and Benefits

As with any project-based financial analysis, the value generated by the CoP should be evaluated in the context of the expected returns. After actual costs and benefits are identified and quantified, they can be compared to expected values for costs and benefits, or derived measures such as return on investment (ROI), net present value (NPV), or discounted cash flow (DCF) can be assessed. If the CoP is not meeting its targets for value generation, the sponsors must take action.

CHECK – Step 4: Produce Actionable Recommendations

The information gathered during the "check" stage of the PDCA cycle must be evaluated in light of the business case and charter to ensure that the community is achieving the desired results for both its participants and its sponsors.

ACT

ACT – Step 1: Implement Recommendations; Revisit Business Case, Revisit Charter

When new process improvements are to be implemented, the business case and charter should be revisited to ensure that any adjustments to the direction of the CoP are made. Process improvements should support the mission of the community, or they will not add the desired value.

ACT – Step 2: Rejuvenate Knowledge Base

Vestal (2003) recommends that the knowledge repository, which is core to a CoP, be periodically revisited by the community leaders and cleansed to remove spurious information. This would include incomplete documents that were never (and will never be) finished; however, an audit trail for ideas that did not come to fruition might be useful to determine why some ideas thrived while others failed. At this time, the community leaders can also refresh the knowledge base to provide up-to-date, relevant artifacts. Timeliness is critical for sustaining a membership that perceives that value is being added for them.

ACT – Step 3: Start the Process Again

PDCA codifies a cycle of continuous improvement. Once the business case is re-visited, the community charter is updated, and recommendations are enacted, the process of measuring and re-evaluating continues. The pattern of value creation and value regeneration thus becomes the status quo.

Future Trends

Network Discovery Applications

Automating the identification of organizational networks is an area of current re-search; two potential applications include being able to study the emergence and evolution of CoPs over time, or to identify latent CoPs that could benefit from ad-ditional investments within an organization. Products are currently being developed to satisfy the data collection requirements. For example, The Morphix Company (http://www.morphix.com) offers the MetaSight product as a tool for building an adaptive learning organization. By tracing the flow of e-mail within an organization as well as outside its boundaries, a real-time network graph is produced that shows connections as well as subject matter clusters.

E-Science and Cyberinfrastructure

The term "e-science" was developed by John Taylor of the UK Office of Science and Technology in a 1999 grant proposal: "e-Science is about global collaboration in key areas of science and the next generation of infrastructure that will enable it" (Hey & Trefethen, 2003). Although e-science will require high-performance computing facilities such as clusters of workstations, advanced computational models and analysis systems, and access to the grid, Hey and Trefethen assert that the ultimate goal of advancing science through vital online "collaboratories" is far from being achieved. The social and intellectual aspects of online and in-person scientific collaboration through communities must be investigated and advanced to achieve these goals.

In the United States, e-science has been more commonly referred to as "cyberinfra-structure," the result of a policy document issued by the National Science Foundation (NSF Cyberinfrastructure Council, 2006), although the overall goal is identical to the European effort. According to the NSF definition, "cyberinfrastructure integrates hardware for computing, data and networks, digitally-enabled sensors, observatories and experimental facilities, and an interoperable suite of software and middleware services and tools." Through its investments, the NSF aims to "develop a human-centered cyberinfrastructure that is driven by science and engineering research and education opportunities." Many opportunities exist for integrating CoPs into this model.

Digital Ecosystems

The concept of digital ecosystem combines the social aspects of communities with high-performance computing resources *and* self-organizing, autonomous software. Much like e-science, these concepts are being pioneered in the European community and are critical aspects of FP7, the 7th six-year plan for research to be funded by the European Framework Programme (FP) (European Commission, 2005). Collaboration and emerging technologies are two of the focus areas for this research program.

The concept of humans and computing embedded in an adaptive ecosystem targeted to learning for the achievement of specific goals is indicative of a CoP-style presence. In addition to the social challenges, there are many challenges specific to the computing environment which include systemically shifting from a centralized to an emergent data management model, and designing and building software systems that are self-similar for optimal maintainability. (Dini, Rathbone, Vidal, Hernandez, Ferronato, Briscoe, et al., 2005) The development of successful digital ecosystems will depend on continued research into knowledge sharing behaviors and characteristics between communities. The limited research that has been done to date (Alvesson, 2000) indicates that the characteristics of CoPs which encourage knowledge sharing within a community may actually suppress it between communities. Understanding these critical success factors will be essential for the growth of viable digital ecosystems.

Conclusion

Effective CoPs rely on the continuous cultivation of social capital and intellectual, which can be enhanced and advanced by implementing a targeted collection of enabling technologies. The growth of a CoP is most effectively facilitated by a dedicated team, whose role is to organize and lead discussions and events, and ensure that learning opportunities are made available to community members.

Although CoPs often make use of established technologies such as e-mail, instant messaging, and discussion groups, it is the unification of these enabling technologies into a strategically cultivated learning environment that defines the community.

Social capital, intellectual capital, and tools must be strategically positioned so that the desired performance improvements are achieved when a CoP is implemented. These performance improvements must match the identified gap between current and preferred performance levels.

References

Alvesson, M. (2000). Social identity in knowledge-intensive companies. *Journal of Management Studies, 37*(8), 1101-1123.

American Society for Process Control (APQC). (2001). Process Classification Framework. Retrieved on February 12, 2007, from http://www.apqc.org/pcf

Callahan, M. (1997). *From training to performance consulting*. Alexandria, VA: American Society for Training and Development.

Castro, M. C. (2006, March). *The Macuarium set of community of practice measurements*. Madrid: Macuarium Network.

Cox, A. (2005). What are communities of practice? A comparative review of four seminal works. *Journal of Information Science, 31*(6), 527.

Cross, R., Laseter, T., Parker, A., & Velasquez, G. (2005). *Assessing and improving communities of practive with organizational network analysis*. Charlottesville, VA: Network Roundtable at the University of Virginia.

Davenport, T. H., & Prusak, I. (1998). *Working knowledge*. Cambridge, MA: Harvard Business School Press.

Dini, P., Rathbone, N., Vidal, M., Hernandez, P., Ferronato, P., Briscoe, G., et al. (2005, July). *The digital ecosystems research vision: 2010 and beyond*.

European Commission. (2005, January 4). *Research themes in FP7*. Retrieved November 17, 2006, from http://ec.europa.eu/research/future/themes/index_en.cfm

Evangelou, C., & Karacapilidis, N. (2005). On the interaction between humans and knowledge management systems: A framework of knowledge sharing catalysts. *Knowledge Management Research and Practice, 3*(4), 253-260.

Hey, T., & Trefethen, A. (2003). E-Science and its implications. *Phil. Trans. R. Soc. Lond. A, 361,* 1809-1825.

Kimball, L., & Ladd, A. (2004). Facilitator toolkit for building and sustaining virtual communities of practice. In P. Hildreth & C. Kimble (Eds.), *Knowledge networks: Innovation through communities of practice* (pp. 202-215). Hershey, PA: IGI Global, Inc.

Lave, J., & Wenger, E. (1991). *Situated learning: Legitimate peripheral participation*. Cambridge, UK: Cambridge University Press.

Lesser, E. L., & Storck, J. (2001). Communities of practice and organizational performance. *IBM Systems Journal, 40*(4), 831-842. Retrieved October 15, 2006, from http://www.research.ibm.com/journal/sj/404/lesser.html

Millen, D. R., Fontaine, M. A., & Muller, M. J. (2002). Understanding the benefits and costs of communities of practice. *Communications of the ACM, 45*(4), 69-73.

Nahapiet, J., & Ghoshal, S. (1998). Social capital, intellectual capital, and the organizational advantage. *Academy of Management Review, 23*(2), 242-266.

Nonaka, I. (1991). The knowledge creating company. *Harvard Business Review, 69,* 96-104.

Nonaka, I., & Takeuchi, H. (1995). *The knowlege-creating company: How Japanese companies create the dynamics of innovation.* New York: Oxford University Press.

NSF Cyberinfrastructure Council. (2006, January 20). *NSF's cyberinfrastructure vision for 21st century discovery (5.0).* Washington, D.C.: National Science Foundation.

Schloss, D. F. (1898). *Methods of industrial remuneration* (3rd ed.). London: Williams & Norgate.

Schultze, U., & Leidner, D. (2002). Studying knowledge management in information systems research: Discourses and theoretical assumptions. *Management Information Systems Quarterly, 26*(3), 213-242.

Shewhart, W. A. (1939). *Statistical method from the viewpoint of quality control.* New York: Dover.

Vestal, W. (2006). Sustaining communities of practice. *KM World, 15*(3), 8-40.

Wenger, E. (2001, March). *Supporting communities of practice: A survey of community-oriented technologies.* North San Juan, CA: Etienne Wenger.

Wenger, E. (2006). *Communities of practice: A brief introduction.* Retrieved October 27, 2006, from http://www.ewenger.com/theory/communities_of_practice_intro.htm

White, N. (n.d.). *Self-assessment resources.* Retrieved November 15, 2006, from http://www.fullcirc.com/community/assessmentlinks.htm

Internet Session: SETI@Home, an Unlikely Community of Practice

http://setiathome.berkeley.edu/

The SETI@Home project, which actively uses the desktop computing facilities of volunteers around the globe, processes huge volumes of radio astronomy data each day to pursue the goal of detecting intelligent life outside Earth. The project was proposed in 1995 and formally launched in 1999.

What makes this a community of practice? First, there is a membership base. These people can access the SETI@Home Web site to post messages, find answers, form teams with other individuals, and view profiles of other individuals and teams. They share a common purpose and have all volunteered their personal computers to participate in the data analysis process. The process is continuous instead of task-based; data analysis could continue for years or decades, depending upon the results that are found. There is a "User of the Day" if members wish to become acquainted with other participants.

Case Study: Communities of Practice for Quality Improvement: A New Model for Healthcare Provider Collaboration & Best Practices Sharing by iCohere (http://www.icohere.com/IPRO_CoPCase.pdf)

Review the case study provided at the URL above, which provides an overview of how one firm delivered benefits through implementation of a CoP.

Questions:

1.   What do you think was the biggest benefit realized by the implementation?

2.   Why is visibility of the quality improvement process important?

3.   How was the new operational model different from the 1:1 marketing model?

Useful URLs

1.   Etienne Wenger, Communities of Practice: Learning as a Social System: http://www.co-i-l.com/coil/knowledge-garden/cop/lss.shtml

2.   iCohere, Community of Practice Design Guide: http://www.icohere.com/CoP-DesignGuide.pdf

3. World Bank, Community of Practice Questions and Answers. http://siteresourc-es.worldbank.org/KFDLP/Resources/461197-1148594717965/CoP_QA.pdf

4. Steve Denning, Communities for Knowledge Management: http://www.ste-vedenning.com/communities_knowledge_management.html

5. Etienne Wenger and William Snyder, Communities of Practice: the Organi-zational Frontier: http://hbswk.hbs.edu/archive/1317.html

6. Joe Jarzombek, Software Assurance: Highlighting Changes within our Soft-ware Community of Practice: http://www.stsc.hill.af.mil/CrossTalk/2006/09/0609FromTheSponsor.html

7. Communities of Practice and Dunbar's Number: http://blog.mopsos.com/ar-chives/000075.html

8. David Raths, Practice Makes Perfect: http://www.infoworld.com/articles/pe/xml/01/11/05/011105pecommunity.html

9. Valdis Krebs & Jerry Falkowski, Discovering Communities of Practice at IBM: http://www.orgnet.com/emergent.html

Further Readings and Interactive Activities

10. United States Patent 7127440, Knowledge Management System and Method (method for establishing a Community of Practice). http://www.freepatent-sonline.com/7127440.html

11. Soren Kaplan, Communities of Practice for Collaborative Knowledge Sharing (an interactive Web presentation). http://www.conferences.icohere.com/pre-sentations/virtual2004/soren/player.html

12. Michael J. Muller, Patterns of Participation in Two Communities of Practice: Community of Engagement vs. Community of Reference. http://domino.research.ibm.com/cambridge/research.nsf/0/6a6879a65d997f3f85256c24005792de/$FILE/TR2002-03.pdf

13. Maura Borrego, et al. Developing an Engineering Education Research Com-munity of Practice through a Structured Workshop Curriculum. http://www.mines.edu/research/cee/1042_DEVELOPING_AN_ENGINEERING_EDU-CATION_RESE.pdf

14. Etienne Wenger et al. Seven Principles for Cultivating Communities of Practice. http://www.askmecorp.com/pdf/7Principles_CoP.pdf

Chapter X

The Hidden Deception of Knowledge Management Systems:
Search, Rigidity, and Declining Radical Innovation

Michael J. Mannor, Michigan State University, USA

Abstract

Drawing on the Carnegie tradition of bounded rationality, knowledge theory, and research on core rigidities, this research examines the potential unintended consequences of knowledge management systems on organizational routines. Although knowledge management systems promote interpersonal knowledge transfer, individual cognitive biases toward satisficing rather than optimal search are exaggerated by knowledge management systems that create a convenient proximal search environment of existing organizational knowledge that biases individuals against broader search. This behavioral bias toward proximal search then leads to the rigid persistence of organizations in existing knowledge traditions and declining radical innovation. To help address these concerns, the chapter concludes with an analysis of how this rigidity can potentially be overcome through the strategic management of knowledge management infrastructure.

Introduction

At First Choice Communications[1], a small but rapidly growing telecommunications and Internet company, a consistent challenge for competing effectively was successful management of knowledge in the organization. New people with diverse knowledge were being hired into the organization, experienced people often hoarded their knowledge, and ambiguity about where knowledge resided was slowing creative endeavors. First Choice thought that it had solved these innovation barriers by implementing a state-of-the-art knowledge management system. However, after only a few months, it was clear that the new system was changing the business in unexpected ways. In addition to the expected changes increases in employee knowledge transfer, unexpected changes to underlying individual routines and processes were also occurring. With new competitors aggressively entering their markets every day, First Choice needed to find the root of these problems and fix them fast.

An important development in the ongoing development of information technologies for contemporary organizations is the emergence of knowledge management systems. These systems hold much promise for organizations, particularly knowledge-intensive firms (Starbuck, 1992), in part due to their ability to allow organizations to make major steps forward in their efforts to create "learning organizations" (Senge, 1990) that can better store, access, and navigate their existing knowledge bases to gain competitive advantage over their rivals.

Despite the great promise knowledge management systems hold for organizations, the hidden side effects of many information technology (IT) "revolutions" are their influence on internal organizational processes and routines, which can be dramatic, unplanned, and dangerous (Willemssen, 2002). Although much may be understood about the technical merits of such IT innovations, much less is understood about how these new systems change the dynamic organizational routines and processes that guide organizational action (Pentland, 1995). Similar to the way that architectural innovations are recognized as the most deceptively disruptive to incumbent firms in an industry because they change the underlying processes and components through which organizations develop products (Henderson & Clark, 1990), IT revolutions can similarly disrupt routines that support innovation inside organizations. In fact, enterprise-wide adoption of new IT solutions such as knowledge management systems not only change the way an organization process information, they change the underlying routines for the way knowledge is combined, used, and shared in organizations. These changes require dramatic adjustments to existing organizational routines, but these changes in routines receive much less attention than other factors of technology implementation and management. Thus, understanding and controlling these changes are an important task for the strategic management of firms, and for the realization of potential benefits from information technology.

In the adoption of new knowledge management systems, several different objectives are often pursued simultaneously and are supported differently by the new systems. First, many firms look to knowledge management systems to assist with the organizational diffusion of existing organizational knowledge. By developing knowledge networks, corporate directories, and best practice guides (O'Dell & Grayson, 1998; Ruggles, 1998) firms can speed the diffusion and transfer of existing knowledge from the "haves" to the "have-nots." This is an important function of knowledge management systems and is the primary goal of many knowledge management initiatives. In addition, many organizations implement knowledge management systems in the hopes of creating new-to-anyone knowledge in the organization that can be leveraged for organizational advantage (Nonaka, 1994). In this knowledge creation endeavor, the centralization of organizational knowledge from the new knowledge management system is intended to spur the growth of new ideas by making it easier for employees to search for and find knowledge in the pursuit of new ideas. Both of these goals are important consequences of knowledge management systems, with the knowledge creation function particularly important to new product development and ultimately firm growth and profit.

However, despite growing attention to knowledge management systems in the literature (Alavi & Leidner, 2001), little is still understood about the impact of knowledge management systems on routines. In this research I specifically focus on this internal systems perspective, highlighting the hidden deception of knowledge management systems in terms of their impact on organizational search routines. I argue that although advantages certainly exist to the use of knowledge management systems to transfer and diffuse knowledge in organizations, an important downside to their adoption may be their role in creating systematic organizational biases in the way the organization searches for information. In essence, I propose that individual cognitive biases to search for satisficing rather than optimal alternatives (March & Simon, 1958) in a limited search environment (Axelrod, 1997; Levinthal, 1997) are exaggerated by the adoption of knowledge management systems. These behavioral biases lead to the development of core rigidities (Leonard-Barton, 1992) that act to stifle radical innovation in organizations. Thus, the overall research question of this investigation is to understand both the full intended and unintended impacts of knowledge management system adoption in organizations.

To understand the nature of these diverse implications, this research proposes a new model of knowledge management system influence that integrates and builds on three key streams of research. First, this research builds on conceptual foundations regarding the functions of knowledge management systems in organizations from the knowledge management systems literature (Alavi & Leidner, 2001; Nonaka, 1994). Second, this research draws from the behavioral theory of the firm (Cyert & March, 1963; March & Simon, 1958) to explore the role of bounded rationality and the nature of search and learning in organizations. Finally, theoretical advances from the core rigidities literature in strategic management are leveraged to inform of the consequences of these behavioral biases for innovation in firms (Leonard-Barton, 1992).

Conceptual Development

Knowledge Management and Knowledge Management Systems

To begin with it is important to be clear with definitions. Knowledge management is defined as identifying and leveraging the collective knowledge in an organization to help the organization compete (von Krogh, 1998). Building on this, knowledge management systems (KMS) are defined as a class of information systems applied to managing this organizational knowledge and are developed to support and enhance processes of knowledge creation, storage/retrieval, transfer, and application (Alavi & Leidner, 2001). As outlined earlier, knowledge management systems help organizations in many ways. Knowledge management systems can help with the coordination of virtual teams, with mapping the sources of organizational knowledge, and with preserving learning from previous organizational experiences. In particular, research has suggested that firms use knowledge management systems for internal benchmarking (KPMG, 1998; O'Dell & Grayson, 1998), directly sharing knowledge (Gazeau, 1998), developing corporate directories (Davenport & Prusak, 1998), and establishing organizational knowledge networks (Ruggles, 1998).

More than just a static database or functional perspective, knowledge management is conceptualized as a set of intertwined activities (Alavi & Leidner, 2001). These intertwined activities include four key management functions which form the foundation of the current exploration of knowledge management systems. The four key functions are knowledge transfer, knowledge creation, knowledge storage/retrieval, and knowledge appropriation (Alavi & Leidner, 2001; Holzner & Marks, 1979; Pentland, 1995) and are summarized in Table 1.

To begin with, knowledge transfer is the dimension of knowledge management that involves the movement and sharing of knowledge from knowledge sources to locations where it is needed and can be used. In particular, in this capacity knowledge management systems foster an environment where intergenerational learning can occur by allowing heuristics, short-cuts, improved processes, and problem solutions to be passed on from one generation of products to future generations. Knowledge management systems also allow tacit knowledge to be better codified and dispersed, lessening the need for mentorship programs and allowing learning to occur individu-

Table 1.

Knowledge Management Functions	Definition
Knowledge Transfer	Involves the movement and sharing of knowledge from knowledge sources to locations where it is needed and can be used
Knowledge Creation	Involves the development of new content to be added to the organization's tacit and explicit knowledge bases
Knowledge Storage/Retrieval	Involves the storage, organization, and retrieval of organizational knowledge residing in various component forms throughout the organization
Knowledge Appropriation	Involves the application and leverage of knowledge toward organizational outcomes rather than the knowledge itself

Sources: Alavi and Leidner (2001), Grant (1996), Holzner and Marx (1979), Pentland (1995), Stein and Zwass (1995), and Walsh and Ungson (1991)

ally by employees who need the information. This type of "just-in-time learning" (Alavi & Leidner, 2001) leads to an environment where search becomes very efficient and organizational knowledge becomes much more widely distributed.

Second, knowledge creation is the dimension of knowledge management that involves the development of new content to be added to the organization's tacit and explicit knowledge bases. In this function knowledge management systems promote the discovery of new insights into existing knowledge by making existing knowledge more accessible. Analysis techniques such as data mining allow organizations to search through potentially vast archives of accumulated knowledge to draw links between disparate sources of knowledge (Alavi & Leidner, 2001). By combining these unconnected sources firms can leverage their existing assets to achieve better utilization of their historical investments into knowledge resources.

Third, knowledge storage/retrieval is the dimension of knowledge management that involves the storage, organization, and retrieval of organizational knowledge residing in various component forms throughout the organization. In this function, organizations can leverage the efficiencies of technology inherent in knowledge management systems to make the identification and mapping of existing organizational knowledge more accessible. Similar to organizational memory, this dimension of knowledge management focuses both on the content and acquisition of knowledge in the organization. The content is the design of the knowledge management system in terms of what knowledge is retained in addition to how the knowledge is retained. The acquisition component is focused on how this knowledge can be accessed by organizational members. Common devices for these efforts are databases, Web sites, and Intranets. In addition, organizations vary significantly in terms of what knowledge they choose to retain for future use in their knowledge management systems. Some organizations may make a strong concerted effort to convert tacit knowledge to explicit knowledge (Polyani, 1963) that can be stored in a knowledge management system and others are content to simply digitize existing company manuals and documents. Other organizations may be still more ambitious and attempt to retain information learned from partners in strategic alliances, technical consortia, or other forms of interorganizational collaborations.

Finally, knowledge appropriation is the dimension of knowledge management that involves the application and leverage of knowledge toward organizational outcomes. In this appropriation stage, knowledge management systems can assist organizations in turning their knowledge into innovative products and services. This phase is particularly important, as this is where investments into knowledge management systems are made worthwhile for firms by potentially giving organizations the opportunity to create competitive advantages from their knowledge assets (Grant, 1996). Due to the complex nature of knowledge and knowledge appropriation inside organizations, these advantages are also more likely to be the type of rare, valuable, nonsubstitutable, and inimitable advantages (Barney, 1991) that can be sustained over significant periods of time. Although this dimension of knowledge management remains under-explored (Alavi & Leidner, 2001), it holds great promise for strategic outcomes such as firm growth and innovation.

Organizational Search Routines and Core Rigidities

Clearly knowledge management systems can provide many benefits to organizations. However, they also have the potential to seriously influence and disrupt the underlying processes of routines in organizations. Thus, for a full picture of the impact of knowledge management systems in organizations we need to explore how the adoption of these new technical systems influences the inner social systems and behavioral patterns of work in organizations.

Routines are defined by Pentland (1995) as "grammars of action" that act to structure the daily process of work in organizations. Routines can be as simple as the routine for addressing a customer in a vendor-client interaction, or as complex as the routine for processing evidence by police at a crime scene. Routines tend to be relatively stable over time, but are subject to disruptions presented by organizational contingencies (Nelson & Winter, 1983). Thus, when significant shocks to the organizational system occur, there is a period of readjustment in which routines may be altered and new routines adopted for continued use. The adoption of new knowledge management systems provides a significant shock to the nature of work done in organizations, particularly in research and development-intensive and service organizations in which knowledge management is the primary activity of the firm. Accordingly, a period of readjustment is likely to occur after the adoption of such systems.

The key question for the current study is how this readjustment will change the nature of work in the organization. Certainly not all routines will change as a result of a new knowledge management system adoption. The routines most likely to be subject to readjustment are the routines surrounding the search for and use of knowledge, as these are the outcomes most influenced by the change. To understand these changes, we must understand how individuals search for and use knowledge. According to Cyert and March (1963), building on earlier work by March and Simon (1958), individuals engage in search for information/knowledge when they need to solve a problem. This "problemistic search" approach applies to a broad range of problems from issues of organizational survival to the search for a new job by an unhappy worker or the search for a new product that better fulfills the demand of customers (Cyert & March, 1963). In each case the individual is motivated by a problem and the search is targeted toward knowledge and solutions that address the problem at hand.

A key question, of considerable interest to scholars through the years, is how far the individual will search to find a solution to their problem. Economic traditions suggest that the "rational man" is an individual who will exhaustively search all possible alternatives, review the total cost/benefit ratio of each alternative, and arrive at an optimal decision. Behavioral scientists have questioned this logic by arguing that individuals have limited cognitive processing abilities and are instead boundedly rational (Simon, 1955). This bounded rationality leads them to engage in satisficing rather than optimal search where they choose the best solution from a limited set of alternatives rather than the global optimal solution (March & Simon, 1958). In a practical sense, one can imagine the decision of a working person who is nearly out of gas on the way to work. The decision of which gas station to fill up at is most likely a decision between a small set of convenient options, which may or may not result in the best possible price of gasoline. The person could use calculations to determine all of the possible gas stations within reach with a short supply of gas, call each to determine their current pricing structure, and then choose the best possible alternative. Instead, the person is more likely to simply choose the lowest price of the gas stations the person passes on the way to work. Following this logic, when boundedly rational individuals encounter a problem they are unlikely to engage in optimal search, but will instead accept a suboptimal proximal search of more convenient alternatives.

Returning to the question of how the adoption of new KMS will impact the readjustment of knowledge search and use routines in organizations, these ideas of bounded rationality and proximal search are particularly relevant. In a pre-KMS organization, individuals who encounter problems are likely to use a wide variety of search techniques to find solutions to problems. The decision of how far these individuals will search is partially driven by individual factors of experience and expertise, and partially driven by the availability of solutions. Some will engage in wider search, some in narrower search, but without a central repository of knowledge available, the search routines engaged will have considerable variability.

The adoption of a KMS, however, provides a central repository of knowledge accessible by all. In a post-KMS organization, the individual who encounters a problem no longer needs to engage in wide search for applicable knowledge, as some degree of relevant knowledge will be proximal and convenient in the knowledge management system. Thus, due to the individual's boundedly rational behavioral tendency toward proximal and convenient search, rather than wide and optimal search, the individual is likely to adjust the knowledge search routines to satisfice more quickly.

Core Rigidity

A final area of research that provides insight into the influence of knowledge management systems in organizations is the strategic management literature on core rigidities. Core rigidities are the inflexibilities in cognitive perspectives that occur when an organization becomes significantly invested in a certain logic or set of technologies to the neglect of other logics and technologies over time (Leonard-Barton, 1992). Leonard-Barton explains that core rigidities are the flip side of core capabilities and are "not neutral in nature." They are deeply embedded knowledge sets that actively create problems for both new and existing projects, even projects that are congruent with current core capabilities (Leonard-Barton, 1992). Although Orlikowski (2002) argues that such rigidities can sometimes be a positive element in organizations (i.e., "the Kappa way"), the key element for the current argument is that such powerful organizational mentalities can overwhelm the desire to look "outside of the box" for new or novel solutions to problems. Over time the capabilities that develop to support the chosen logic and technology begin to cut the organization off from alternative logics and technologies. This rigidity acts to both reduce the possibility of out-of-the-box ideas as well as poorly positioning the organization for potential market changes.

Building on the ideas of routines advanced in the previous section, the behavioral tendency of individuals in a post-KMS organization to engage in more proximal and convenient search of existing organizational knowledge is likely to exaggerate the problem of core rigidities in such companies. Although all firms have to deal with the possibility of core rigidities to some degree, because of the changes in organizational routines to favor proximal search, these routines will begin to perpetuate the dominant logics of these organizations and deceptively push these organizations into strong core rigidities. These rigidities will then become manifest in a focus on incremental ideas, inflexible reinforced organizational cultures, and declining radical innovation.

Theory and Propositions

Bringing together these ideas, the adoption of new knowledge management systems are proposed to influence organizational routines in two key ways. These ideas are outlined in Figure 1. The first effect is a positive impact on routines for the transfer of existing organizational knowledge within the firm in terms of intergenerational learning and knowledge search efficiency. This improved knowledge transfer is then proposed to positively impact the appropriation of this existing organizational knowledge by increasing the rate of innovation in organizations. The second effect is a negative impact on routines for new knowledge creation, in terms of the breadth and distance of knowledge search, due to the hidden construction of core rigidities. These reduced search routines are then proposed to lead to knowledge appropriation activities that are less capable of producing radical innovations due to the diminished exposure to diverse and out-of-the-box ideas. The proposed model is included as Figure 1 and the key constructs are described in Table 2.

Knowledge Transfer and the Processes of Individual Learning

Stepping through the model, the first stage is the positive association between the adoption of knowledge management systems and the transfer of knowledge within

Figure 1.

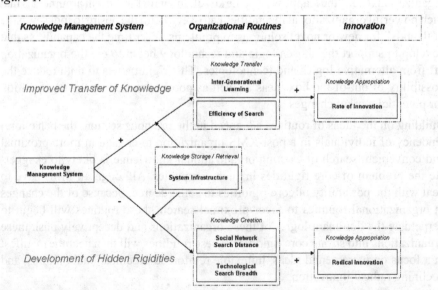

Table 2.

Definitions of Key Model Constructs	Definition
Knowledge Management Systems	Information technology systems that support the creation, transfer, storage, retrieval, and appropriation of firm expertise and knowledge
System Infrastructure	The structure of the knowledge management system, qualitatively, as internal, external, or hybrid
Intergenerational Learning	Learning from one cohort of an organization's products and services that is applied to new cohorts of products and services
Efficiency of Search	The ratio of the successful search results to the input of search behaviors in an organization
Social Network Search Distance	The total distance away from the focal firm, primarily in terms of social network ties, that the organization investigates in their search activities
Technological Search Breadth	The number of different technologies that the organization investigates in their search routines
Rate of Innovation	The raw number of innovations produced by the focal firm per year
Radical Innovation	The creativity, novelty, uniqueness, and overall divergent nature of new innovations produced by the focal firm

Sources: Alavi and Leidner (2001), Hall, Jaffe, and Trajtenberg (1993), and Abernathy and Utterback (1978)

the firm. This is proposed based on several factors. First, I argue that knowledge management systems are likely to increase search efficiency in firms that adopt such systems. In short, the adoption of new knowledge management systems brings together the knowledge resources held in an organization more efficiently and effectively than was have ever been possible before. Instead of individuals needing to rely on social networks or hierarchical structures to "find" knowledge that is likely dispersed throughout an organization, the individual can now look to a single comprehensive resource that encapsulates much of the organizations knowledge stock into a single user interface. In addition to tracking down individuals within the organization that may be potential sources of information, firms that do not have a KMS may engage in a search that leads outside of the firm. This may include relying on resources available through public databases (i.e., U.S. patent and trademark office resources) or through social network ties, but in any case takes more time and more effort. A KMS can improve the efficiency of this process by providing a single central knowledge repository where search activities can be focused to find answers with much less effort or extended search. Together these arguments support the following proposition.

Proposition 1: Organizational adoption of knowledge management systems increases the efficiency of search routines within the organization.

In addition to search efficiency gains, knowledge management systems also help to make intergenerational knowledge and learning more readily available for new products and services. Organizations that do not have knowledge management systems often rely on individual memory from previous product experiences to guide the transfer of learning from one generation of products to another. In addition to the faultiness of individual memory, these memories are often personally biased and may not accurately reflect the full learning from previous organizational experiences. The accuracy and completeness of this intergenerational knowledge can be critical in avoiding the mistakes of the past, and thus help to both speed and improve future innovations. Working to solve these problems, knowledge management systems help the organization to formalize the transfer of knowledge and make intergenerational learning easier and more widely disseminated. Instead of one or a few individuals trying to recall past learning, the experiences of all historical organizational research efforts can be distilled into a single source. Instead of making the same mistakes over time or relying on the often biased memory of individuals regarding what was learned from previous generations, this information is made widely available and easily accessible. Together these arguments support the following proposition.

Proposition 2: Organizational adoption of knowledge management systems increases the degree of intergenerational learning within the organization.

Knowledge Creation and the Construction of Hidden Rigidities

The next important outcome of knowledge management system adoption is the effect of such systems on knowledge creation in firms. For many organizations the potential for gains in knowledge creation capabilities are a primary factor in the decision to invest in knowledge management systems. Unfortunately, the effects of knowledge management systems on knowledge creation routines may be largely unintended and negative in their ultimate influence on organizations.

The primary negative influence is the influence of knowledge management systems on behavioral biases that lead to shorter, more proximal and convenience-based searches that fail to integrate new and novel ideas. Building on the behavioral theory argument that individuals engage in search that often trades optimizing for satisficing (Cyert & March, 1963), the impact of knowledge management systems on search routines would have a generally narrowing effect. Although without knowledge management systems individuals are already prone to behavioral biases and satisficing search routines, these biases become more exaggerated. In fact, the adoption of a knowledge management system is likely to aggravate these already limited and convenience-based search activities because it provides a vast collection of proximal solutions to be searched. Instead of looking outside of the firm or to related technologies for ideas and innovations from other organizations, individuals are likely to fall victim to their boundedly rational tendency to satisfice in search.

The effects of this narrowed search are evident in several changed knowledge creation routines. First, a primary process of knowledge creation involves the development of systems of meaning, whereby new knowledge is created through interpersonal interactions among experts. However, the negotiation of knowledge meaning between experts is generally the result of interpersonal interactions that occur in the attempt to resolve problems. Instead of promoting these types of helpful knowledge negotiations between experts, knowledge management systems create a narrowed search by offering an alternative media format where individuals do not need to engage others to solve as many problems. Thus, instead of encouraging knowledge negotiations between experts, knowledge management systems encourage self-directed search for more immediate and less novel answers from codified organizational knowledge rather than the dynamic interaction with peers.

This bias toward limited social search is supported by the work of Nonaka and Konno (1998) who argue that knowledge creation in organizations depends on the creation of a "ba," or a place for knowledge interaction to occur. Of the four types of ba explored by these authors, the most applicable to the study of knowledge management systems is the "cyber ba," a virtual space of interaction where knowledge can be combined to create new knowledge (Nonaka & Konno, 1998). Although this virtual space helps to share existing knowledge, the problem is that it limits the need for social network search or interpersonal interactions. Further, the cyber ba simply recycles existing organizational knowledge. In this sense, knowledge management systems inhibit creative or novel knowledge creation because it reinforces what is already known by the organization, and existing knowledge continually gets reprocessed in the organization rather than novel new knowledge being created.

The underlying similarity in these arguments is the degree to which knowledge management systems encourage or discourage social network search. For increased novelty and creativity, a wide and varied social network search is needed. However, knowledge management systems provide a central and opportune location for knowledge acquisition, acting to discourage extended social network search and increasing the convenience of proximal search. Without a wider social network search, organizations become increasingly entrained in existing patterns of thought and dominant logics for action. Instead of engaging in an extensive social network search to gather new knowledge, this becomes more unnecessary and a decreasing tendency in the routine search for solutions to problems. Accordingly, these arguments support the following proposition.

Proposition 3: Organizational adoption of knowledge management systems decreases the distance of social network search by individuals in the organization.

In addition to decreased social network search, a second search narrowing effect is also likely to be realized because of the behavioral tendency toward proximal search. Important to the discovery of new ideas are the insights of ideas from related but distinct technologies. In many cases, breakthroughs for products are inspired by innovations in related products. Throughout history major drug developments, automotive designs, and breakthroughs in computing technologies have shared credit with related technologies that inspired their novelty. This model of searching for inspiration from related technologies is known as technological search breadth and gauges the degree to which different technologies are investigated as part of the search process. On the high end, an extensive technological search would include the search of many related and potentially distant technologies, where a more limited search would only investigate significantly-related technologies. However, because knowledge management systems encourage narrowed and more proximal search, researchers are less likely to search other technologies to find solutions to current product obstacles. Over the course of multiple generations these behaviors have become the standard routines and are institutionalized into core rigidities. These arguments lead to the following proposition.

Proposition 4: Organizational adoption of knowledge management systems decreases the breadth of search by individuals in the organization.

Knowledge Storage & Retrieval (System Infrastructure Matters)

An important point to note is that knowledge management systems are designed in different ways, which can lead to different effects on knowledge transfer and knowledge creation routines. Although millions of different classifications might be created to describe different knowledge management systems, three categories of designs are proposed to illuminate the issues explored in this research. The three designs are knowledge management systems with an internal focus, an external focus, or a hybrid approach.

The dominant approach is to design knowledge management systems with an internal focus. An internal focus is so popular that many users of knowledge management systems might not realize that other infrastructure types exist. An internally focused knowledge management system is one that simply focuses all system features and functionality at mapping, exploring, and storing existing organizational knowledge.

Corporate directories, knowledge maps, and similar subsystems all support an internally focused knowledge management system. An externally focused knowledge management system is one that focuses most system features and functionality at mapping, exploring, and storing knowledge outside the organization for internal organizational use. Such systems often tie together basic science from university labs, competitor knowledge from technical consortia groups, and may also incorporate new perspectives from strategic partner knowledge stocks. These types of systems are uncommon but serve to make wide knowledge search much easier for organizational members. The final type of knowledge management system is a hybrid system. This type of knowledge management system incorporates both elements of internal and external systems into one central repository of both existing and external knowledge for organizational use.

The important question for the current research is how these different types of knowledge management system infrastructures influence the other relationships proposed in the theoretical model. The influence is proposed to be significant. Although knowledge management systems that only unite internal business logics, ideas, and knowledge enhance the opportunity for knowledge transfer and diffusion, such systems reinforce the behavioral rigidities suggested. This creates an important tradeoff. By focusing the knowledge management system on existing stocks of organizational knowledge the organization is providing the most extreme type of an internal knowledge recycling system. Because knowledge incorporated in the system is not new to the organization, this perpetuates the entrainment of organizational members in existing business logics and dominant organizational paradigms. By consistently recycling existing organizational knowledge, the behavioral biases that encourage proximal search will lead to strong internal rigidities where outside ideas may eventually become not only ignored but actually rejected because they are outside of the mold of the developed internal business logic. Further, because of the prevalence of the dominant knowledge perspectives, the opportunity for new organizational members to change the dominant perspective becomes weaker and weaker over time. Powerful and influential opinion leaders in research and development efforts who have become entrained in the logic utilize their influence to overpower new idea-holders, thus sustaining the dominant logic through socialization and institutionalization efforts.

On the other hand, knowledge management systems that incorporate external knowledge sources into the system design specifically break out of the dominant logic frames that lead to these rigidities. Once again, however, we see a tradeoff. Although external systems actively break down hidden rigidities, these systems do not assist in the transfer of existing knowledge within the organization. Thus, externally-based systems do an excellent job of bringing in the basic science of university labs, the competitor knowledge of technical consortia, and the powerful knowledge of strategic partners, but may fail in diffusing existing organizational knowledge through the organization. A solution to these problems is the design of hybrid knowledge management systems. Hybrid systems overcome these problems by bringing together the best of both worlds. By simultaneously bringing together a comprehensive source of existing organizational knowledge together with an interface that easily integrates the knowledge resources of business partners and outside agencies, these systems can effectively balance the need for knowledge diffusion and transfer with the need for new ideas to prevent the creation of hidden rigidities. Together these arguments lead to the following propositions.

Proposition 5a: The infrastructure of the knowledge management system will moderate the relationship between knowledge management system adoption and knowledge transfer such that an internal or hybrid focused knowledge management system will enhance the knowledge transfer inside the firm, but an external system will limit the degree of knowledge transfer inside the firm.

Proposition 5b: The infrastructure of the knowledge management system will moderate the relationship between knowledge management system adoption and knowledge creation such that an internally-focused knowledge management system will further reduce the knowledge creation in the firm, but an external or hybrid system will enhance the degree of knowledge creation in the firm.

Knowledge Appropriation

Finally, the last part of the proposed model explores the implications of the improved learning and developed rigidities for organizational outcomes. Although a direct relationship with organizational performance might be posited, Ray, Barney, and Muhanna (2004) and others have argued that choosing intermediate dependent variables are more appropriate when studying internal business processes. Accordingly, and following the development of the four knowledge perspectives developed by Alavi and Leidner (2001), this research will focus on the ability of an organization to appropriate value from their knowledge. In appropriating value from knowledge in organizations, firms often have multiple goals. Some firms focus on the development of absorptive capacity (Cohen & Levinthal, 1990), the training of new associates, or the ability to create innovative new products and services. Among these, particularly critical to the achievement of competitive advantage, is the ability of an organization to use its knowledge to innovate. Focusing on this important outcome of firm knowledge and learning, two separate innovation outcomes are proposed to be influenced differently by the development of new routines for knowledge transfer and knowledge creation.

Rate of Innovation

First, enhanced knowledge transfer routines are proposed to improve the rate of innovation in organizations. A key driver of quantity in production, from manufacturing to R&D, is the efficiency of production processes. Building on the idea that knowledge management systems facilitate quicker and more efficient search activities, these faster searches are likely to lead to an increase in the overall quantity of innovations produced. Bad ideas are discarded more quickly, good ideas are identified more quickly, and overall the process of innovation is pushed faster and more efficient. Thus, through their role in making organizational search routines more efficient, knowledge management systems are likely to increase the efficiency of the overall R&D process. This increased efficiency will then allow the same resources to be engaged in a higher quantity of research and development than previously possible, leading to a larger number and higher rate of innovations produced by the organization.

In addition, the increased availability of intergenerational knowledge is also likely to speed up the rate of new innovation by organizations. Organizations that are better at learning from their past mistakes can use this knowledge to make better decisions. In addition, the transfer of knowledge from previous learning can be used to as a guide to choosing more fruitful paths for investigation and allow the researcher to avoid useless combinations of resources (Fleming & Sorensen, 2004). Together these arguments lead to the following proposition.

Proposition 6: Increased search efficiency and intergenerational learning in organizational search activities positively influence the quantity of innovations produced by the organization.

Radical Innovation

Finally, the creation of hidden rigidities in the breadth and distance of search are proposed to decrease the degree of creativity, originality, and novelty of the innovation created in organizations. As argued above, although knowledge management systems influence the creation of knowledge in the organization, the fact that the knowledge is derived from recycled existing organizational knowledge is likely to impact the novelty of the results. This overexposure of organizational researchers to existing knowledge stocks directly results in less exposure to new and novel ideas from outside the firm. Research on creativity has stressed that truly creative outcomes depend largely on the integration of new and novel ideas, often from diverse disciplines and sources in search for breakthroughs (Rosenkopf & Nerkar, 2001).

To be able to incorporate these diverse sources into organizational research efforts, firms must both search through distant social networks and diverse technologies to create real breakthroughs. In fact, notable findings from weak ties literature suggest that the "strength" of weak ties is their ability to expose individuals to out-of-the-norm ideas and concepts that can inspire creative outcomes (Granovetter, 1973). Further, truly creative outcomes are often the result of combining several unrelated technologies in novel ways (Fleming, 2001).

Thus, the result is that although knowledge management systems are argued to spur more innovation, unfortunately the innovation produced will tend to be more of the same type of innovation that the firm has done in the past. In a world where breakthrough innovation is capable of transforming industries and redefining markets (Tushman & Anderson, 1986), the increased rigidity in knowledge traditions can seriously limit the ability of the organization to achieve competitive advantage. Together these arguments lead to the following proposition.

Proposition 7: Increased search distance and search breadth in organizational search activities positively influence the degree of creativity, originality, and novelty of innovations produced by the organization.

Discussion and Implications

The Hidden Repercussions of IT Innovations

This research provides an interesting examination of the hidden repercussions of IT innovations. Although the technical merit of innovative systems such as enterprise resource planning (ERP) systems, customer relationship management (CRM) systems, and knowledge management (KM) systems are impressive, it is important to also understand the potential for hidden changes in underlying organizational processes. In the case of knowledge management systems, the changes in organizational search routines might very well go unnoticed. However, the results of institutional rigidity and the inability to create radical innovations are likely to be very clear.

This research highlights the need for the knowledge management literature, and potentially other IT literatures, to look deeper into the organizational processes influenced by such innovations. Future research might apply similar logic to the adoption of sales management tools, customer relationship systems, or further explore other routines that may be influenced by knowledge management system adoption. In fact, the future of IS research in many areas may be to look at how IS changes not just the efficiency/productivity of workers but also how it changes the nature of the work done in organizations. In many cases the ability of firms to leverage their IT assets, and ultimately achieve successful organizational outcomes, may be at stake.

Overcoming the Deception: Practical Implications for Managers

In addition to its theoretical implications, this research has serious potential implications for practicing managers and senior executives. First and foremost, knowledge management systems may be impacting organizations in ways that managers do not understand. This is particularly relevant for managers of radical innovation-dependent organizations such as medical research institutes and pharmaceutical firms who need to find breakthroughs to survive. Instead of waiting for long term repercussions, executives can take steps early in the adoption and development of knowledge management systems to achieve intended results. Blindly turning on the switch and hoping for the best might have unintended consequences, but it is possible to get the best from both worlds. Building routines that utilize the knowledge management system but still have mechanisms for wider search (and rewards for such search), or developing knowledge management systems that utilize a hybrid internal and external structure, can get the best of both worlds. The functionality of the knowledge management systems can both build broad search directly into the system in addition to assisting in the transfer and diffusion of knowledge. In this way firms can ensure that their employees are engaging in wide and diverse search, as the evolution of organizational routines will begin to include these dimensions and become integrated into the typical use patterns.

In conclusion, this research takes a first step in exploring the wide and diverse influence of knowledge management systems inside organizations. Continuing research into the nature of this influence is needed to further expand our understanding of these diverse implications. Although knowledge management systems hold much promise for advancing organizational learning and allowing firms to better leverage their assets, the underlying consequences of such innovations need to be carefully examined before turning on the switch.

References

Abernathy, W. J., & J. M. Utterback. (1978). Patterns of innovation in technology. *Tech. Rev., 80*, 41-47.

Alavi, M., & Leidner, D. E. (2001). Knowledge management and knowledge management systems: Conceptual foundations and research issues. *MIS Quarterly, 25*(1), 107-136.

Axelrod, R. M. (1997). *The complexity of cooperation: Agent-based models of competition and collaboration.* Princeton University Press.

Barney, J. B. (1991). Firm resources and sustained competitive advantage. *Journal of Management* (17), 99-120.

Cohen, W. M., & Levinthal, D. A. (1990). Absorptive capacity: A new perspective on learning and innovation. *Administrative Science Quarterly, 35*(1), 128-152.

Cyert, R. M., & March, J. G. (1963). *A behavioral theory of the firm.* Englewood Cliffs, NJ.

Davenport, T. H., & Prusak, L. (1998). *Working knowledge.* Boston: Harvard Business School Press.

Fleming, L. (2001). Recombinant uncertainty in technological search. *Management Science, 47*(1), 117-132.

Gazeau, M. (1998, June). Le management de la connaissance. *Etats de Veille*, 1-8.

Granovetter, M. (1973). The strength of weak ties. *American Journal of Sociology, 78*(6), 1360-1380.

Grant, R. M. (1996). Toward a knowledge-based theory of the firm. *Strategic Management Journal,* (17), 109-122.

Hall, B. H., Jaffe, A., & Trajtenberg, M. (2001). *The NBER patent citation data file: Lessons, insights and methodological tools (NBER Working Paper 8498).*

Henderson, R. M., & Clark, K. B. (1990). Architectural innovation: The reconfiguration of existing product technologies and the failure of established firms. *Administrative Science Quarterly, 35*(1), 9-30.

Holzner, B., & Marx, J. (1979). *The knowledge application: The knowledge system in society.* Boston: Allyn-Bacon.

KPMG Management Consulting. (1998). *Case study: Building a platform for corporate knowledge.*

Leonard-Barton, D. (1992). Core capabilities and core rigidities: A paradox in managing new product development. *Strategic Management Journal, 13*, 111-125.

Levinthal, D. (1997). Adaptation on rugged landscapes. *Management Science, 43*, 934-950.

March, J. G., & Simon, H. (1958). *Organizations.* New York: John Wiley & Co.

Nelson, R. R., & Winter, S. G. (1982). *An evolutionary theory of economic change.* Cambridge, MA: Belknap Press.

Nonaka, I. (1994). A dynamic theory of organizational knowledge creation. *Organization Science, 5*(1), 14-37.

Nonaka, I., & Konno, N. (1998). Concept of "Ba" building a foundation for knowledge creation. *California Management Review, 40*(3), 40-54.

O'Dell, C., & Grayson, C. J. (1998). If only we knew what we know: Identification and transfer of internal best practices. *California Management Review, 40*(3), 154-174.

Orlikowski, W. J. (2002). Knowing in practice: Enacting a collective capability in distributed organizing. *Organization Science, 13*(3), 249-273

Pentland, B. T. (1995). Information systems and organizational learning: The social epistemology of organizational knowledge systems. *Accounting, Management and Information Technologies, 5*(1), 1-21.

Polanyi, M. (1962). *Personal knowledge: Toward a post-critical philosophy.* New York: Harper Torchbooks.

Ray, G., Barney, J. B., & Muhanna, W.A. (2004). Capabilities, business processes, and competitive advantage: Choosing the dependent variable in empirical tests of the resource-based view. *Strategic Management Journal,* (25), 23-37.

Rosenkopf, L., & Nerkar, A. (2001). Beyond local search: Boundary-spanning, exploration, and impact in the optical disk industry. *Strategic Management Journal, 22*(4), 287-306.

Ruggles, R. (1998). The state of the notion: Knowledge management in practice. *California Management Review, 40*(3), 80-89.

Senge, P. M. (1990). *The fifth discipline. The art and practice of the learning organization.* London: Random House.

Simon, H. A. (1955). A behavioral model of rational choice. *Quart. J. Econom., 69*, 99-118.

Starbuck, W. H. (1992). Learning by knowledge-intensive firms. *J. Management Stud., 29,* 713-740.

Stein, E. W., & Zwass, V. (1995). Actualizing organizational memory with information systems. *Information Systems Research, 6*(2), 85-117.

Tushman, M. L., & Anderson, P. (1986). Technological discontinuities and organizational environments. *Administrative Science Quarterly, 31*, 439-465.

von Krogh, G. (1998). Care in knowledge creation. *California Management Review, 40*(3), 133-153.

Walsh, J. P., & Ungson, G. R. (1991). Organizational memory. *Academy of Management Review, 16*(1), 57-91.

Willemssen, J. C. (2002, October 1). *OMB's temporary cessation of information technology funding for new investments* (Testimony before U.S. Congress).

Endnote

[1] First Choice Communications is a fictional name to created to protect the identity of the actual organization.

Chapter XI

The Current Bottleneck of Knowledge Management and How Information Technology can be Successfully Used to Reduce It

Ricardo Salim, Cautus Networks Corporation, USA, &
Software de Venezuela, S.A., Venezuela

Carlos Ferran, Pennsylvania State University, USA

Abstract

Knowledge is generated and propogated by cultural selection, a process that—like it genetic counterpart, natural selection—consumes much time and resources in contrasting every new (or mutated) information with reality. However, if we hasten to minimize the field tests or marketing tests—forms of cultural selection—we run into the risk of not testing the knowledge sufficiently and make a deficient contrast with reality. In this chapter we present the concept of pragmatic minimization as the compromise of minimizing the amount of resources invested in contrasting the newly acquired knowledge with reality, while not falling into a lack of realism—blind idealism—or a cominatorial explosion of mental possibilities. Then, we advocate "simulated praxis" and a "more pragmatic artificial intelligence" as new avenues to optimally solve the problem of pragmatic minimization.

Introduction

Prior research[1] spanning several centuries allowed us to identify the knowledge management (KM) bottleneck as the increased demand for knowledge over the current limits in pragmatic minimization.

The chapter develops the concept of pragmatic minimization using three observations:

1. Just as the genetic code evolves by natural selection of random mutations of macromolecular information, knowledge is generated and propagated by cultural selection of essentially random changes in neurological information (innovations, inventions). This process occurs in three phases: (a) a syntactic phase in which the information is altered and exclusively kept in the syntactic or formal dimension of information; (b) a pragmatic phase in which the new (or altered) information is contrasted with reality (field test, marketing test) and is culturally accepted or discarded (forgotten or placed in an archive for future potential retesting); and (c) a semantic phase in which the new information is incorporated and diffused into the relational information network that we call culture, in particular, that which we call knowledge.

2. The phase of knowledge generation and transfer that consumes more time and resources is its pragmatic phase; the phase in which we bring it to praxis. In other words, the phase in which we contrast the newly generated information with reality. This is the phase that constitutes today's knowledge management bottleneck and therefore the one that needs to be minimized if we want to satisfy the ever increasing demand for knowledge. We call this need pragmatic minimization.

3. In our rush to minimize the pragmatic phase we run into the risk of not testing the knowledge fully and making a deficient contrast with reality that weakens its pragmatic anchors by (a) falling into voluntarism or idealistic belief that the facts will conform or must conform to our idea, or (b) letting our imagination fly into a prolific explosion of syntactic-semantic combinations, where each

one is as feasible as the prior while they do not land into the harsh dimension of reality.

Once the concept of pragmatic minimization has been developed as the compromise between minimizing the amount of resources invested in contrasting the newly acquired knowledge with reality, while not falling into blind idealism or a combinatorial explosion, the chapter proceeds to discuss how information technologies (IT) is the only option available to advance pragmatic minimization further than what traditional pedagogy and current knowledge management has been able to do. Moreover, it will show how if IT is excluded from knowledge management, none of its propositions are better than traditional pedagogy.

Following this idea, the chapter then proposes "simulated praxis" and a "more pragmatic artificial intelligence" as new avenues to optimally solve the problem of pragmatic minimization.

"Simulated praxis" is a way to overcome the current limits of pragmatic minimization by electronically simulating reality to test the ideas. The chapter will discuss how developments like virtual reality simulations are becoming the new test tubes for knowledge. It proposes as new avenues of research the use of virtual reality as an instrument to do practical tests of ideas. Virtual reality was initially represented in applications like flight simulators that were (and still are) used to train pilots but today it has extended to training surgeons, simulating chemical reactions, and biochemical tests to develop medicines.

A "more pragmatic artificial intelligence" is—in comparison with the traditional, more semantic inclination of artificial intelligence—oriented toward praxis and represented by developments in business intelligence systems applied to the Internet. The chapter discusses some attempts to develop Internet intelligent systems by companies like Yahoo! and Google.

After reading the chapter, the reader will have a solid set of criteria to evaluate the various attempts and tendencies present in knowledge management to overcome the current limits of pragmatic minimization.

Knowledge and Information

In the fields of philosophy, semiotic, and information theory, there is a generally accepted classification of information that differentiates between the information's syntactic, semantic, and pragmatic aspects (Brier, 1995; Carnap & Bar-Hillel, 1952; Ferran & Salim, 2003; Morris, 1971; Mosterín, 1991; Nauta, 1972; van der Lubbe, 1997).

Let us briefly illustrate this classification of information. The correspondence, relationship, or material (and/or energetic) meaning of certain information—for instance a design carved on a piece of marble—gives such information a pragmatic dimension. Its correspondence, relationship, or meaning in respect to other information—for instance a reference from and to other design—gives it a semantic dimension. And as its meaning becomes smaller, it only has a syntactic dimension; it becomes a form without content. Thus, a few lines with no relationship whatsoever to a material object or to another piece of information is considered syntactic information. If the same group of lines serves as the guide to the construction of a house, it is considered pragmatic information. And, when comprising a file, archive, or index with other designs, plans, sketches, projects, it is said to have a semantic content.

The dimensions of information are useful to clarify frequent misunderstandings around the concept of information; particularly in the current discussion in the knowledge management field on whether knowledge is information or not, if there is a difference between the two, and which are these differences. It has been said that information is a passive object located in books and in the memory of people, where it is waiting to be used or not. On the other hand, it has been said that knowledge, besides being able to stay "passive" in a book or in someone's memory, is also capable of "acting" from the brain, directing the movements of muscles or producing more knowledge (Galup, Dattero, & Heeks, 2002; Guignard, 1999). It is also said that information is "explicit knowledge" but not "implicit knowledge" (Polanyi, 1966).

Clearly, these attempts by knowledge management to distinguish between information and knowledge have resorted to ad hoc conceptual frameworks and not to stable frameworks. On the other hand, the dimensions of knowledge comprise a more formal, precise, and useful framework. For instance, it is clear that the ability to "act" over matter is inherent to the pragmatic dimension of information in contrast with the "passivity" of other types of information with a more syntactic or semantic dimension. Likewise, the so-called "implicit knowledge," manifested by "what it does" instead of "what it says" is mainly pragmatic information while "explicit knowledge" has more to do with the semantic dimension. Knowledge—due to its tendency towards the pragmatic dimension—is in organisms the equivalent of software in computers, while the data or "passive information" stored inside their memories are solely semantic or syntactic information.

Knowledge Generation and Transfer

Knowledge management often divides its subject into two main subjects: knowledge generation and knowledge transfer. Thus in Krog (2001) we can read: "In the literature on knowledge management, we can distinguish two core knowledge processes: knowledge creation and knowledge transfer."

After reviewing the literature referred to on the previous quote, we confirmed that such creation and transfer processes are not the discoveries of knowledge management, but evocations or reformulations of processes extensively researched by disciplines as diverse as biology and information theory, including all the cognitive sciences.

Genetic evolution consists on the generation of random mutations of genotypic information plus the natural selection of the mutation that increased the probability of the phenotype's ability to reproduce (Ayala & Kriger, 1984; Lewontin, 1974). When reproducing, the phenotype transfers the mutation to a new generation. If it does not achieve this, the mutated genotype becomes extinct, that is, all of its phenotypes perish leaving no descendants. So, information generation and transfer are processes that begun with genetic evolution (Gatlin, 1972; Griffiths, 2000; Holzmüler, 1984; Quastler, 1953).

A large chain of genetic mutations produced an evolutionary adaptation that has allowed some species—humans in particular—to generate nongenetic information that has the same or even higher capacity than that of the genetic information to increase the probability of successful reproduction. Furthermore, this is accomplished without the need to turn into another species or of necessarily paying with its life and extinction due to a failed innovation. This is information that started by being transferred between the organism's cells, especially of the nervous system, then between brain cells, and finally between individuals; the latter through imitation and learning behaviors. It is called cultural information or knowledge. This information is also transferred between families and organizations, and nowadays even between individuals, organizations, and machines (Caldwell, 2000; Donald, 1991; Gabora, 1995; Jonscher, 1999; Mosterín, 1986).

Nonetheless, for both genetic and cultural information there is an implicit process between information generation and information transfer. This process is the proof that the new information increases the possibility of surviving and reproducing. In the case of genetic information, such proof is natural selection (Darwin, 1859; Sober, 1984). If after a mutation the species increase its reproduction probability, the mutation is transferred to more descendants and it is established as naturally selected. In the case of cultural information, the proof starts with the adoption of the innovation by the dominating groups in the species but then it is propagated and accepted at formal and informal markets, generally in the form of goods and services that incorporate the innovation (Basalla, 1988; Gamble, 1983; Hartung, 1976).

Knowledge Processes and Dimensions of Information

Knowledge generation begins with the generation of information that is hardly related or committed to reality; it is more or less random events, brainstorms, sketches, preliminary designs, drafts, and so forth. It starts mainly with syntactic information since its meaning in concrete energetic-material terms or of other types of existing information is scarce. Then, the first attempts to turn the ideas into reality begin with the first practical tests of the information. They go from sketches or plans to the construction of the prototype or final draft, its test and correction before the full scale construction, the start of mass production or publishing, and even the test in restricted markets before the finishing touches, the production of the final batches, or the launching of the product to the great public. It is the phase in which information acquires its full pragmatic dimension, and in which the energetic-material restrictions appear. Finally, it is usually the tested information (i.e., idea, design) that acquires a significant semantic dimension, as it is related to previous or simultaneous experiences (information), essentially comparing its costs and benefits. It is the information that must be prone to be explicitly stated and transferred or spread in the organization; that is, capitalized in the form of knowledge obtained from the experiments, investigation, development, and market behavior. It is basically comprised by documentation, registry, formalization, legal protection of finished copyright, and its conversion into didactic material for the rest of the organization.

We can establish a correspondence between knowledge processes and the dimensions of information in that knowledge generation corresponds to syntactic information that gains a pragmatic dimension. Knowledge transfer corresponds to the pragmatic information when it acquires a semantic dimension. Information is knowledge only when it already has a pragmatic dimension, that is, when it has been tested.

Pragmatic information may be current and alive or past and experienced. The former is strictly pragmatic information while the latter is a semantic reference to pragmatic information, an accumulated experience or a settled memory.

Pragmatic Minimization

A model of a house is not always enough to evaluate it, but it usually is less costly than the house itself. Otherwise, no one would waste their time, materials, and work to do the model; they would test the house itself. The same could be said about the design of the model in reference to the model itself, of the draft in reference to the project, of the sketch in reference to the design; and by the same token, let us say in descending order, the idea compared to the design, the image, the fantasy, the dream compared to their respective successors. The smaller, less massive, less detailed, or less materialized the model, the smaller the cost usually is. However, its approximation and evaluation power compared to the real object is also smaller. So there is a need for a compromise between the cost of the model and its evaluating power. It is necessary to minimize the model, but not beyond an optimal point in which the cost of a bad evaluation starts to be greater than the minimization savings.

The syntactic phase of knowledge is rich in syntactic information, which generally is not very expensive. The pragmatic phase has to deal with energetic-material restrictions and therefore its costs are generally higher. The semantic phase is less costly, but it needs the pragmatic phase. Thus, to have a viable and cost effective generation of knowledge we require the minimization of the pragmatic phase without making the mistake of straying too far from reality.

Unlike genetic evolution, which requires the abortion of phenotype, its death, or the extinction of a whole species to discard a mutation of the genotype, knowledge is capable of inferring the result of an erratic idea with far fewer pragmatic indications, and sometimes with the simple comparison of the new idea against similar ones, previously subjected to experimentation and preserved into memory. This accelerates evolution and reduces energetic-material costs. In other words, knowledge lays a syntactic-semantic bridge that avoids—as much as possible—the slow and costly contacts with matter and energy of the pragmatic phase. We call this ability pragmatic minimization, with its complimentary syntactic-semantic maximization.

The fugacity, velocity, automatic nature, or the unconsciousness of certain "events of the mind," compared to the parsimony or poignancy of the "events of the material world," sometimes make the moves of the forms or of the erratic ideas towards materialization imperceptible, which is the time in which most of them are aborted.

When we can not perceive the materialization attempts, we are left with the illusion that we "mentally" selected the shapes and ideas. This illusion is then reinforced when later occurrences of similar shapes or ideas are indeed mentally aborted without the need of putting new attempts into practice. Thus, the erratic idea of taking a step towards nonsolid ground could be aborted so fast on the first attempt, that later on we do not even consciously remember that the first time there was at least one materialization attempt.

It is the illusion that the shapes and the ideas face each other in their own mental, ideal world with no need for material or pragmatic confrontation, until the best shape or idea is mentally selected, and only then it is materialized or put into practice. It is an illusion that has its origin in the possibility given by our thoughts to minimize the contrast with reality, necessary to get the result; that is, the possibility of semantic gain with minimum pragmatic effort.

The Idealist Order and the Evolutionary Order

Given a genetic mutation, nothing shortlists it. Only when reproduced on other portions of matter, and in that same measure, it is selected. Evolution does not say the best will win, but that the winner is the best. Evolution is a realistic or pragmatic order.

But knowledge in not always generated on the evolutionary order (following the Syntactic, Pragmatic and Semantic phases). In many cases, the phases sequence is first syntactic, then semantic and finally pragmatic. It is an idealist or formalist order in the sense that first an idea is selected and then it is put into practice. In contrast, on the evolutionary order, ideas try to become practice, and that idea which in fact becomes practice is then, for that same reason, selected.

Both orders start from a "pure" form that lacks meaning (syntactic phase), but while on the idealist order we continue by assigning significance in terms of other shapes (semantic phase) and end up with the material or practical meaning (pragmatic phase), on the evolutionary order we continue with the material or practical meaning (pragmatic phase) and end up with the meaning in terms of other shapes (semantic phase).

According to the formalist—or idealist—position, given certain shapes (syntax), the best one is selected from its comparison with other shapes (semantic), and then put into practice (praxis). According to the pragmatic position, given certain shapes (syntax), the ones that are put into practice (praxis), are considered the best (in comparison with the ones that did not make it) since they were put into practice (semantic). According to the formalist position, out of the different colors (syntax), the best to blend with the environment at the pole is the one that looks the most like the snow (semantic), and that is why it was adopted by the polar bear (praxis). According to the realistic or pragmatic position, out of the different colors (syntax), the one of the bear that survived on the pole (praxis) was, for that very reason, the best for its survival (semantic).

Semantic Heritage

The idealist position is not completely illusory. It is "practical" or "realistic" to save as much as possible on the hard and costly experimentation on our own flesh, taking advantage of the pragmatic minimization, that is, of the possibility granted to us by thoughts to reduce experimentation—the material test of the shapes—to a minimum and even do without it in the case of shapes similar enough to others previously aborted on their practical tests. In other words, it is convenient that the shapes or ideas inherit the semantics of their similar, of its models, and patterns as much as possible and that they inherit the results of the pragmatic tests of other ideas and avoid their own pragmatic testing.

Semantic heritage facilitates inferences, thus providing fluidity and letting the imagination fly. It allows us to project ideas, formulate hypothesis, and plan. In other words, it lets us think before we act.

Idealistic Perversions as the Limits to Pragmatic Minimization

The abuse of the capacity to minimize the energetic-material test of the information leads to perversions such as blind idealism, which is totally disconnected from reality or to a combinatorial explosion of possibilities due to the lack of "tough" pragmatic filters, capable of performing an early trimming of the combinatory branches that could cause an excessive semantic lushness.

Blind Idealism

Deep inside the semantic heritage there is an illusion. If we trust it too much, if we completely forget about the need for performing at least a minimum ratification or reality-check to keep us from losing contact with reality itself, we fall into blind idealism, that is, the naive conviction that the facts will shape or should shape themselves to an idea that someone considers perfect, without the need of this idea to learn or take anything from its confrontation with the former. This illusion is a dangerous and brainless arbitrariness. It is coarse creationism. It is the perversion of ideologies, superstition, fanaticism, delirium, and its phantasmagoria.

In contrast, methodic doubt turns the scientific method into something successful; the cautious humbleness in front of the facts (the market, for instance) is perhaps what makes liberalism something prosper. Thinkers such as Karl Popper and Friedrich Hayek have insisted on this (Shearmur, 1989). Rosenberg (1974) presents an interesting comment on the iterations of information with the market, in particular that of knowledge.

The controversy between idealism and pragmatism is very old. Plato and Aristotle are its classic exponents. The adjective "platonic," applied to love, for instance (sometimes in a disdainful or mocking fashion, and other times as a compliment) makes reference to an idealized love that never "descends" to the act, to the practice of making love. In the center of his fresco "School of Athens," Raphael portrays Plato pointing to the sky with his finger, and Aristotle pointing to the ground.

Combinatorial Explosion

Blind idealism is not the only perversion of semantic heritage or of pragmatic minimization. When there are no pragmatic anchors, the *flight of the imagination* may end up not just on a *blind idealism* that at least tries to impose itself on matter, but on a frenetic explosion of syntactic-semantic combinations, where each one of them is as possible as the other, as long as they do not bump into the limitations of matter or energy. This way the flight is lost into the tangled combination of myriad possibilities. It becomes a pathologically imaginary world, deeply autistic, and thus with no practical viability. In fact, even beginning with a modest number of combinable elements, there is nothing to prevent a combinatory explosion from happening when all its combinations are plausible. For instance, the potential outcomes of throwing a single dice ten times are in the order of the tens of million; for throwing them twenty times are in the hundreds of trillion; and for throwing thirty the figure is just too big to express (24 digits). The only way to prevent a combinatorial explosion –that sooner than later exhausts the capabilities of any natural or artificial brain– is to cut most of the combinatorial branches from the trunk. Normally the material –pragmatic– restrictions take care of this. If we cannot count on them, then we could try resorting to logical restrictions, but we know these depend on their premises, which at the end are arbitrary (subjective), and that lead us back to *blind idealism*.

So, again, pragmatic minimization is convenient but only up to a certain point. In this case, the limit is where the game of the ideas is in danger of falling into a combinatorial explosion.

The Knowledge Management Bottleneck

Knowledge is information—mainly pragmatic and semantic information— but not all information is knowledge, since syntactic information is not. The offer of information is abundant. On the Internet and in the media a huge amount of information is offered at a very low cost or just given away. However, a very small amount of that information is knowledge, and what in the end is knowledge is lost to those who can not distinguish it from what is not. So the abundant information offer does not satisfy the demand for knowledge, as shown by the high costs of professional education. Let us illustrate this.

The last decade alone has generated a huge amount of information on knowledge management. As a sample, on a day of November, 2006, the search engine Yahoo! on the "exact phrase" mode yielded about 11, 600,000 search results for the words "Knowledge Management" and 1,410,000 for that same exact phrase, plus the acronym PDF (that is, those search results that refer to a text that is usually an article). Even if only one of every 1,000 of these texts had information on the subject that would be relevant and not redundant, we would still be talking about 1,400 texts (and this number of different and significant articles in such a restricted subdiscipline of knowledge management, that only relates to business and the academy, is really an impressive number). Something similar happens with any subject that is "in fashion." For instance, "Enterprise Resource Planning" yields 4,030,000 thousand search results, and "Enterprise Resource Planning" + PDF, yielded 496,000 of them.

Of course, if CEOs believe that their companies are suffering a knowledge capitalization problem, or if the CEOs were suffering from a severe pain in a kidney, the CEOs would probably not look up the solution on the Internet or in a traditional library, nor will they try to generate solutions on their own. Chances are they will seek the help of a specialist, who in turn would have already studied the nonredundant and relevant information on the subject, and who would also be up-to-date on current innovations. Neither the Web nor the traditional libraries are made, at least for now, to replace proven knowledge, that is, knowledge that has been validated and gradually acquired in an organized fashion during a professional career. Naive innovation, on its own, is always an expression of the risky and not advisable practice of self-medication.

The cost of knowledge, whether it is in the form of services rendered by professionals, experts, consultants, specialists, or in the form of licenses or goods that incorporate knowledge, such as patents, software, or high tech devices, is usually high particularly when compared to other inputs and supplies that both companies and countries require (Blankley, Scerri, Molotja, & Saloojee, 2005). Peter Drucker (1993) has described this clearly:

Knowledge does not come cheap. All developed countries spend something like a fifth of their GNP on the production and dissemination of knowledge. Formal schooling - schooling of young people before they enter the labor force - takes up about one tenth of GNP (...). Employing organizations spend another 5 percent of GNP on the continuing education of their employees; it may be more. And 3 to 5 percent of GNP is spent on research and development - on the production of new knowledge.

Inside organizations, these knowledge formation costs are translated into expensive payrolls of professionals and experts. The alternative to hiring these experts is to put aside the semantic heritage and go through brand new trial and error; that is, to build the pragmatic dimension of information required out of their own experience. However, this obviously poses a high risk of causing even much higher costs to simply reinvent the wheel.

The cost of pragmatically testing the information—whether it is performed beforehand and is known by experts, or it is performed by the organization itself and thus accumulating its own experience—is the bottleneck that keeps the excess information offer from satisfying the knowledge demand.

It is therefore critical to move forward on the pragmatic minimization without falling into the above mentioned perversions. This is the only way to widen the current bottleneck of knowledge management.

Knowledge Management and Traditional Pedagogy

Without openly acknowledging it, knowledge management as a discipline has not produced a definite solution to the problem of knowledge generation and transfer. Having shown important advances on both sides, the really important problem shared by both has been left intact: the proof of knowledge. We will see that in this sense it has not even surpassed the methods already developed by traditional pedagogy.

One of the most elaborated subjects on the knowledge management literature is the distinction between tacit knowledge and explicit knowledge. We identify tacit knowledge with the pragmatic phase of the knowledge cycle and explicit knowledge with the syntactic and semantic phases. Thus, the way in which a painter moves the brush is what we, in terms of Polanyi (1966), "know" but can hardly say. It is pragmatic information that is hard to transform into semantic information.

Now then, even if it is not transformed into explicit knowledge, tacit knowledge could be turned into a tangible asset. For instance, we could develop a video course on painting that presents the painter moving a brush in a didactic fashion and this course could be burned into as many DVDs as the market demands. This way the tacit knowledge of the painter is transformed (with more or less fidelity) into a tangible asset that can be sold. Then, from a business standpoint, it is worth asking: If explicitation is not necessary to make knowledge tangible, what is the purpose of insisting in explicitly stating tacit knowledge? As we saw, we can exploit it, sell it, make it useful for others, and transfer it without the need of making it explicit.

Probably the answer is that knowledge management, by its own experience, has reached the same conclusion that traditional pedagogy reached very long ago: that we need to reduce tacit knowledge as much as possible, that is, the need for the syntactic-semantic maximization and pragmatic minimization. To not try to make the knowledge explicit is to renounce the advantage of using mental processes like inference and idea association that save us from the slower gestural imitation or practical exercise.

Indeed, for thousands of years, pedagogy (teaching) has developed the concepts and methods for teaching theory and practice and had evolved towards teaching more theory and less practice. Using our terminology, it has evolved towards the maximization of the semantic transfer and the minimization of the pragmatic transfer. Proof of this, without a doubt, is the proportion of hours that formal education dedicates to theory in the classroom, compared to what it dedicates to practice in the labs, field tests, and internships. It is common place to say that during teacher-student lectures, only theoretical knowledge is taught and that the real learning takes place, later, when we put into practice "in the streets" what we learned.

This is a very old discussion. Kessels and Korthagen (2001), for example, state that "several authors, especially in the philosophical domain, referred to the classical controversy between Plato's and Aristotle's conceptions of rationality (episteme vs. phronesis)."

And later:

Nowadays we can find many classifications in the literature that clarify different conceptions of knowledge: for example, public versus personal knowledge, molecular versus holistic knowledge, knowledge as given versus knowledge as problematic, knowledge by acquaintance versus knowledge by description, declarative versus procedural knowledge, knowing how versus knowing that. Haven't we made too much progress in 2,500 years to return to the very beginning of the debate? As a matter of fact, it appears not. Centuries ago, the same type of problems now confronting teacher educators were thoroughly studied by philosophers, resulting in a fruitful theoretical framework of which most modern researchers are not aware.

Knowledge management, on the other hand, has been realizing that the "tangibilization" of knowledge without explicitly stating it, even though it solves some management problems, is still a slow and incomplete form of knowledge transfer compared to its explicitation. The sales success of "practical teaching" products, such as our painter's video, is more of a market management success than of a knowledge management success. What we are selling in that video is an incomplete knowledge set which is still slow to transfer back into a person's knowledge inventory. Perhaps a more appropriate example than the painter is the knowledge management attempt to transfer "the best practices" through imitation. This is what we attempt to do in the so-called "workshops," "practical courses," and books with titles such as *Ten Key Steps to Success*. They are mostly pragmatic information that may have been "made tangible" or not and are generally more dramatic than effective. They only transfer parts or superficial aspects of the knowledge; they provide appearances, poses, fancy words, and so forth.

Lasnik's (2003) article has a presentation of the pros and cons of the different pedagogic methods we have mentioned here under the concept of "tangibilization of pragmatic knowledge." Its bibliography is also pertinent for all this section (Demarest, 1997; Zucker, Darby, & Armstrong, 2002). To successfully transfer knowledge, we first need to make it explicit and only in the cases where it is irreducibly tacit should we make it "tangible" without making it explicit.

Knowledge management has not achieved considerable improvements in the transfer speed of tacit knowledge that cannot be made explicit. Perhaps the problem is presented for the first time, and in a very concise fashion, on this quote found in "Personal Knowledge Towards a Post-Critical Philosophy" (Polanyi):

Discussions of KM begin by addressing the question, 'What is knowledge?' The most popular tenet here rests on the forms of knowledge that can be expressed for codification. The "robust" assumption is that tacit knowledge is difficult to extract from the human mind, thus limiting the manipulation and transfer of this type of knowledge.

But from a diverse sample of recent literature we infer that no important achieve- ments have been reached and that the speed of knowledge transfer is still very limited by the time dedicated to the human interaction between teacher or expert and pupils or apprentices.

Indeed, almost four decades after Polanyi explained the problem, we read again, for instance, by Zucker et al. (2002), the following: "Commercializing knowledge involves transfer from discovering scientists to those who will develop it com- mercially"

However, "our basic argument is that knowledge close to breakthrough discoveries needs to be transformed into words, codes, and/or formula before it can be easily transferred."

A success story, typically modest, is reported by Boiral (2002). This article describes how by applying some managerial methodologies to the tacit knowledge contained in the experience of individuals in an environmental control organization, they were able to use this knowledge to improve the identification of environmental pollution, react to it, and prevent it more efficiently. However, this report does not provide any substantial knowledge management achievement that may be generalized.

From the description of knowledge transfer discussed by Krogh, Nonaka, and Aben (2001), we also infer that the achievements of knowledge management in reference to knowledge transfer do not go much further than those of traditional pedagogy. Neither does Nadler (2003) report any major findings in this respect: "Our review of the learning and training literature revealed four common methods for training people to be more effective negotiators: didactic learning, learning via information revelation, analogical learning, and observational learning."

Indeed, "didactic" learning methods and "information revelation" correspond to traditional learning through pedagogy or through the simple reading of explicit information, respectively. The "analog" and "observation" methods refer to tacit knowledge, but "the observation group showed the largest increase in performance, but the least ability to articulate the learning principles that helped them improve, suggesting that they had acquired tacit knowledge that they were unable to articu- late" (Nadler et al., 2003).

Therefore we can conclude that the achievements of disciplines such as knowledge management in respect to knowledge transfer lean more towards the identification and explanation of the problem in business terms, than towards their solutions. These solutions, even though they have new names such as "coaching," are still, in essence, those of the traditional pedagogy, assisted or not by information technologies. It is common to find in the WWW promotions such as: "Much more than information technology (IT), knowledge management (KM) overlaps project and relationship management. You can transfer information with a fax or email. You can transfer knowledge with effective training and you can transfer wisdom with coaching and mentorship" (http://www.soulwork.net/Systemic/knowledge_management.htm).

However, we still need to ask ourselves if there is any substantial difference between *effective training* or *coaching and mentorship* and the traditional activity of pedagogy. Are they different to the traditional interaction between the teacher, tutor, trainer, or professor and the students, trainee, intern, or apprentice? If there is a difference, it is not evident and much less explicit in the knowledge management literature.

In summary, we can say that the only real innovation of knowledge management compared to traditional pedagogy is that the former acknowledges the existence of valuable knowledge in nonacademic settings and the opening of these spaces for the multiplication of such knowledge. For instance, that is the case of brainstorming (de Bono, 1992) and the IC-multiplier effect (Edvinsson, 2002). However, is not the first one a business variation of the traditional forums, arenas, intellectual exchange campaigns, and so forth? And, is not the second an organizational variation of the multiplying effect of knowledge, common to traditional educational institutions, such as universities, or the more popular seminars or workshops?

Nonetheless, neither pedagogy nor knowledge management can ignore the limits of pragmatic minimization. When they bump into those limits, they can offer nothing better than pragmatic knowledge, having to dedicate to it whatever resources it may require. And most certainly the option that passes through "tangibilized" tacit knowledge is better than the one that only resorts to intangible tacit knowledge. So we have that the tangibilization of pragmatic knowledge is currently the only support available when facing the case of tacit knowledge that resists explicitation. To learn more about explicit knowledge the reader may consult Polanyi (1966), Nonaka and Noboru (1998), Davenport and Prusak (1998), Boiral (2002), Dixon (2000), and Swart and Kinnie (2003).

Knowledge Management and Organizational Solutions

Knowledge management has resorted to disciplines related to information technology and business science. Generally, its premises resort to both, sometimes in a balanced fashion, and others taking one as the main one and the other as an auxiliary. The ones that take business sciences as their main support generally base their solutions on the introduction of organizational changes. This organizational tendency, although mentioned and discussed using different terminology is particularly attributed to Ikujiro Nonaka who postulated it in writings like *The Knowledge-Creating Company: How Japanese Companies Create the Dynamics of Innovation* (Nonaka & Takeuchi, 1995), *The Concept of "ba": Building a Foundation for Knowledge Creation* (Nonaka & Noboru, 1998), and *A Theory of Organizational Knowledge Creation: Understanding the Dynamic Process of Creating Knowledge* (Nonaka, Toyama, & Byosière, 2001).

To a large extent, Nonaka's proposals' appeal laid on his implicit promise of explicitating or at least transferring the tacit key of the notorious success of some Japanese organizations in knowledge creation. And it could be thought that the promise has been fulfilled, judging by some successes reached by certain western organizations that "copied" management methods from their rivals or equivalent Japanese organizations. Nonetheless, it can not be said that all of that success is due to Nonaka's revelations, or that it solely refers to knowledge creation. A good part of it refers to methods such as the famous "total quality" and other "good practices," even though it is not clear how much corresponds to knowledge generation. In any case, knowledge management in general has not shown substantial advances in this sense.

Let us turn to the pharmaceutical industry. This is one of those industries for which innovation is a critical issue and so they have resorted intensely to the sciences and techniques of knowledge generation and treatment. Their innovation cost are still so high that this is one of the arguments that they use to justify the prohibitive prices of its products for some patients and whole regions of the world which are in desperate need of medical supplies but can not afford them. Furthermore, as Seeley (2004) says, "Drug companies need money to develop innovative products. Patients need innovative products whether they can pay for them or not. And a drug pricing policy that forgets either of these vital points is likely to be a disaster."

Therefore we cannot disqualify this justification as simple evil or capitalist greed (Reisman, 1980).

In any case, there are not many signs indicating that organizational changes have managed to substantially reduce the cost or time of innovation. So, since the September 2006 edition of *KM Monthly* magazine on its Web version (at http://www. destinationkm.com), one search using the option "All of dKM" of the phrase "success stories" yielded 56 articles. The most promising ones are, on one side, not very convincing and, on the other, they mainly refer to solutions supported by information technologies, not by organizational changes.

Knowledge Management and Information Technologies

For a short while knowledge management contemplated using artificial intelligence as a way to apply information technologies to its field.

In the 70s and on the first part of the 80s, artificial intelligence was developed as the software of what later would be "the thinking machine." It mainly focused on explicating through the application of computerized inference rules or "automatic test of theorems," the knowledge implicit in the supplied information. Some results were promising, but they did not represent a solution to the problem of the unpredictable nature of knowledge generation. Indeed, since it was limited to making explicit certain types of implicit information, its contribution could only be partially useful for the tacit knowledge transfer problem, and maybe for some compatibility problem between transmitter and receiver.

The school used the so called "expert systems" proposed and was partially able to generate partially erratic variations of a pattern and try them with the automatic tests of theorems. This simulated what for us are the syntactic and semantic phases (being the latter not based on pragmatic results but on directly applying it to the syntactic information). Even if the results had been more successful, they would not have solved the main hurdle: minimizing the pragmatic test without completely obviating it.

There were also attempts to simulate the pragmatic phase of knowledge. We can see a revealing summary of these steps in cognitive science, from computers to anthills as models of human thought, by Gärdenfors (1999):

With the development of computers in the 1940s and 1950s, a new model for human thinking became available. The initial period of cognitive science was driven by the analogy that the brain functions like a computer. Consequently, thinking was viewed as the processing of symbols. This was also the methodology of classical artificial intelligence. As a result of criticism of the symbol manipulation paradigm, there have recently been two main kinds of reaction to it. The first one is connectionism, where thinking is modeled as associations in artificial neuron networks. Some connectionist models are tightly connected to developments in the neurosciences, while others are more general models of cognitive processes such as concept formation.

Up to here, the author, using a terminology different to ours, refers to the attempts that stay at the semantic and syntactic-semantic phase. More on this could be found with the opinion of D. C. Marr (1990), a well known researcher of the "conectionist" tendency, which was formulated during the years of marked decline of artificial intelligence. The summary of "cognitive science" continues with the phase we here call pragmatic:

The second reaction consists of theories of embodied and situated cognition, where cognition is seen as taking place not only in the brain, but in interaction with the body and the surrounding world. In line with this, modern studies of robotics are based on so called reactive systems, the actions of which depend directly on the world instead of a symbolic model of it. The situated view on cognition will also be central for future developments of man-machine interaction, in particular in educational tools that exploit information technology.

On that same work the author dedicates his fourth chapter, "The Rise and Fall of Artificial Intelligence," to talk about the poor results of the non-pragmatic attempts as a whole:

However, expert systems never reached the adroitness of human experts and they were almost never given the opportunity to have the decisive word in real cases. A fundamental problem is that such systems may incorporate an extensive amount of knowledge, but they hardly have any knowledge about the validity of their knowledge. Without such meta-knowledge, a system cannot form valid judgments that form the basis of sound decisions. As a consequence, expert systems have been demoted to the ranks and are nowadays called 'decision support systems.'

And on the eighth chapter, "The Future of Cognitive Science," he places in the future the potential achievements of attempts that include pragmatic confrontation:

The goal of contemporary cognitive science is not primarily to build a thinking machine, but to increase our understanding of cognitive processes. This can be done by various methods, including traditional psychological experiments, observations of authentic cognitive processes in practical action, or by simulating cognition in robots or programmes. Unlike the early days of AI when it was believed that one single methodology, that of symbolic representation, could solve all cognitive problems, the current trend is to work with several forms of representations and data.

The previous paragraphs summarize the current state of trying to reach a solution via artificial intelligence and of what in our terms is the criticism to the pragmatic weakness of its main tendencies. However, we must recognize that this is not the most frequent criticism present on the literature. What is found most frequently is what we could call "humanism," which in its most extreme manifestations makes the mistake of substituting gods for human beings as the exclusive centers of all creation and argues against machines, sometimes in pseudo-scientific terms, and others using openly mystic language with such vagueness as "the infinite richness of the mind," "the unrepeatable nature of the human experience," "free will," and so forth. A sample of moderate criticism is discussed by Jonscher (1999). In an editorial synopsis of this work we find a typical expression: "Charles Jonscher presents the other side of the argument. He shows us that (...) no calculating machine can match the creative power of the human mind."

But the very breakthroughs of artificial intelligence, although so far modest, suggest that we should not subscribe to this "humanistic" criticism which is a candidate to the ineffable museum of the impossible, where among many others we find the famous report by Lord Kelvin made in 1895, about the impossibility of machines heavier than air being able to fly.

Pragmatic Minimization and Information Technologies

Computer science applications that synthesize music with the quality, quantity, and velocity of a Mozart are sold in stores or given for free on the Internet, alongside the ones that play chess on a grand master level and among many other applications based on the combinatory play. Nowadays, the exceptionality of Mozart is reduced to the fact that he was exceptional from his time until the appearance of modern synthesizers. A modern computer with synthesizing devices and sound players can memorize a composition by "hearing" it just once, as well or even better than Mozart. It can abstract its syntax or rhythmic, harmonic, or instrumentation patterns and, in case it identifies them with some preset, it detects formal (syntactic) imperfections and suggests how to correct them. It can generate new syntax with or without human feedback and it can activate all playback mechanisms with the sounds of the largest imaginable orchestra. It could execute the composition with strict fidelity or with any margin for improvisation. If given information in a proper fashion about the tastes of a possible human audience, it can easily adapt to it. It can make innumerable semantic relations with other scores, arrangements, and performances previously acclaimed at mind boggling speeds, find rhythmic, harmonic, melodic or instrumental similarities, compose "bridges," references or musical combinations between them, change their rhythms and instruments, and infer compositional projections; all of these with the advantage that if the human consumers does not like the result, they can simply erase it without inflicting a cruel disappointment on another human being, and without even losing any hard drive space. So the synthesizer works as a generator and the taste of the promoter or businessperson—or that of a selected audience—plays the role of the selector.

But we must remember that computerized music compositions—even those that comply with the highest standards—can be made in quantities and speeds which are several orders of magnitude higher than the capacity of any audience to enjoy and remember them or to hate and forget them. Therefore, as we already said, the problem is not about generating potential innovations but about the ability to process those innovations.

It is worth asking oneself if computers can help improve the pragmatic processing capability of the syntactic-semantic innovations. The answer is that they can only do it to the extent that they deepen the pragmatic minimization. Otherwise, to give the computers the ability to test the formulas generated by them, combining energy and material supplies, using industrial processes and market tests as if they were music notes, would surpass any financing capability. It is unthinkable (not only from an ethical but an economical point of view) to let computers play chess with human pieces and industrial machinery.

Simulated Praxis and its Limitations

A very obvious possibility to make good use of the combinatory speed of computers for pragmatic selection is to also make good use of their processing speed to simulate the practical test of the combinations with increasing realism. This way we would use computers to boost what the scientific community has known for centuries as "mental experiments" and what in this chapter we call pragmatic minimization. This is the promise of a "virtual reality" which is already used on flight simulators to help pilots practice before taking a real plane into the air. (By the way, the use of the expression "virtual reality" to name show-biz products or consumer electronics has distorted its original meaning. Indeed, before becoming a buzz-phrase, the use of the adjective "virtual" with the noun "reality" implied all that had the virtues and potentials of reality for a limited group of effects and purposes, for instance, for audiovisual purposes. But today, instead of this, it implies an alternate and even opposed reality. In this chapter we will limit ourselves to the original meaning of the expression).

Computer simulations have their limitations in terms of the material test. Limitations given by the high possibility that one or more of the simulated components could differ from its real counterpart. There are classic examples, like that of the stone that falls from the mast. Here we will transfer that example from the imagination to the computer simulation. We could assign a speed to the image of the stone on the computer screen, calculated using the corresponding laws of physics. We could supply data such as the height of the mast, the weight of the stone, the speed of the ship, and others. The initial speed of the stone would be zero, taking the mast as a reference. Now, if the ship is not at rest with respect to the sea plane, an ill-prepared simulation or imagination would show that the stone touches the floor far away from the mast's base, because the mast, unlike the stone, would have moved at the speed of the ship while the stone was falling, which is a mistake, because the movement of the ship and of the mast take place with respect to the sea plane, and the initial horizontal speed of the stone with respect to that plane is not zero, but the speed of the ship. And even supposing that this mistake would not be made because the original speed of the stone was foreseen, there is still another possibility of error even harder to prevent, that is, the horizontal friction of the stone with the air, which would not have any effect if the ship was at rest. In any case, what is important here is to highlight the ease with which a mental experiment or simulation could make a mistake that a real life test would not make. And in most cases the possibility of making a mistake is much less obvious, much more subtle, and far more complex.

Nonetheless, it will generally be more economical to perfect the simulations than try to prove in practice, with real matter and energy, a whole array of possibilities. Indeed, if we do not try this option, we will have to accept that whatever we consider today an exceptional advance of knowledge will be the maximum advance ever, that knowledge will continue to advance at a human pace and that the exceptional advances would keep on being the result of a fortunate combination of the human resources of the world, its circumstances, and its opportunities. In other words, we would not make good use of the combinatory power of computer science, at least not of its whole power. To read more on the dehumanization of knowledge you can read "In the Age of the Smart Machine: The Future of Work and Power" (Zuboff, 1988).

A More Pragmatic Artificial Intelligence

The present state of artificial intelligence is weak from the pragmatic point of view. This weakness is at least partially rooted in the fact that the first designs of its software, encouraged by the power of logical processing of the then novel computers, bet with excessive optimism on a game of words and ideas on logical inference; they made the mistake of ignoring the material confrontation of ideas instead of minimizing it as much as possible and they also made the mistake of falling into one of the idealist perversions, that is, the combinatorial explosion.

Indeed, the languages and logical inference applications or automatic test of theorems proliferated, and with them also proliferated a huge capacity for generating information of a certain syntactic validity and even of a high semantic selection. But this occurred without an equivalent capacity to test and therefore allow them to select the information that was useful or that had some practical meaning. The possible breakthroughs made by logical inference cannot be recognized and get buried under the landslide of the other many possible inferences.

The only possibility for computers to contribute to widen the bottleneck of knowledge management, instead of clogging it even further, seems to be to reduce the asymmetry between artificial generation and pragmatic selection of information by increasing the interaction of computers with the energetic-material world.

What we call in this chapter simulated praxis is a way to increase the interaction between computers, not directly through energetic-material reality, but through its most reliable digital representation possible, that is, with the most virtual simulation of reality possible. In other words, virtual reality provides artificial intelligence with its corresponding artificial reality.

But there is a possibility for artificial intelligence to validate itself against everyday reality, without affecting the objective of pragmatic minimization. The growing facilities and penetration of the Internet makes a massive interaction with users possible. These users introduce enough information (in terms of quantity and variety) to the net, to substitute the artificial generation with a more current and "live" erratic information (however a thorough analysis on the advantages and disadvantages of the latter is not within the reach of this chapter, and we can always go back to the artificial generation in case this is found to be negative). On the other hand, though not on purpose and with no special effort, Internet users are living and real-time selectors of the information circulating on the Internet. If well managed, their preferences, interests, curiosities, approvals, disapprovals, and so forth comprise such a massive survey or statistic that it could be considered a live census. They are the most agile and at the same time the massive links with reality any intelligence could have at its disposal.

Of course, such intelligence should have the ability to interact with that huge flow of information, which discards human intelligence by itself, given its limitations in reference to massive processing of information. Artificial extensions of human intelligence are then required, which as a whole comprise artificial intelligence. And this intelligence is the one that would make a good management of the manifestations of Internet users. Intelligence is, indeed, required, for instance, not to compare in absolute values, but in relative values, the popularity of a young music band measured in "clicks" on Web pages with the number of academic publications quoting a certain author or text. A whole new high intelligence and sensitivity system is required to detect, for instance, a sudden change in the manifestation of interest for certain information and its possible relationship with other variations or events reflected on the net.

This shifts the use of artificial intelligence from the syntactic and semantic phases to the phase of pragmatic minimization. Minimization would be given by the capacity to detect at an early stage and intelligently discriminate the variations in the reaction of the mass of users to the information circulating the Internet.

Certain modern computer systems, such as those included under the denomination of data mining (Hand, Mannila, & Smyth, 2001), business intelligence systems, market intelligence systems (Cody, Kreulen, Krishna, & Spangler, 2002), and many others, are oriented to the processing of indirect massive information, that is, information obtained not as "input" of a specific system, but as a summary of the "inputs" and even of the "outputs" of the largest possible variety of systems. This data not necessarily share the same database, but are distributed in many of them inside a big data warehouse (Pyle, 2003) or connected to one or more closed networks (intranets), or even to the Internet. So the search level of these systems is similar to that of the famous Internet engines (such as Yahoo! and Google). But its capacity to process the successive answers is far more automatic and systematic. They do not require as much interaction as the human user does in the process of reducing or widening the range of potential answers for selecting the most relevant answers. They use pattern recognition, statistical analysis, and other techniques, some of them with a very high complexity level.

On the other side, the data that comprise the "mine" explored by these systems, even though they may be obtained by accumulation of the "inputs" and "outputs" of systems that are not specifically designed to obtain or produce such data, have a growing tendency to come from systems whose input is open to all Internet users; from the small subscription or poll forms of the particular Web pages, to the several interest groups chat-rooms, to the enormously large collectively constructed knowledge bases. A well known example is promoted at http://en.wikipedia.org/wiki/Main_Page where it says, "Welcome to Wikipedia, the free encyclopedia that anyone can edit. 1,785,378 articles in English."

(By the way, the article corresponding to data mining on Wikipedia [http://en.wikipedia.org/wiki/Data_mining] is the best bibliographic reference I can quote on the subject.)

The growing investments on research and development for more powerful computers and communication systems increase and complement the expectations that systems as those mentioned above and, in general, artificial intelligence systems focused on pragmatic minimization (though not called that way) may clear the bottleneck of knowledge management.

Conclusion

Using terminology of information theory, we defined pragmatic minimization and identified its limit with the main bottleneck of knowledge management. Then we showed the relevance of resorting to information technologies as a means to extend such limit, thus accelerating the necessary confrontation between theoretical and practical knowledge.

Indeed, we pointed out that what knowledge management thinks it identifies as knowledge generation and knowledge transfer problems at companies and in the business realm, are in substance the same problems pedagogy has been facing for a long time, and that the solutions proposed by the former are not substantially better than the ones that long ago were placed into practice by the latter, except on what refers to the intensive use of information technologies. We point out that this is what knowledge management should dedicate most of its effort, especially focusing on the techniques of simulating reality (also called virtual reality) and of intelligence of the massive information market through the Internet.

References

Ayala, F. J., & Kriger, J. A. (1984). *Genética moderna*. México: Fondo Educativo Interamericano.

Basalla, G. (1988). *The evolution of technology*. Cambridge: Cambridge University Press.

Blankley, W., Scerri, M., Molotja, N., & Saloojee, I. (Eds.). (2005). *Measuring innovation in OECD and non-OECD countries*. HSRC Press.

Boiral, O. (2002). Tacit knowledge and environmental management. *LRP Long Range Planning, 35*, 291-317. Retrieved January 25, 2008, from www.lrp-journal.com

Brier, S. (1995). Cyber-semiotics: On autopoiesis, code-duality and sign games in bio-semiotics. *CYBERNETICS & HUMAN KNOWING (A Journal of Second Order Cybernetics & Cyber-Semiotics), 3*(1).

Caldwell, B. (2000). The emergence of Hayek's ideas on cultural evolution. *Review of Austrian Economics*, 13, 5-22.

Carnap, R., & Bar-Hillel, Y. (1952). *An outline of a theory of semantic information*. Massachussetts Institute of Technology, Reseach Laboratory of Electronics.

Cody, W. F., Kreulen, J. T., Krishna, & Spangler, W. S. (2002). The integration of business intelligence and knowledge management. *IBM Systems Journal, 41*(4), 697-713.

Darwin, C. (1859). *The origin of species*. London: John Murrap.

Davenport, T. H., & Prusak, L. (1998). *Working knowledge: How organizations manage what they know*. Harvard Business School Press.

de Bono, E. (1992). *Serious creativity*. New York: HarperBusiness.

Demarest, M. (1997). Understanding knowledge management. *LRP Long Range Planning, 30*(3), 374-384. Retrieved January 25, 2008, from www.lrpjournal. com

Dixon, N. M. (2000). *Common knowledge: How companies thrive on*.

Donald, M. (1991). *Origins of modern mind: Three stages in the evolution of culture and cognition*. Cambridge, MA: Harvard University Press.

Drucker, P. F. (1993). *Post-capitalist society*. New York: HarperCollins.

Edvinsson, L. (2002). *Corporate longitude*. Bookhouse.

Ferran, C., & Salim, R. (2003). The Internet and the digital divide. *Asian Information-Science-Life, 2*(1).

Gabora, L. (1995). Meme and variations: A computer model of cultural evolution. In L. Nadel & D. Stein (Eds.), *Lectures in complex systems*. Boston: Addison-Wesley.

Galup, S. D., Dattero, R., & Heeks, R. C. (2002). Knowledge management systems: An architecture for active and passive knowledge. *Information Resources Management Journal, 15*(1), 22-27.

Gamble, T. J. (1983). The natural selection model of knowledge generation: Campbell's dictum and its critics. *Cognition and Brain Theory, 6*(3), 353-363.

Gärdenfors, P. (1999). Cognitive science: From computers to anthills as models of human thought. *Human IT, 2.*

Gatlin, L. (1972). *Information theory and the living system.* Columbia University Press.

Griffiths, P. E. (2000). *Genetic information: A metaphor in search of a theory.* University of Sydney.

Guignard, P. (1999). *A powerful and easy-to-use Internet enabled expert system which knows the limit of its knowledge.* Paper presented at the Conference on Knowledge Management KNOW'99, Sydney.

Hand, D., Mannila, H., & Smyth, P. (2001). *Principles of data mining.* Cambridge: MIT Press,.

Hartung, J. (1976). On natural selection and the inheritance of wealth. *Current Anthropology, 17,* 606-614.

Holzmüler, W. (1984). *Information in biological systems: The role of macromolecules.* Cambridge University Press.

Jonscher, C. (1999). *Evolution of wired life: From the alphabet to the soul - catcher chip: How information technologies change our world.* John Wiley & Sons, Inc.

Kessels, J., & Korthagen, F. (2001). The relation between theory and practice: Back to the classics. In F. A. J. Korthagen (Ed.), *Linking practice and theory: The pedagogy of realistic teacher education (eBook).* Mahwah, N.J.: Lawrence Erlbaum Associates, Inc.

Krogh, G. V., Nonaka, I., & Aben, M. (2001). Making the most of your company's knowledge: A strategic framework. *LRP Long Range Planning, 34,* 421-439. Retrieved January 25, 2008, from www.lrpjournal.com

Lasnik, V. E. (2003). *Courseware cosmetics to human cognetics: A pragmatic, innovative pedagogy for distributed learning design & development.* Retrieved January 25, 2008, from http://www.stc.org/ConfProceed/2003/PDFs/STC50-044.pdf

Lewontin, R. (1974). *The genetic basis of evolutionary change.*

Marr, D. C. (1990). Artificial intelligence: A personal view. In M. Boden (Ed.), *The philosophy of artificial intelligence.* Oxford University Press.

Morris, C. (1971). *Writings on the general theory of signs.* Hague: Mouton.

Mosterín, J. (Ed.). (1986). *La cultura como información.* Valencia: Tirant Lo Blanch.

Mosterín, J. (1991, October). Variedades de información. *Ciencia, Pensamiento y Cultura, 550*(91), 121-144.

Nadler, J. T., Leigh, Van Boven, Leaf. (2003). Learning negotiation skills: Four models of knowledge creation and transfer. *Management Science, 49*(4), 529 -512.

Nauta, D. (1972). *The meaning of information*. The Hague: Moton.

Nonaka, I., & Noboru, K. (1998, Spring). The concept of "ba": Building a foundation for knowledge creation. *California Management Review ABI/INFORM Global, 40*(3).

Nonaka, I., & Takeuchi, H. (1995). *The knowledge-creating company: How Japanese companies create the dynamics of innovation.*

Nonaka, I., Toyama, R., & Byosière, P. (2001). A theory of organizational knowledge creation: Understanding the dynamic Process of creating knowledge. In M. Dierkes, A. Berthoin Antal, J. Child, & I. Nonaka, (Eds.), *Handbook of organizational learning and knowledge* (pp. 491-517). New York: Oxford University Press.

Polanyi, M. P. (1962). *Personal knowledge towards a post-critical philosophy.* The University of Chicago Press.

Polanyi, M. (1966). *The tacit dimension*. Garden City, NY: Doubleday & Co.

Pyle, D. (2003). *Business modeling and data mining*. Morgan Kaufmann.

Quastler, H. (Ed.). (1953). *Information theory in biology*. Urbana: Unveristy of Illinois Press.

Reisman, G. (1980, February). Price controls and shortages. *The Freeman: Ideas on Liberty.*

Rosenberg, N. (1974). Science, invention and economic growth. *The Economic Journal, 84*(333), 90-108.

Seeley, L. B. (2004, October 1). The cost of innovation: Highlights from "large molecules, large dreams: A forum on global drug pricing and sustainable medical innovation." *Pharmaceutical Executive.*

Shearmur, J. (1989). Popper, Hayek, and classical liberalism. *The Freeman: Ideas on Liberty.*

Sober, E. (1984). *The nature of selection.*

Swart, J., & Kinnie, N. (2003). Sharing knowledge in knowledge-intensive firms. *Human Resource Management Journal, 13*(2).

van der Lubbe, J. C. A. (1997). *Information theory*. Cambridge University Press.

Zuboff, S. (1988). *In the age of the smart machine: The future of work and power.* New York: Basic Books.

Zucker, L. G., Darby, M. R., & Armstrong, J. S. (2002, January). Commercializing knowledge: University science, knowledge capture, and firm performance in biotechnology. *Management Science, INFORMS, 48*(1), 138-153.

Endnote

[1]   A literature review of over 350 texts –some seminal, some collateral- that span several centuries of thinking, covers the topic in depth and actuality, providing an additional value to the chapter. However, based on space restrictions the review is not included in its entirety.

Chapter XII

A Framework for Introducing Knowledge Management in the Banking Sector:
State of the Art and Empirical Results

Friedrich Roithmayr, Johannes Kepler University Linz, Austria

Kerstin Fink, University of Innsbruck, Austria

Abstract

The management of knowledge has become a major research field in different disciplines in the last years. A key issue is the future development of knowledge management as a "fashion" or "trend" initiative. A longitudinal empirical study conducted by the authors analyzing the literature of knowledge management from 1994 until 2004 comes to the conclusion that knowledge management is already transformed into a "trend". Furthermore, this chapter deals with the integration of knowledge management in the banking sector by applying the building block approach from Probst, Raub & Romhardt. Currently knowledge management is used in an unbalanced manner and not considering all knowledge-intensive processes.

Problem Description

In the last decade there has been a large interest in knowledge management and knowledge management systems. Enterprise knowledge management software includes sales of content management and portal licenses, which have been growing at a rate of 35% annually (Laudon & Laudon, 2006). For each IT-investment decision of an enterprise the question arises whether the investment goes into a "fashion" or into a "trend" (Roithmayr & Steininger, 2006). In this chapter the authors follow up two objectives. One key objective is to find the state of the art of knowledge management in practice and theory. Is knowledge management a "fashion" or is it a "trend"? From the methodical point this research is done with a literature review. Outgoing from these results the authors analyzed in the second key question the impact of knowledge management in the banking sector. In theory and practice there are many types of business processes associated with different objectives.

To begin with, there is an important distinction between data, information, knowledge, and knowledge-in-action (Fink, 2004). *Data* are a set of discrete, objective facts about events. Data are unorganized and unprocessed facts (Tiwana, 2000). In an organizational context, data are most usefully described as structured records of transactions. When a customer goes to a gas station and fills the tank of the car, the transaction can be partly described as data, such as purchase process, how many gallons, and the amount of payment. The data tell nothing about why the customer went to the service station and cannot predict if the customer is likely to come back. Such facts say nothing about whether the service station is well or badly organized and whether it is failing or thriving. Data describe only a part of what happened; data provide no judgments or interpretation and no sustainable basis of action. While the row material of decision making may include data, data cannot tell you what to do. Data are the essential materials for the creation of information.

Information is described as a message, usually in the form of a document or an audible or visible communication. As with any message it has a sender and a receiver. Information is meant to change the way the receiver perceives something, to have an impact on the receiver's judgment and behavior. It must inform. The word "inform" originally meant "to give shape to" and information is meant to shape the person who gets it and to make some difference in the person's outlook or insight. Information can be described as systematized data, this means that information is data that have been sorted, analyzed, and displayed. Data are transformed into information by adding value in various ways:

- **Contextualized:** We know for what purpose the data were gathered.
- **Categorized:** We know the units of analysis or key components of the data.
- **Calculated:** The data may have been analyzed mathematically or statistically.
- **Corrected:** Errors have been removed from the data.
- **Condensed:** The data may have been summarized into a more concise form.

Most people have an intuitive sense that *knowledge* is broader, deeper, and richer than data or information. Knowledge derives from minds at work. Knowledge is a fluid mix of framed experience, values, contextual information, and expert insight that provides a framework for evaluating and incorporating new experiences and information. It originates and is applied in the minds of knowers (Davenport & Prusak, 1998; Mockler & Dologite, 2002). In organizations, it often becomes embedded not only in documents or repositories, but also in organizational routines, processes, practices, and norms. Knowledge is a mixture of various elements. Knowledge derives from information as information derives from data. If information is to become knowledge, humans must do virtually all the work. The transformation to knowledge happens through

- **Comparison:** How does information about this situation compare to other situations we have known?
- **Consequences:** What implications does information have for decision and actions?
- **Connections:** How does this bit of knowledge relate to others?
- **Conversation:** What do other people think about this information?

Methods and tools for modelling business processes (e.g., ARIS, ADONIS) primarily handle data and information but are not adequate knowledge-oriented, although first steps in this direction can be observed (e.g., ARIS Version 7.0).

Research Methodology

The authors formulated the following:

Research Question_1 (RQ_1): *Is knowledge management a "fashion" or a "trend"?*

This question will be analyzed with two *empirical studies*. In the first study, the position of knowledge management is analyzed from a scientific view and a practical view. The empirical study was conducted at the Department of Information Systems-Information Engineering at the University of Linz (Austria) in cooperation with the Department of Information Systems at the University of Innsbruck (Austria). The goal was to find the impact of knowledge during the last 10 years. The research design was based on the examination of abstracts as well as on keywords in German and English literature from the years 1994 to 2005. Figure 1 gives an overview of the data sample.

The second empirical study gives an overview about the state of the art of business process improvement (BPI) approaches. Within a research project with SIEMENS Munich (Roithmayr & Kobler, 2006) the authors analyzed the life cycle of knowledge management processes in enterprises using the Tele Delphi Method (Fink Roithmayr, & Kofler, 2001). These two empirical studies build the basic research framework for finding the state of the art of knowledge management in theory and practice.

Figure 1. Data sample of empirical studies

	number of journals		number articles	number keywords
	englisch	german		
Scientific journals	15	3	11.777	30.113
IT-technical journals	5	1	40.910	49.249
IT-articles in newspapers	4	1	20.670	30.716
sum	**24**	**5**	**73.357**	**110.078**

Research Question_2 (RQ_2): *In the second research question the authors ask in which dimension knowledge management is integrated in business processes of a bank.*

Based on the framework of Probst et al. (1997) a detailed case study was developed for finding the impact of the knowledge processes in a bank. Basically, for the bank it is interesting to know in which processes knowledge is embedded. Depending on this view, the bank should improve existing business processes or change to new business processes (knowledge processes). Banks have recognized that it is necessary to improve their business processes. This process is called business process improvement. Business processes in banks follow two types of improvements: the *"comprehensive approach"* and *"specific issues within an organization."*

Comprehensive approaches give a framework which normally can be used for a great variety of processes. They consist of several methods with the overall objective of process improvement (e.g., Six-Sigma) or propose a best-practice solution (e.g., ITIL). Every organization has specific requirements for their business processes. BPI must also align their processes on the specific issues within the organization. Internal improvement of functions or single processes can take positive effects on processes (e.g., organizational culture as precondition for improvement). Banks have recognized that modern knowledge-intensive organizations are increasingly dependent on transferring and sharing knowledge, experiences, and insights among employees. Although knowledge communities can be found in many organizations, they have in common the objective of knowledge sharing; their forms and functions appear to be quite diverse. In the presented case study it becomes obvious that all process models in the bank have a lack of intangible assets. Therefore, it seems necessary to introduce a broad knowledge methodology.

Knowledge Management: State of the Art

The first empirical study conducted at the Department of Information Systems-Information Engineering at the University of Linz (Austria) in cooperation with the Department of Information Systems at the University of Innsbruck (Austria) had the objective to find the impact of knowledge during the last 10 years. The research design was based on the examination of abstracts and keywords in German and English literature from 1994 to 2005. Figure 2 gives an overview of the key results. The left side of Figure 2 shows the development of knowledge management from the point of the scientific publications. In English written scientific papers the results show a continuous rise of the importance of knowledge management while in German written scientific papers the increase of the importance of knowledge management

Figure 2. The importance of knowledge management from 1994 until 2005 [RoSt06] (Roithmayr & Steininger, 2006)

Scientific View   **Practical View**

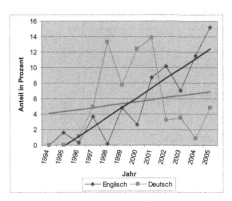
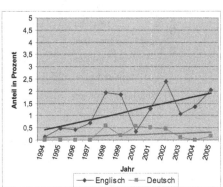

is not so highly ranked. Figure 2 (right side) visualizes the results obtained from publications with a practical focus. In German written practical paper the issue of knowledge management has a lower impact than in English written journals.

Reflecting the results on Research Question_1 (RQ_1) the authors conclude that knowledge management is not a "fashion," it will become (or is) a "trend." To verify the thesis that knowledge management is a "trend" the authors conducted a second empirical study.

Dealing with knowledge management, it is important to find the position of knowledge management processes in practice. Intangible assets (Sveiby, 1997) are property which lack physical substance but give valuable rights or benefits to the owner (i.e., patents, copyrights, culture, research, organizational knowledge). Measuring, managing, and expanding intangible assets are becoming critical success factors to improve the performance of an organization and its processes. The challenge is to determine the importance of the intangible assets with regard to the performance of each process. The study was conducted in autumn of 2006 using an online questionnaire. The data sample comprehended 234 worldwide active specialists in business processes management. Two results of this study will be presented. Figure 3 shows the objectives which are observed in association with knowledge management processes, while Figure 4 illustrates the position of knowledge management processes in a life cycle concept. Figure 3 shows that 55% of the respondents introduce knowledge management processes for reducing costs and 54% introduce the processes for improving reliability and security. As illustrated

Figure 3. Objectives for knowledge management

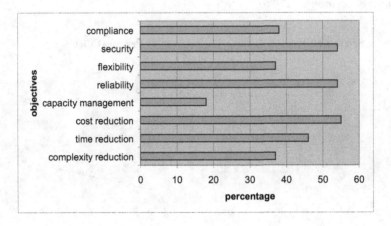

in Figure 4, knowledge management is positioned in the arising cycle curve and has therefore much improvement potential.

The results of the second empirical study amplify the thesis that knowledge management is a "trend" and therefore an important factor for improving business processes. Based on the results from these two empirical studies the authors evaluated in a case study the importance of knowledge management in business processes in a bank.

Figure 4. Position of knowledge management in the life cycle concept

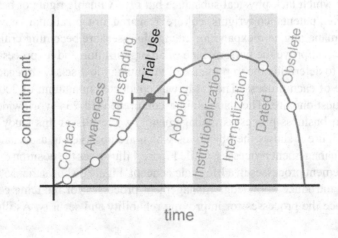

Components of Knowledge Management

Knowledge management can be seen as a set of processes to create, gather, store, maintain, and disseminate the bank's knowledge. Business process is a way in which organizations coordinate and organize work activities, information, and knowledge to produce a product or service. Knowledge alone is not enough to get competitive advantage; much more, the use of knowledge is necessary and we call it "knowledge in action." Knowledge management has a special value if it applies to dealing with knowledge-intensive processes (Fink & Ploder, 2007). Knowledge-intensive processes for instance capture the expertise of a human in limited domains of knowledge. Such processes are important for dealing with the competitive advantage of the bank. Knowledge management refers to the set of business processes developed in an organization to create, store, transfer, and apply knowledge. In the investigation we follow the knowledge component concept of Probst et al. (1997).

Knowledge Management in the Banking Sector

The need for action results from globalization, technological changes, value changes, and the differentiation in banking services. Banks are submitted to a strong change. In Europe the competition was intensified by introducing the common currency in Euro. The introduction of the Euro makes the capital markets more largely liquid, and in particular, more transparent. Another need of action can be seen by the increasing importance of the technology. The increasing employment of technology leads to changes in the processes of customer relationship (electronic banking) but also in internal processes of a bank. Figure 5 shows a structure of the knowledge adjustment. Knowledge can be embedded in business processes in a four-quadrant manner. Knowledge, which is primarily embedded on internal-oriented business processes (operative oriented knowledge focus), is centered in supporting the employees of the bank. On the other side, knowledge can be identified, which is primarily embedded in external oriented business processes (market oriented knowledge focus) and is centered on supporting the customers of the bank. Processes can also have an internal and external knowledge focus (a dual knowledge focus is market- and operative-oriented). If processes have neither an internal knowledge orientation nor an external knowledge orientation these processes are not knowledge oriented. As you see in Figure 5, knowledge in the explored bank medium is internal- and low external-oriented. An improvement to a dual oriented knowledge focus is suggested. Empirical studies attest that successful enterprises have a dual process and therefore also knowledge focus (König, 2003).

Figure 5. Structure of knowledge adjustment

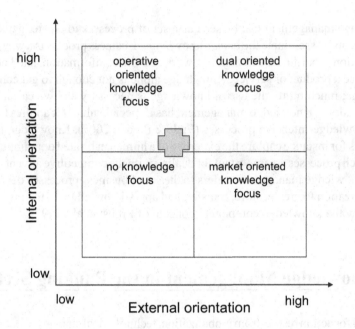

The Banking Sector as a Knowledge Intensive Organization

Knowledge management models can be applied basically on all forms of organizations. However, there are criteria on the completion of introducing knowledge management. The knowledge-intensive portfolio gives the possibility to position the knowledge intensity of an enterprise (Figure 6). On the one side, the production of services needs different knowledge, while on the other side, the business idea as well as the professional knowledge can be estimated from low to high ranking.

Field C includes processes with a low professional knowledge and low entrepreneurial know how. An example is the mining industry. Figure 6 shows that the professional know-how in the banking sector lies from medium to high, but the entrepreneurial know-how lies from low to medium.

Figure 6. Knowledge intensive enterprises

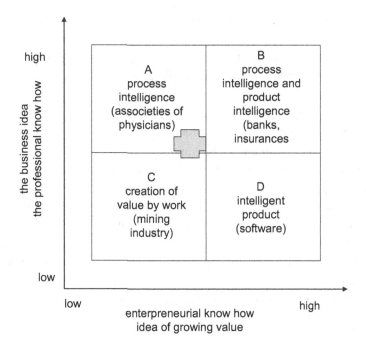

Knowledge in Business Processes

Following the approach from Probst et al. (1997), the authors developed a knowledge checklist for the allocation process of a personal loan. Figures 8 and 9 give an overview about the methodology used in the knowledge elements of Probst et al.'s systematic approach. This knowledge profile was the base of a questionnaire which was answered by 78 banking process specialists (data sample) (Razenböck, 2006). In this chapter the most important results are presented in Figure 7. The grey area in the individual components shows the realized level of knowledge management. The results in the components "defining knowledge objectives" and "knowledge evaluation" align with the study of Pfeffer and Suton (2003). From the empirical results the authors conclude

- *Knowledge objectives* are not enough or explicitly defined, especially norma-tive and strategic knowledge objectives. In the vision and mission statement no knowledge relation can be found.

- *Knowledge evaluation* (Roithmayr & Fink, 2007) has a least significant im-portance. The reason could be seen in insufficient methodology for knowledge measurement (Fink, 2004). The controlling concept is index-oriented and has no qualitative approach.

- *Knowledge development* must be improved and takes place in projects, but there is no systematic documentation.

- *Knowledge distribution* must be improved by the application of systematic approach. There is also no IT support for knowledge distribution.

- *The element of "knowledge gaining" is very well supported.* This is understand-able, because in banking sector methods of knowledge gaining (i.e., market research, stakeholder management) have a long tradition (Fink, Roithmayr, & Ploder, 2006).

- The high frequency of *knowledge usage* shows the importance of knowledge management.

- *Knowledge preservation* must be systematically organized. The used knowledge is not enough preserved.

Figure 7. Embedded knowledge

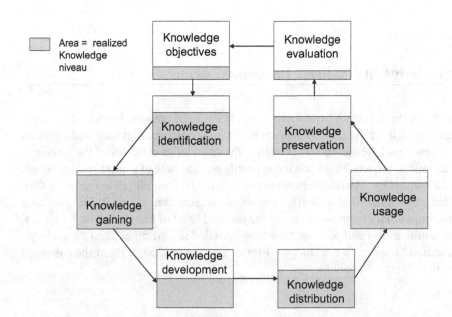

- *Knowledge identification* is well developed. But this is understandable because employees use methodologies for identifying knowledge sources.

Summary

As results of the empirical studies the authors can conclude that knowledge management is not a "fashion" but rather a "trend," which answers the Research Question_1 (RQ_1). Especially Figure 2 shows the continuous increasing of the number of publications in scientific papers and also the same "trend" in practical-oriented publications. The empirical results presented in Figure 4 refers to the same direction. Knowledge management is in many enterprises in the "trial use" phase of the life cycle of knowledge management.

With the second research question (Research Question_2 [RQ_2]) the authors asked in which dimension knowledge management is integrated in business processes of a bank. The case study shows different results. The approach of Probst et al. (2003) is a good basis for introducing knowledge management in an organization. Important is the methodological approach used in the individual elements of the used model (see Figures 8 and 9). The results show that knowledge is embedded in an unbalanced manner into the different elements of the model. One reason could be that knowledge objectives and knowledge evaluation are not strategically positioned enough in the explored enterprise.

References

Davenport, T., & Prusak, L. (1998). *Working knowledge. How organizations manage what they know*. Boston: Harvard Business Press.

Fink, K. (2004). *Knowledge potential measurement and uncertainty* (1st ed.). Wiesbaden: DUV.

Fink, K., & Ploder, C. (2007, June). A comparative study of knowledge processes in Austrian and Swiss SMEs. In *Proceedings of the European Conference on Information Systems ECIS2007*, St. Gallen, Switzerland.

Fink, K., Roithmayr, F., & Kofler, G. (2001, November-December). Rahmenbedingungen für die Teledemokratie. *Verwaltung & Management*, 333-340

Fink, K., Roithmayr, F., & Ploder, C. (2006, May 21-24). Multi-functional stakeholder information system for strategic knowledge management: Theoretical concept and case studies. In M. Khosrow-Pour (Ed.), *Emerging trends and chal-*

lenges in information technology management (pp. 152-155). Paper presented at the2006 Information Resourcees Management Association International Conference, Washington, D.C. Hershey, PA/London/Melbourne/Singapore: IGI Global, Inc.

König, W. (2003). International vergleichende Untersuchung des Einsatzes von Electronic Commerce: Schwerpunkte effizienter Unternehmen. D. Ehrenberg & H. J. Kaftan (Eds.), *Herausforderungen der Wirtschaftsinformatik in der Informationsgesellschaft* (Wissenschaftliche ed.). Leipzig: Am Gutenbergplatz Leipzig.

Laudon, C. K. & Laudon, J. P. (2006). *Management information* systems (p. 417). Upper Saddle River, NJ: Pearson Education.

Mockler, R., & Dologite, D. (2002). Strategically-focused enterprise knowledge management. In D. White (Ed.), *Knowledge mapping & management* (pp. 14-22). Hershey, PA: IRM Press.

Myers, M. (1997). Qualitative research in information systems. *MIS Quarterly, 21*(2), 241-242.

Pfeffer, J., & Suton, R. I. (2003). *The knowing-doing gap* (p. 20).

Probst, G., Raub, S., & Romhardt, K. (2003). Wissen managen: Wie Unternehmen ihre wertvollste Ressource optimal nutzen. 4. Aufl., Gabler, Wiesbaden.

Razenböck, A. (2006). *Betriebliches management von wissen.* University of Linz, Department of Information Systems–Information Engineering.

Roithmayr, F., & Fink, K. (2007). *Knowledge measurement.* Vienna: Best of 2003 SAP Business School Vienna.

Roithmayr, F., & Kobler, M. (2006). *Business process improvement: Intermediate report* (pp. 2-3). Linz: Department of Business Informatics–Information Engineering.

Roithmayr, F., & Steininger, K. (2006). *Moden und trends in der wirtschaftsinformatik.* Universität Linz, Institut für Wirtschaftsinformatik–Information Engineering.

Sveiby, K. (1997). *The new organizational wealth.* San Franciso: Berrett-Koehler-Publishers.

Tiwana, A. (2000). *The knowledge management toolkit.* Upper Saddle River, NJ: Prentice Hall.

Figure 8. Knowledge profile-1

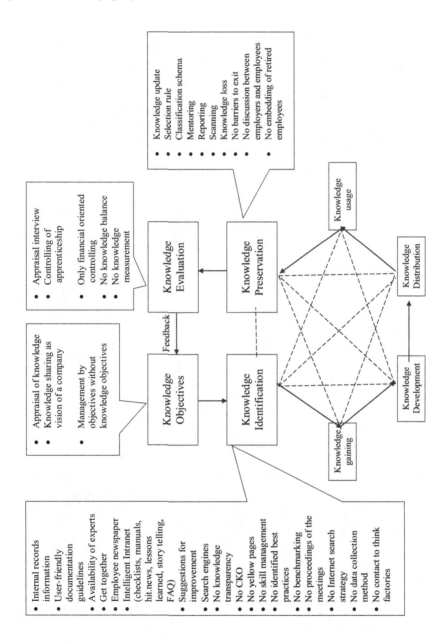

Figure 9. Knowledge profile-2

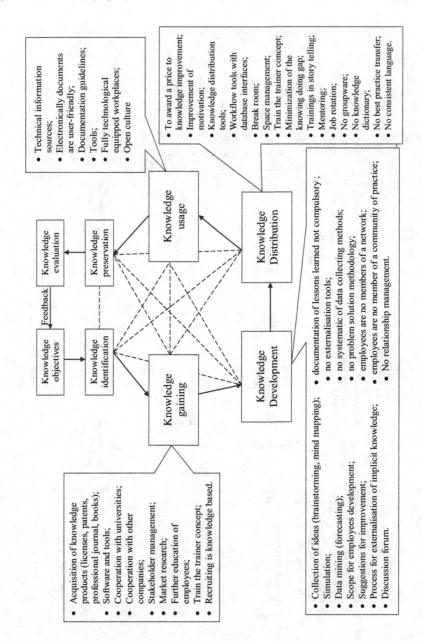

Chapter XIII

Managing Interorganizational Networks

Nancy Linwood, DuPont, USA

Brian Langton, DuPont, USA

Abstract

This chapter introduces the challenges facing interorganizational knowledge management networks. Examples from DuPont, the knowledge management working group of the federal government, as well as the Construction Industry Institute give concrete examples of how these challenges were faced and overcome. The authors hope that their industry experience and years of working in these networks help the readers to apply these principles to their own networks.

Introduction

Interorganizational networks are formed because large organizations and companies know they may not communicate well. Any knowledge management network has at its core people who understand the organization very well. There are always opportunities to save money, manage information, and collaborate more effectively. Knowledge-based networks may appear to work seamlessly but in order to deliver value, some guiding principles need to be applied. A larger orgnization such as DuPont benefits immeasurably from formal and informal networks, but behind the scenes this is the result of creative leadership and individual contributions. Most large organizations have groups which do not "play well" with each other for various reasons. Like many virtual organizations, people come together to work on common problems, but still have to answer to their management when it comes to budget, time, and resource allocations.

Managing interorganizational networks for knowledge management is difficult unless you have several things: clear vision and scope, clear sponsorship, and actual projects to complete that show value. Many times, this type of network finds itself unsponsored, without a clear goal or product, and the afterthought of the organization. This is even clearer at times when knowledge management is not necessarily a favorite initiative of upper management.

The knowledge management network in DuPont, a large multinational corporation, has been in place since at least 1999. The purpose of the DuPont knowledge management and collaboration network is to act as a champion and driver across DuPont businesses in order to improve productivity and create growth. The team works together to provide examples of new tools and processes, to publicize resources and activities that are available, to serve as role modes and stewards, and to publicly recognize good practices.

Deliverables and Demonstrating Value

As with any organization in a business that requires profit, a network cannot survive without deliverables and showing real value. Most networks are very good at knowledge sharing and "show-and-tell." The meetings can turn into this quite easily if not redirected. Show-and-tell has value, but the network cannot sit on its laurels and expect that this fills the void and demonstrates the value of the organization.

Other meaningful tasks to complete include collecting and testing good and best practices, and acting as the "test bed" for new tools and processes. Many new corporate processes, such as testing collaborative tools, need to involve a cross-section of the organization. A good knowledge management network can provide a ready-made group of energetic and experienced testers. This in turn can allow new products and tools to be more easily evaluated, saving time.

Getting the Right People Involved

In many knowledge management networks, membership is self-directed. You tend to find early adopters, "techies," and others like that who join and participate. Unfortunately, unless there is management support, often members are drawn off to more important projects. An important task of these networks is to encourage members and to draw in new members. It is especially important to watch the organization for new appointments of people who have responsibility for knowledge management activities. These activities can vary in name from collaboration, to networking, to document management. Those people should be invited to attend and given roles in the network. They can also help drive projects which demonstrate real value to the organization. Such projects are things like evaluation of tools, surveys of workflow or document management practices, and so forth. In 2006, the DuPont knowledge management and collaboration network partnered with Corporate IT and Research and Development and Crop Protection to pilot the new Google Search Appliance. This cross-functional team designed the process to be tested, spent several weeks checking to see how the tool worked within DuPont's security parameters, and wrote an extensive white paper recommendation to Corporate IT. As a result of the careful analysis, DuPont purchased the Google Search Appliance. The value of network involvement was proven because of buy-in from several segments of DuPont. Also, Corporate IT was not burdened with the evaluation. In 2007, DuPont's legal IT department was able to read the white paper and use it to make a decision on using Google for searching legal documents. The real value of a knowledge management organization is in seamlessly allowing these knowledge sharing activities. When the people in the network hold meetings, it allows those who regularly communicate only through e-mail a chance to make a more thorough connection in person. It also gives participants a chance to make comments and connections in person that might be inappropriate in a written communication. DuPont found that IT people are drawn to the knowledge management network. A study, by Kulkarni, Ravindran, and Freeze (2006, p. 3), found that "IT plays an important role in the firm's ability to apply existing knowledge effectively." Many new initiatives depend on the IT capability to even start to come to fruition. IT capability has to be in place to provide the infrastructure and connections necessary for the systems.

Sponsorship

A big problem for any interorganizational group is finding sponsorship. Any network needs a strong sponsor to enable growth and give focus to the group. Any group can get started, but without a strong sponsor, the people will not feel that they have management support to spend time on projects. A sponsor can also focus the group on projects that are relevant and in line with management objectives. Groups can flounder around picking projects and never know what they should focus on completing. The DuPont knowledge management and collaboration network had no sponsor for several years. Recently, a research director agreed to become the sponsor.

The Knowledge Management Working Group (KMWG) of the U.S. Government is an excellent example of what can be accomplished in the public sector. The KMWG (KM-LIST@listserv.gsa.gov) seems to have no sponsor, other than the federal government. Recently, the leadership of the group abruptly changed. There was a flurry of e-mail and phone calls clarifying the direction and purpose of the group. Without formal direction, the group dynamics were at risk of changing and weakening. Rapidly, long-standing members reestablished themselves as leaders, and the group quickly rebounded from the confusion. A strong sponsor would have made all the confusion and change unnecessary. It would also have given long-standing members permission to step up and take leadership of the group earlier.

Social Networking Analysis

Social networking tools are used to analyze groups and find how members interact with each other. While the tools involve surveying the group, and may take a lot of members' time, they offer valuable insights into how the group works and where it needs to be strengthened. Some tools require analyzing e-mail to see who writes to whom, and developing a chart showing the relationships. Other tools require the whole team to fill out a survey evaluating the strength of their communications and dependence on other team members. This sort of evaluation requires a commitment from the team in order for it to work. The results show patterns of behavior which allow team members to see who is consulted. This tool is useful to map who talks to whom, and pinpoints communication gaps in the team, both in coverage from certain businesses, and in connections among and between team members. The downside of this sort of analysis is that team members, who regularly communicate with everyone, show up unevenly as having a lot of expertise. This analysis does not show why people are consulted. An example of a chart prepared from such an analysis follows.

A better way of determining expertise might be expert locator software, such as that from Tacit (www.tacit.com). This software finds people with expertise in the subject of interest, and sends e-mail to the group asking for assistance. People self-select if they wish to reply, and relationships are formed. The software aids in expertise location because large organizations are poor at introductions and expertise awareness. Many people may not know that the person down the hall or in the next building, let alone another country, has expertise in the problem that needs a solution.

Figure 1.

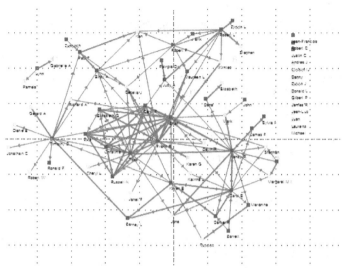

The KM Working Group of the U.S. Government recognized the strength of social networking tools. A lively discussion was started online after someone in the group shared an article on the efficacy of these tools.

The U.S. Government is like many other large organizations with similar needs. Each agency has its own budgets, and it is very easy to waste money solving a problem that another agency has already researched. This group meets regularly in Washington to bring together people with an interest in knowledge management. It is unique in that it also allows outsiders to participate, both in meetings and online discussions. This allows the government's contractors to offer their insights (free of charge of course), improves organizational effectiveness, and also involves the larger knowledge management community in the discussions.

Web 2.0 Tools for Collaboration

Networks like this offer ample opportunities to experiment with new collaboration technologies. The network can be the vanguard of the organization for things like wikis, RSS, blogs, and so forth. Members often are skilled in these new tools, and are eager to set them up for the group to use. Regular usage gives other members skills they can take back to their organizations, seamlessly extending the proliferation of new technology. The *National Geographic Magazine* is large publisher with many different internal and external collaborators. Their contributors can be all over the world, taking pictures, writing articles, or sharing ideas. Karen Huffman, Manager of Knowledge Initiatives of the *National Geographic* shared her successes using podcasts and wikis (mediawiki) and RSS feeds to improve collaboration at the magazine. Huffman regularly hosts 20 minute coffee sessions to teach her colleagues how to use the new technologies (http://www.oclc.org/capcon/member-ship/news/OCLC_CAPCON_shares,_.htm).

Communities of Practice

According to Wikipedia (http://en.wikipedia.org/wiki/Community_of_Practice) the concept of a community of practice (CoP) refers to the process of social learning that occurs when people who have a common interest in some subject or problem collaborate over an extended period to share ideas, find solutions, and build innovations.

The term was first used in 1991 by Jean Lave and Etienne Wenger who used it in relation to situated learning as part of an attempt to "rethink learning" at the Institute for Research on Learning. In 1998, the theorist Etienne Wenger extended the concept and applied it to other contexts, including organizational settings. More recently, communities of practice have become associated with knowledge management as people have begun to see them as ways of developing social capital, nurturing new knowledge, stimulating innovation, or sharing existing tacit knowledge within an organization. It is now an accepted part of organizational development (OD).

Designed vs. Emerging

In the business world, and in particular for interorganizational networks, it is important to distinguish "designed" networks from "emerging" or "naturally forming" networks. Examples of designed networks might be organized team sports, clubs such as the "Elks Lodge" or the "Knights of Columbus," and even to some degree churches and schools. These communities are well defined, often with charters, by-laws, and well defined roles for all members. There is often a structured leadership and obvious hierarchy within the organization

Professional networks frequently do not have the luxury of such a well-defined structure. There may be one leader, and perhaps some officers for duties such as managing meeting minutes and organizing future meetings. Sometimes there is a simple charter and perhaps some method of selecting leaders and officers. But there is a key difference in that the network stays together as a product of members contributing useful information. In order for a network to remain healthy or to be successful, there must be a steady stream of new information and accomplishments from which the community members derive some benefit.

Healthy and Successful Networks

In contrast to some networks which are more structured within one organization, interorganizational networks must be formed by communities of individual with common interests and a shared purpose. Naturally forming "communities of practice" are typically made up motivated experts who are interested in sharing knowledge and common goals with other experts who have similar areas of expertise.

Often there are significant barriers to the formation, health, or success of such networks. Interorganizational competition is an obvious problem. In many cases, network members are driven by business practices and market forces to protect innovation and hoard organization knowledge. Usually, members must also balance time demands from full-time jobs and work pressures which limit network participation or free time available. In order for a network to be healthy, like any community, most of the participants must contribute in a positive way. It is easier and often more common for participants to take information and professional contacts from such networks while being very guarded about their own information or expertise for business reasons.

In order for an interorganizational network, or any community, to be truly successful there must be a strong bond of common interest and also strong leadership from an individual or a small group of individuals who can demonstrate and encourage positive community behaviors. There must be one or more role models who both practice and attract value-adding contributions to the community. Participation and contributions—of time, knowledge, expertise, and real-life examples—must also be rewarded in some way. In most cases, some kind of recognition within the community as an expert and as a valued community member is the only reward available.

Case Study: CII: Construction Industry Institute® (The University of Texas at Austin) (http://www.construction-institute.org)

The Construction Industry Institute, based at The University of Texas at Austin, is a consortium of more than 90 leading owner, engineering-contractor, and supplier firms from both the public and private arenas. These organizations have joined together to enhance the business effectiveness and sustainability of the capital facility life cycle through CII research, related initiatives, and industry alliances. A learning organization with a wealth of knowledge and information, CII is unique in the engineering and construction industry.

The Construction Industry Institute is a collection of representatives from diverse engineering and construction firms across the world. Several of the participants are Fortune 500 companies. Various committees meet quarterly and a conference is held annually with topics, panels, papers, and presentations designed to share information on industry topics according to guidelines found in the literature (e.g. Wenger & McDermott, 2002; Wenger, McDermott, & Snyder, 1999).

It is often the case that large organizations will have persistent relationships with other companies that are in their own industry. These relationships generally begin from relationships between individuals within the respective organizations, and can become more formalized over time. These interactions are often cordial, and can be brought to the forefront due to mutual participation in trade shows, consortia, special interest committees, and professional organizations. Each collaboration partner might informally visit the other company for information sharing, discussion of emerging industry trends and standards, and perhaps to explore possible opportunities for joint ventures. Such relationships might exist between companies that are actually competitors in the marketplace, but are more likely between companies that are similar but not in direct competition. Ultimately, sustained healthy business relationships of this kind depend on intracompany networks of individuals who can collaborate with openness and professionalism while being careful not to disclose trade secrets or otherwise behave in any unethical manner.

It is not unusual for mutually beneficial interaction between large companies to take place within the framework of a consortium. According to Wikipedia (http://en.wikipedia.org/wiki/Consortium), "a consortium is an association of two or more individuals, companies, organizations or governments (or any combination of these entities) with the objective of participating in a common activity or pooling their resources for achieving a common goal." Often, a consortium is formed for non-profit purposes, such as colleges or universities joining together "to share human and material assets as well as to link academic and administrative resources."

One example of a for-profit consortium, also an example of a joint-venture, was Six Companies, Inc. formed to construct the Hoover Dam. Another example of a for-profit consortium is when a group of banks collaborate to give a loan. This is more commonly known as a syndicated loan. A more permanent joint activity is usually called an institute.

An example of one such interorganizational network is FIATECH (http://en.wikipedia.org/wiki/FIATECH). "FIATECH is a non-profit construction-industry research, development, and deployment (RD&D) consortium that focuses on the fast-track development and deployment of technologies to improve the life-cycle processes of capital projects. Membership includes facilities owners, operators, contractors, suppliers, government agencies and academic institutions." Participants in the consortium include many major U.S. corporations. The Board of Directors includes members from DuPont, KBR, Jacobs Engineering, Procter & Gamble, Fluor, and Dow Chemical.

One of the most notable of such arrangement is the World Wide Web Consortium (W3C), a committee with more than 400 member organizations formed to develop and maintain standards for the Web. Formed by Tim Berners-Lee, W3C created standards for the hypertext transfer protocol (HTTP), the hypertext markup language (HTML), and the universal resource locator (URL). These standards are the basis of the Internet as we know it today.

Modern corporations of any size often depend heavily on arrangements that involve "outsourcing" certain kinds of work. Many companies use significant numbers of "contract employees" to perform services within the company that are not part of that company's "core competency" or to provide specialized services that may be difficult to staff internally in an increasingly competitive job market. Such roles might involve "flexible" staffing to meet needs for temporary demand or capital investment—allowing for easier increases or decreases in total labor costs—or may involve semipermanent employees in a variety of roles that, for a variety of reasons, are not ideal for permanent employees. For example, technical information technology professionals with a particular set of skills may be involved in assignments for years at a time until technology environments advance and new sets of contract employees may be required.

In companies with important outsourced work arrangements, sometimes described as "leveraged organizations," the company generally forms a set of almost symbiotic relationships with companies that provide contract employees. The leveraged company depends on the contracting company to find and train enough workers to meet business needs, and to manage contract employee benefits at a level that allows for steady contract employments as needed. The leveraged company and the various potential contract companies all participate in loose network ties to the industry and the job market involved. All stay up to date on trends and professional advancements, and recruiters from regional, national, or even global networks identify and match up contract employees to jobs as demands shift.

Strong trends in global sourcing and "off shoring" are the culmination of this same approach. Networked relationships must exist between companies with contract employment demands, contract companies with global reach and understanding of outsourcing methods, and strong networks must exist between the various contracting and recruiting agencies so that needs can be aligned with capabilities across vast geographic and cultural differences.

Conclusion

Managing interorganizational knowledge management networks is not easy. It is a little like herding cats, in that no one listens to the leader, and everyone has their own agenda and their own inner direction. But, like cats, everyone sees the value of the end reward of sharing the "cat chow," or, sharing the new tools and processes that are tested and developed. If you can get the right sponsorship, involve key people, and direct their energy in productive ways, there are many returns on investment for an organization to sponsor such a network.

References

Kulkarni, U., Ravindran, S., & Freeze, R. (2006). A knowledge management success model: Theoretical development and empirical validation. *Journal of Management Information Systems, 23*(3), 309-347.

Wenger, E., & McDermott, R. (2002). *Cultivating communities of practice.* Boston: Harvard Business School Press.

Wenger, E., McDermott, R., & Snyder, W. (1999). *Communities of practice: Learning, meaning, and identity.* Cambridge University Press.

About the Contributors

Miltiadis D. Lytras is an assistant professor in the Computer Engineering and Informatics Department-CEID (University of Patras). His research focuses on Semantic Web, knowledge management, and e-learning, with more than 100 publications in these areas. He has coedited 25 special issues in international journals (e.g., *IEEE Transaction on Knowledge and Data Engineering, IEEE Internet Computing, IEEE Transactions on Education, Computers in Human Behaviour*, etc.) and has authored/(co)edited 12 books [e.g., *Open Source for Knowledge and Learning management, Ubiquitous and Pervasive Knowledge Management, Intelligent Learning Infrastructures for Knowledge Intensive Organizations,* and *Semantic Based Information Systems*] . He is the founder and officer of the Semantic Web and Information Systems Special Interest Group in the Association for Information Systems (http://www.sigsemis.org). He serves as the (co)editor in chief of 12 international journals [e.g., *International Journal of Knowledge and Learning, International Journal of Technology Enhanced Learning, International Journal on Social and Humanistic Computing, International Journal on Semantic Web and Information Systems, International Journal on Digital Culture and Electronic Tourism, International Journal of Electronic Democracy, International Journal of Electronic Banking,* and *International Journal of Electronic Trade*] while he is associate editor or editorial board member in seven more.

Meir Russ received his PhD from The Ohio State University in strategic management, entrepreneurship, and international business. He also has an MBA and a B.Sc.E.E. from Tel Aviv University. He is currently an associate professor with the University of Wisconsin, Green Bay. Dr. Russ currently teaches undergraduate and graduate classes in management and marketing. He also teaches a strategic emergency preparedness, planning and implementation class in the Certificate for Emergency Management Master of Administrative Science Program at UW-GB. His research interests include knowledge-based strategies, the use of knowledge management for hospital preparedness, and the new-knowledge based economic development, among others. In addition to his academic focus, Dr. Russ serves in a consulting capacity with a number of multinational companies in the area of global strategic management and knowledge management.

Ronald Maier graduated from Johannes-Kepler-University of Linz, Austria, in management information systems. He holds a PhD in management information systems from The Koblenz School of Corporate Management—Otto Beisheim Graduate School of Management (WHU), Germany. His PhD thesis was on quality of data modelling (in German). He completed his habilitation at the University of Regensburg with the habilitation thesis *Knowledge Management Systems. Information and Communication Technologies for Knowledge Management*. He worked as visiting assistant professor at the Terry College of Business, University of Georgia in Athens, GA from 1998-1999; from 2002-2007 he was with the School of Business and Economics, Martin-Luther-University Halle-Wittenberg, Germany, and held a chair in MIS, Information Systems Leadership. Since February 2007, he has been a university professor in information systems at the School of Management of the Leopold-Franzens-University of Innsbruck, Austria. He has published articles on knowledge management and knowledge management systems in a number of research journals, books, and conference proceedings. His research interests include data management and business intelligence, business process management, knowledge management, and technology-enhanced learning.

Ambjörn Naeve (www.nada.kth.se/~amb) has a background in both mathematics and computer science and received his PhD in computer science from KTH in 1993. With his *Garden of Knowledge* project (1996-98) he initiated the research on interactive learning environments at KTH, where he presently heads the knowledge management research group (http://kmr.nada.kth.se). He is also the coordinator of research on interactive learning environments at the Uppsala Learning Lab at Uppsala University. The KMR group has been involved in Semantic Web research and development since 1999. The work of the KMR group focuses on how to make use of Semantic Web technology in order to enable more efficient forms of technology-enhanced learning and administration, and support the emergence of a *public knowledge and learning management environment*. Prominent among the KMR tools are the frameworks *SCAM* (http://scam.sourceforge.net) and *SHAME* (http://kmr.nada.kth.se/shame), the concept browser *Conzilla* (www.conzilla.org), and the electronic portfolio system *Confolio* (www.confolio.org). The KMR-group is active within several international networks in technology-enhanced learning and Semantic Web, notably, *Prolearn* (www.prolearn.eu), *SIGSEMIS* (www.sigsemis.org), and *Sakai* (http://sakaiproject.org). Ambjörn Naeve is also a well-known industry consultant with extensive experience in conceptual modeling for software engineering and business applications. He is the inventor of Conzilla and has developed a conceptual modeling technique called *unified language modeling* (http://kmr.nada.kth.se/cm), which is specially designed to depict conceptual relationships in a linguistically coherent way - that is, to "draw how we talk about things."

* * *

Richard Adler is the founder and chief architect of DecisionPath, Inc. He designed ForeTell, the company's knowledge-based software platform and directs development of domain-specific ForeTell decision support solutions. Throughout his career as a software architect and consultant, Dr. Adler has focused on knowledge representation, capture, transfer, and deployment issues. He has designed and helped develop diverse knowledge-based tools and mission-critical systems, including an intelligent network management system for NASA's Space Shuttle Launch Processing System, frameworks for coordinating distributed systems, and communities of practice. Dr. Adler has published on topics including counter-terrorism, organizational change management, intelligent systems, distributed computing, simulation, and component software technology.

Mariel Alejandra Ale is a professor of information system engineering at Universidad Tecnológica Nacional (UTN) – Facultad Regional Santa Fe (Argentina). She received her degree in information systems engineering in 1999 from Universidad Tecnológica Nacional–Facultad Regional Santa Fe, Argentina, and is currently a PhD student at Universidad Tecnológica Nacional–Facultad Regional Santa Fe. Since 2003, she has been working for CIDISI Research Center in Information Systems Engineering. Her current research interests include knowledge management systems, ontologies, knowledge representation and retrieval, and total quality management.

Maria Elizabeth Bianconcini de Almeida is professor of the post graduation program in education curriculum and of the department of computer science of the Pontifical Catholic University. She is a Doctor in education by the Pontifical Catholic University of São Paulo. She is a specialist and researcher in training of educators for the incorporation of information and communication technology in educational practice and in distance education with support in the digital media and digital inclusion. She is coordinator of the technologies and school management project.

Omar Chiotti was born in Argentina in 1959. He received his degree in chemical engineering in 1984 from Universidad Tecnológica Nacional (UTN) and is PhD from Universidad Nacional del Litoral (UNL) in 1989. Since 1984, he has been working for the Argentina's National Council of Scientific Research (CONICET) as a researcher. He has been a professor of information systems engineering al UTN since 1986. Currently, he is the director of CIDISI Research Center in Information System Engineering. His current research interests include e-collaboration, knowledge management, and multiagentsystems.

Leif Edvinsson. Since 2000, Leif Edvinsson has been the world's first professor adjunct at Lund University on Intellectual Capital. In January 2006, he was also appointed professor adjunct at The Hong Kong Polytechnic University. In January 1998, Leif received the prestigious Brain Trust "Brain of the Year" award (UK). He has been a special advisor on service trade to the Swedish Ministry of Foreign Affairs as well as Ministry of Industry, a special advisor to the United Nations International Trade Centre, and is a cofounder of the Swedish Coalition of Service Industries. During 2004 he was one of the prime advisors for the German Ministry of Economics on initiating the now very successful project on Wissenskapital and IC reporting. He is also one of the high-level experts working for the European Commission on guidance for IC reporting. He has also been very active in transfer his experiences to Asia, working with, among others, METI in Japan.

Martin J. Eppler holds the chair of information and communication management at the University of Lugano (USI), Switzerland where he teaches strategy and knowledge management and conducts research on knowledge communication, visualization, and strategy communication. He has published over 70 academic papers and seven books on knowledge communication. He is a fellow of Cambridge University and a guest professor at the Central University of Finance and Economics in Beijing. He is the inventor of the visual knowledge management suite lets-focus.com. He has been an advisor to organizations such as KPMG, Ernst & Young, DaimlerChrysler, the United Nations, UBS, the Swiss Military, Swiss Re, and others.

Carlos Ferran is an assistant professor of management information systems at the Pennsylvania State University in Great Valley. He received his DBA in MIS from Boston University, a graduate degree in MIS from Universidad Central de Venezuela, a Cum Laude Master in finance, and a Licentiate in management sciences (BS) from Universidad Metropolitana. Dr. Ferran has been a visiting professor at IESA (Venezuela), INALDE (Colombia), and IAE (Argentina). He worked in the software industry for 10 years, acted as an IT/IS consultant for over 10 years, and held the position of CIO for an important financial group in Venezuela. His research interests span technology mediated communication (particularly videoconferencing), accounting information systems, knowledge management, and the digital divide. He serves in the editorial board of several professional journals and is currently the editor of *Revista de la Asociación de Sistemas de Información para Latinoamérica y el Caribe* (an AIS journal).

Kerstin Fink is a professor in the Department of Information Systems, Operations Management and Logistics, at the University of Innsbruck, Austria. Her research interests include information and knowledge management/measurement, information system management, stakeholder information systems, and knowledge-intensive process modelling. She has an excellent research record and has participated in various R&D projects like:

- Knowledge management and measurement project for software companies (e.g., SAP).
- Stakeholder information system for the Bank Austria.
- Development of a case study center at the Department of Information Systems, University of Innsbruck, in the field of knowledge management and system planning.

María Rosa Galli is a professor of information system engineering and industrial engineering at Universidad Tecnológica Nacional (UTN)–Facultad Regional Santa Fe (Argentina). She received her degree in chemical engineering in 1983 from Universidad Nacional de Mar del Plata, Argentina, and a PhD in chemical engineering from Universidad Nacional de Litoral (Santa Fe), in 1989. Since 1984, she has been working for de Argentina's National Council of Scientific Research (CONICET) as a researcher. Currently, she is directory member of CIDISI Research Center in Information System Engineering. Her current research interests include knowledge management systems, ontology, e-collaboration, semantic interoperability, and multiagents systems.

Mr. Greg Jones is an executive coach specializing in entrepreneurial growth. In his role as a change agent he has created educational and development interventions for high-growth life cycle shift industries. His clients include organizations within the agricultural, higher education, nonprofit, and niche product sectors. Mr. Jones holds an undergraduate degree in organizational leadership and an MBA with a knowledge management and executive coaching focus from Franklin University in Columbus, Ohio. In addition to his design and development endeavors, Mr. Jones serves on the board of directors of a conservation organization. His research and publication areas include instructional design, executive coaching, knowledge management, training and development, and organizational life cycles.

Jeannette K. Jones, RCC, is a full-time faculty member with American Interconti-nental University (AIU)-Online Campus in the MED program area. Prior to joining AIU, she was responsible for curriculum design of graduate and undergraduate programs and online faculty development instruction at the university level. Her research interests include knowledge management strategies and technologies; online learning theory, practice, and design; coaching methodologies; and breast cancer survivor skills. In addition to her academic credentials, Dr. Jones is a registered corporate coach certified through the World Association of Business Coaches. Dr. Jones' most recent publications include articles in the 2005 and 2006 issues of the *International Journal of Knowledge and Learning* and the *International Journal of Knowledge, Culture, and Change Management*. Dr. Jones received her BS in human resource management from George Mason University in Fairfax, Virginia, her MBA from Averett College in Danville, Virginia, and her Ed.D. in instructional technology and distance education from Nova Southeastern University in Ft. Lauderdale, Florida.

Brian Langton has worked at DuPont Engineering and Information Technology as an employee for 6 years and as a contractor for the 5 years previous to that. He is an IT specialist with a background in servers, databases, applications, collaboration, and knowledge management. Brian was a leader of the engineering KM program for 5 years and is currently a project manager for Intellectual Property Protection. He was previously employed as a systems analyst, systems engineer, and IT consultant for the travel industry, the electronic and paper publishing industry, and for point of sale systems. He attended Boston University

Nancy Linwood has been employed at DuPont for 25 years. She is currently holding dual roles for Central Research and Development's Information and Computing Technology group. She is the technology consultant for the DuPont Information and Content Management group and also a taxonomy consultant for the eBusiness and Taxonomy Search Solutions Group. Nancy has been involved in DuPont's knowledge management and collaboration network for three years, and is currently serving as chairperson of that network. She has an MSLIS from Drexel University and a BA from the University of Delaware. She has also been an adjunct professor at Delaware State University and Wilmington College.

Michael J. Mannor (mannormi@msu.edu) is a visiting professor in the strategic management group of The Eli Broad Graduate School of Management at Michigan State University. His research focuses on executive leadership and the management of knowledge in organizations, with interests in the domains of radical innovation and entrepreneurship. His research has been published in the *Journal of Applied Psychology*, the best paper proceedings of the Academy of Management, and in several books. Prior to entering academia, Dr. Mannor worked for 5 years in the telecommunications industry.

Neli Maria Mengalli is to get a doctorate in the postgraduation program in education curriculum and professor at the college of education of the Pontifical Catholic University in São Paulo. She worked at the course of training of School Managers for the Use of Information and Communication Technology of the Technologies and School Management Project. In context of the Master's degree dissertation defended in October 2006. Her current project of research includes the educational design for communities of practice in education and the study of collaborative learning environments. She also works for the Inland Teaching Coordination, an institution linked to the Secretary of Education office of the State of São Paulo, Brazil.

Patricia Ordóñez de Pablos is professor in the Department of Business Administration and Accountability, at the Faculty of Economics of The University of Oviedo (Spain). Her teaching and research interests focus on the areas of strategic management, knowledge management, intellectual capital measuring and reporting, organizational learning, and human resources management. She is executive editor of the *International Journal of Learning and Intellectual* and the *International Journal of Strategic Change Management.*

Nicole M. Radziwill is the asistant director for End to End Operations at the National Radio Astronomy Observatory (NRAO) headquarters in Charlottesville, VA, overseeing software development and service delivery. She also served as the division head for Software Development for NRAO's Green Bank, WV site. Before NRAO, she managed consulting engagements and worked in scientific computation at the National Oceanic and Atmospheric Administration (NOAA) in Boulder, CO. She has over a decade of experience managing continuous improvement efforts in business and technology, specializing in improvements that result from information technology. Nicole has a degree in meteorology, an MBA, and is pursuing a doctorate in technology management and quality. She is an ASQ Certified Quality Manager and the Regional Councilor for ASQ's Software division in the mid-Atlantic.

Friedrich Roithmayr is, since 2004, a full professor for information systems-information engineering at the Johannes Kepler University Linz (Austria). Since 2007, he also has been vice-rector for communication and foreign affairs at the same University. Before he was professor at the University of Bamberg (Germany), the University of Duisburg (Germany) and the University of Innsbruck (Austria), he was also guest professor at the University of New Orleans and the University of Leipzig. He is scientific head at the SAP Business School Vienna. His research interests include information and knowledge management, business process management, case studies, stakeholdermangement, and IT project management.

Ricardo Salim is the chief software architect for Cautus Network Corporation. He has over 25 years of experience in developing and implementing enterprise software solutions for small and midsize companies. He has worked as a consultant in IT/IS to over 100 companies and government institution in developing countries. Mr. Salim is a successful entrepreneur that has founded several successful IT/IS companies in various developing and developed countries. He holds a BS in computer science from Universidad Central de Venezuela and is currently a PhD candidate from Universitat Autònoma de Barcelona in Spain. His research is on the areas of accounting information systems, knowledge management, and the digital divide.

Hanno Schauer is a research assistant at the Research Group for Information Systems and Enterprise Modeling (Prof. Dr. Ulrich Frank), University of Duisburg-Essen, Germany. His research interests focus on knowledge management, conceptual modeling, information systems management, and philosophy of science. His particular research interests are at the intersection of these research areas. He gained insightful experience in knowledge management practice in research projects in cooperation with public enterprises and public administrations.

Carola Schauer (birth name Lange) is a research assistant at the Research Group for Information Systems and Enterprise Modelling (Prof. Dr. Ulrich Frank), University of Duisburg-Essen, Germany. She has done research in the areas of conceptual enterprise modelling, e-commerce, and philosophy of science. Currently, she is employed in the IFWIS-project (funded by the German Science Foundation) which aims at comparing the North-American information systems discipline and Wirtschaftsinformatik, its counterpart in German-speaking countries.

Jim Sena is a professor of management and information systems at Cal Poly's Orfalea College of Business. His current teaching assignments include organization systems and technology, management information systems, project management, business and IT strategy, and computer security. He received his PhD in organization theory and computer science from the University of Kentucky. His research interests include knowledge management, sustainable work systems, process analysis and reengineering, research and development of group decision making, and organizational analysis.

R. Todd Stephens is the technical director of the Collaboration and Online Services Group for the AT&T Corporation. Todd is responsible for setting the corporate strategy and architecture for the development and implementation of the enterprise collaborative and metadata solutions. Todd writes a monthly online column in *Data Management Review* and has delivered keynotes, tutorials, and educational sessions for a wide variety of professional and academic conferences around the world. Todd holds degrees in mathematics and computer science from Columbus State University, an MBA degree from Georgia State University, and a PhD in information systems from Nova Southeastern University.

Index

A

agent-oriented and knowledge-based system (AOKBS) 35
antivirus solutions 204
application automation integration 186
application processes 182
artificial intelligence 123, 291, 309
artificial intelligence (AI) 146
artificial intelligence (AI) software 2
asynchronous communication 254
autonomic computing 35

B

banking sector 316
banking sector, knowledge intensive organization 324
Bayesian network (BN) 35
blind idealism 297
blogs 175
Bohn's Scale 8
Bohn's stages of knowledge growth 30
business-to-business (B2B) transactions 184
business automation integration 186
business intelligence (BI) 149
business intelligence (BI) tools 149
business processes 182
business process models 97

business process models, fields of application 98
business process models, modeling concepts 97
business process models, preliminary assessment 100
business strategies 1
business strategy 195

C

C3EEP 1, 5
C3EEP, codification vs. tacitness 5
C3EEP, coding scheme 28
C3EEP, complementary vs. destroying 5
C3EEP, concealment vs. transparency 6
C3EEP, exploration vs. exploitation 6
C3EEP, external acquisition vs. internal development 6
C3EEP, product vs. process 7
C3EEP and KBS-LC frequencies 34
C3EEP frequencies 32
CALM VDE ontology 152
case-based reasoning (CBR) 35
case-based reasoning (CBR) systems 147
CBR systems 155
CDMS VDE ontology 150
change, adaptation, and learning model (CALM) VDE 152